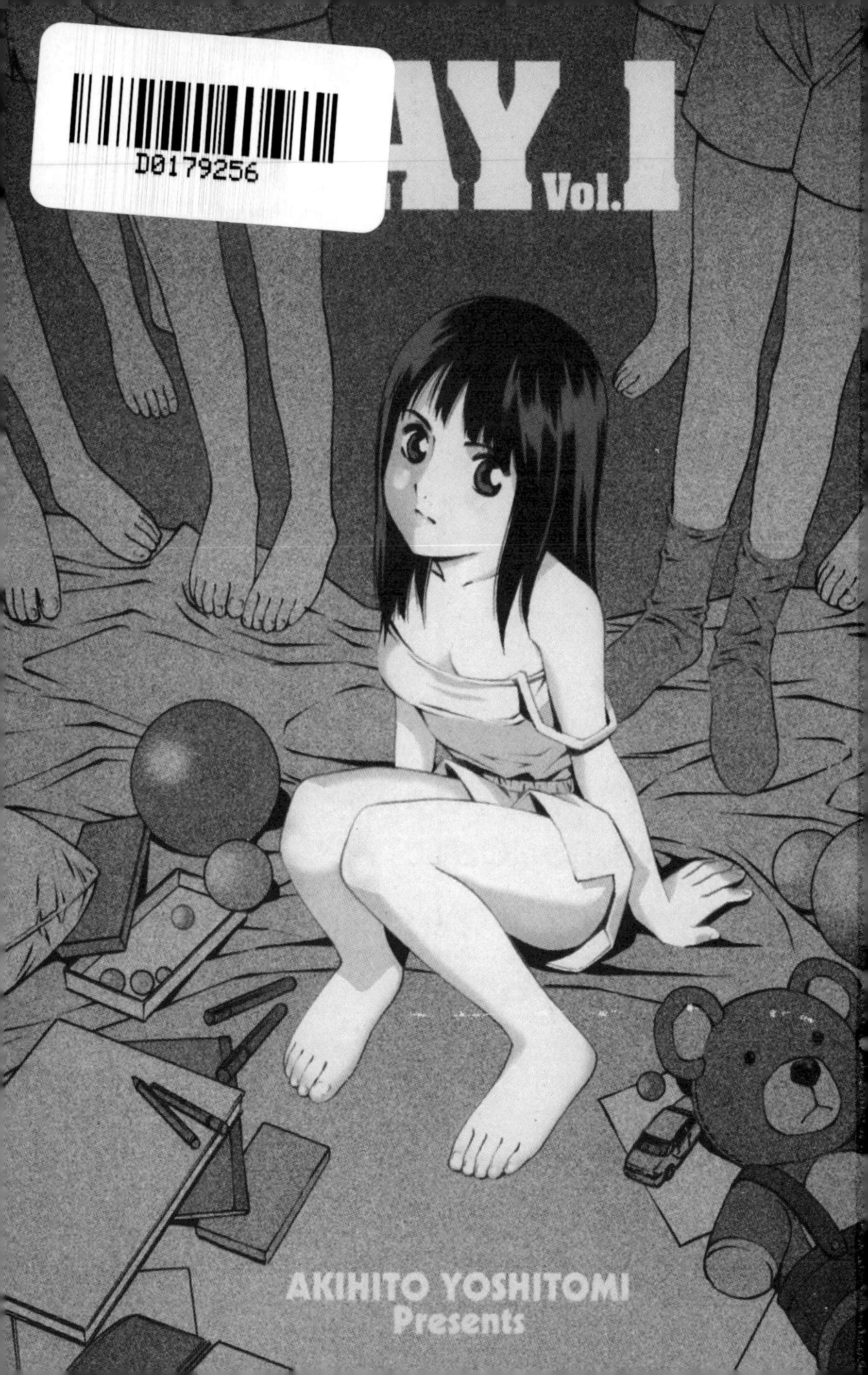
AY
Vol.
AKIHITO YOSHITOMI
Presents

RAY Vol. 1

CONTENTS

Patient.1
The Chain

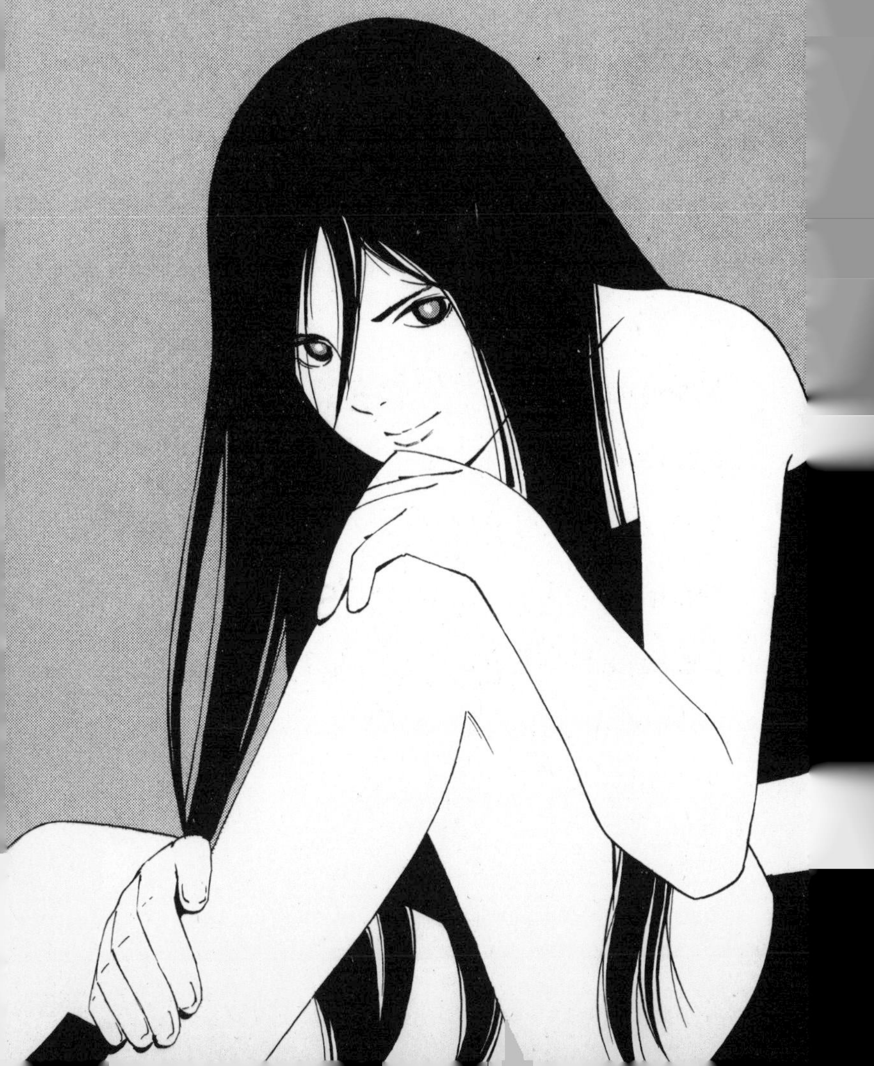

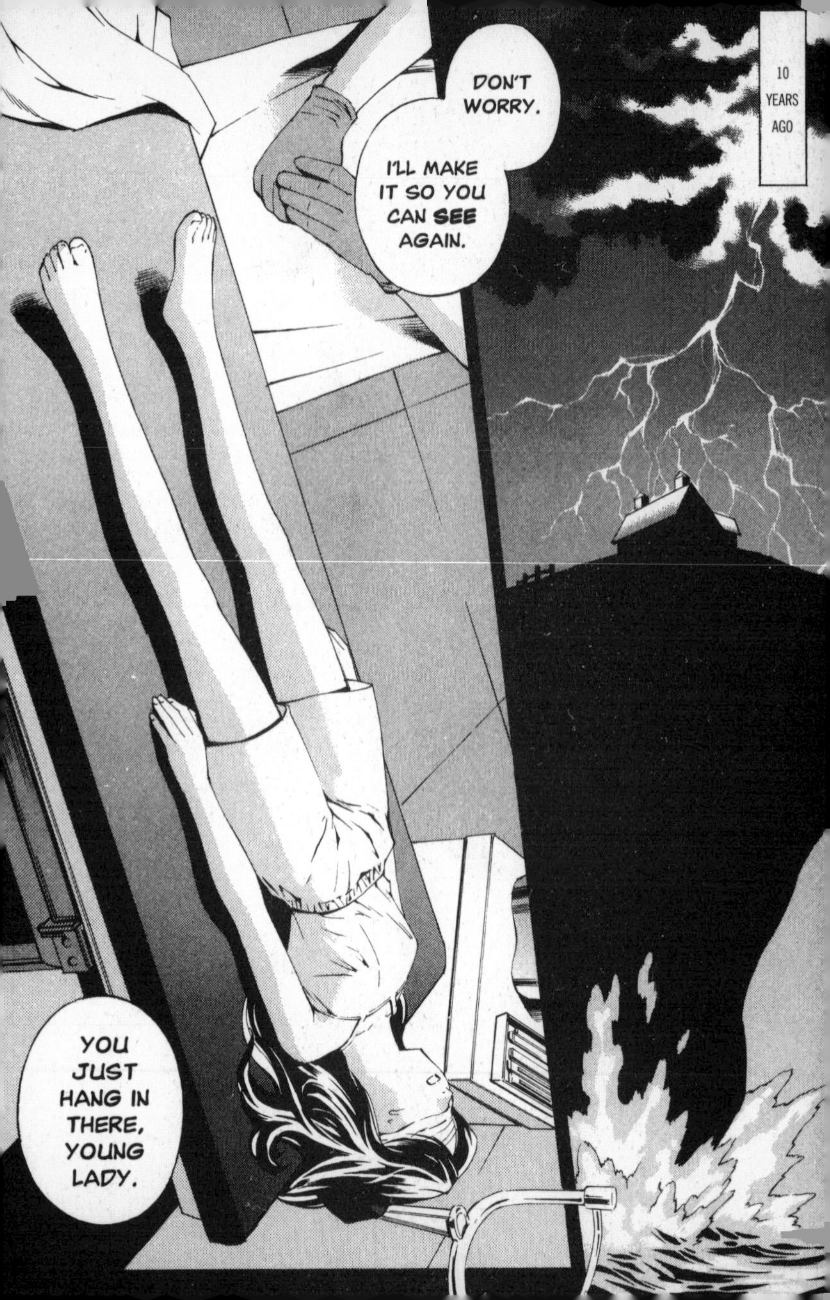
10 YEARS AGO
DON'T WORRY.
I'LL MAKE IT SO YOU CAN SEE AGAIN.
YOU JUST HANG IN THERE, YOUNG LADY.

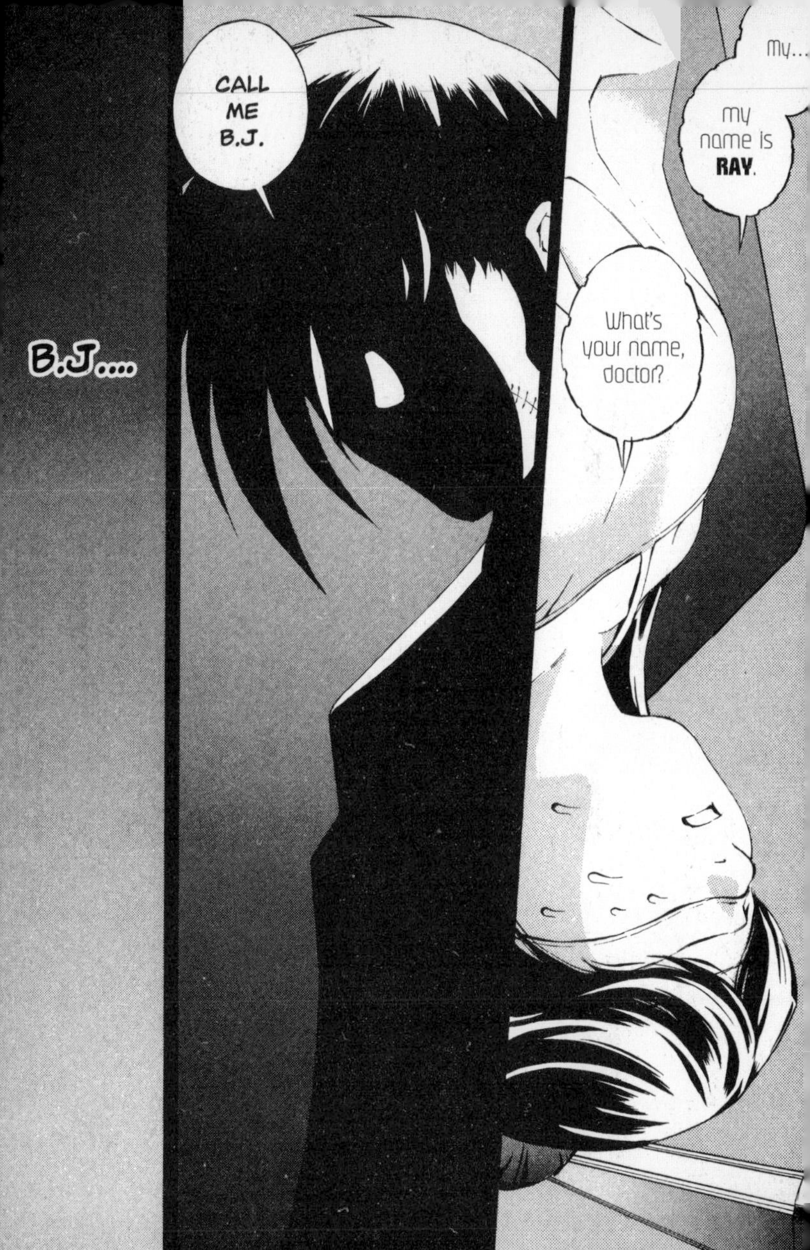
My...
my name is **RAY**.
What's your name, doctor?
CALL ME B.J.
B.J....

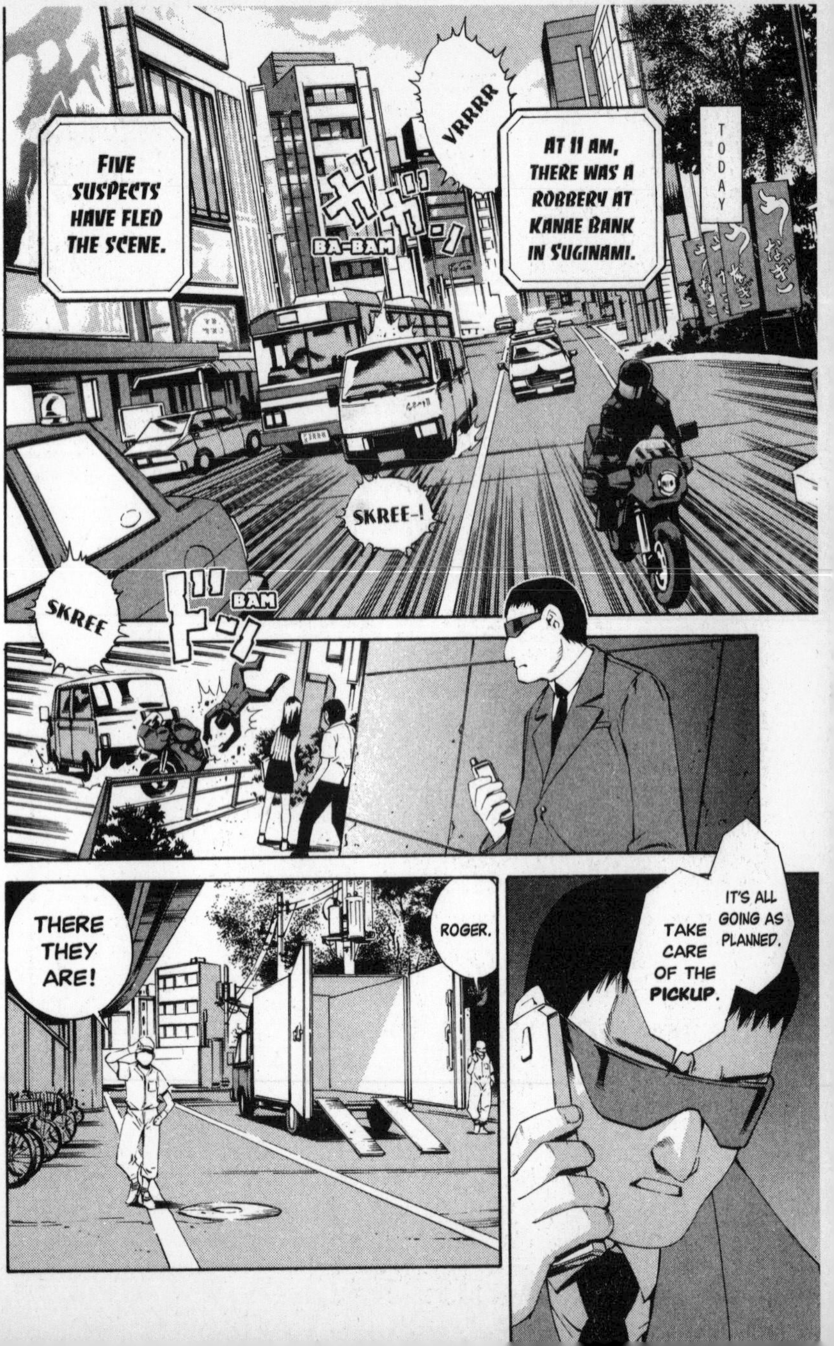
TODAY
At 11 am, there was a robbery at Kanae Bank in Suginami.
VRRRR
BA-BAM
Five suspects have fled the scene.
SKREE-!
BAM
SKREE
It's all going as planned.
Take care of the pickup.
Roger.
There they are!

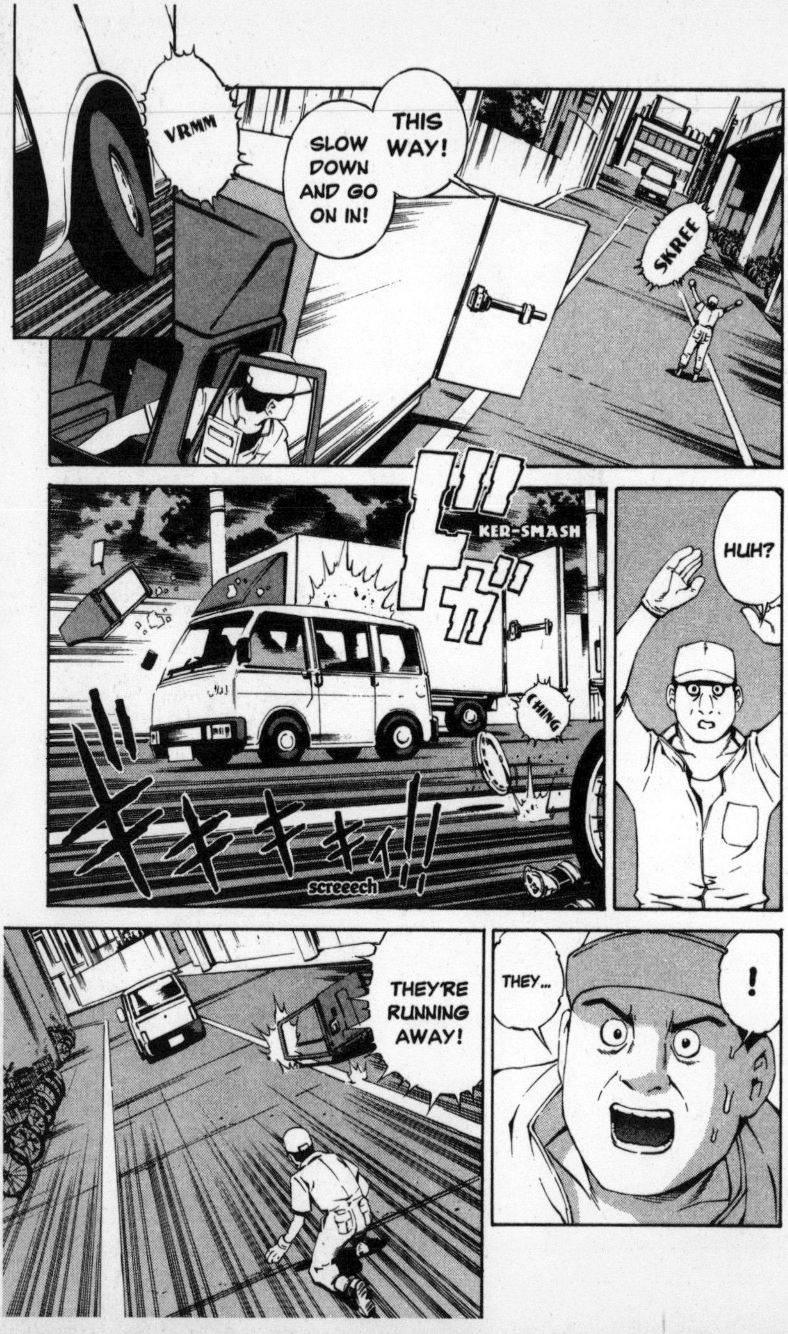
VRMM
THIS WAY!
SLOW DOWN AND GO ON IN!
SKREE
KER-SMASH
CHING
screeech
HUH?
THEY...
!
THEY'RE RUNNING AWAY!

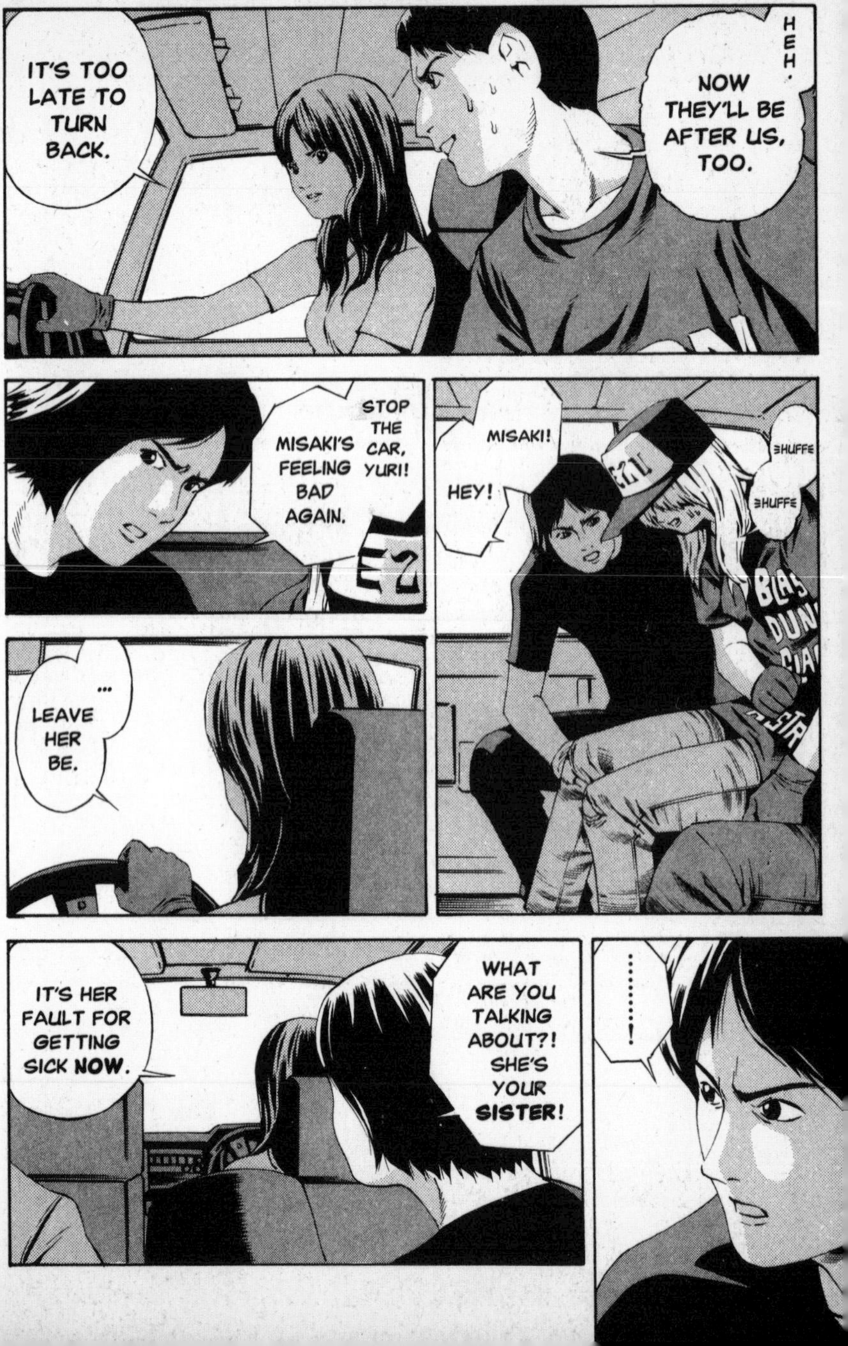
IT'S TOO LATE TO TURN BACK.
HEH.
NOW THEY'LL BE AFTER US, TOO.
MISAKI'S FEELING BAD AGAIN.
STOP THE CAR, YURI!
MISAKI!
HEY!
HUFF
HUFF
... LEAVE HER BE.
IT'S HER FAULT FOR GETTING SICK **NOW**.
WHAT ARE YOU TALKING ABOUT?! SHE'S YOUR **SISTER**!
........!

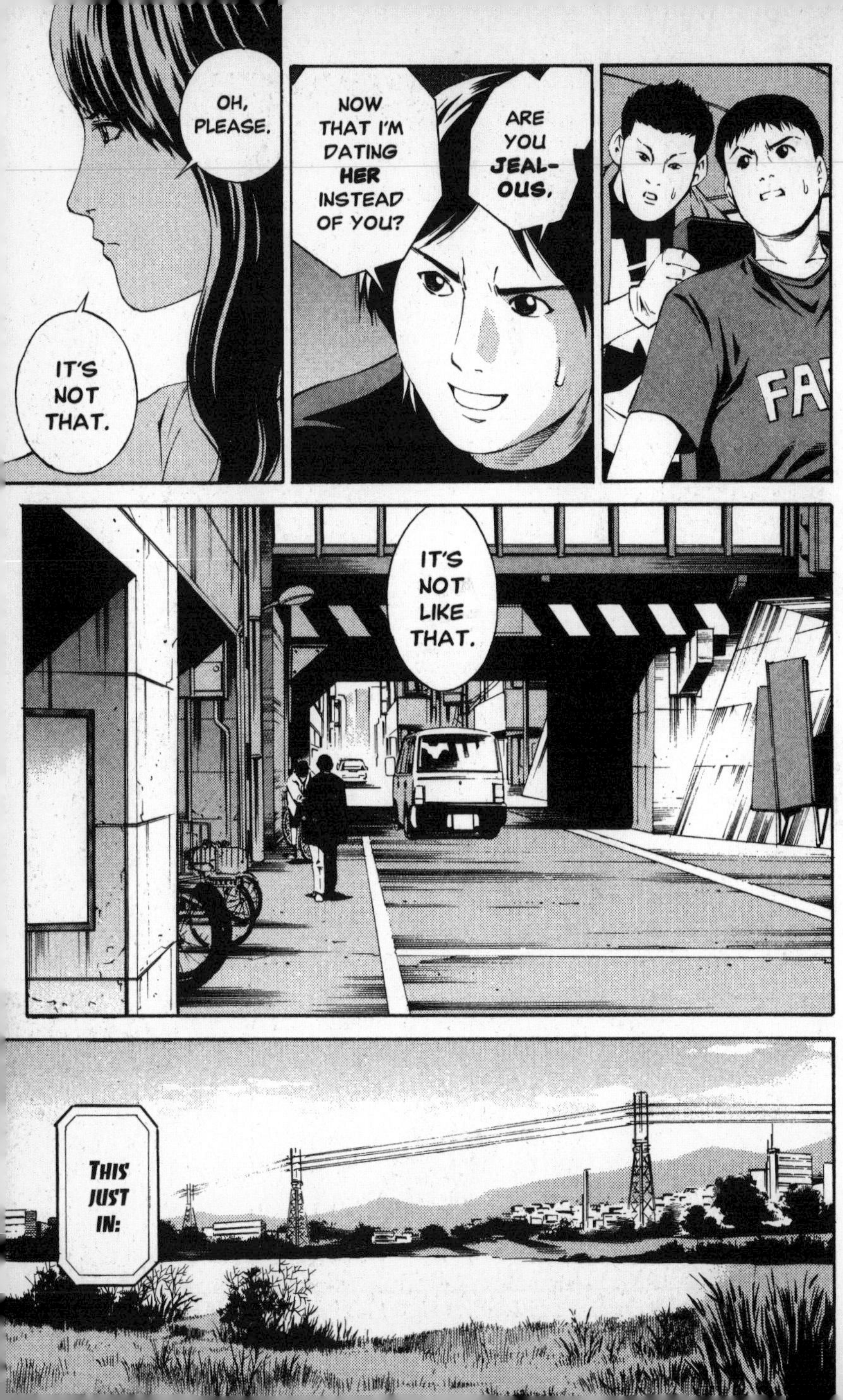
ARE YOU JEAL-OUS,
NOW THAT I'M DATING HER INSTEAD OF YOU?
OH, PLEASE.
IT'S NOT THAT.
IT'S NOT LIKE THAT.
THIS JUST IN:

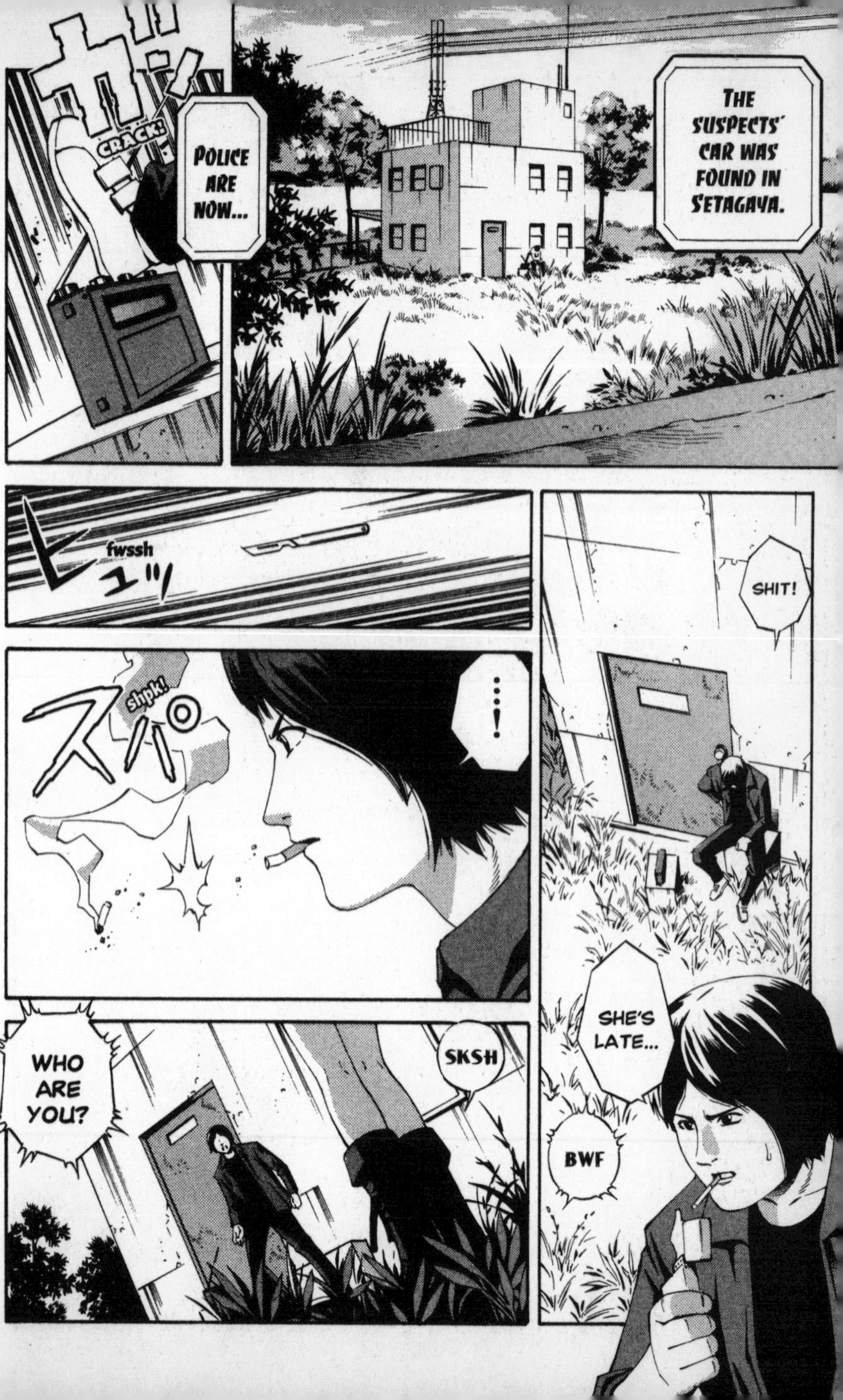
The suspects' car was found in Setagaya.
Police are now...
CRACK!
SHIT!
SHE'S LATE...
BWF
fwssh
...!
shpk!
SKSH
WHO ARE YOU?

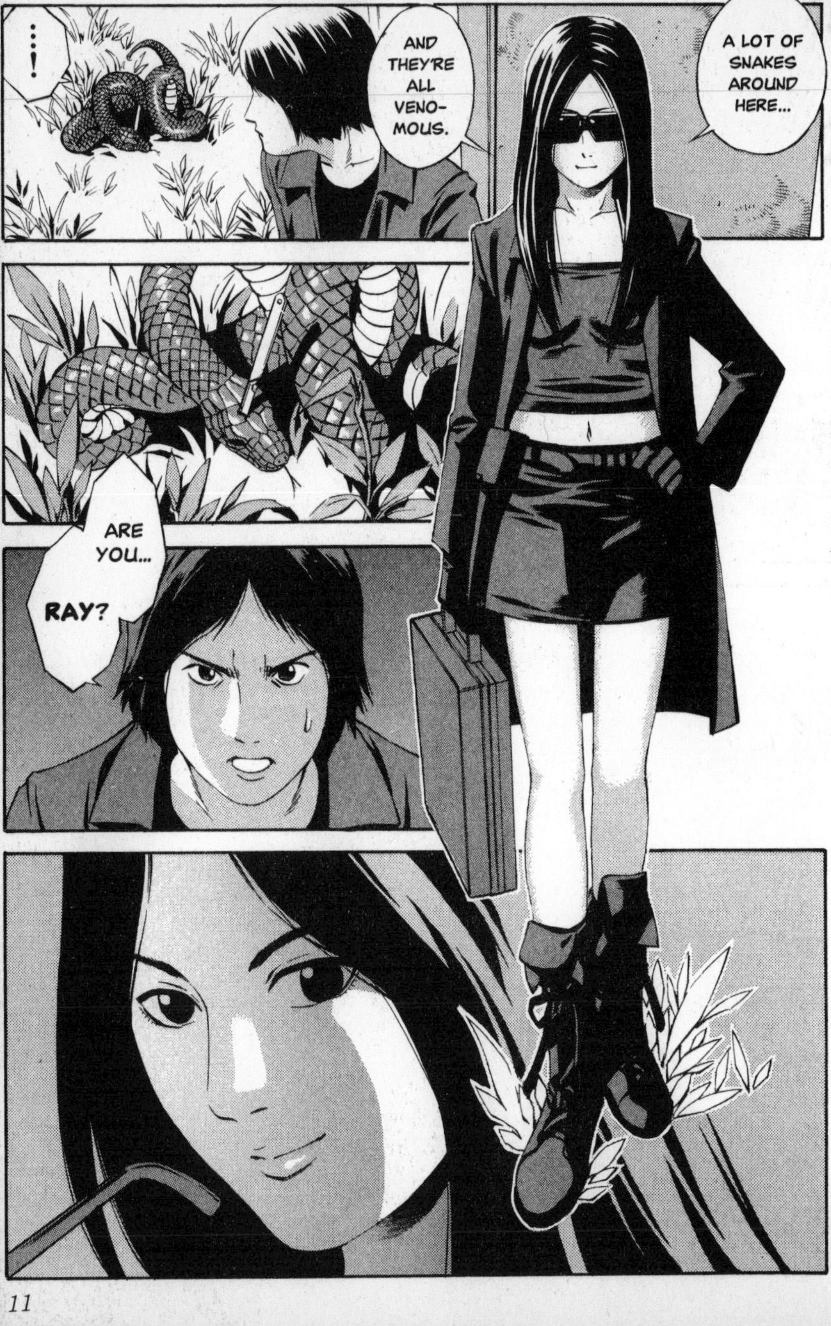
A LOT OF SNAKES AROUND HERE...
AND THEY'RE ALL VENO- MOUS.
...!
ARE YOU...
RAY?

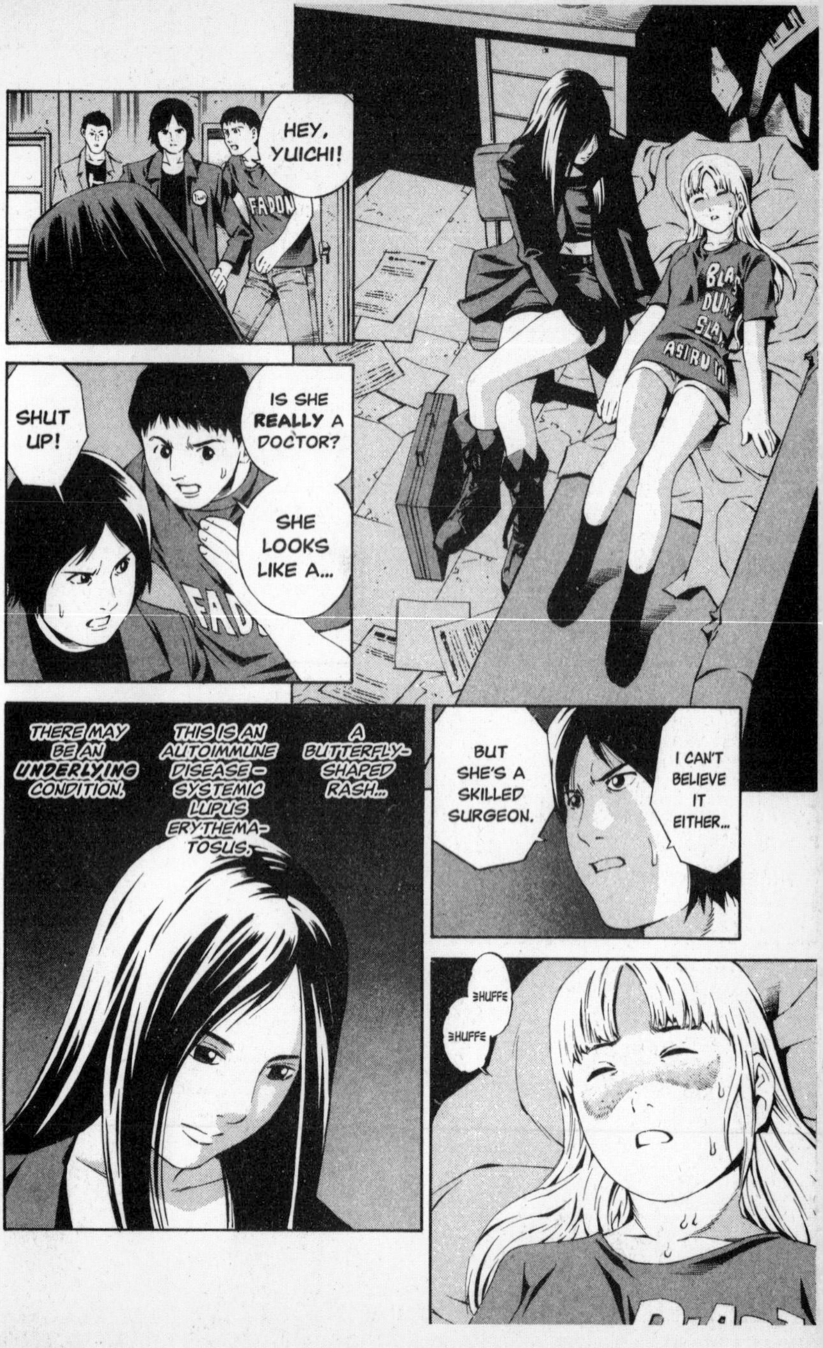
HEY, YUICHI!
IS SHE REALLY A DOCTOR?
SHE LOOKS LIKE A...
SHUT UP!
I CAN'T BELIEVE IT EITHER...
BUT SHE'S A SKILLED SURGEON.
A BUTTERFLY-SHAPED RASH...
THIS IS AN AUTOIMMUNE DISEASE - SYSTEMIC LUPUS ERYTHEMATOSUS.
THERE MAY BE AN UNDERLYING CONDITION.
HUFF
HUFF

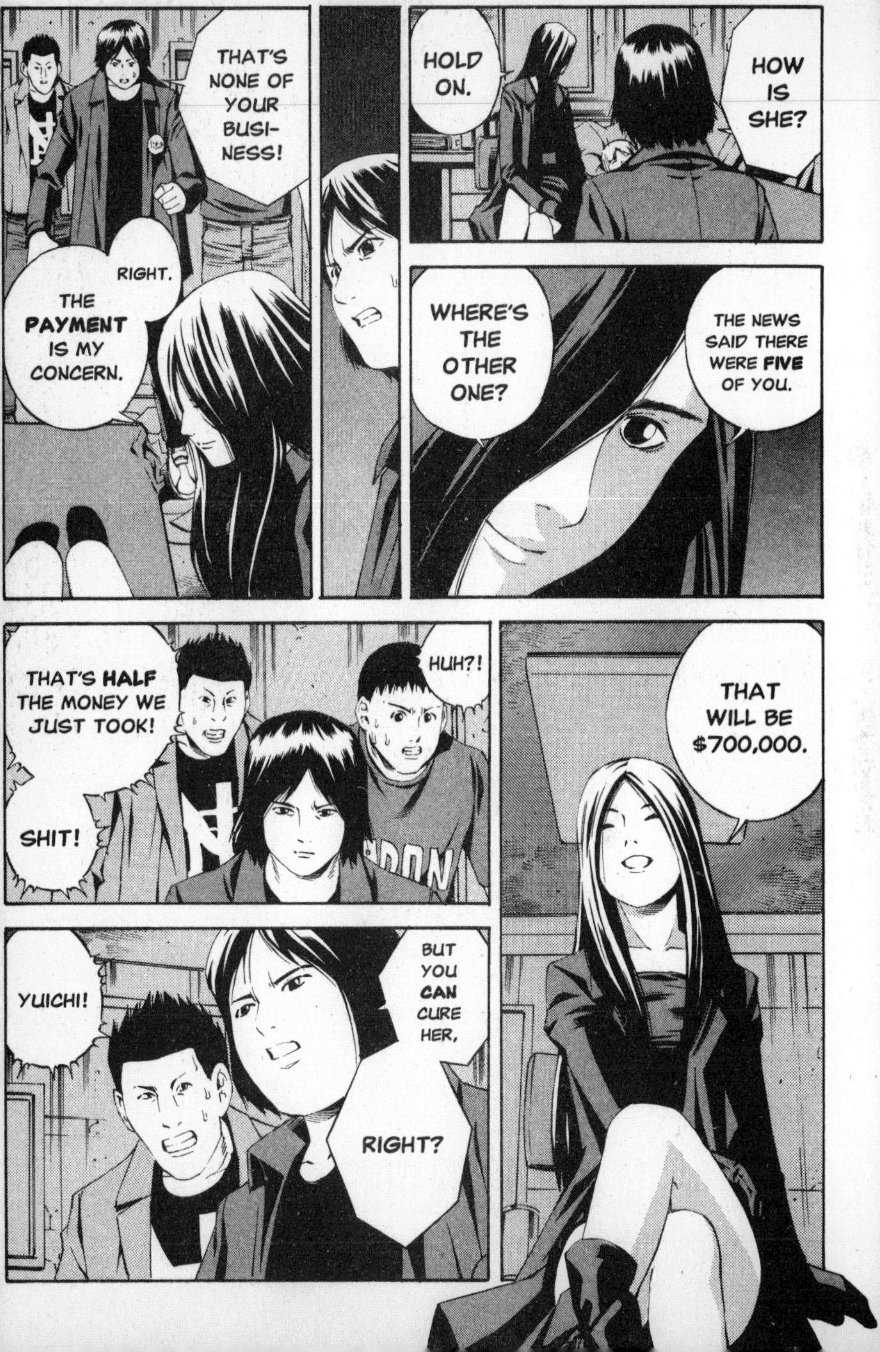
HOW IS SHE?
HOLD ON.
THE NEWS SAID THERE WERE **FIVE** OF YOU.
WHERE'S THE OTHER ONE?
THAT'S NONE OF YOUR BUSI-NESS!
RIGHT.
THE **PAYMENT** IS MY CONCERN.
THAT WILL BE $700,000.
HUH?!
THAT'S **HALF** THE MONEY WE JUST TOOK!
SHIT!
BUT YOU **CAN** CURE HER,
RIGHT?
YUICHI!

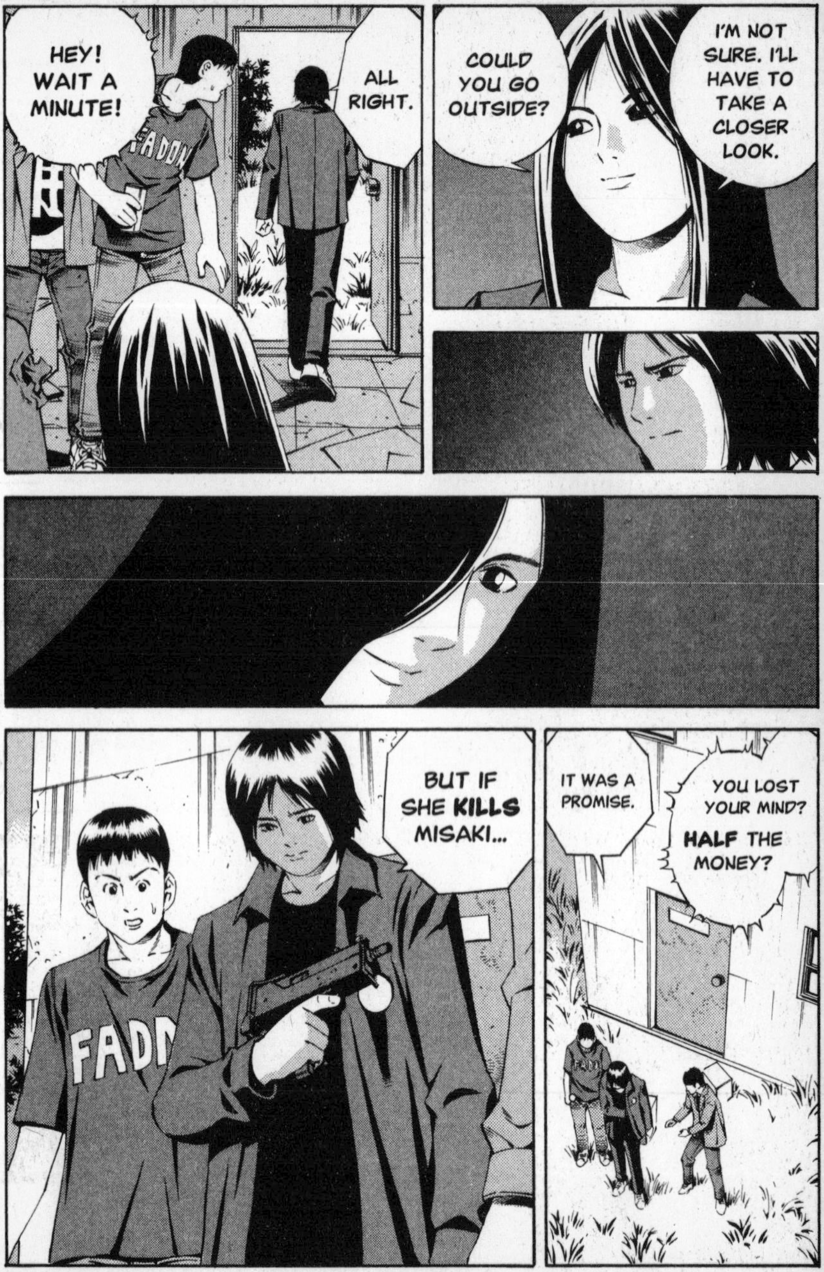
I'M NOT SURE. I'LL HAVE TO TAKE A CLOSER LOOK.
COULD YOU GO OUTSIDE?
ALL RIGHT.
HEY! WAIT A MINUTE!
YOU LOST YOUR MIND? **HALF** THE MONEY?
IT WAS A PROMISE.
BUT IF SHE **KILLS** MISAKI...

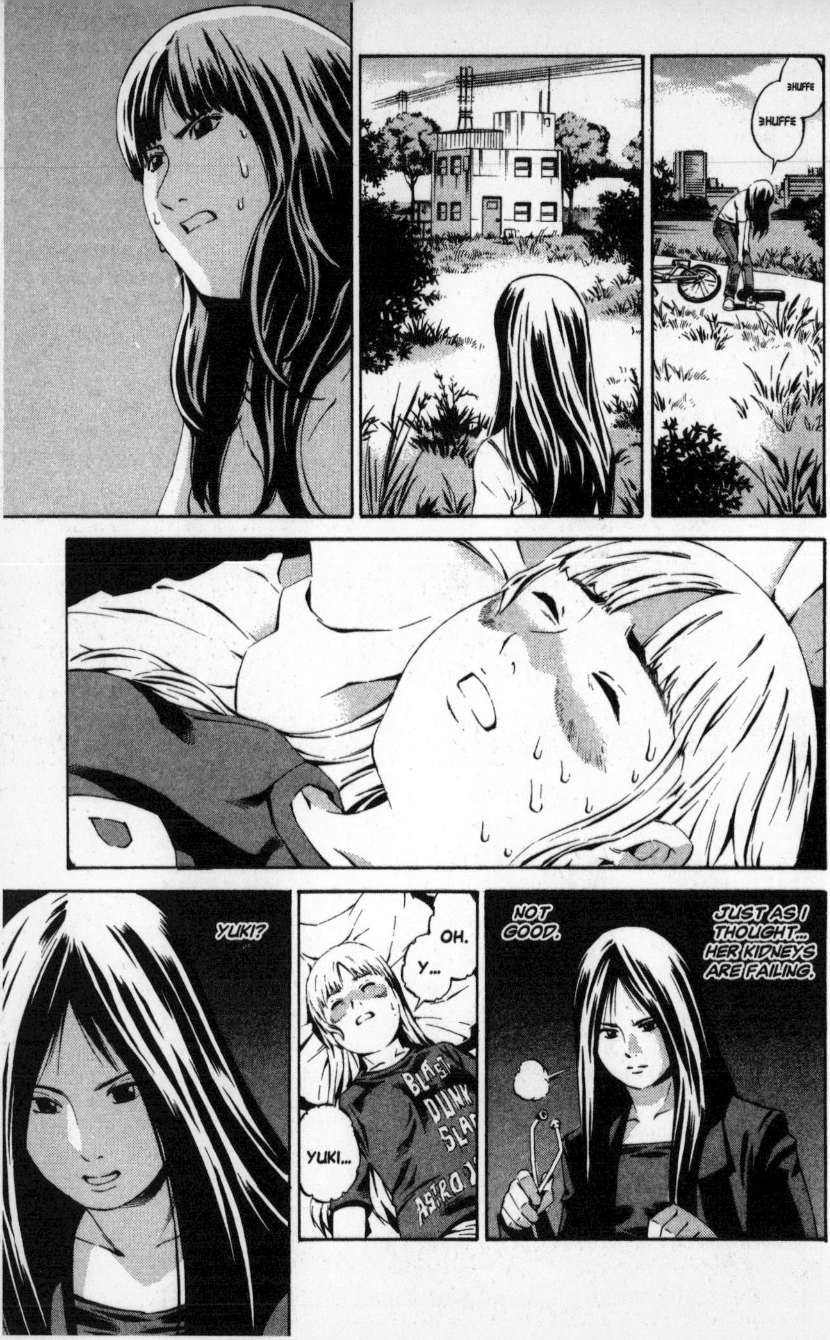
HUFF
HUFF
JUST AS I THOUGHT... HER KIDNEYS ARE FAILING.
NOT GOOD.
OH.
Y...
YUKI...
YUKI?

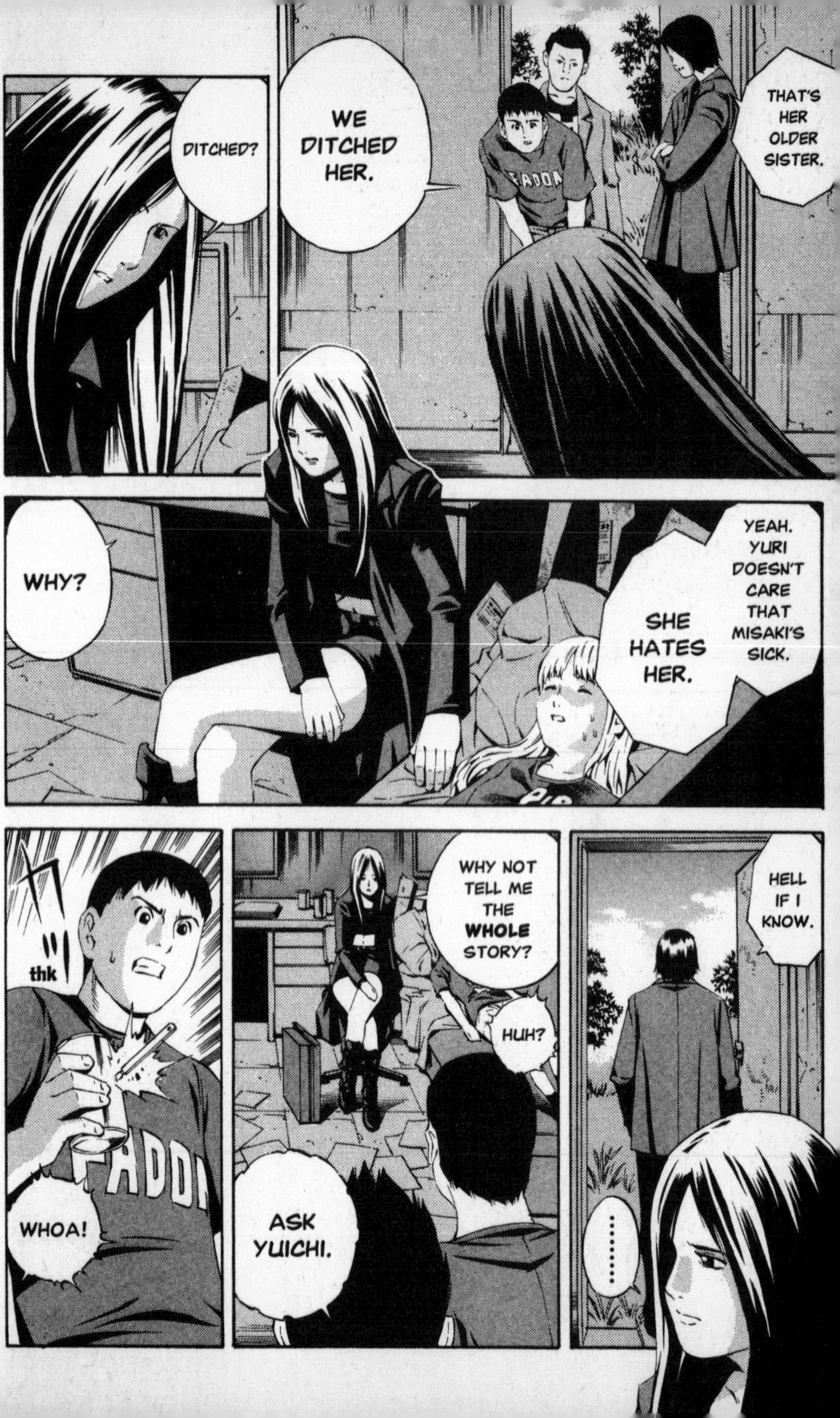
THAT'S HER OLDER SISTER.
WE DITCHED HER.
DITCHED?
YEAH. YURI DOESN'T CARE THAT MISAKI'S SICK.
SHE HATES HER.
WHY?
HELL IF I KNOW.
....
WHY NOT TELL ME THE **WHOLE** STORY?
HUH?
ASK YUICHI.
thk
WHOA!

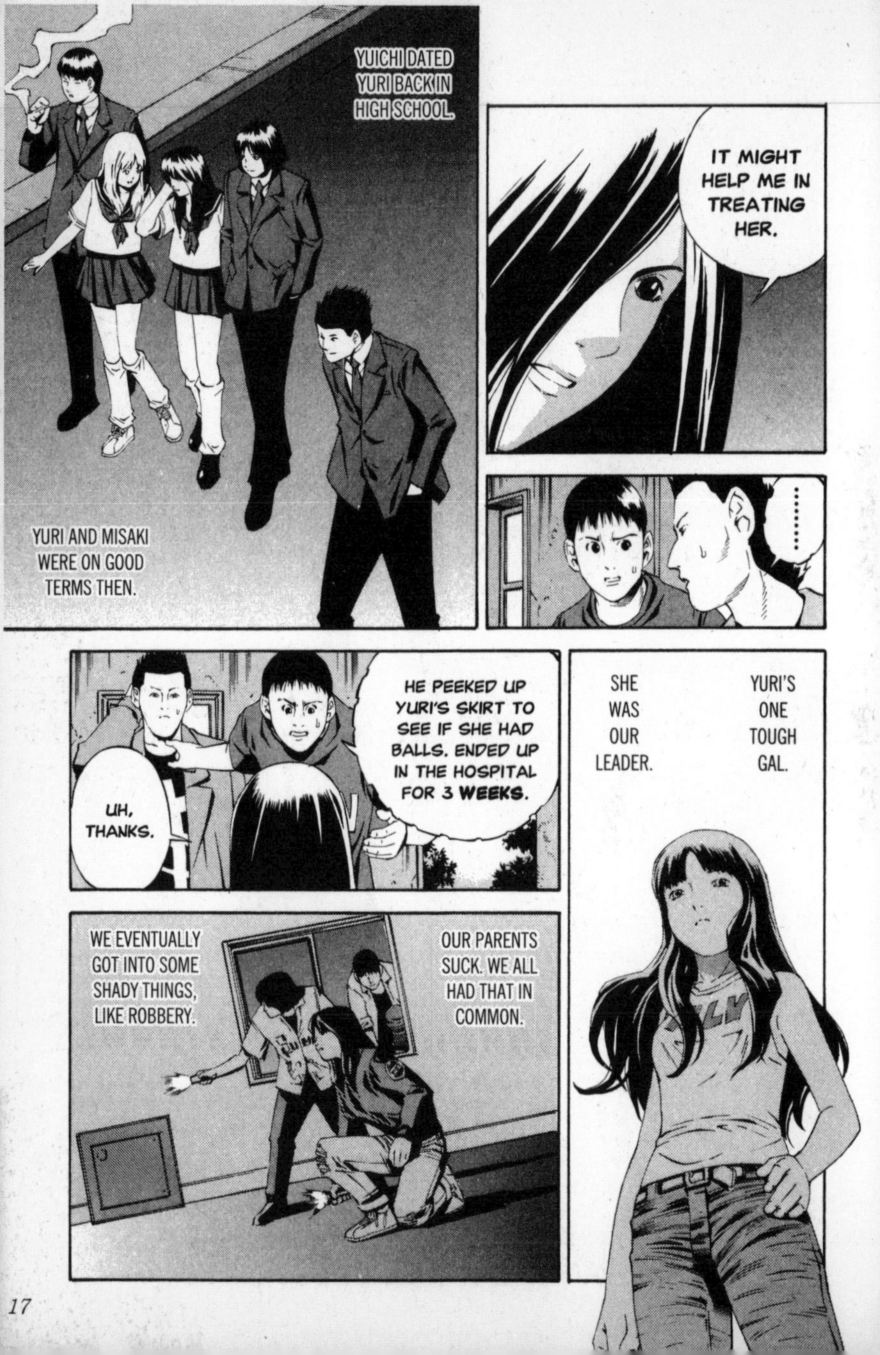
IT MIGHT HELP ME IN TREATING HER.
......
YUICHI DATED YURI BACK IN HIGH SCHOOL.
YURI AND MISAKI WERE ON GOOD TERMS THEN.
YURI'S ONE TOUGH GAL.
SHE WAS OUR LEADER.
HE PEEKED UP YURI'S SKIRT TO SEE IF SHE HAD BALLS. ENDED UP IN THE HOSPITAL FOR 3 WEEKS.
UH, THANKS.
OUR PARENTS SUCK. WE ALL HAD THAT IN COMMON.
WE EVENTUALLY GOT INTO SOME SHADY THINGS, LIKE ROBBERY.

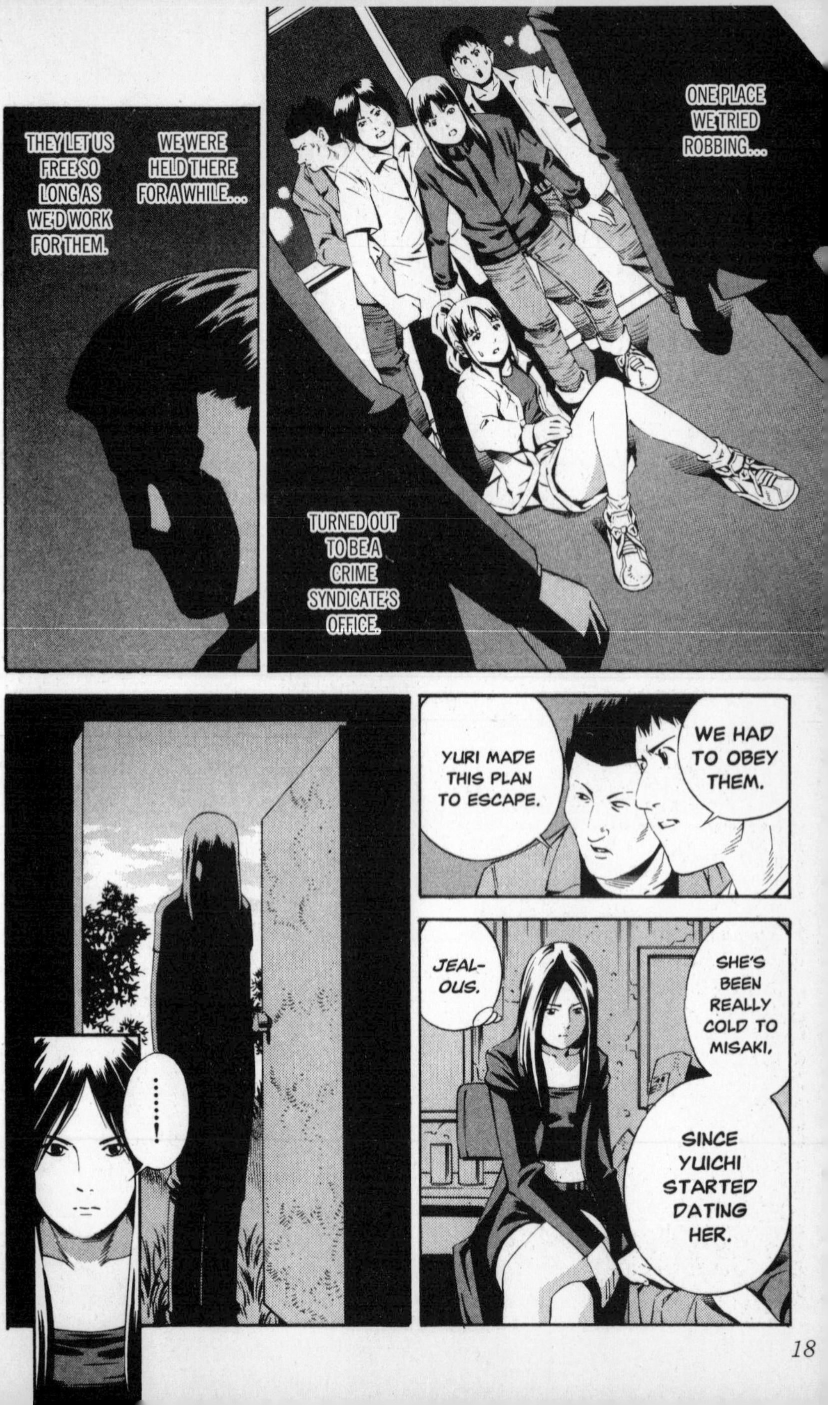
ONE PLACE WE TRIED ROBBING...
TURNED OUT TO BE A CRIME SYNDICATE'S OFFICE.
WE WERE HELD THERE FOR A WHILE...
THEY LET US FREE SO LONG AS WE'D WORK FOR THEM.
WE HAD TO OBEY THEM.
YURI MADE THIS PLAN TO ESCAPE.
SHE'S BEEN REALLY COLD TO MISAKI.
SINCE YUICHI STARTED DATING HER.
JEAL-OUS.
......!

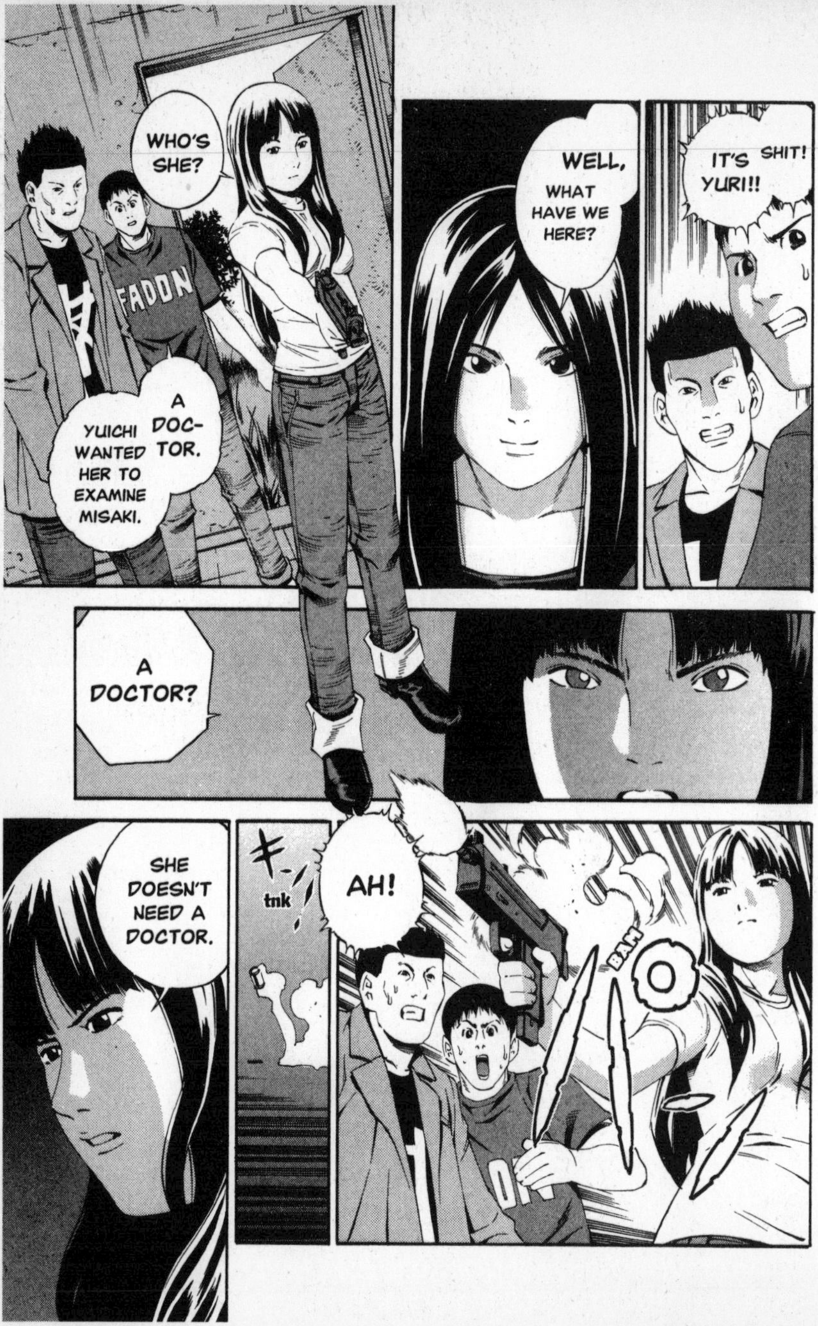

WHO'S SHE?
A DOCTOR. YUICHI WANTED HER TO EXAMINE MISAKI.
WELL, WHAT HAVE WE HERE?
IT'S YURI!!
SHIT!
A DOCTOR?
SHE DOESN'T NEED A DOCTOR.
tnk
AH!
BAM

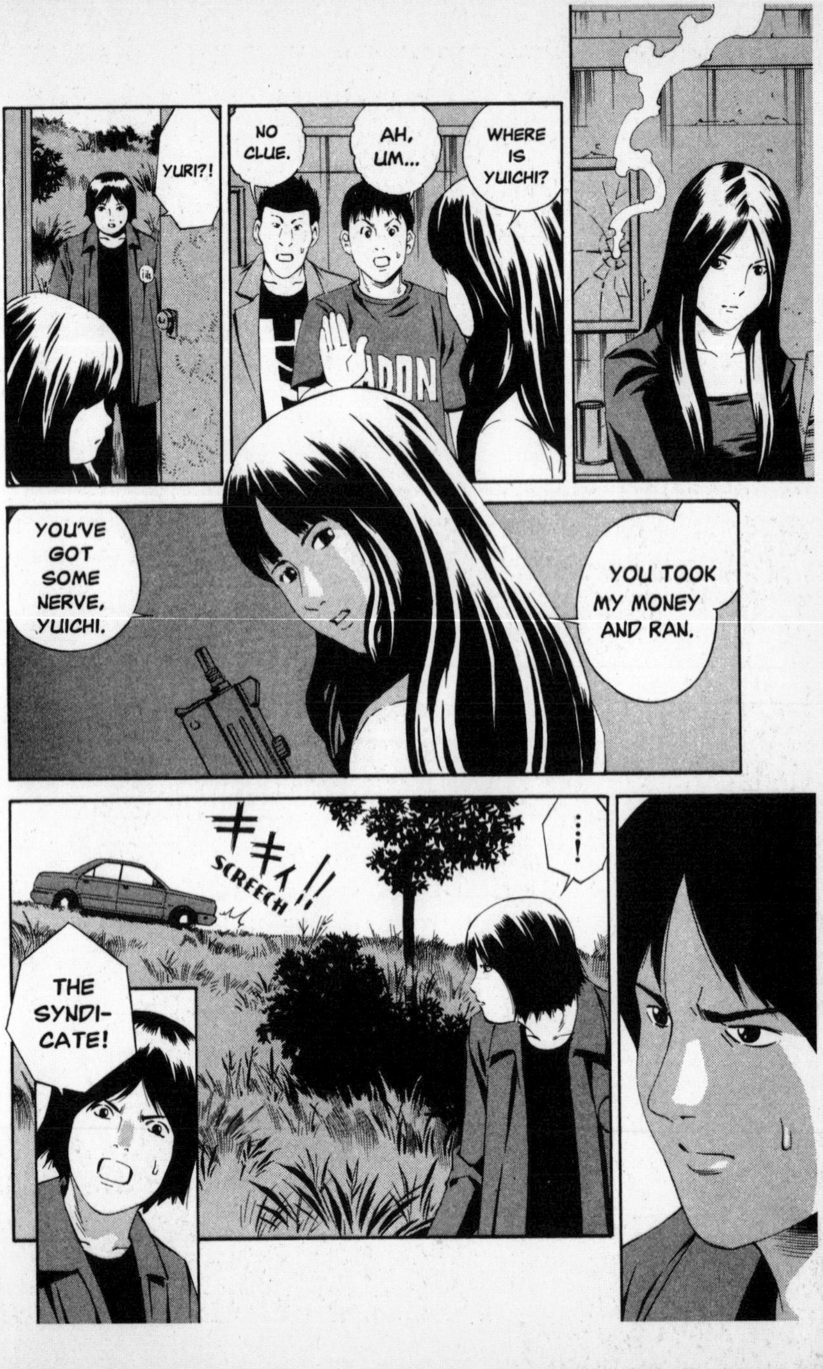
WHERE IS YUICHI?
AH, UM...
NO CLUE.
YURI?!
YOU TOOK MY MONEY AND RAN.
YOU'VE GOT SOME NERVE, YUICHI.
...!
キキィ!! SCREECH
THE SYNDI- CATE!

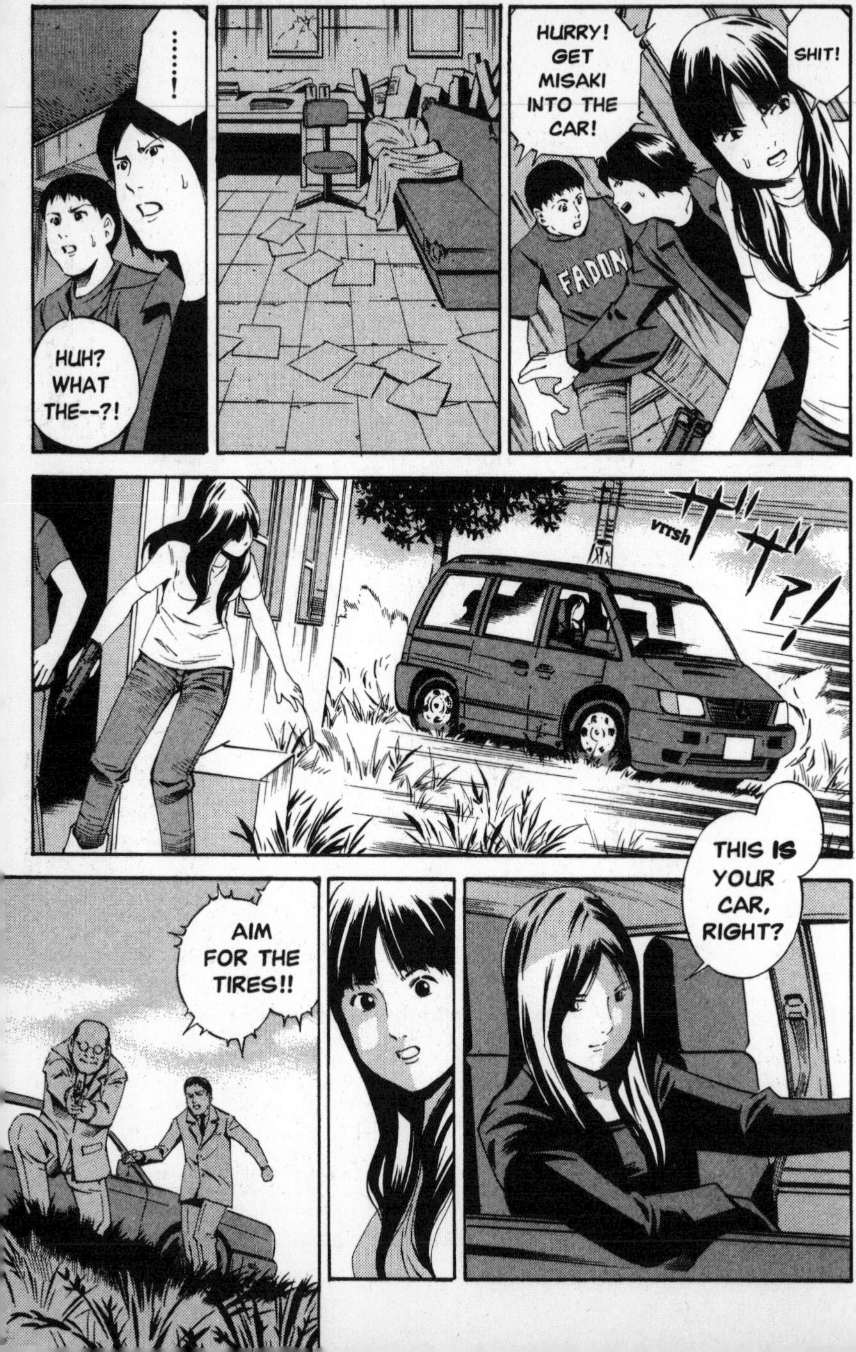
......!
HUH? WHAT THE--?!
SHIT!
HURRY! GET MISAKI INTO THE CAR!
FADON
VRRSH
THIS IS YOUR CAR, RIGHT?
AIM FOR THE TIRES!!

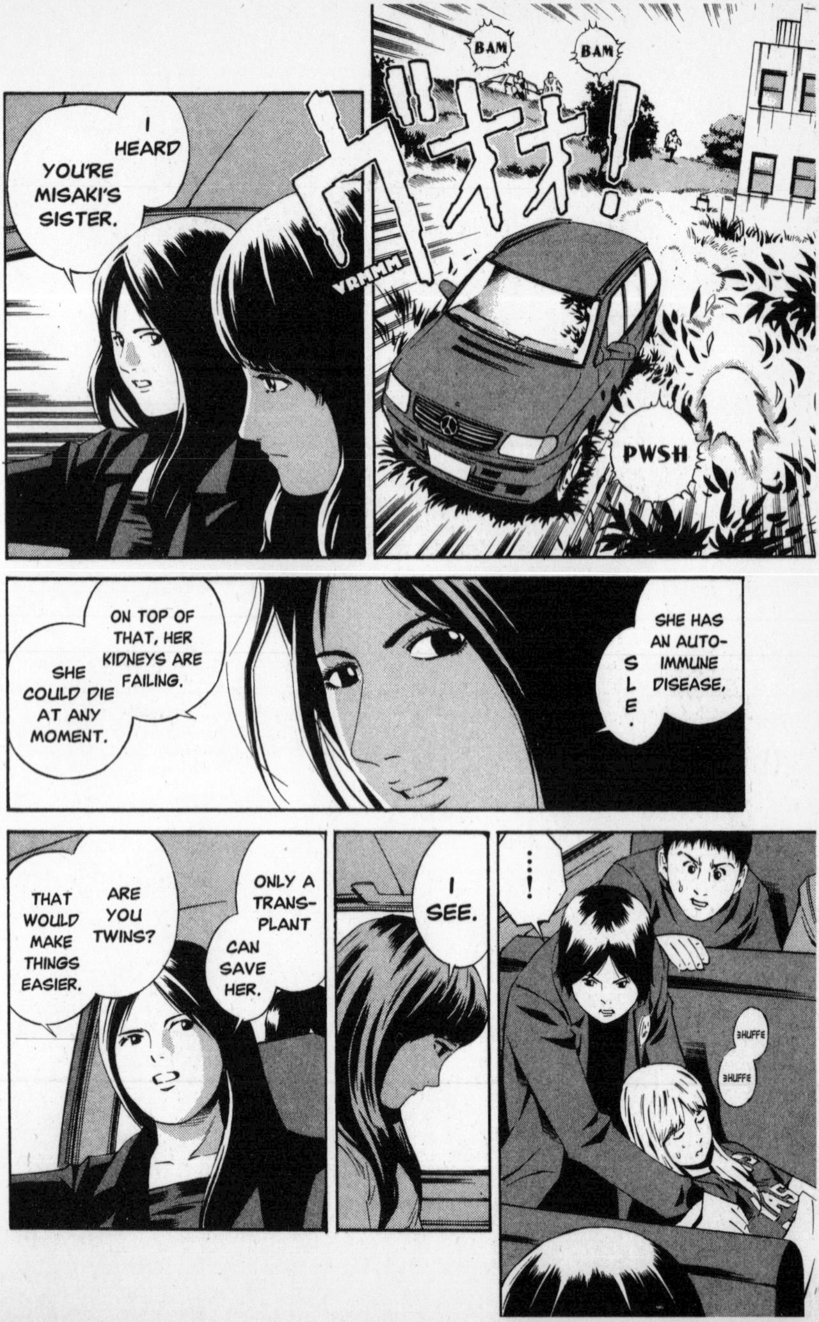
BAM
BAM
ヴォォォ!
VRMMM
PWSH
I HEARD YOU'RE MISAKI'S SISTER.
SHE HAS AN AUTO-IMMUNE DISEASE,
SLE.
ON TOP OF THAT, HER KIDNEYS ARE FAILING.
SHE COULD DIE AT ANY MOMENT.
...!
I SEE.
ONLY A TRANS-PLANT CAN SAVE HER.
ARE YOU TWINS?
THAT WOULD MAKE THINGS EASIER.

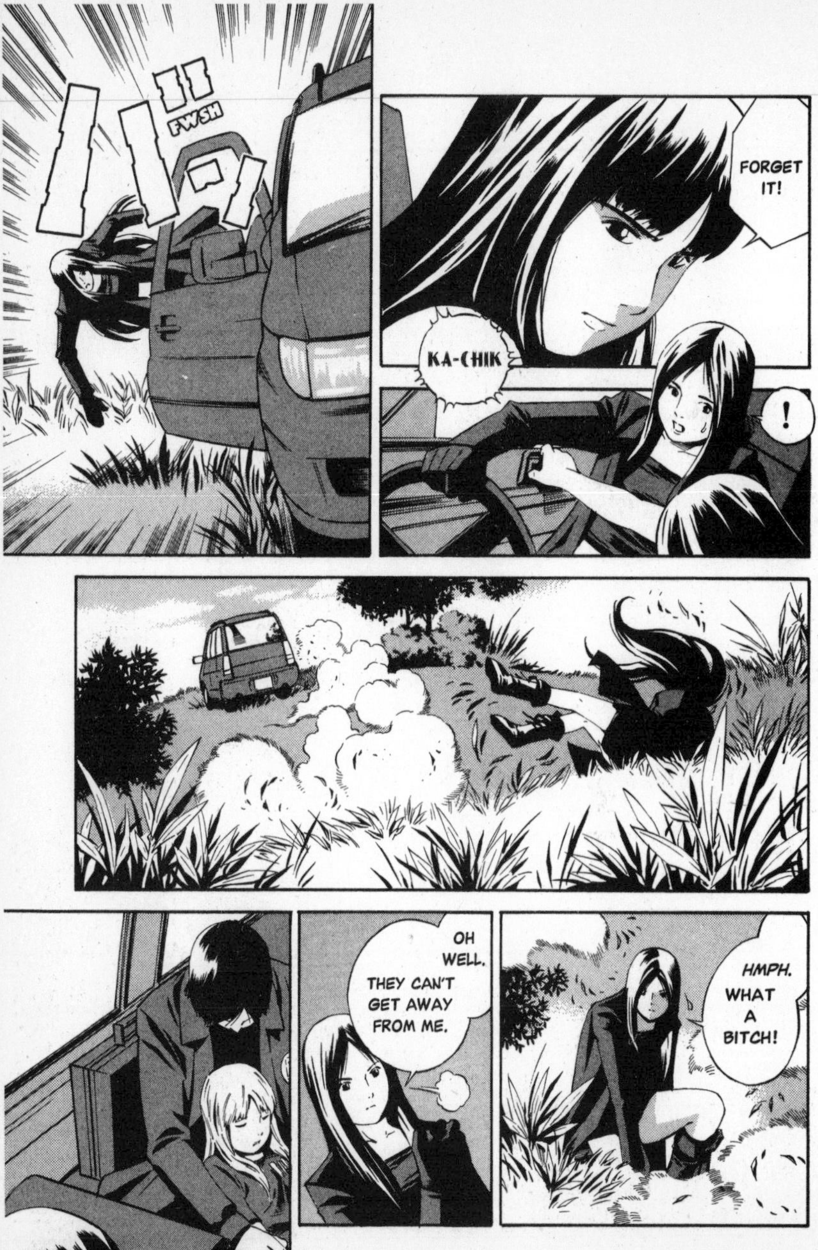
FWSH
FORGET IT!
KA-CHIK
!
OH WELL.
THEY CAN'T GET AWAY FROM ME.
HMPH. WHAT A BITCH!

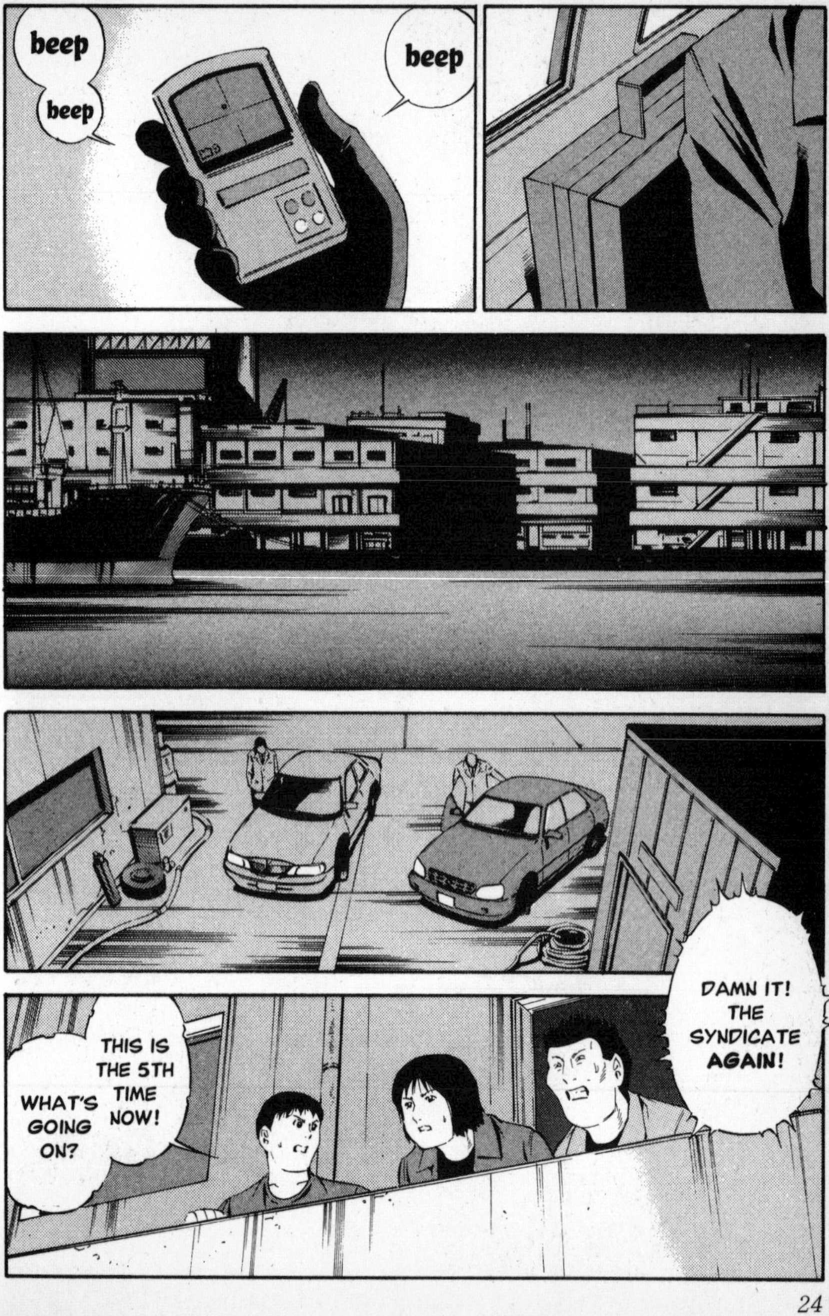
beep
beep
beep
DAMN IT! THE SYNDICATE AGAIN!
THIS IS THE 5TH TIME NOW!
WHAT'S GOING ON?

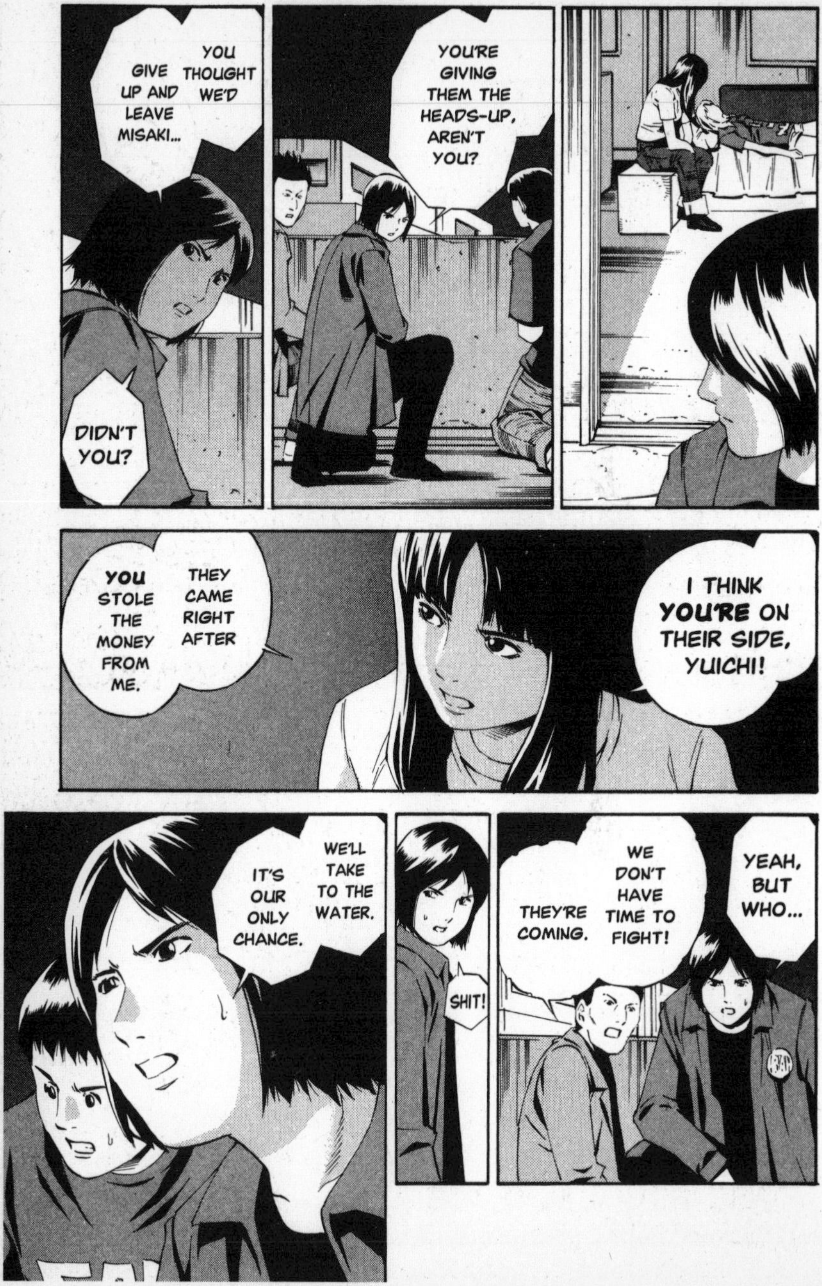
YOU'RE GIVING THEM THE HEADS-UP, AREN'T YOU?
YOU THOUGHT WE'D GIVE UP AND LEAVE MISAKI...
DIDN'T YOU?
I THINK **YOU'RE** ON THEIR SIDE, YUICHI!
THEY CAME RIGHT AFTER **YOU** STOLE THE MONEY FROM ME.
YEAH, BUT WHO...
WE DON'T HAVE TIME TO FIGHT!
THEY'RE COMING.
SHIT!
WE'LL TAKE TO THE WATER.
IT'S OUR ONLY CHANCE.

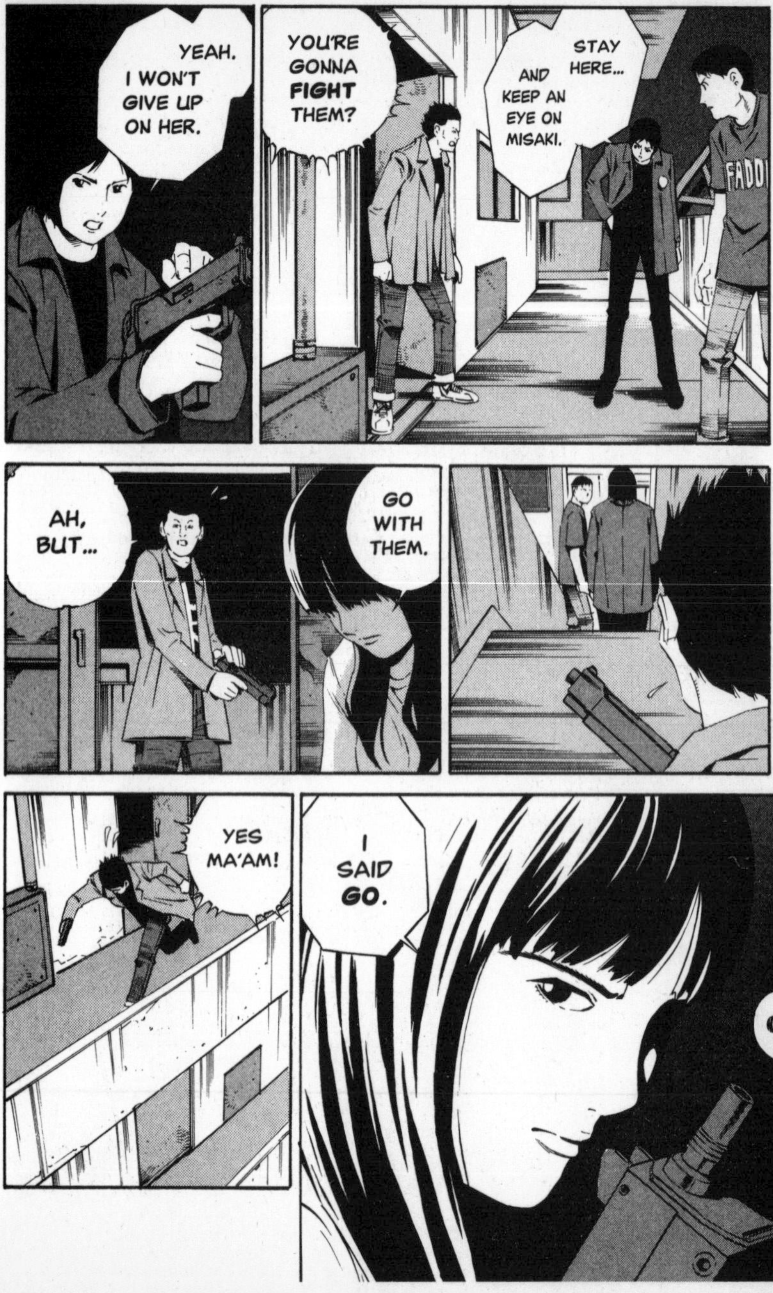
STAY HERE...
AND KEEP AN EYE ON MISAKI.
YOU'RE GONNA FIGHT THEM?
YEAH. I WON'T GIVE UP ON HER.
GO WITH THEM.
AH, BUT...
CHK
I SAID GO.
YES MA'AM!

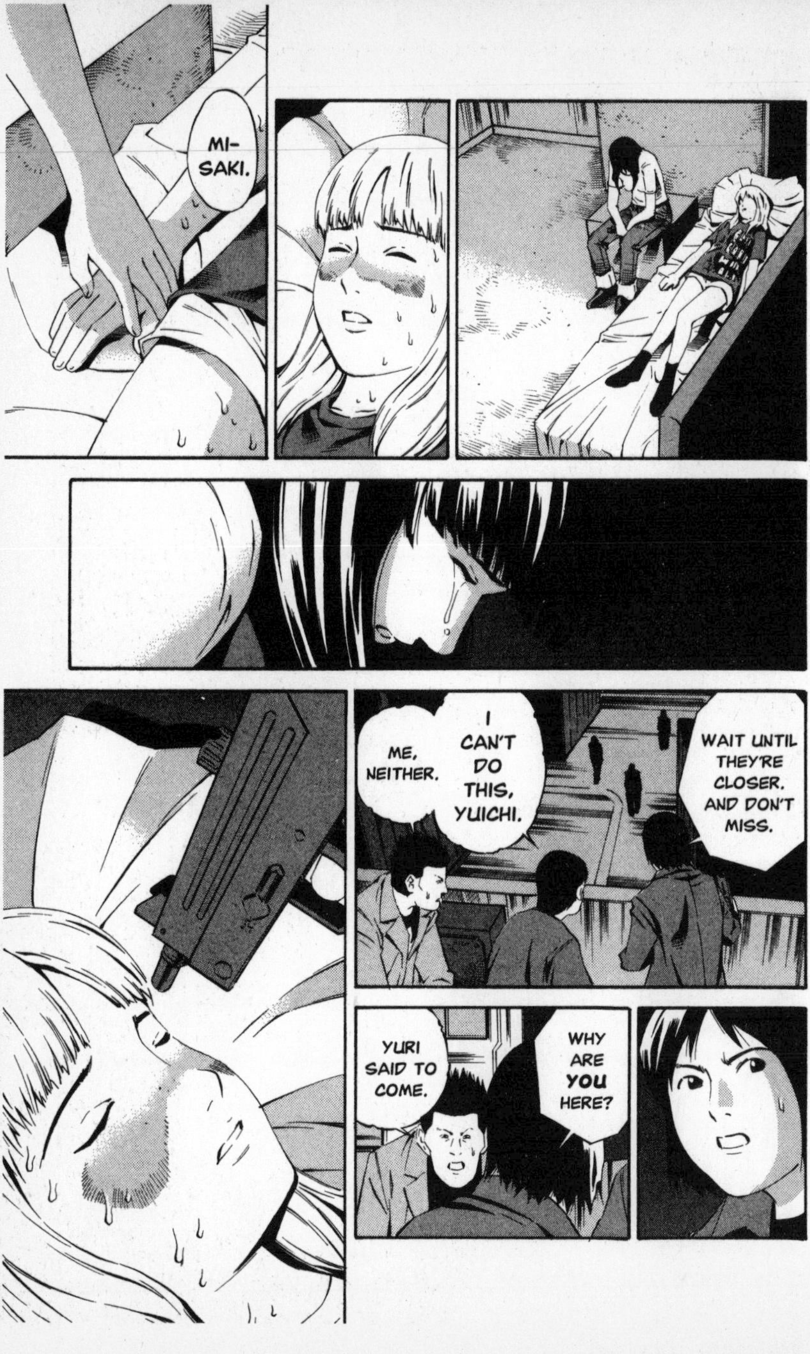
MI-SAKI.
WAIT UNTIL THEY'RE CLOSER. AND DON'T MISS.
I CAN'T DO THIS, YUICHI.
ME, NEITHER.
WHY ARE YOU HERE?
YURI SAID TO COME.

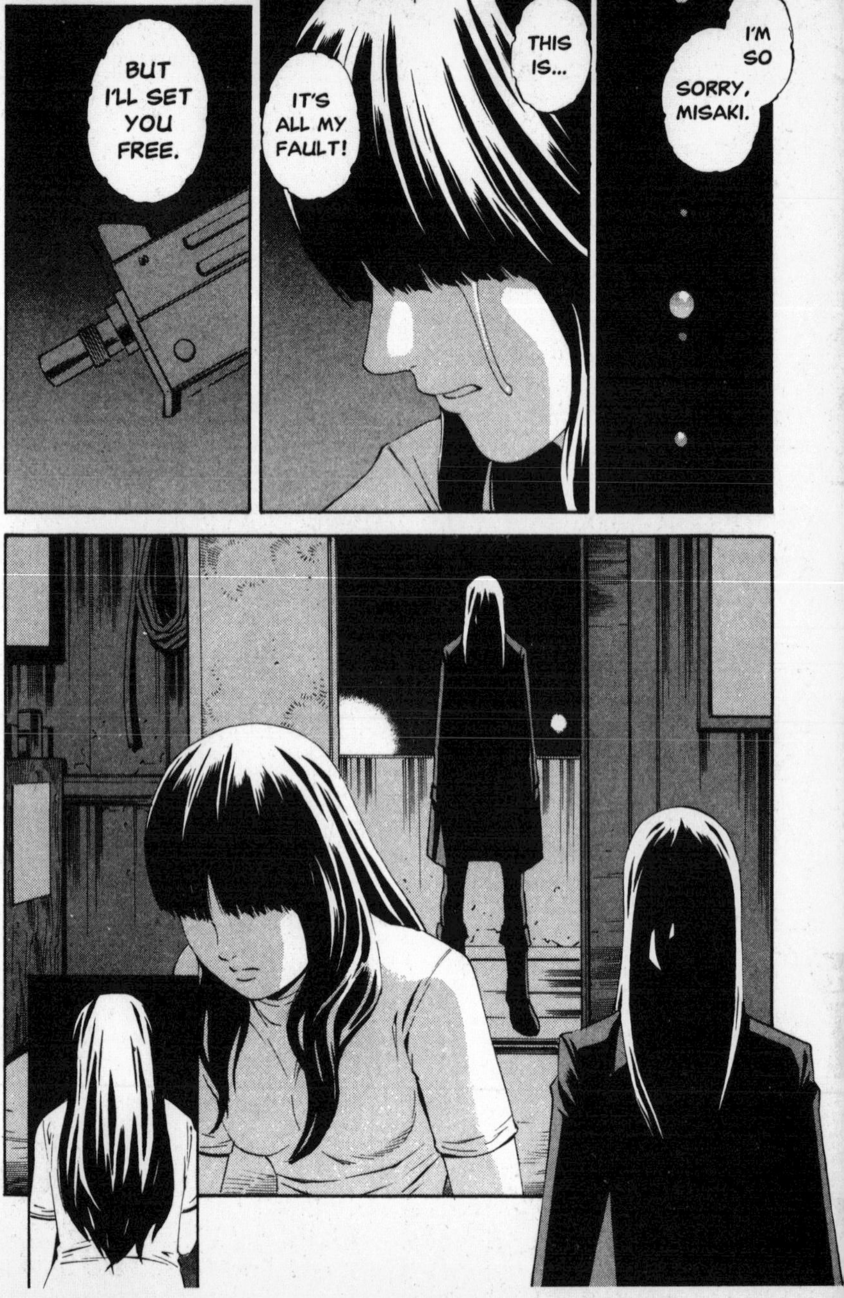
I'M SO SORRY, MISAKI.
THIS IS...
IT'S ALL MY FAULT!
BUT I'LL SET YOU FREE.

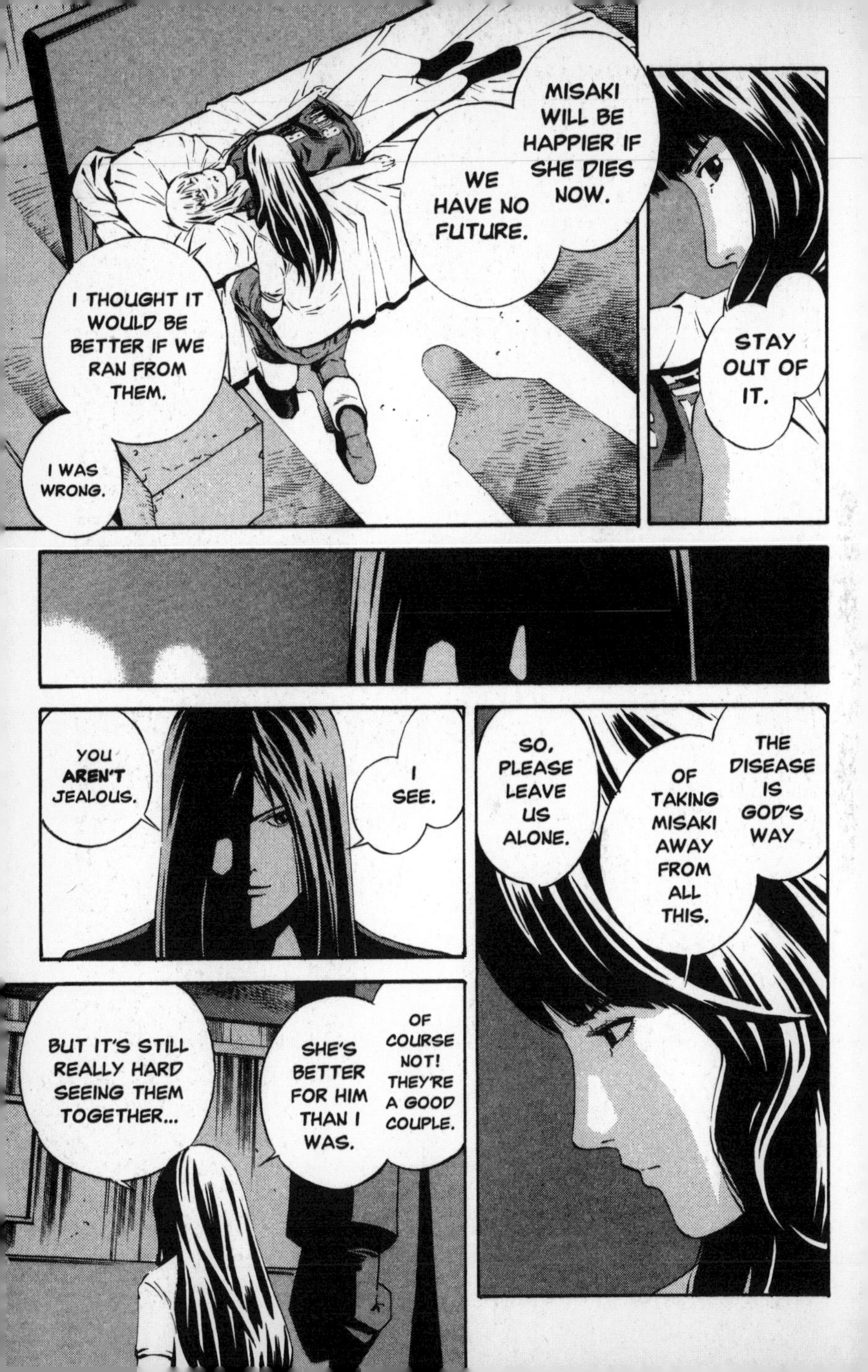
STAY OUT OF IT.
MISAKI WILL BE HAPPIER IF SHE DIES NOW.
WE HAVE NO FUTURE.
I THOUGHT IT WOULD BE BETTER IF WE RAN FROM THEM.
I WAS WRONG.
THE DISEASE IS GOD'S WAY OF TAKING MISAKI AWAY FROM ALL THIS.
SO, PLEASE LEAVE US ALONE.
I SEE.
YOU **AREN'T** JEALOUS.
OF COURSE NOT! THEY'RE A GOOD COUPLE.
SHE'S BETTER FOR HIM THAN I WAS.
BUT IT'S STILL REALLY HARD SEEING THEM TOGETHER...

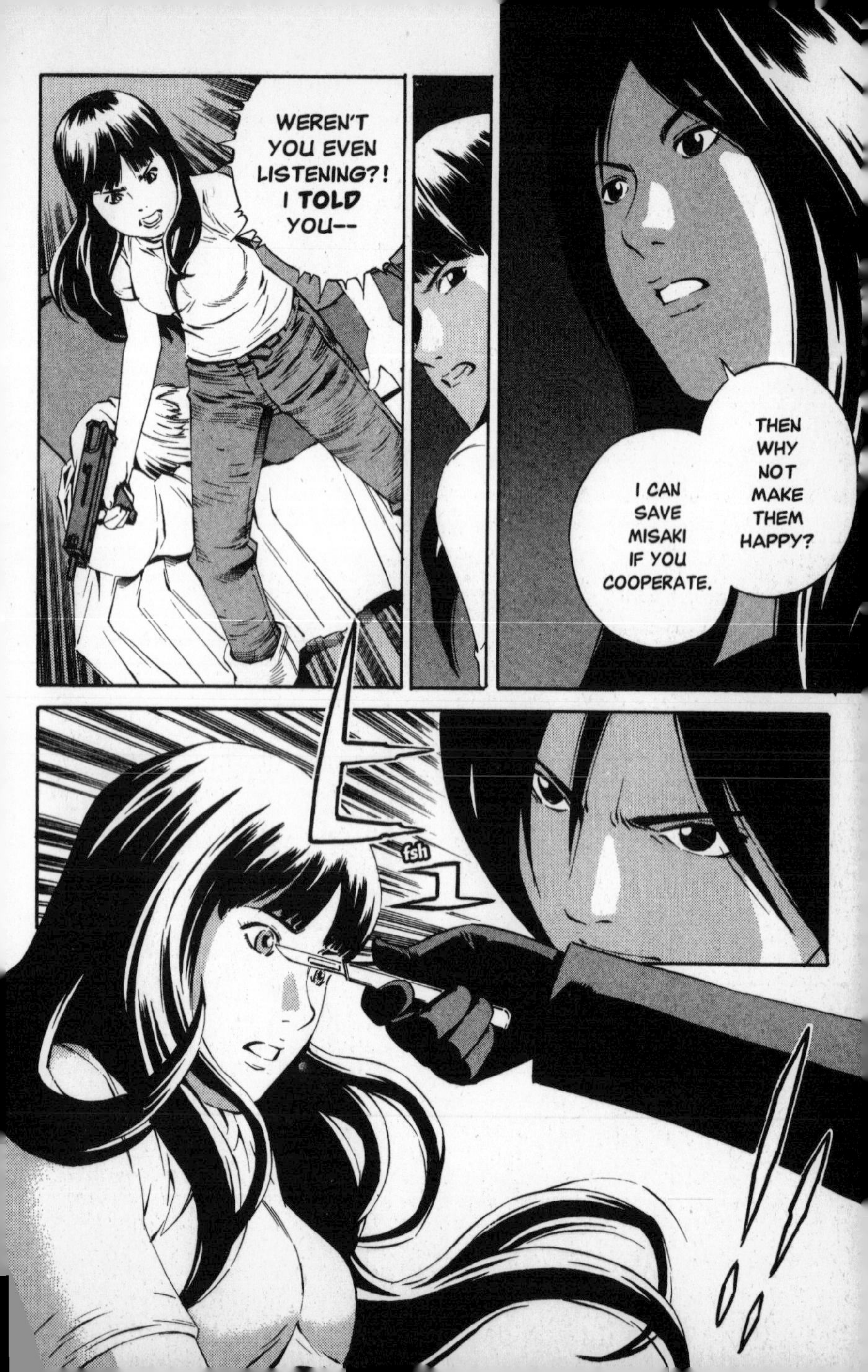
THEN WHY NOT MAKE THEM HAPPY?
I CAN SAVE MISAKI IF YOU COOPERATE.
WEREN'T YOU EVEN LISTENING?! I TOLD YOU--
fsh

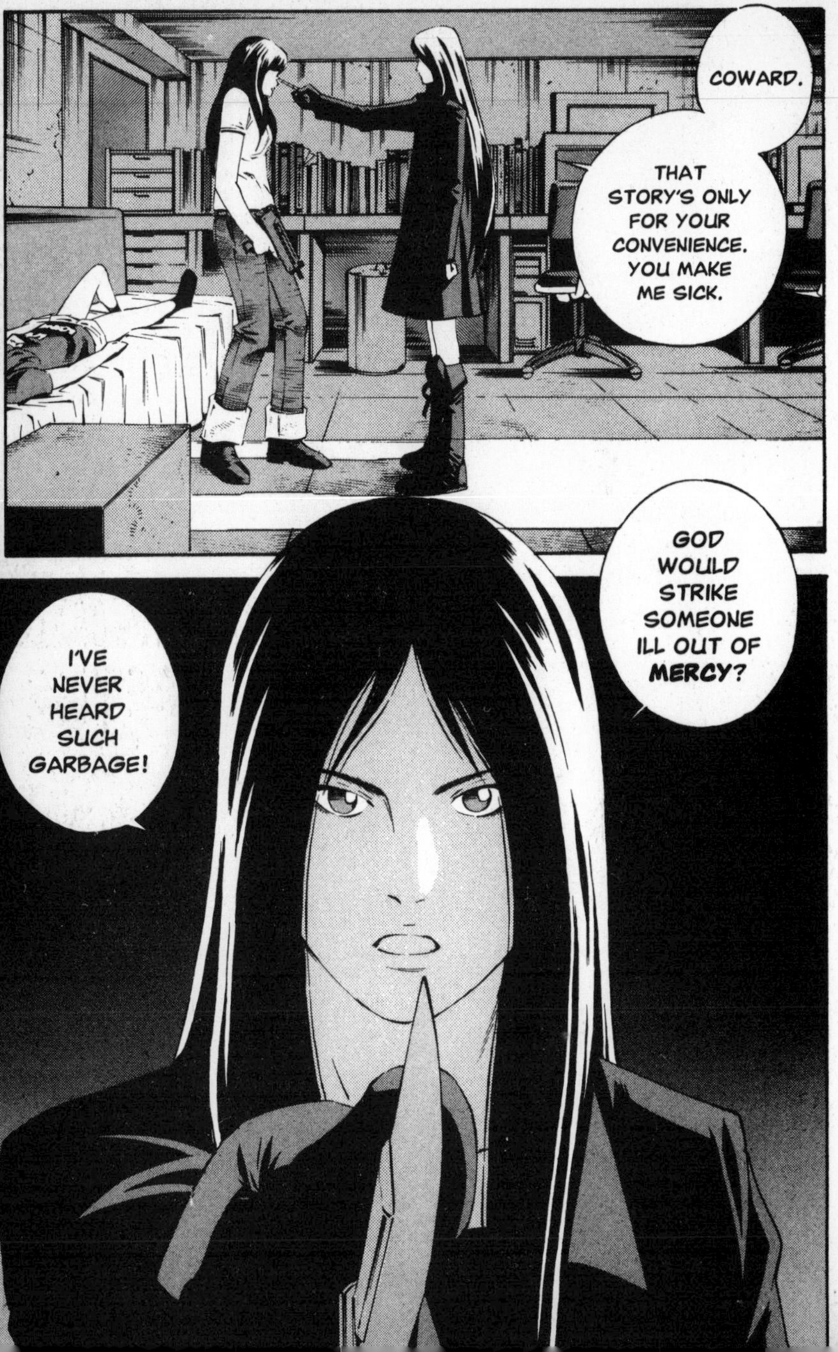
COWARD.
THAT STORY'S ONLY FOR YOUR CONVENIENCE. YOU MAKE ME SICK.
GOD WOULD STRIKE SOMEONE ILL OUT OF **MERCY**?
I'VE NEVER HEARD SUCH GARBAGE!

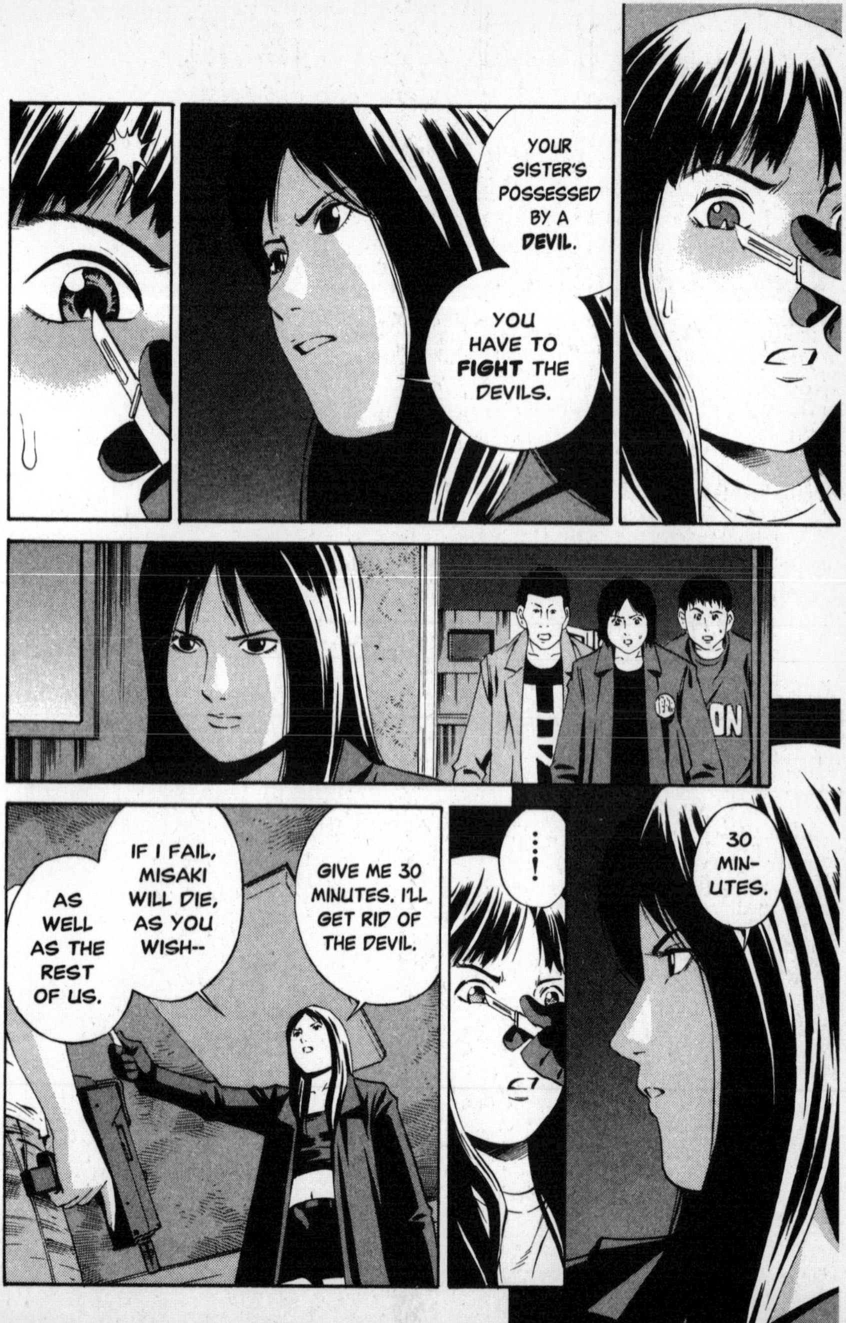
YOUR SISTER'S POSSESSED BY A **DEVIL.**
YOU HAVE TO **FIGHT** THE DEVILS.
GIVE ME 30 MINUTES. I'LL GET RID OF THE DEVIL.
IF I FAIL, MISAKI WILL DIE, AS YOU WISH--
AS WELL AS THE REST OF US.
...!
30 MIN-UTES.

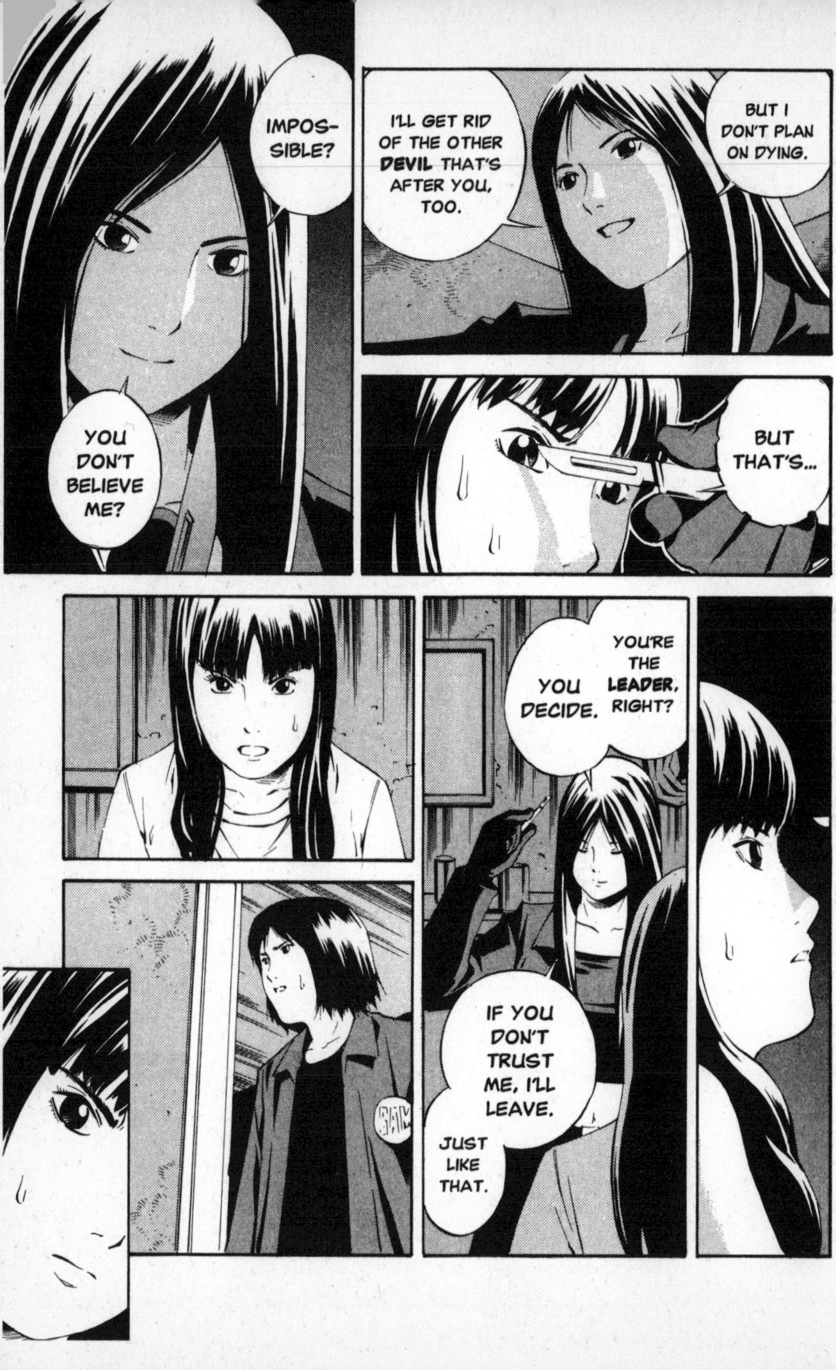
BUT I DON'T PLAN ON DYING.
I'LL GET RID OF THE OTHER DEVIL THAT'S AFTER YOU, TOO.
BUT THAT'S...
IMPOSSIBLE?
YOU DON'T BELIEVE ME?
YOU'RE THE LEADER, RIGHT?
YOU DECIDE.
IF YOU DON'T TRUST ME, I'LL LEAVE.
JUST LIKE THAT.

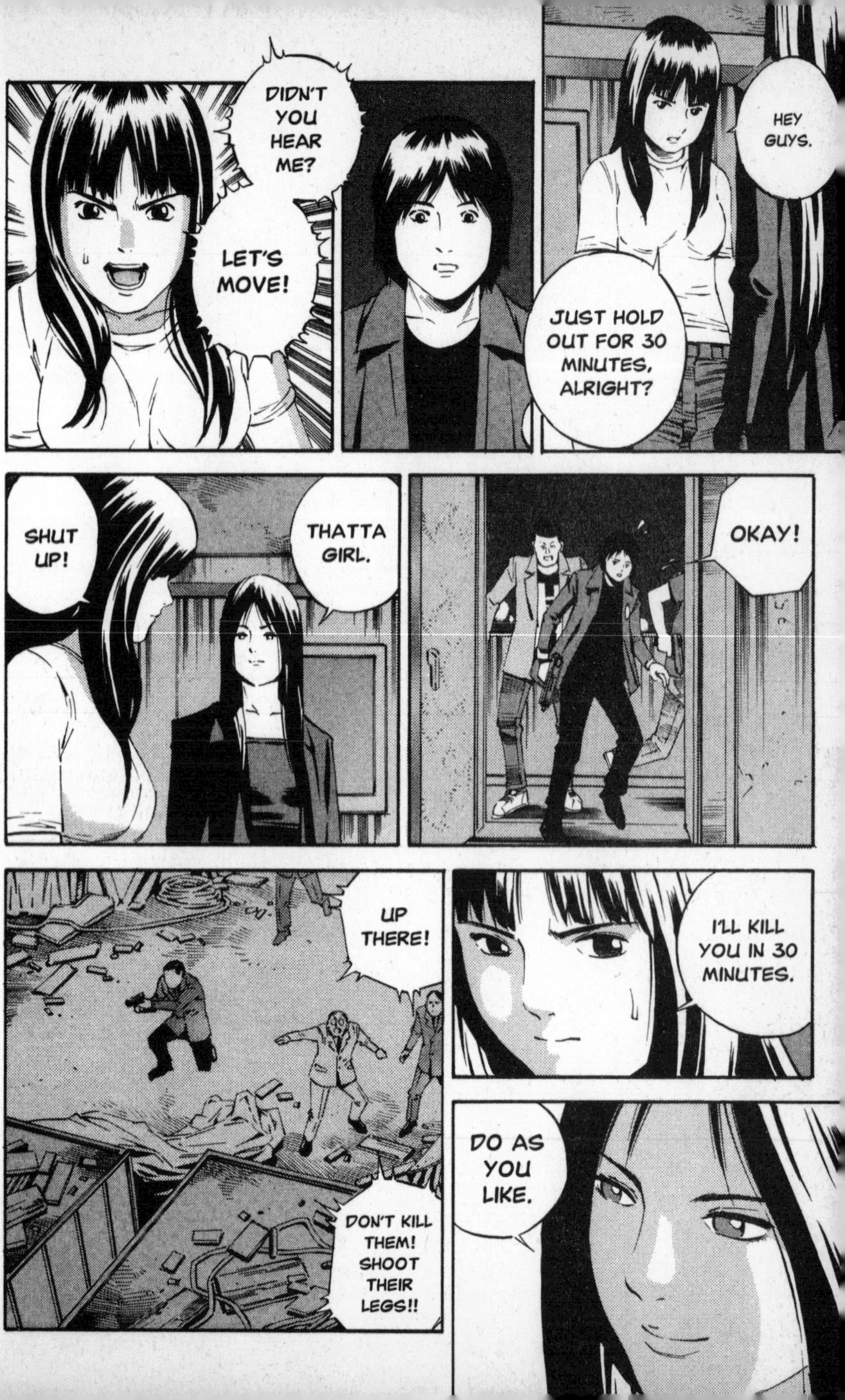
HEY GUYS.
JUST HOLD OUT FOR 30 MINUTES, ALRIGHT?
DIDN'T YOU HEAR ME?
LET'S MOVE!
OKAY!
THATTA GIRL.
SHUT UP!
I'LL KILL YOU IN 30 MINUTES.
DO AS YOU LIKE.
UP THERE!
DON'T KILL THEM! SHOOT THEIR LEGS!!

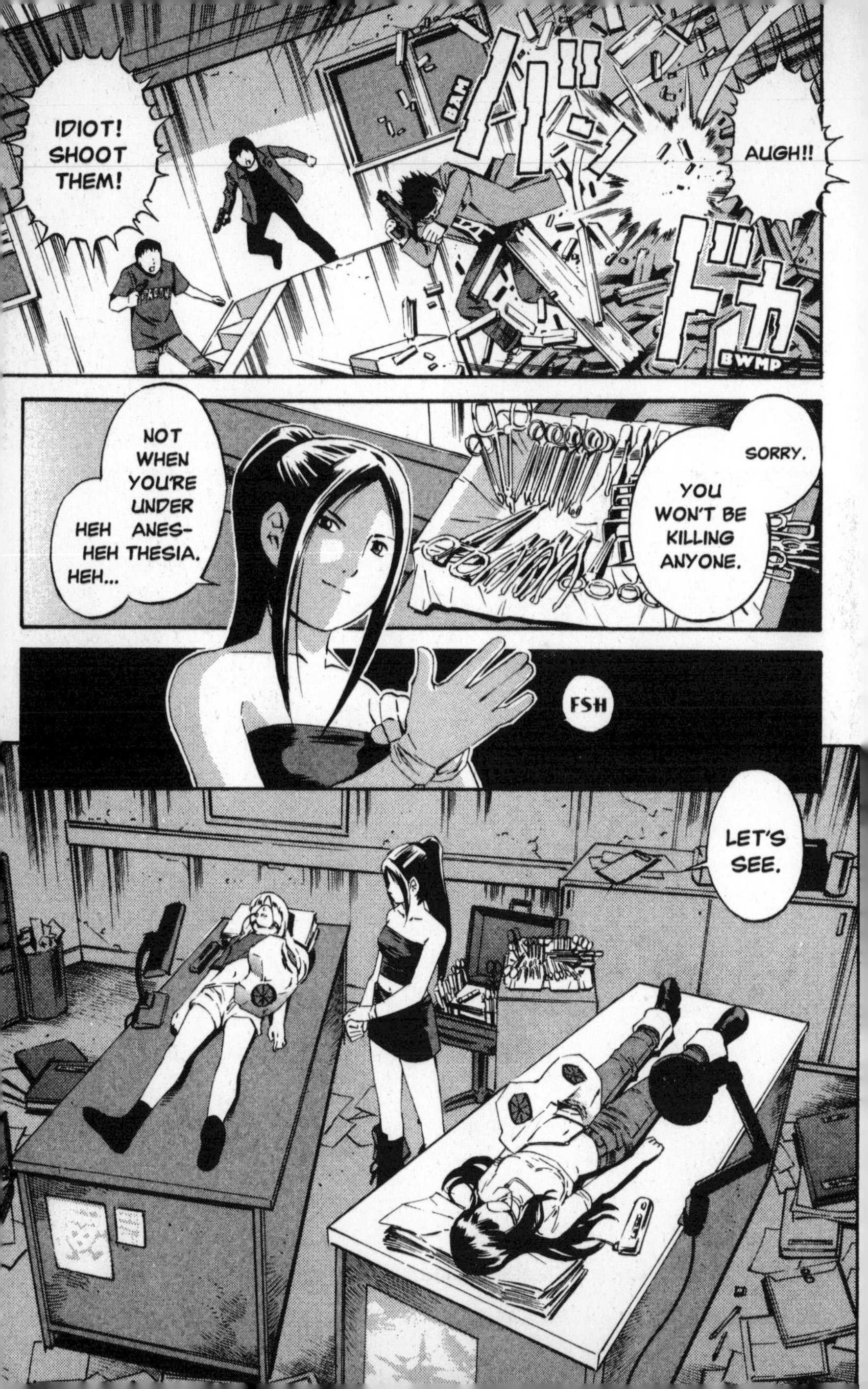
BAM
AUGH!!
BWMP
IDIOT! SHOOT THEM!
SORRY.
YOU WON'T BE KILLING ANYONE.
HEH HEH HEH...
NOT WHEN YOU'RE UNDER ANES-THESIA.
FSH
LET'S SEE.

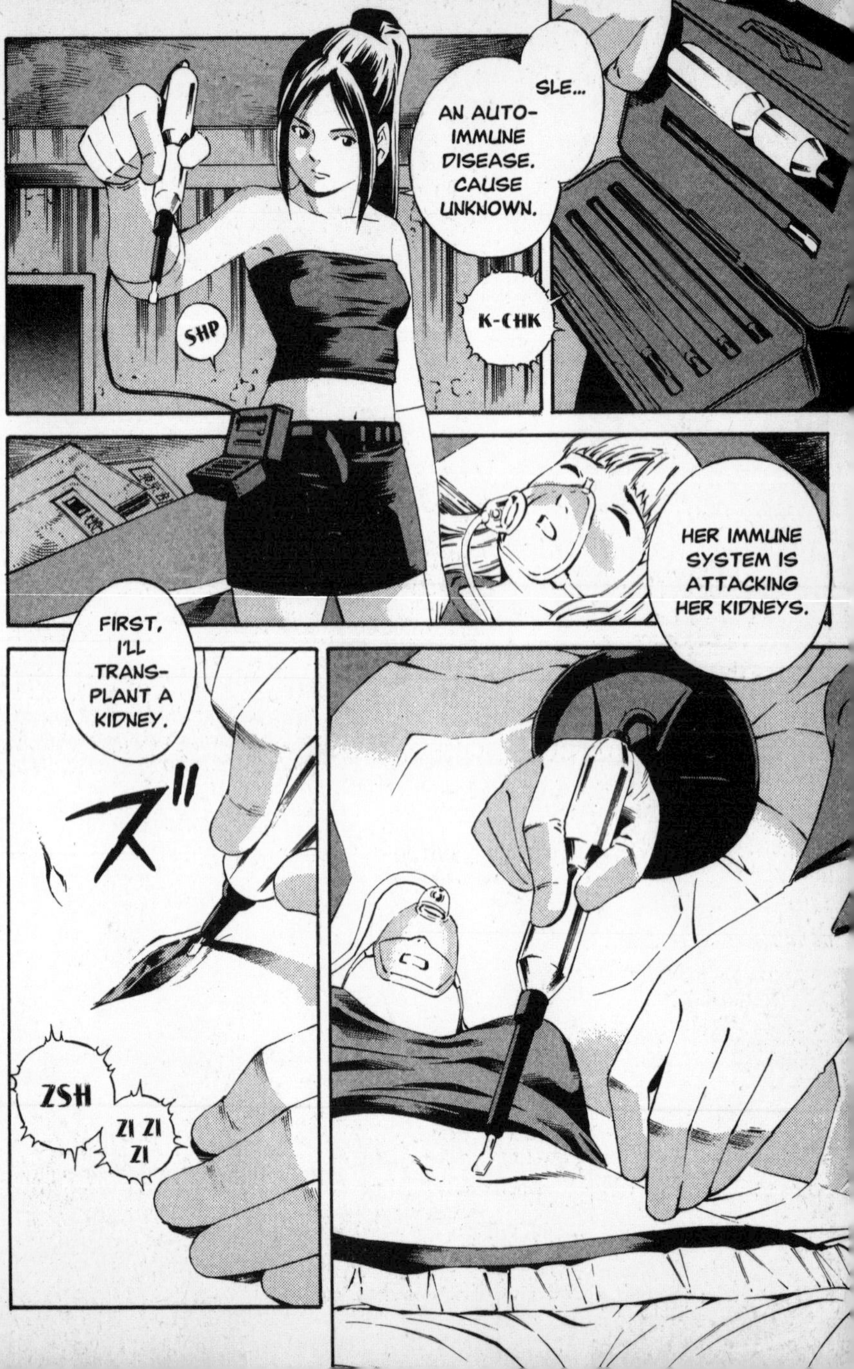
SLE... AN AUTO-IMMUNE DISEASE. CAUSE UNKNOWN.
K-CHK
SHP
HER IMMUNE SYSTEM IS ATTACKING HER KIDNEYS.
FIRST, I'LL TRANS-PLANT A KIDNEY.
ズ
ZSH
ZI ZI ZI

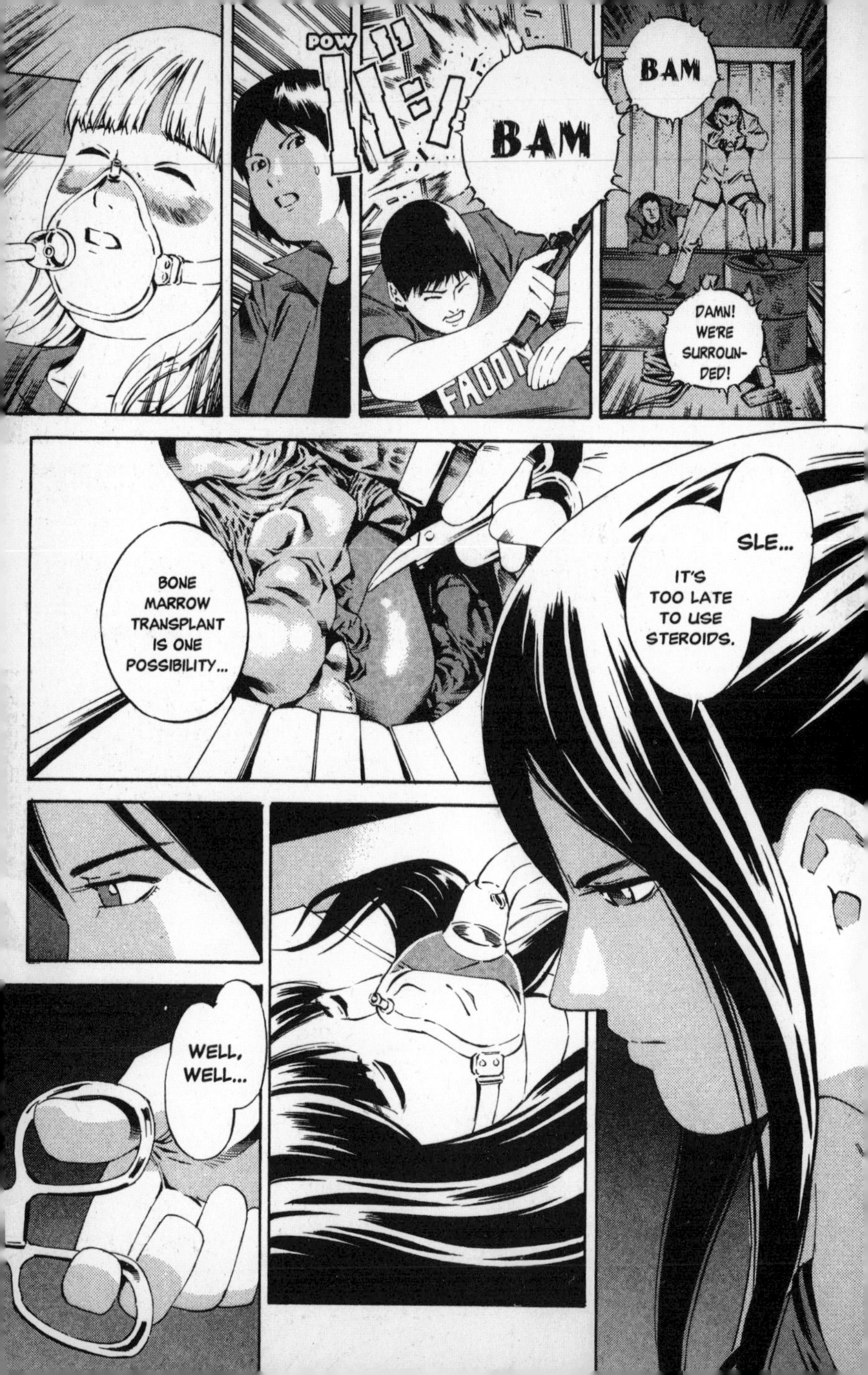
BAM
BAM
POW
DAMN! WE'RE SURROUNDED!
FADO
SLE...
IT'S TOO LATE TO USE STEROIDS.
BONE MARROW TRANSPLANT IS ONE POSSIBILITY...
WELL, WELL...

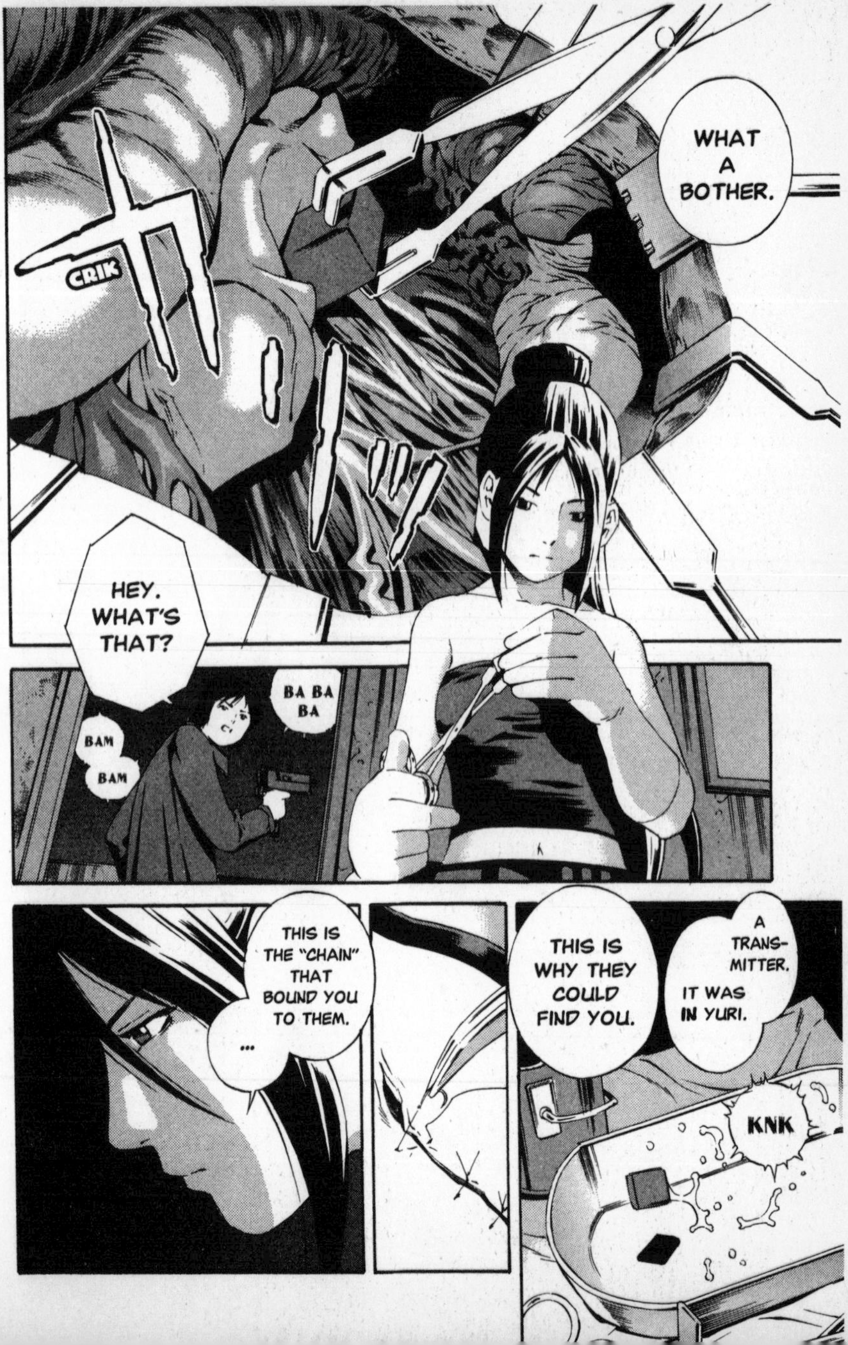
WHAT A BOTHER.
CRIK
HEY. WHAT'S THAT?
BA BA BA
BAM
BAM
A TRANS-MITTER.
IT WAS IN YURI.
KNK
THIS IS WHY THEY COULD FIND YOU.
THIS IS THE "CHAIN" THAT BOUND YOU TO THEM.
...

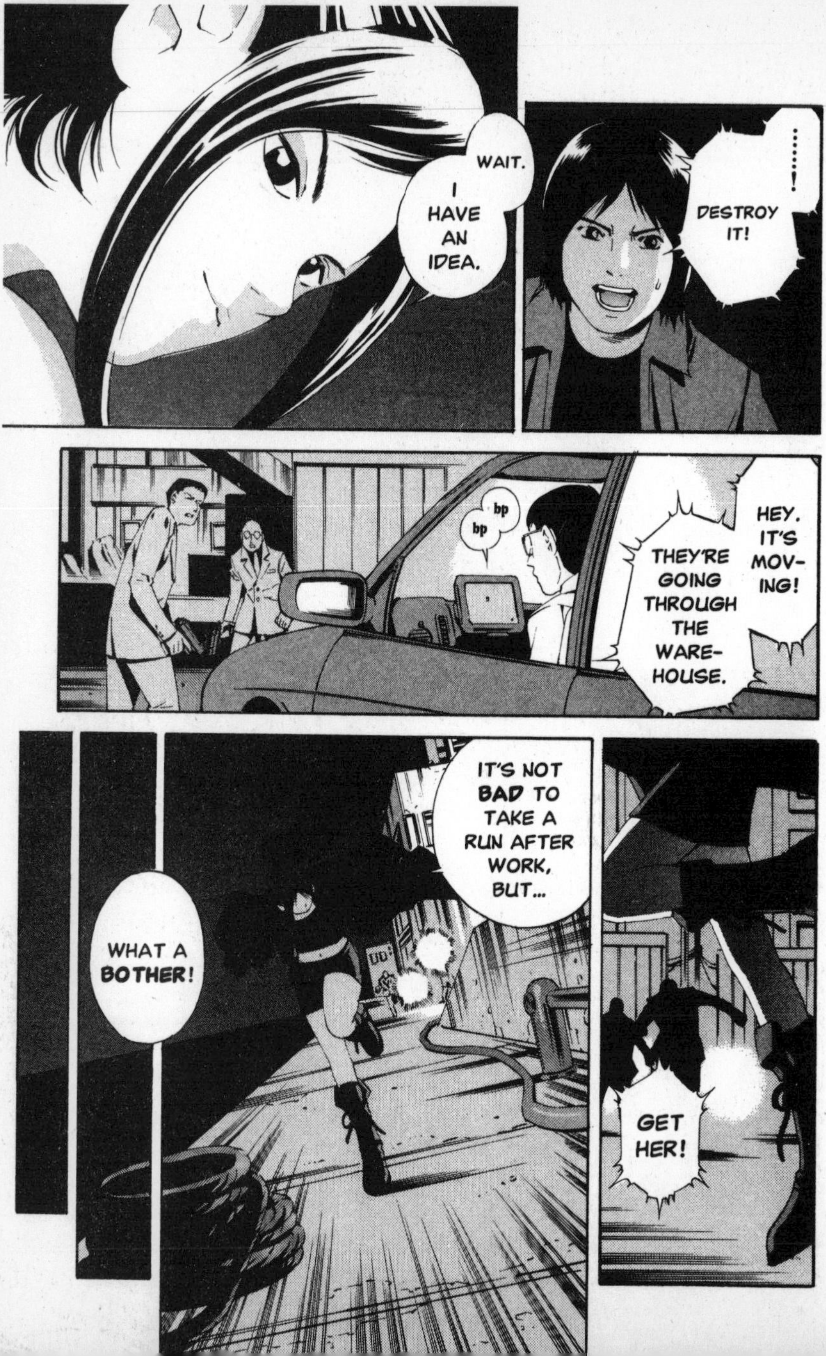
......!
DESTROY IT!
WAIT.
I HAVE AN IDEA.
HEY. IT'S MOV-ING!
THEY'RE GOING THROUGH THE WARE-HOUSE.
bp
bp
GET HER!
IT'S NOT **BAD** TO TAKE A RUN AFTER WORK, BUT...
WHAT A **BOTHER**!

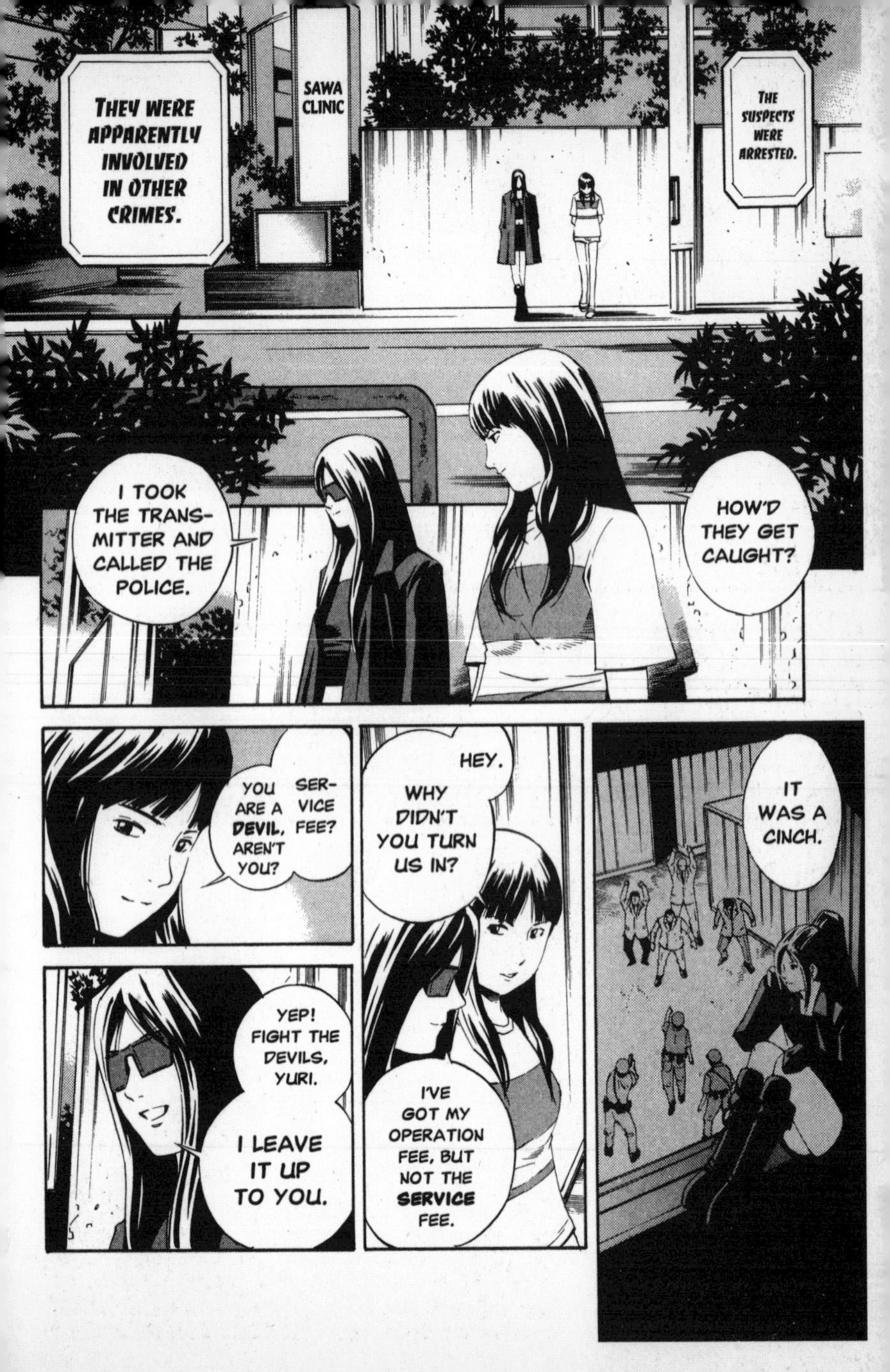
SAWA CLINIC
The suspects were arrested.
They were apparently involved in other crimes.
How'd they get caught?
I took the transmitter and called the police.
It was a cinch.
Hey.
Why didn't you turn us in?
I've got my operation fee, but not the service fee.
Service fee?
You are a devil, aren't you?
Yep! Fight the devils, Yuri.
I leave it up to you.

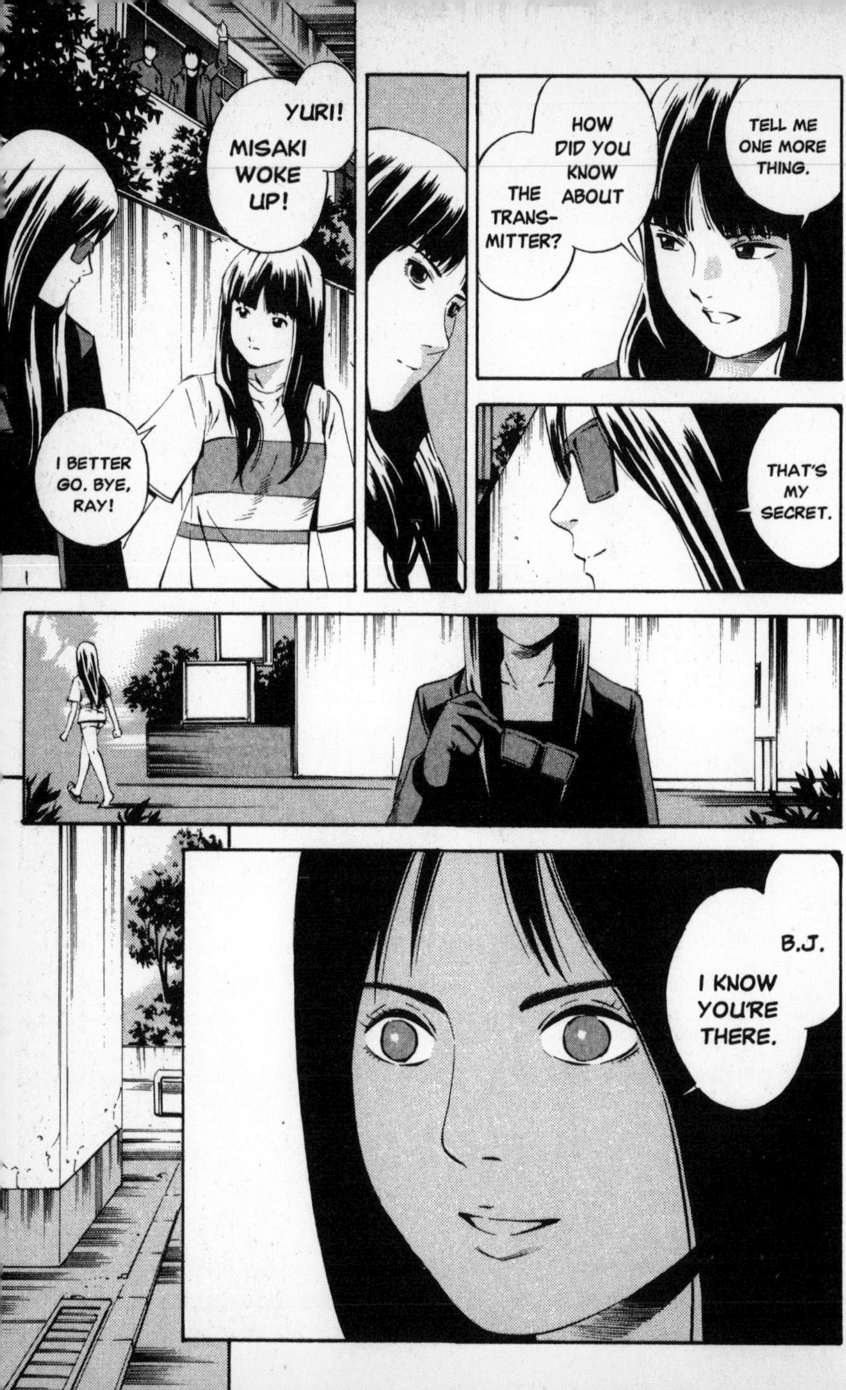
YURI!
MISAKI WOKE UP!
I BETTER GO. BYE, RAY!
TELL ME ONE MORE THING.
HOW DID YOU KNOW ABOUT THE TRANS-MITTER?
THAT'S MY SECRET.
B.J.
I KNOW YOU'RE THERE.

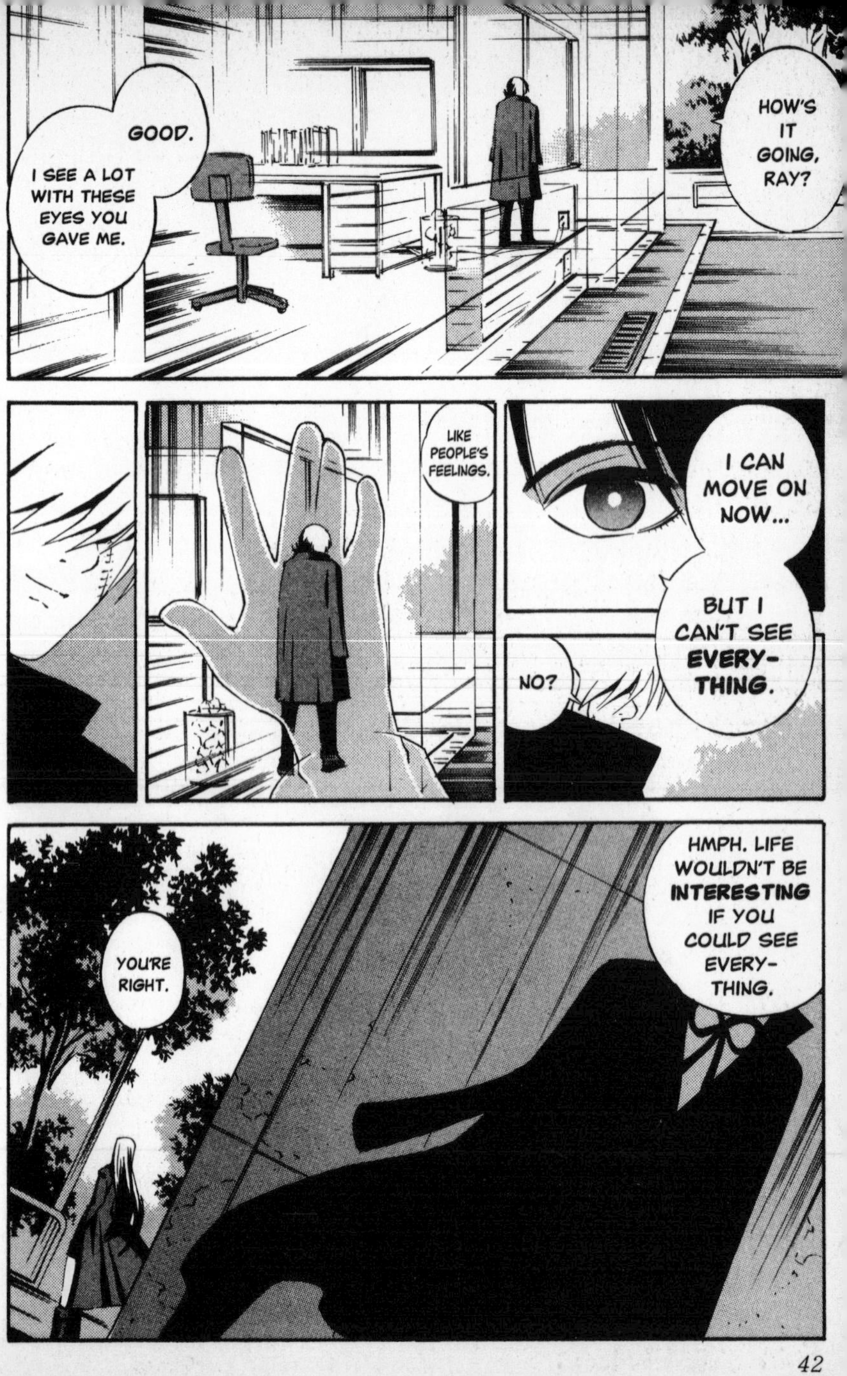
HOW'S IT GOING, RAY?
GOOD.
I SEE A LOT WITH THESE EYES YOU GAVE ME.
I CAN MOVE ON NOW...
BUT I CAN'T SEE EVERYTHING.
NO?
LIKE PEOPLE'S FEELINGS.
HMPH. LIFE WOULDN'T BE INTERESTING IF YOU COULD SEE EVERYTHING.
YOU'RE RIGHT.

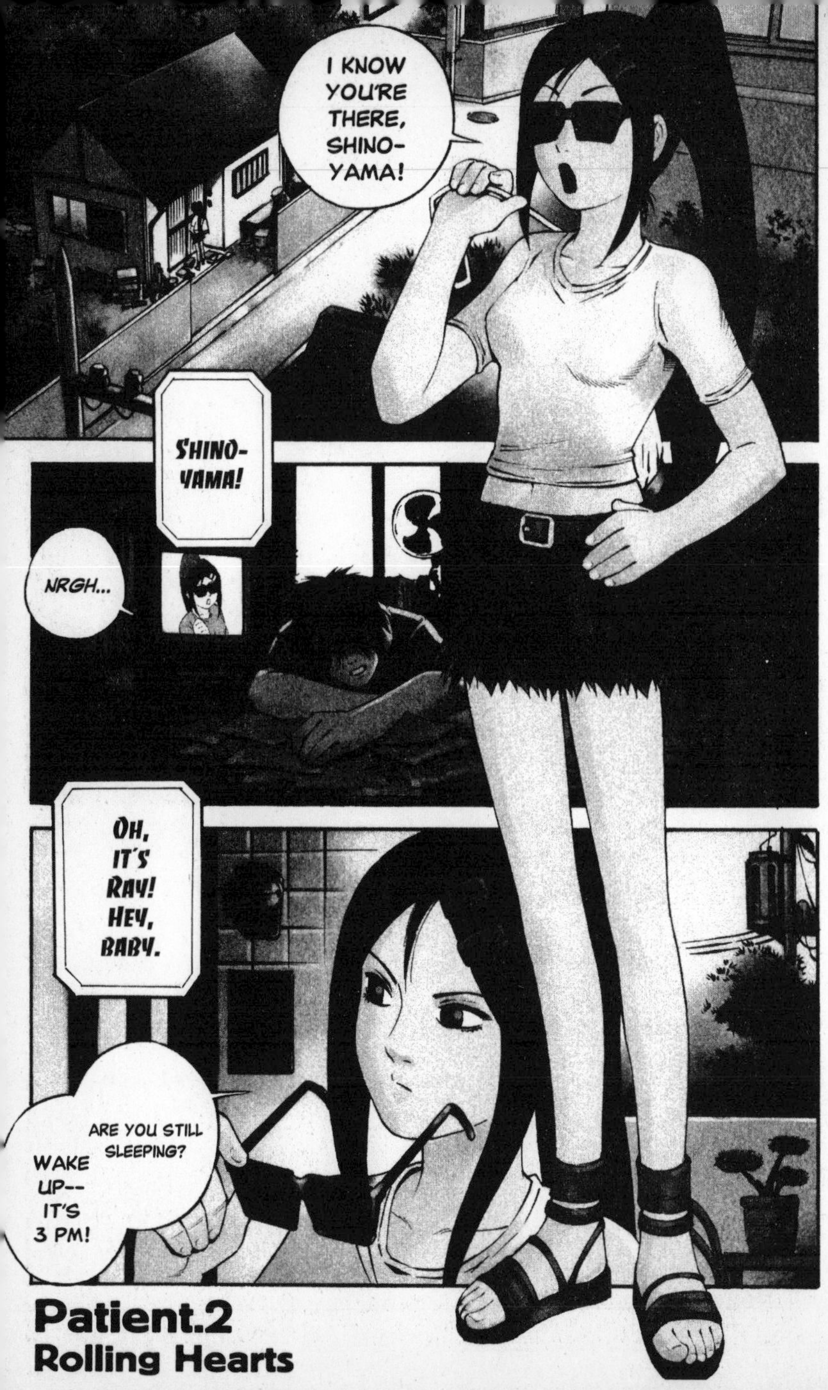
I KNOW YOU'RE THERE, SHINO-YAMA!
SHINO-YAMA!
NRGH...
OH, IT'S RAY! HEY, BABY.
ARE YOU STILL SLEEPING?
WAKE UP-- IT'S 3 PM!

Patient.2
Rolling Hearts

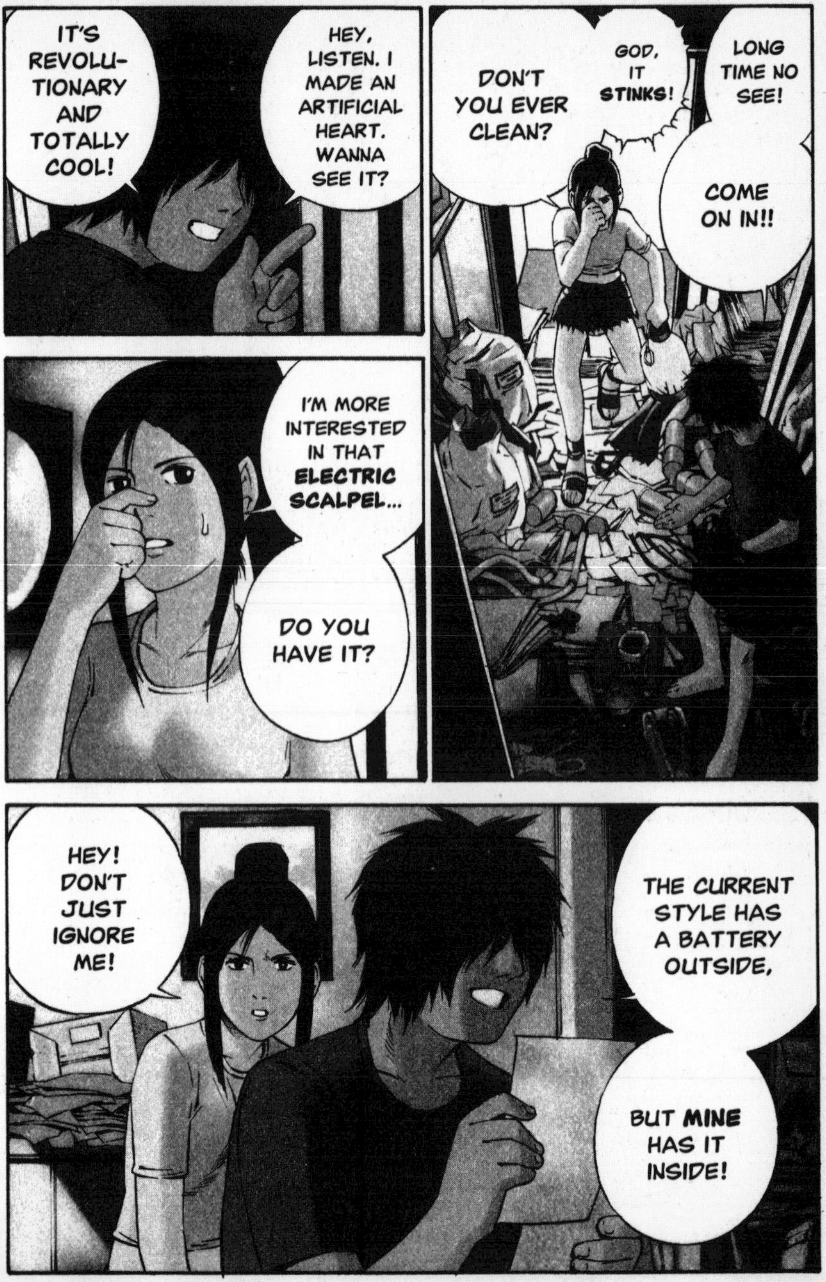
LONG TIME NO SEE!
COME ON IN!!
GOD, IT STINKS!
DON'T YOU EVER CLEAN?
HEY, LISTEN. I MADE AN ARTIFICIAL HEART. WANNA SEE IT?
IT'S REVOLU-TIONARY AND TOTALLY COOL!
I'M MORE INTERESTED IN THAT ELECTRIC SCALPEL...
DO YOU HAVE IT?
THE CURRENT STYLE HAS A BATTERY OUTSIDE,
BUT MINE HAS IT INSIDE!
HEY! DON'T JUST IGNORE ME!

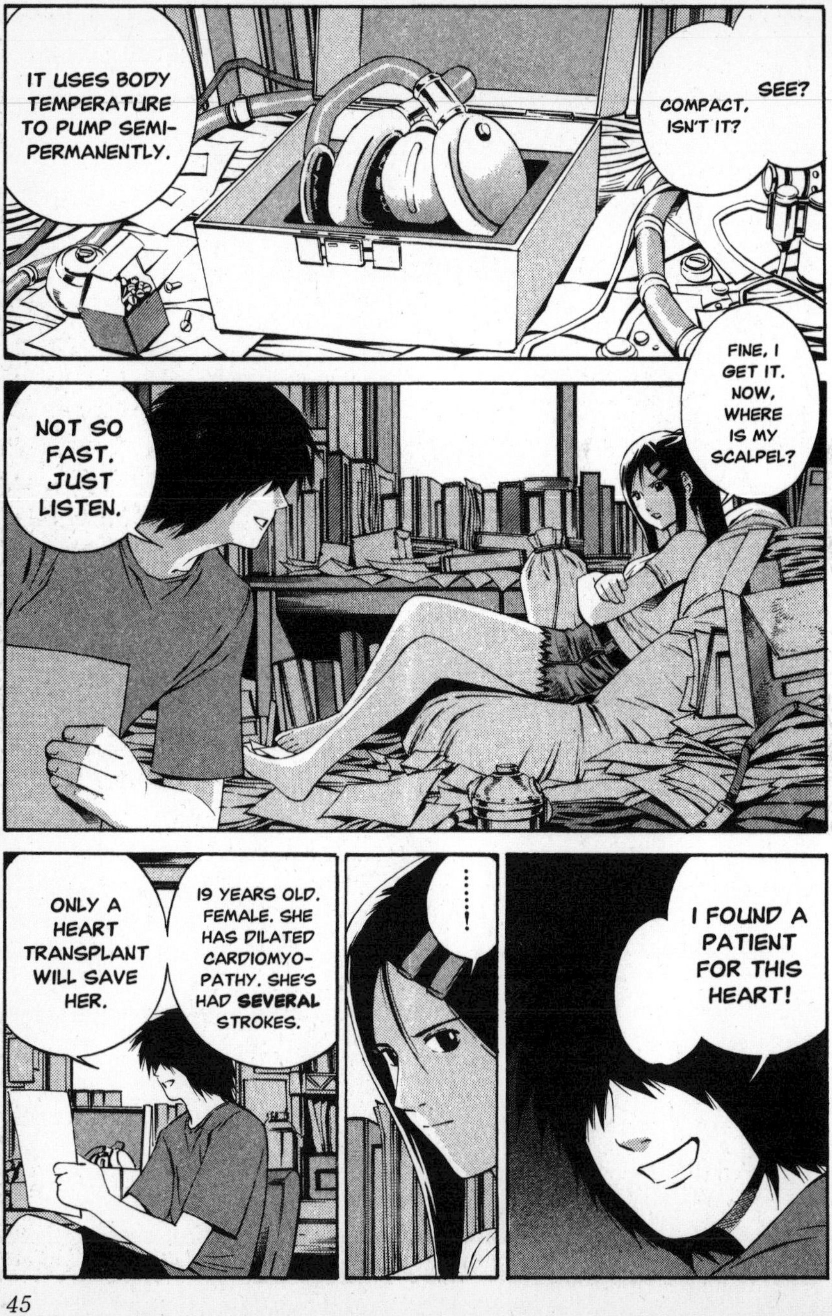
SEE?
COMPACT, ISN'T IT?
IT USES BODY TEMPERATURE TO PUMP SEMI-PERMANENTLY.
FINE, I GET IT. NOW, WHERE IS MY SCALPEL?
NOT SO FAST. JUST LISTEN.
I FOUND A PATIENT FOR THIS HEART!
......!
19 YEARS OLD. FEMALE. SHE HAS DILATED CARDIOMYO-PATHY. SHE'S HAD **SEVERAL** STROKES.
ONLY A HEART TRANSPLANT WILL SAVE HER.

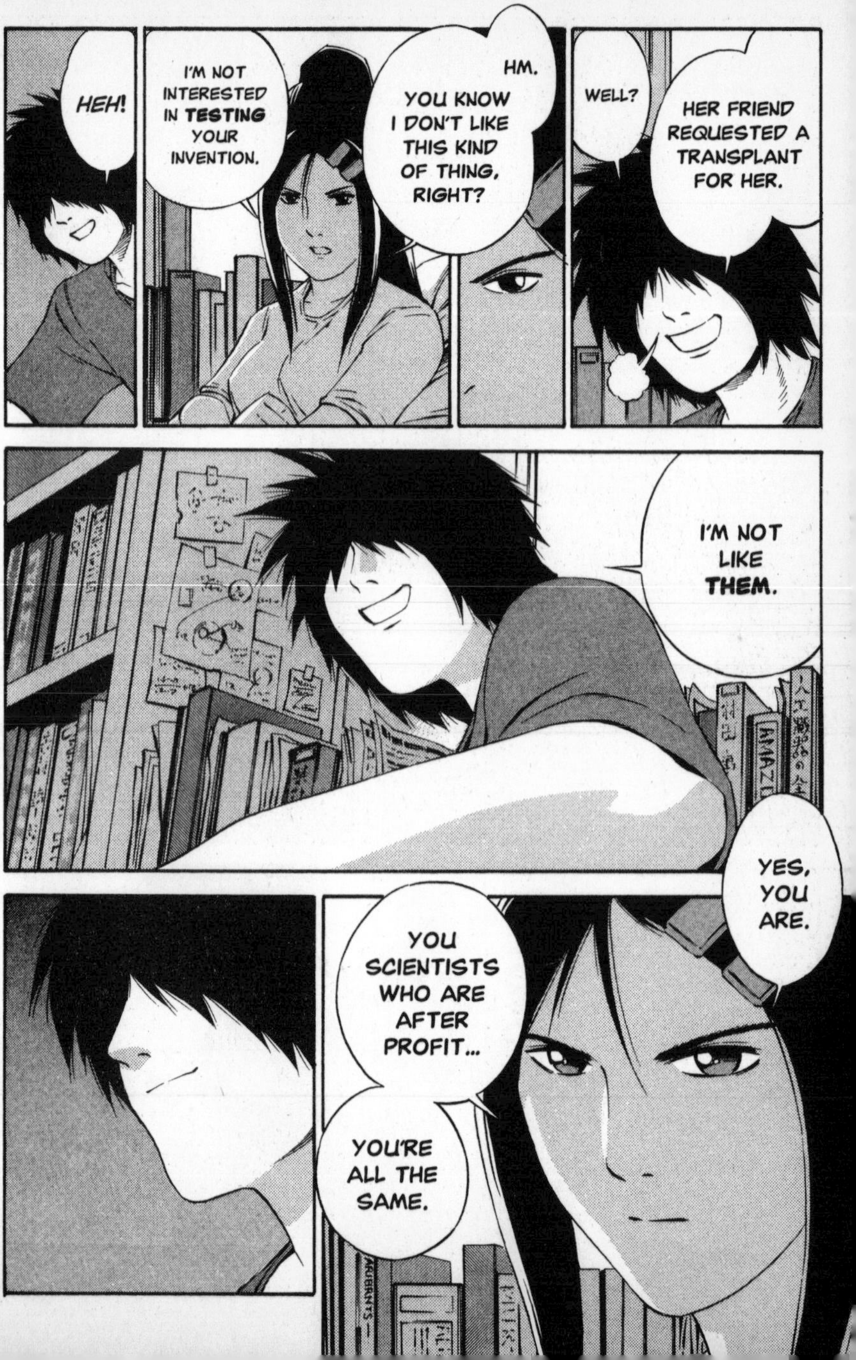
HEH!
I'M NOT INTERESTED IN TESTING YOUR INVENTION.
HM.
YOU KNOW I DON'T LIKE THIS KIND OF THING, RIGHT?
WELL?
HER FRIEND REQUESTED A TRANSPLANT FOR HER.
I'M NOT LIKE THEM.
YES, YOU ARE.
YOU SCIENTISTS WHO ARE AFTER PROFIT...
YOU'RE ALL THE SAME.

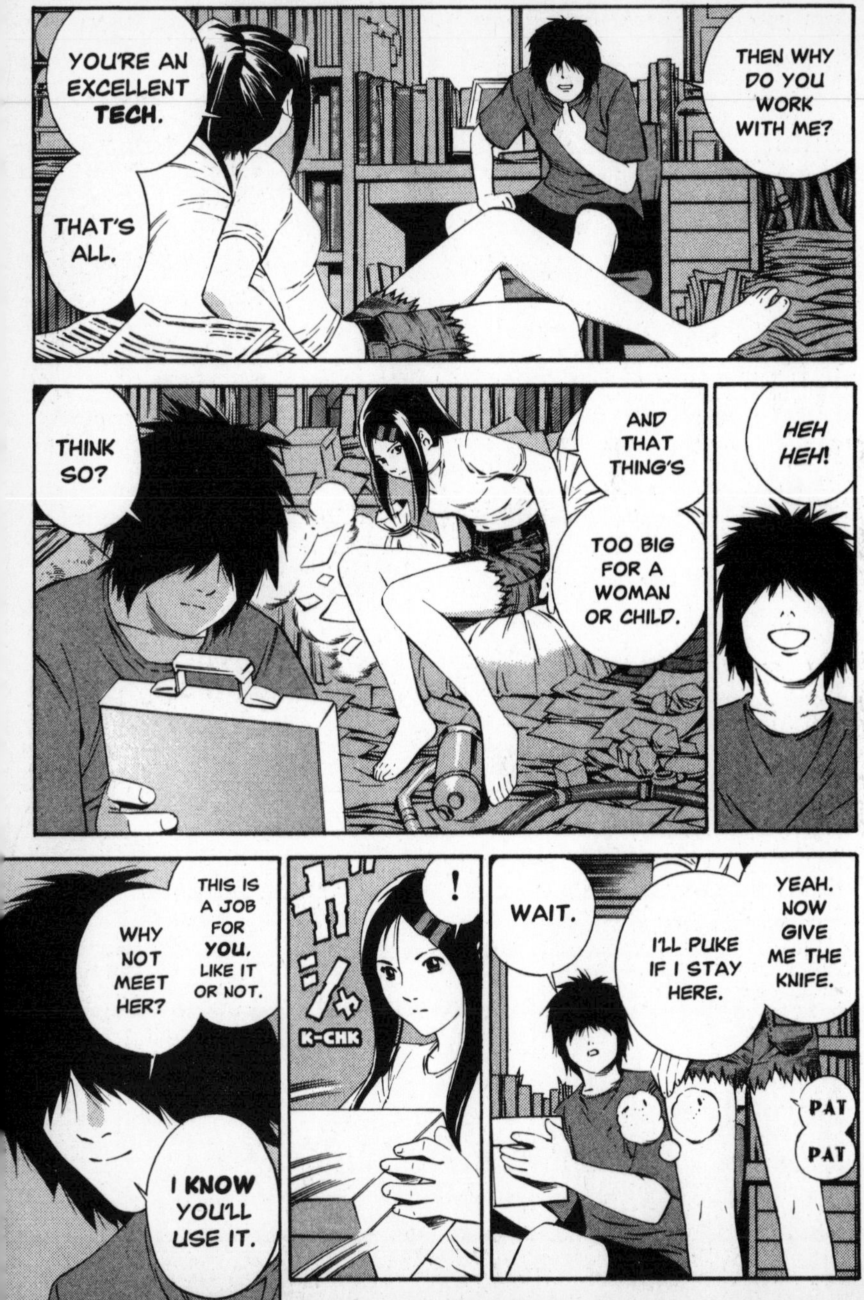
THEN WHY DO YOU WORK WITH ME?
YOU'RE AN EXCELLENT TECH.
THAT'S ALL.
HEH HEH!
AND THAT THING'S
TOO BIG FOR A WOMAN OR CHILD.
THINK SO?
YEAH. NOW GIVE ME THE KNIFE.
I'LL PUKE IF I STAY HERE.
WAIT.
PAT
PAT
!
K-CHK
THIS IS A JOB FOR YOU, LIKE IT OR NOT.
WHY NOT MEET HER?
I KNOW YOU'LL USE IT.

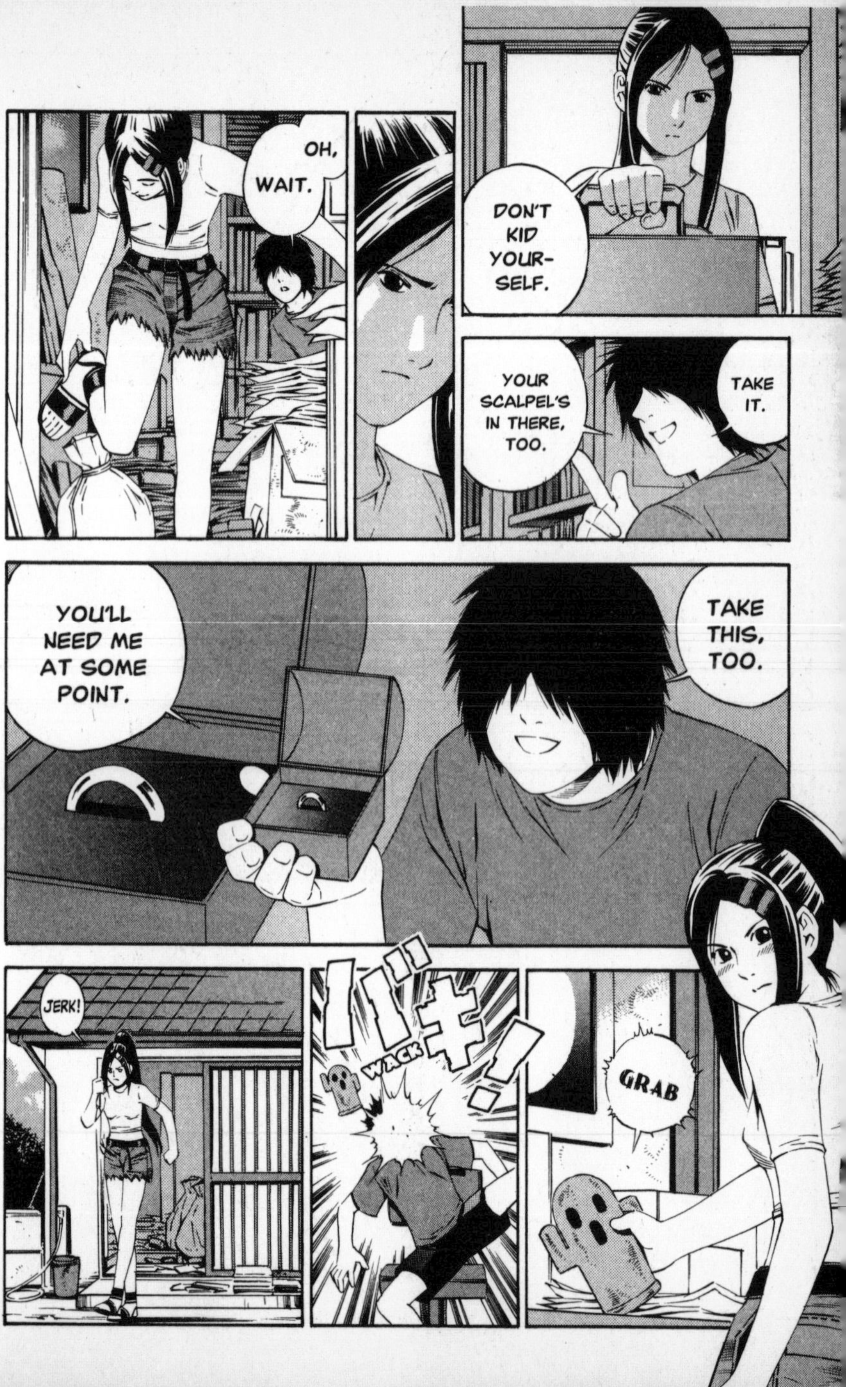
DON'T KID YOURSELF.
TAKE IT.
YOUR SCALPEL'S IN THERE, TOO.
OH, WAIT.
TAKE THIS, TOO.
YOU'LL NEED ME AT SOME POINT.
GRAB
WACK
JERK!

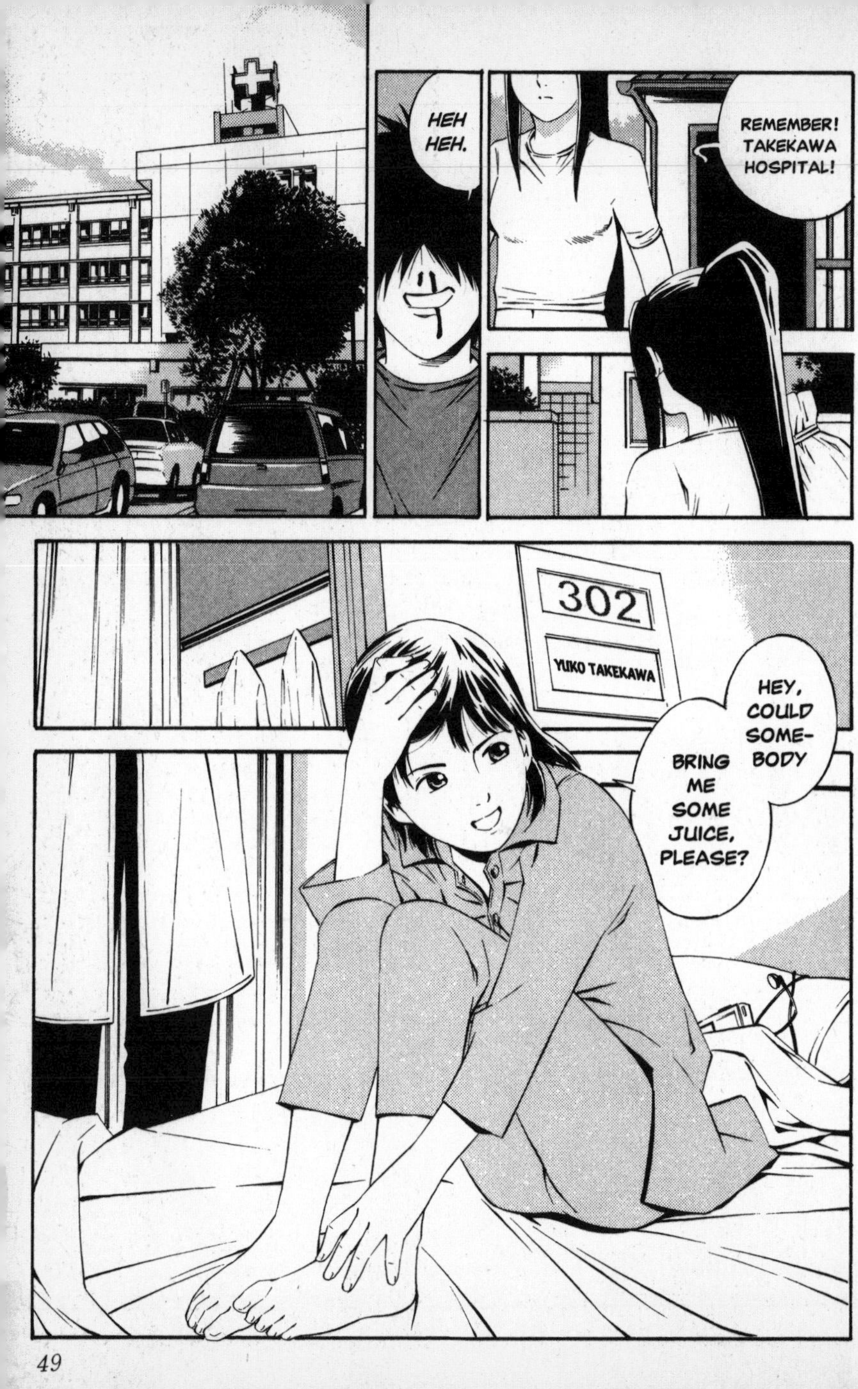
REMEMBER! TAKEKAWA HOSPITAL!
HEH HEH.
302
YUKO TAKEKAWA
HEY, COULD SOME- BODY
BRING ME SOME JUICE, PLEASE?

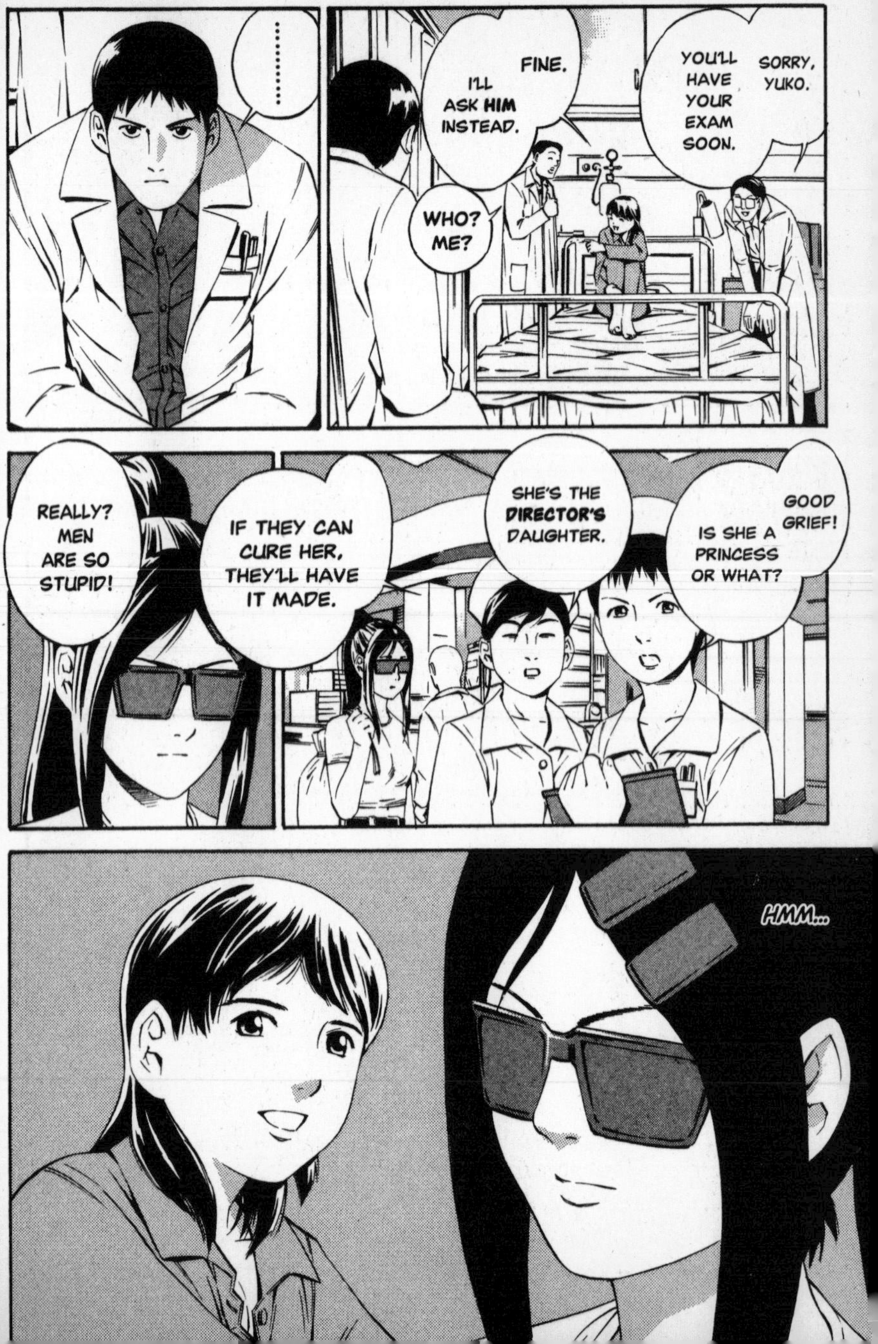
....
SORRY, YUKO.
YOU'LL HAVE YOUR EXAM SOON.
FINE.
I'LL ASK HIM INSTEAD.
WHO? ME?
GOOD GRIEF!
IS SHE A PRINCESS OR WHAT?
SHE'S THE DIRECTOR'S DAUGHTER.
IF THEY CAN CURE HER, THEY'LL HAVE IT MADE.
REALLY? MEN ARE SO STUPID!
HMM...

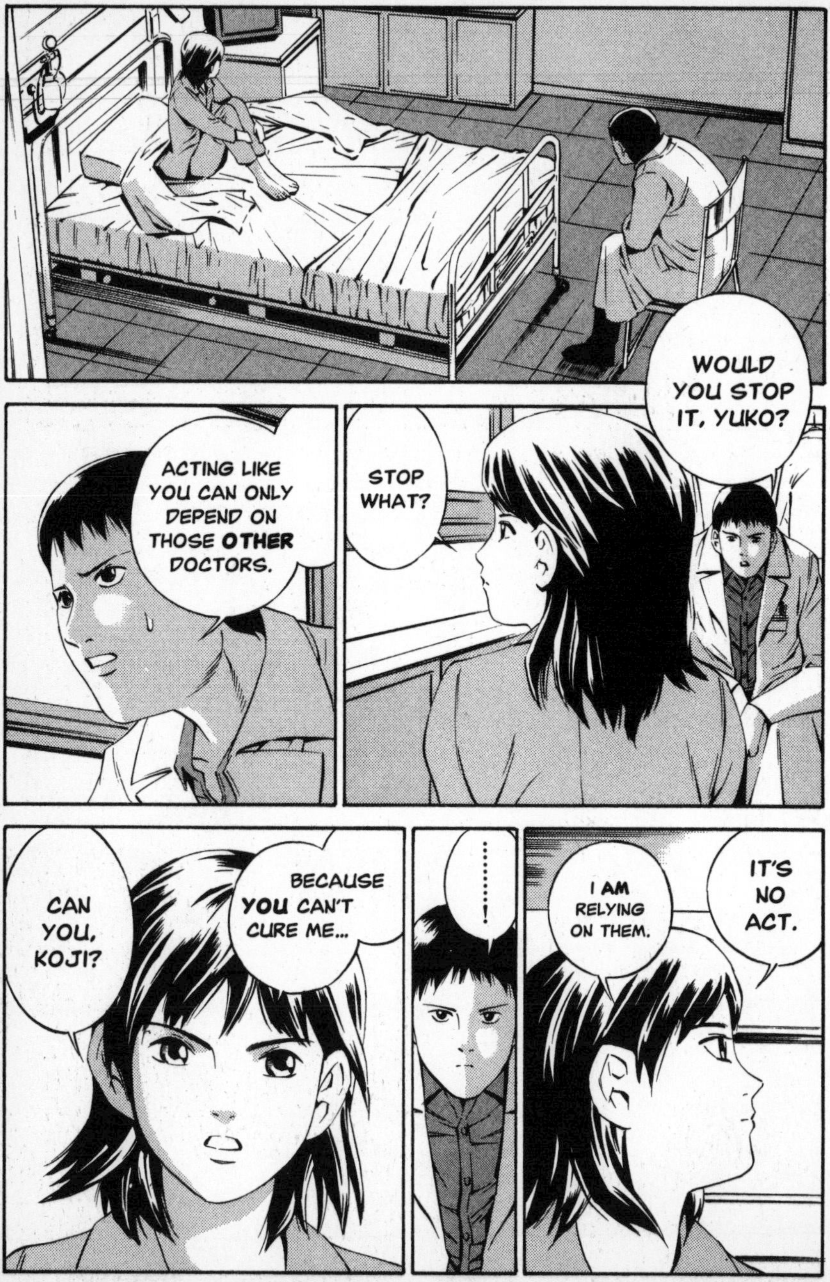
WOULD YOU STOP IT, YUKO?
STOP WHAT?
ACTING LIKE YOU CAN ONLY DEPEND ON THOSE **OTHER** DOCTORS.
IT'S NO ACT.
I **AM** RELYING ON THEM.
......!
BECAUSE **YOU** CAN'T CURE ME...
CAN YOU, KOJI?

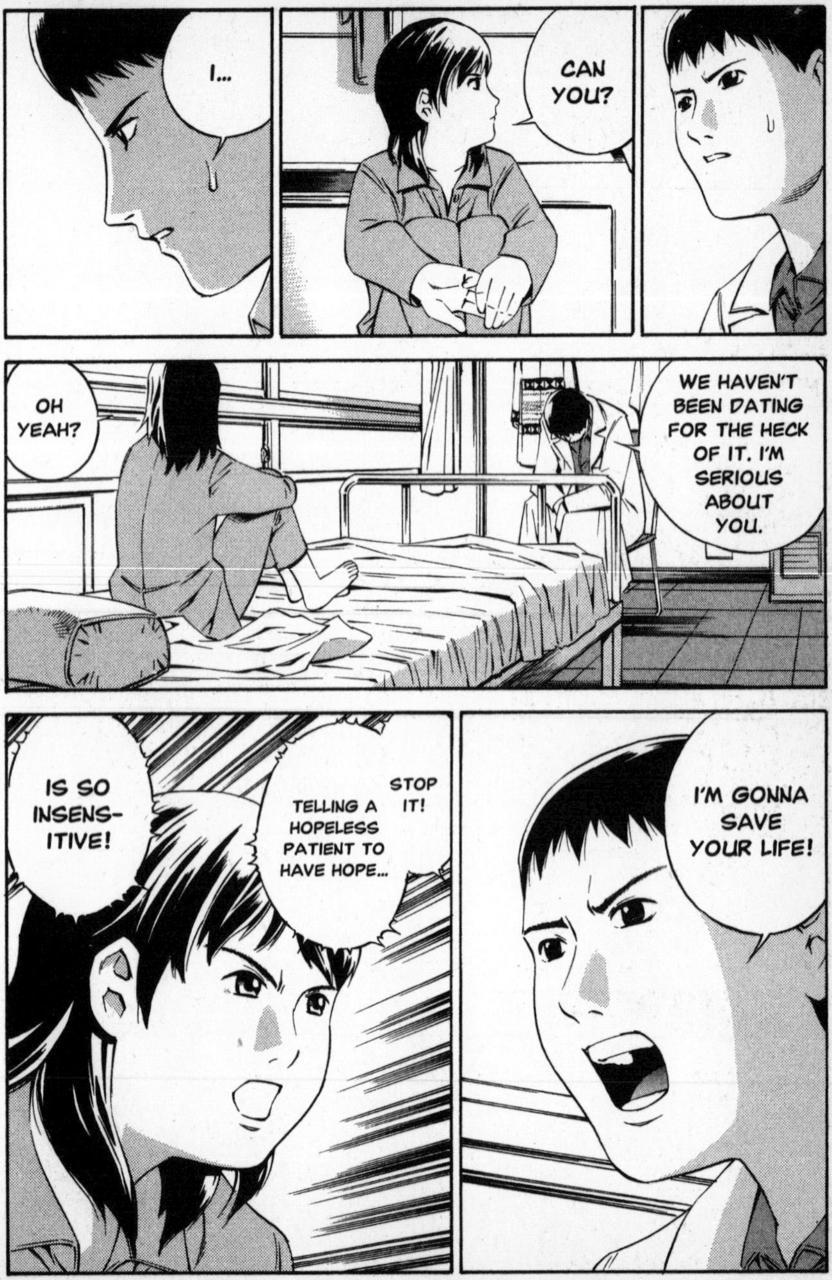
CAN YOU?
I...
WE HAVEN'T BEEN DATING FOR THE HECK OF IT. I'M SERIOUS ABOUT YOU.
OH YEAH?
I'M GONNA SAVE YOUR LIFE!
STOP IT!
TELLING A HOPELESS PATIENT TO HAVE HOPE...
IS SO INSENSITIVE!

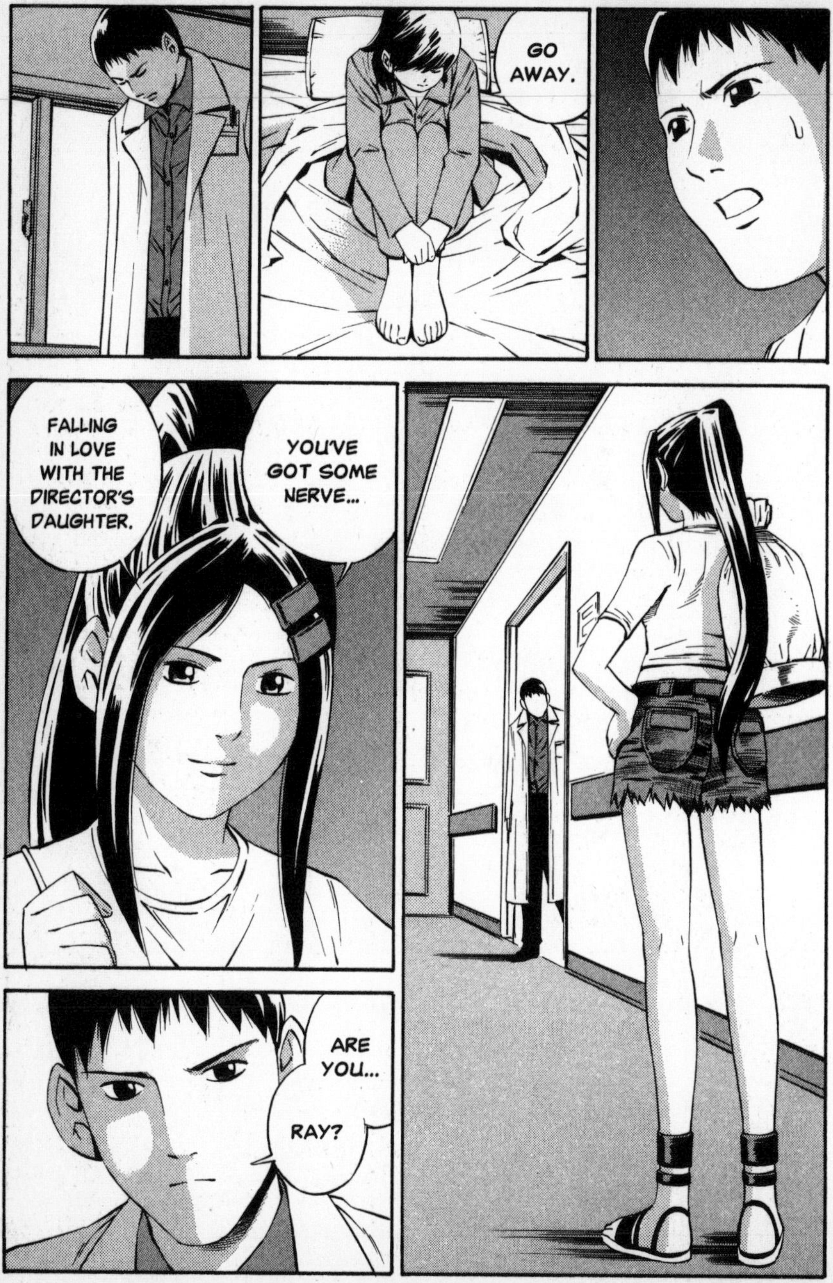
GO AWAY.
YOU'VE GOT SOME NERVE...
FALLING IN LOVE WITH THE DIRECTOR'S DAUGHTER.
ARE YOU...
RAY?

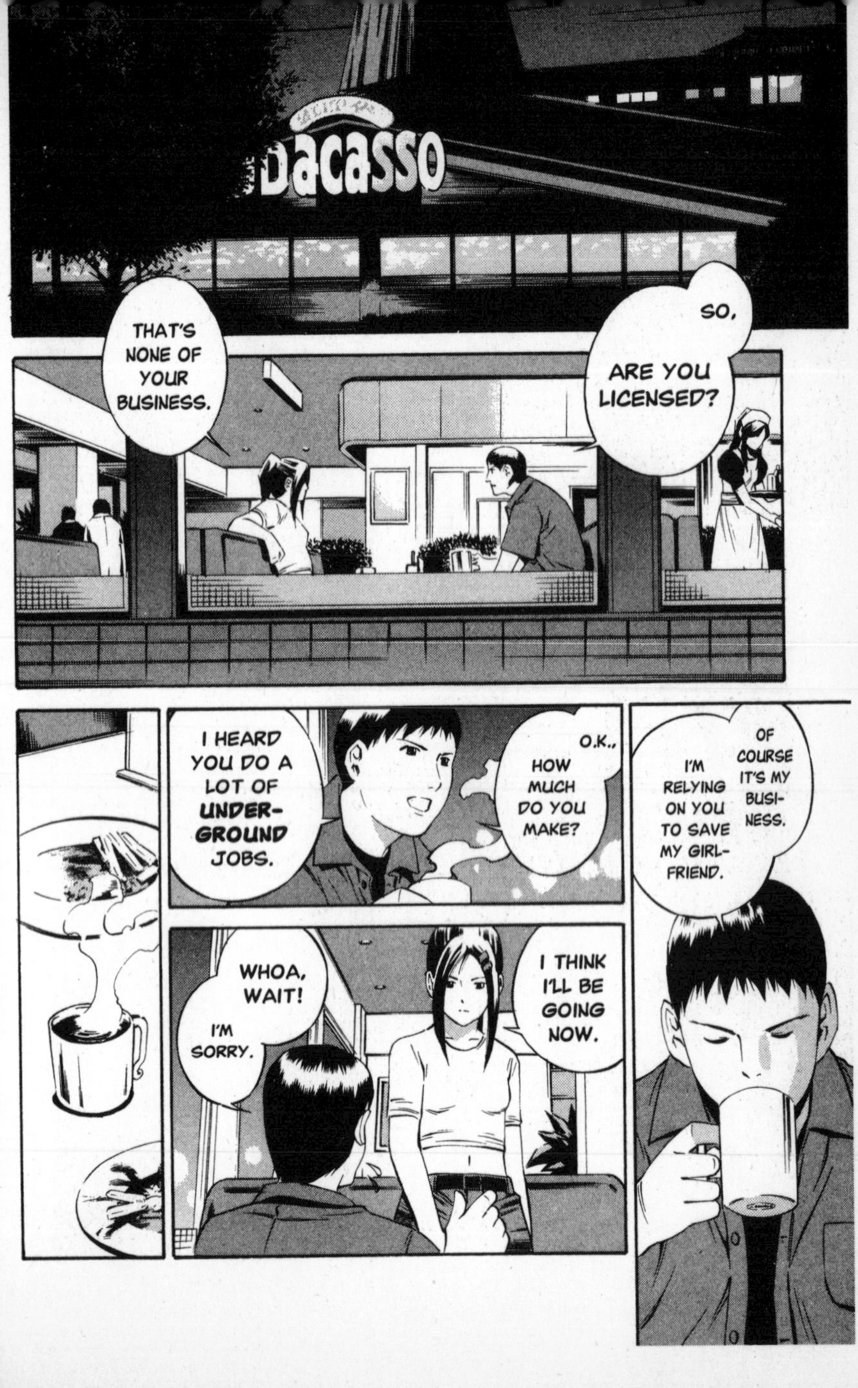
Dacasso
SO,
ARE YOU LICENSED?
THAT'S NONE OF YOUR BUSINESS.
OF COURSE IT'S MY BUSINESS.
I'M RELYING ON YOU TO SAVE MY GIRLFRIEND.
O.K., HOW MUCH DO YOU MAKE?
I HEARD YOU DO A LOT OF **UNDERGROUND** JOBS.
I THINK I'LL BE GOING NOW.
WHOA, WAIT!
I'M SORRY.

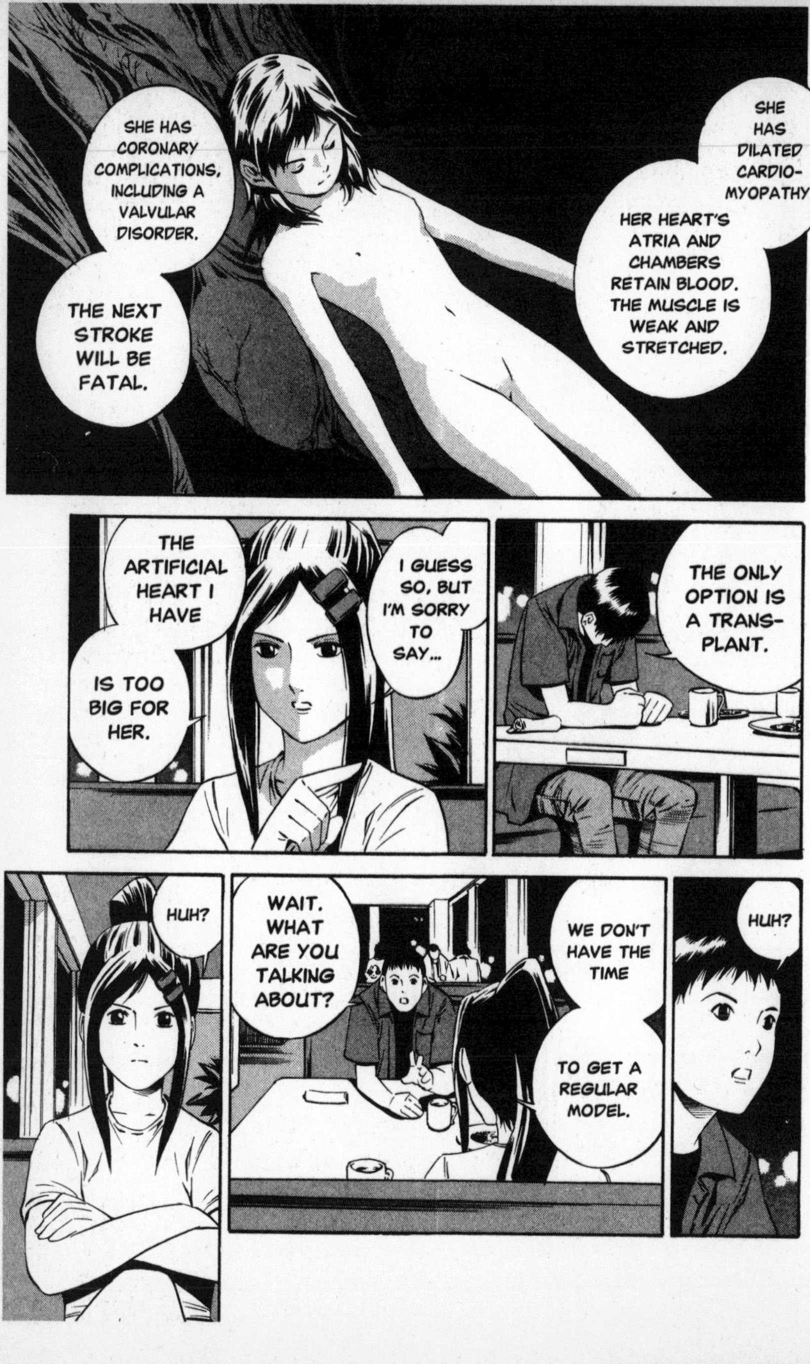
SHE HAS DILATED CARDIO-MYOPATHY.
HER HEART'S ATRIA AND CHAMBERS RETAIN BLOOD. THE MUSCLE IS WEAK AND STRETCHED.
SHE HAS CORONARY COMPLICATIONS, INCLUDING A VALVULAR DISORDER.
THE NEXT STROKE WILL BE FATAL.
THE ONLY OPTION IS A TRANS-PLANT.
I GUESS SO, BUT I'M SORRY TO SAY...
THE ARTIFICIAL HEART I HAVE
IS TOO BIG FOR HER.
HUH?
WE DON'T HAVE THE TIME
TO GET A REGULAR MODEL.
WAIT. WHAT ARE YOU TALKING ABOUT?
HUH?

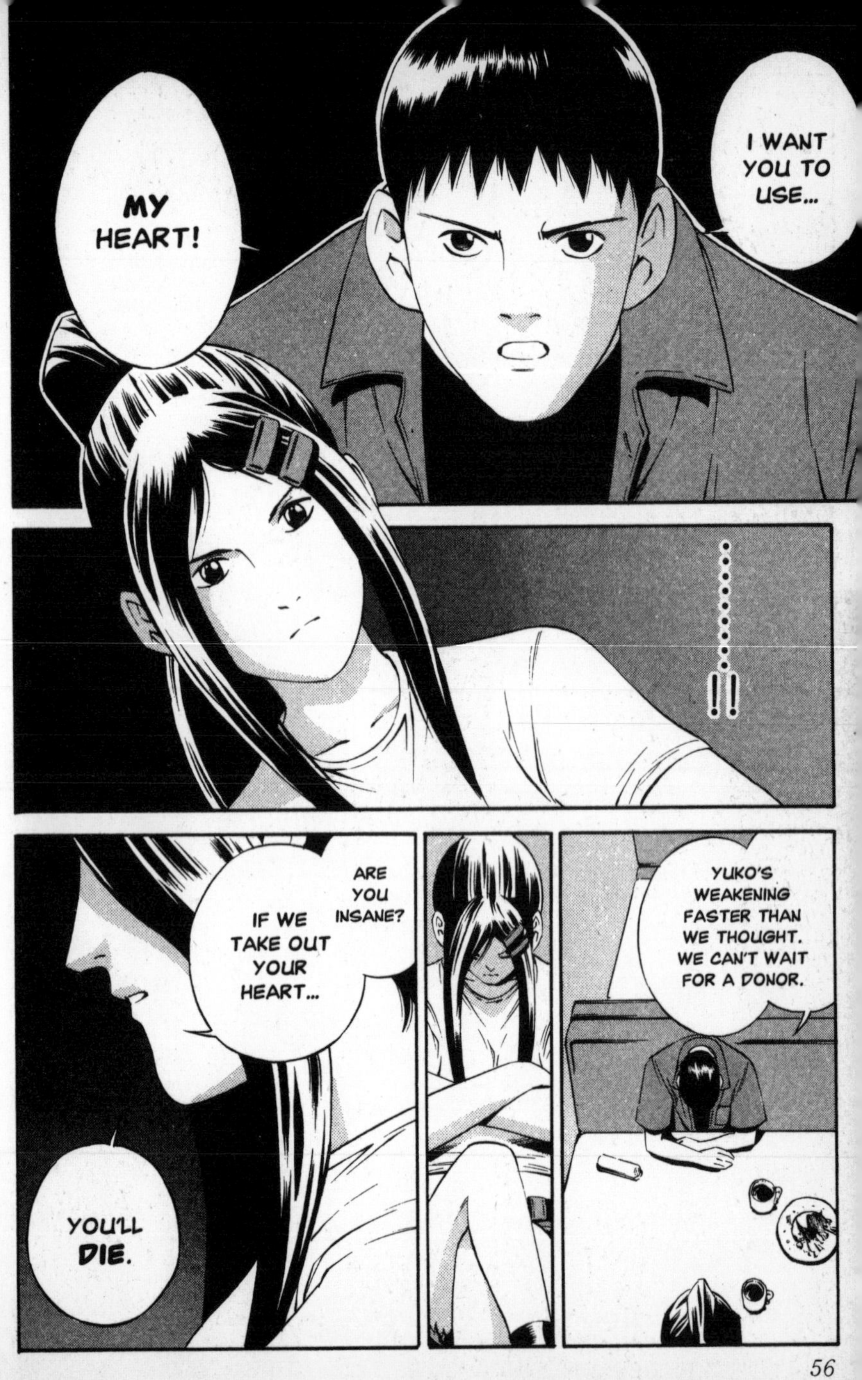
I WANT YOU TO USE...
MY HEART!
..........!!
YUKO'S WEAKENING FASTER THAN WE THOUGHT. WE CAN'T WAIT FOR A DONOR.
ARE YOU INSANE?
IF WE TAKE OUT YOUR HEART...
YOU'LL DIE.

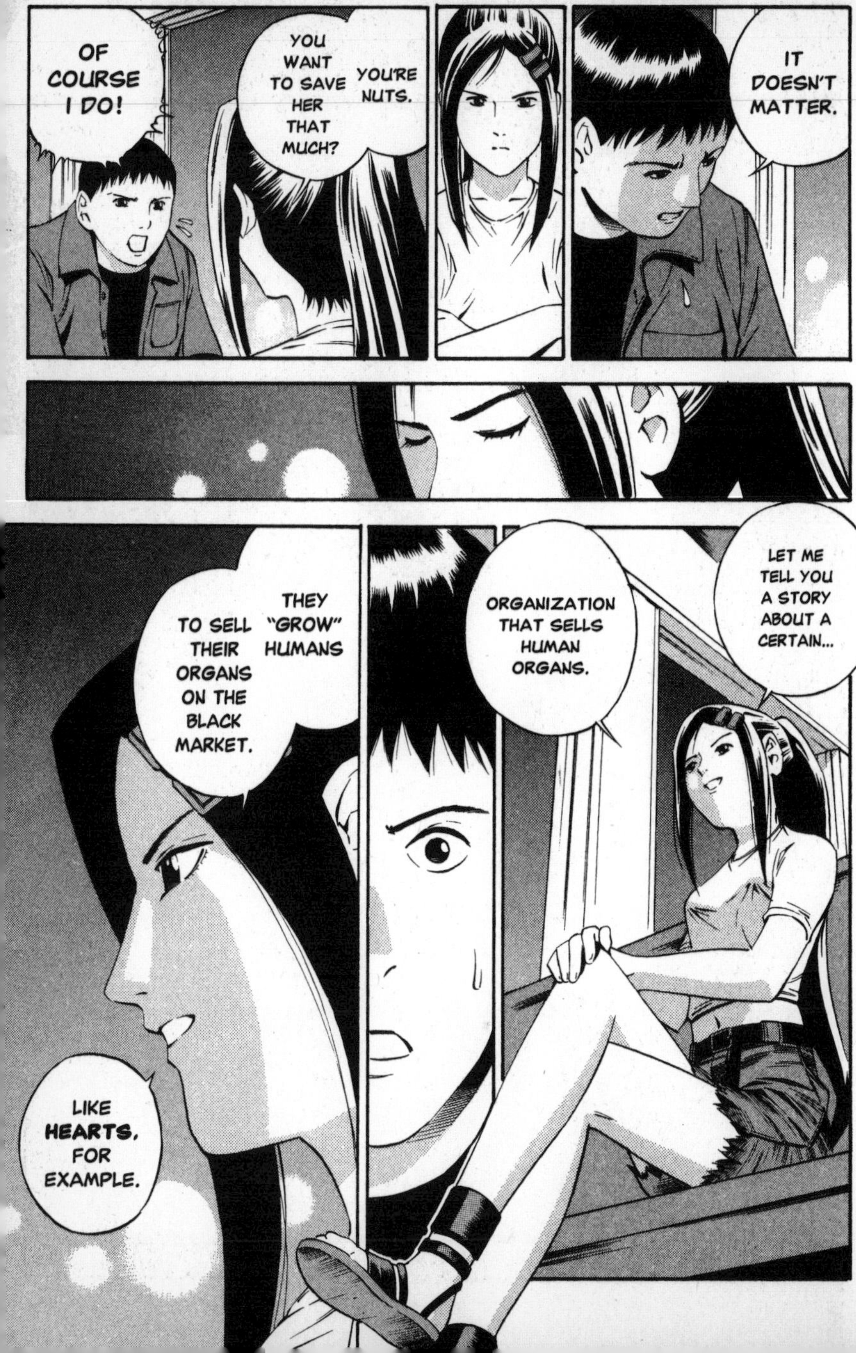
IT DOESN'T MATTER.
YOU'RE NUTS.
YOU WANT TO SAVE HER THAT MUCH?
OF COURSE I DO!
LET ME TELL YOU A STORY ABOUT A CERTAIN...
ORGANIZATION THAT SELLS HUMAN ORGANS.
THEY "GROW" HUMANS
TO SELL THEIR ORGANS ON THE BLACK MARKET.
LIKE **HEARTS**, FOR EXAMPLE.

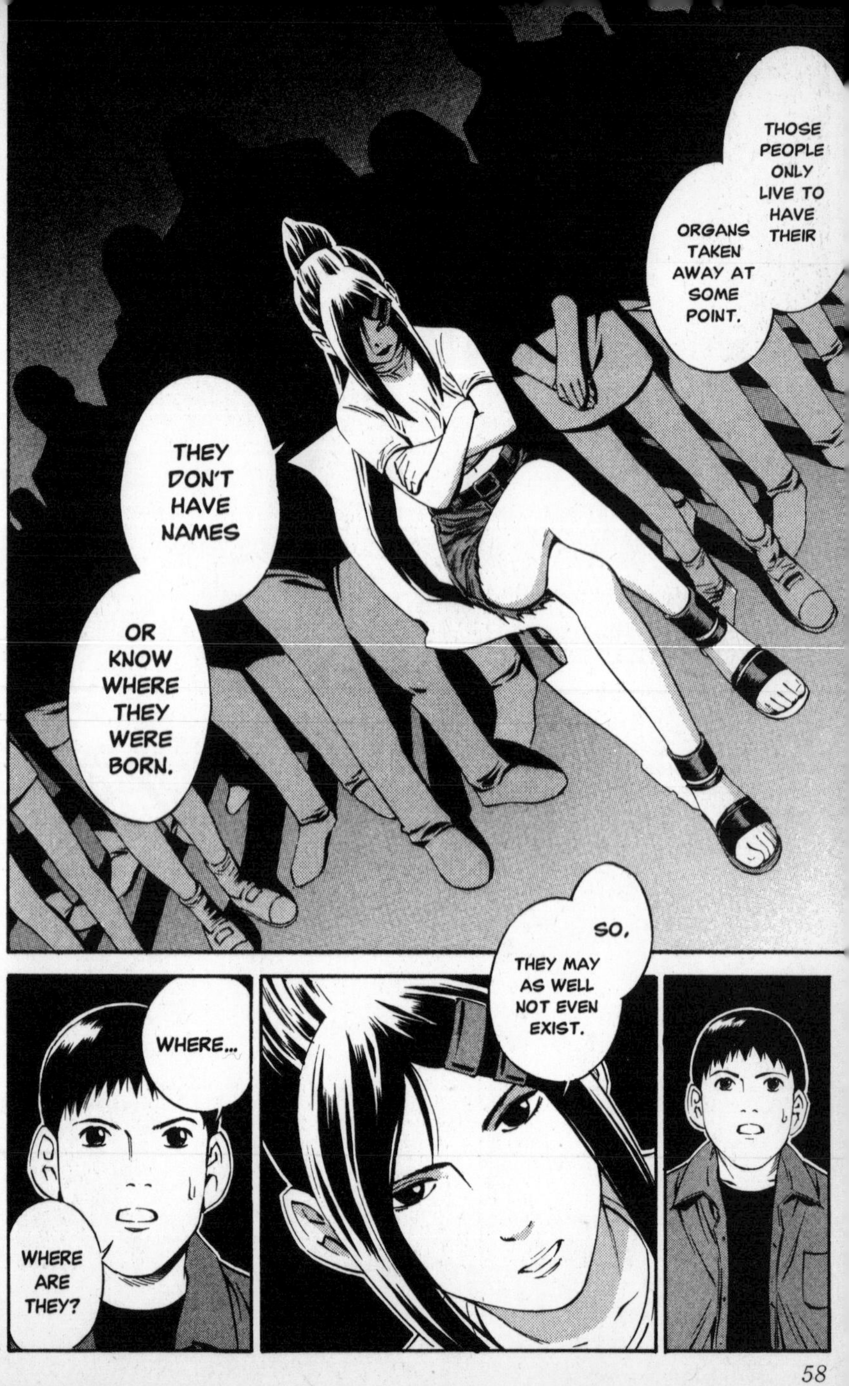
THOSE PEOPLE ONLY LIVE TO HAVE THEIR
ORGANS TAKEN AWAY AT SOME POINT.
THEY DON'T HAVE NAMES
OR KNOW WHERE THEY WERE BORN.
SO,
THEY MAY AS WELL NOT EVEN EXIST.
WHERE...
WHERE ARE THEY?

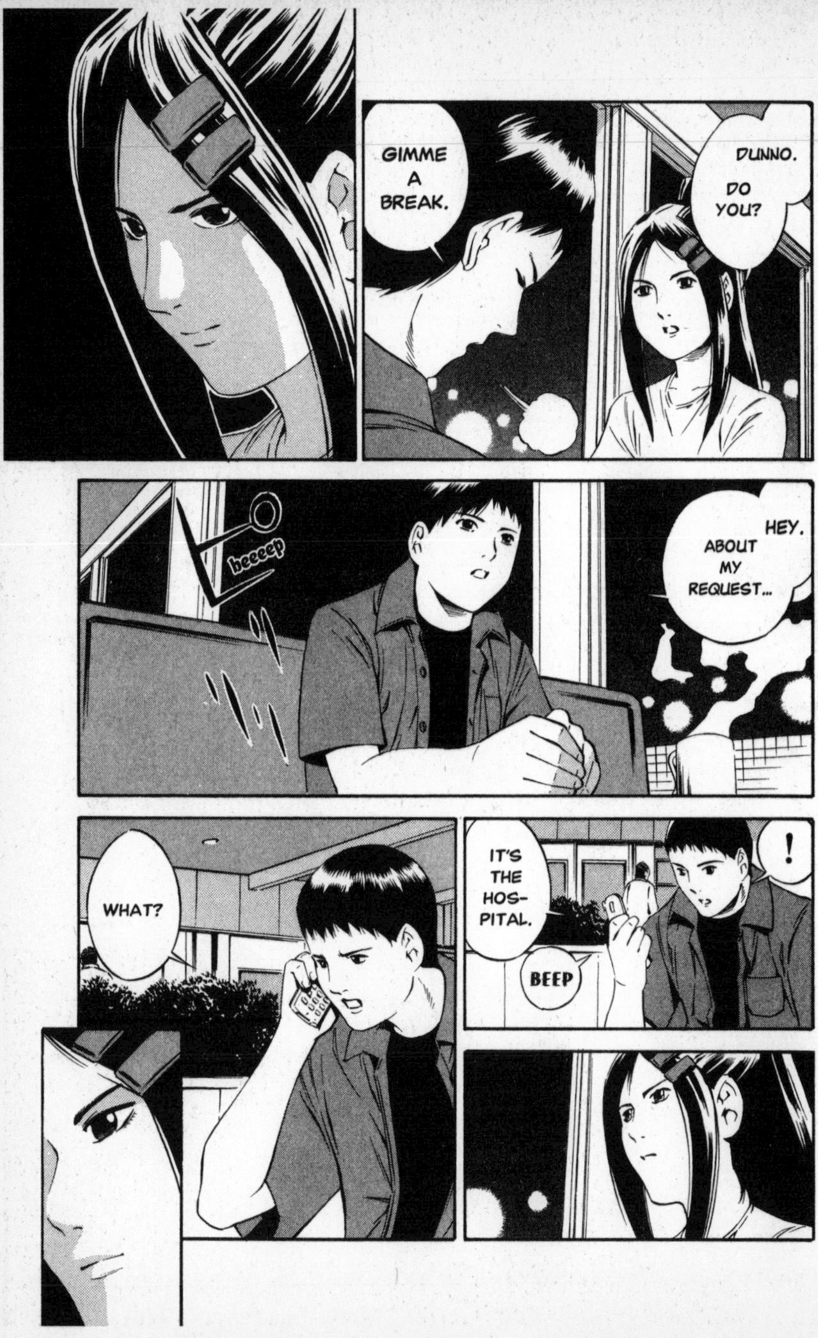
GIMME A BREAK.
DUNNO.
DO YOU?
HEY. ABOUT MY REQUEST...
beeeep
WHAT?
IT'S THE HOS-PITAL.
BEEP
!

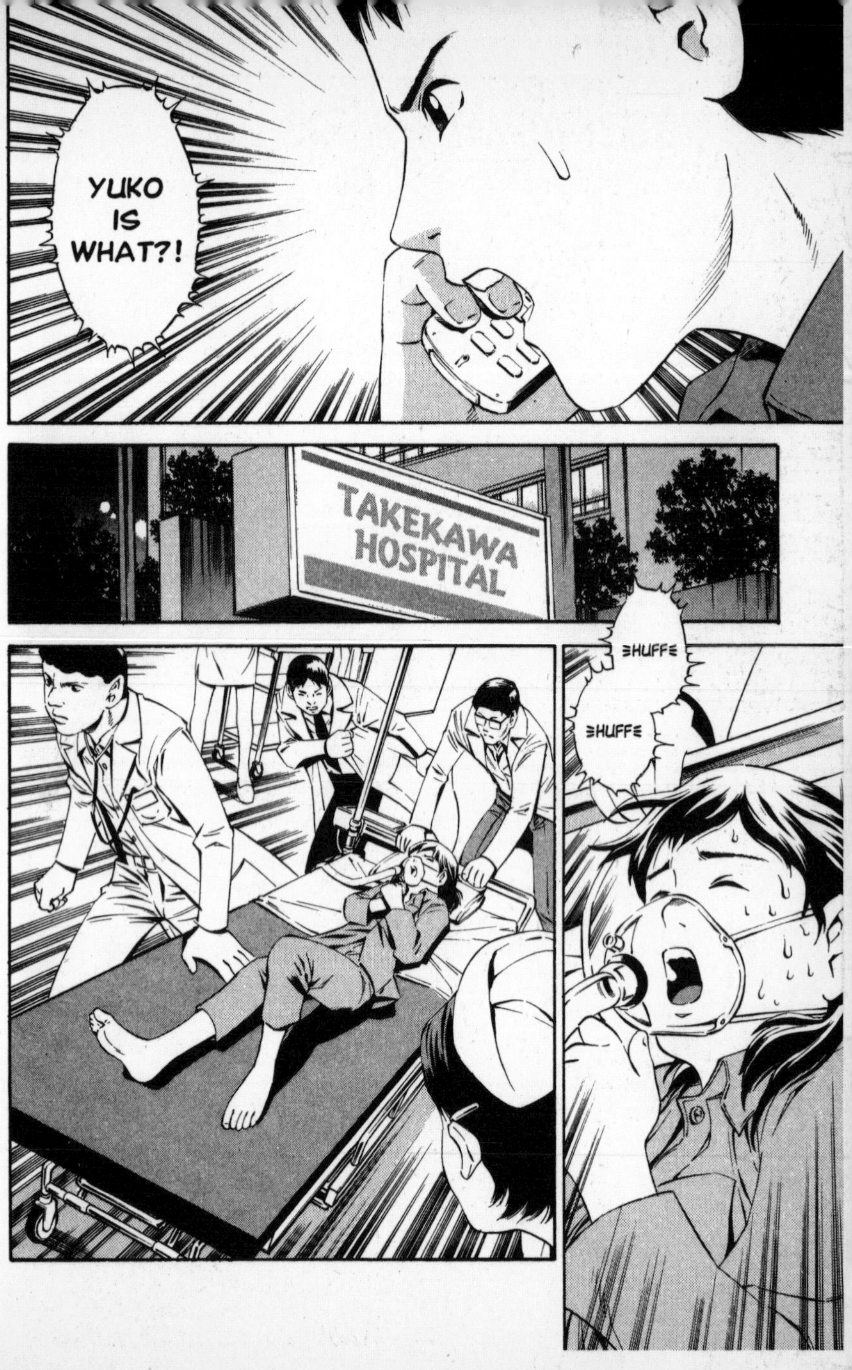
YUKO IS WHAT?!
TAKEKAWA HOSPITAL
≡HUFF≡
≡HUFF≡

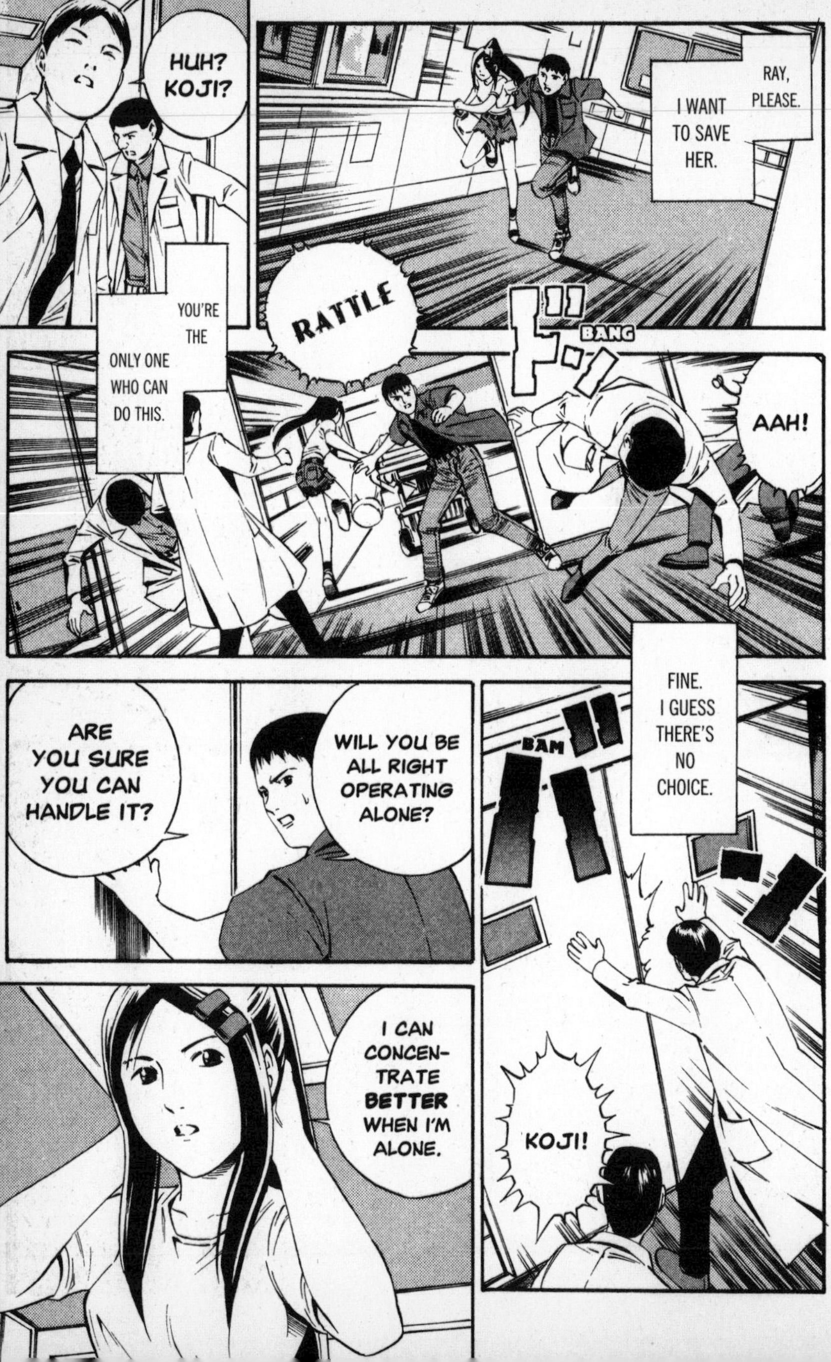

RAY, PLEASE.
I WANT TO SAVE HER.
HUH? KOJI?
YOU'RE THE ONLY ONE WHO CAN DO THIS.
RATTLE
BANG
AAH!
FINE. I GUESS THERE'S NO CHOICE.
BAM
KOJI!
WILL YOU BE ALL RIGHT OPERATING ALONE?
ARE YOU SURE YOU CAN HANDLE IT?
I CAN CONCENTRATE BETTER WHEN I'M ALONE.

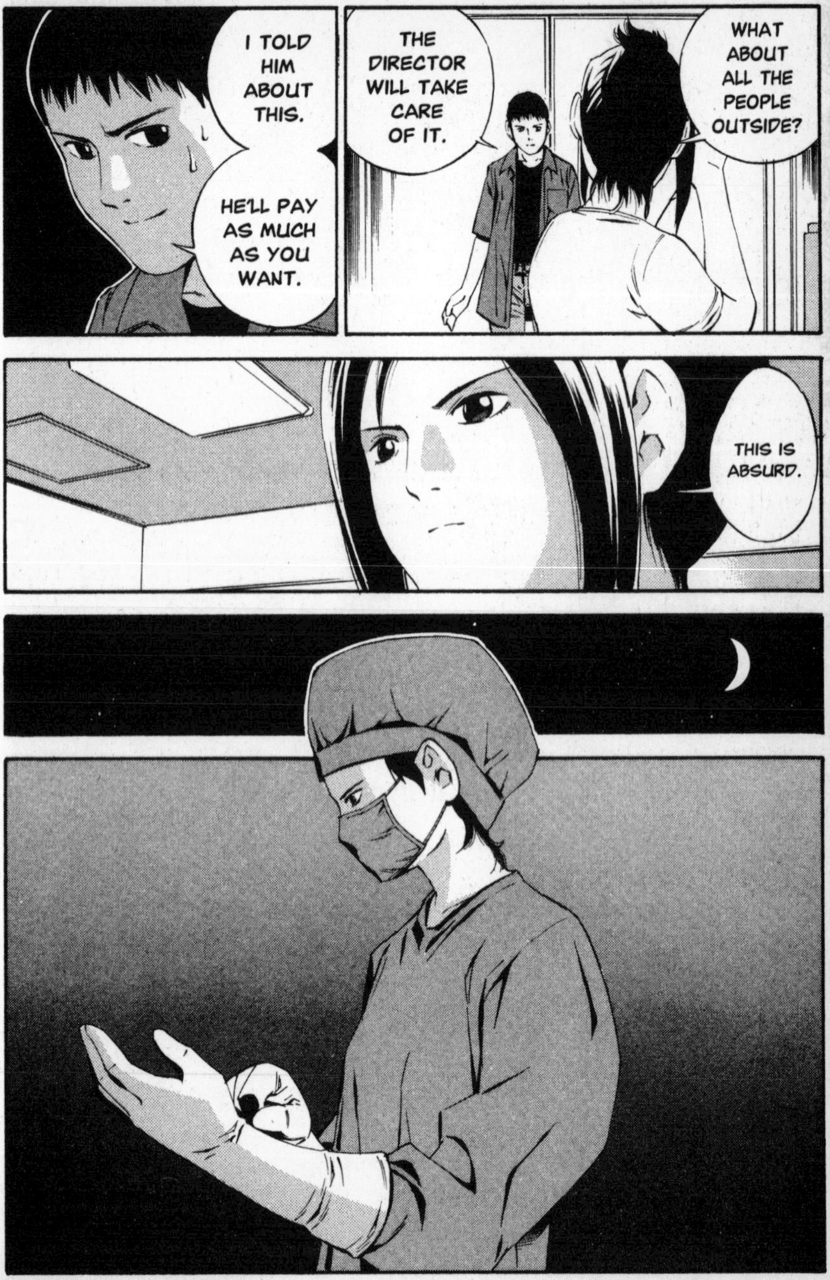
I TOLD HIM ABOUT THIS.
HE'LL PAY AS MUCH AS YOU WANT.
THE DIRECTOR WILL TAKE CARE OF IT.
WHAT ABOUT ALL THE PEOPLE OUTSIDE?
THIS IS ABSURD.

WHAT AM I DOING HERE?
DOES THIS MAKE ME LIKE THEM?
NO.
ZI ZI
I'M NOT LIKE THEM!

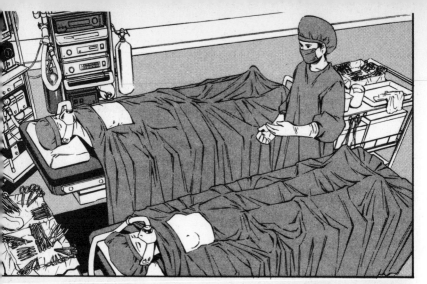

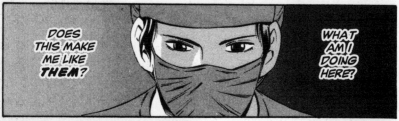

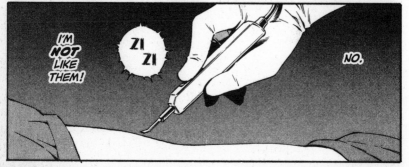

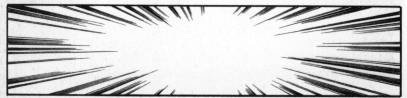

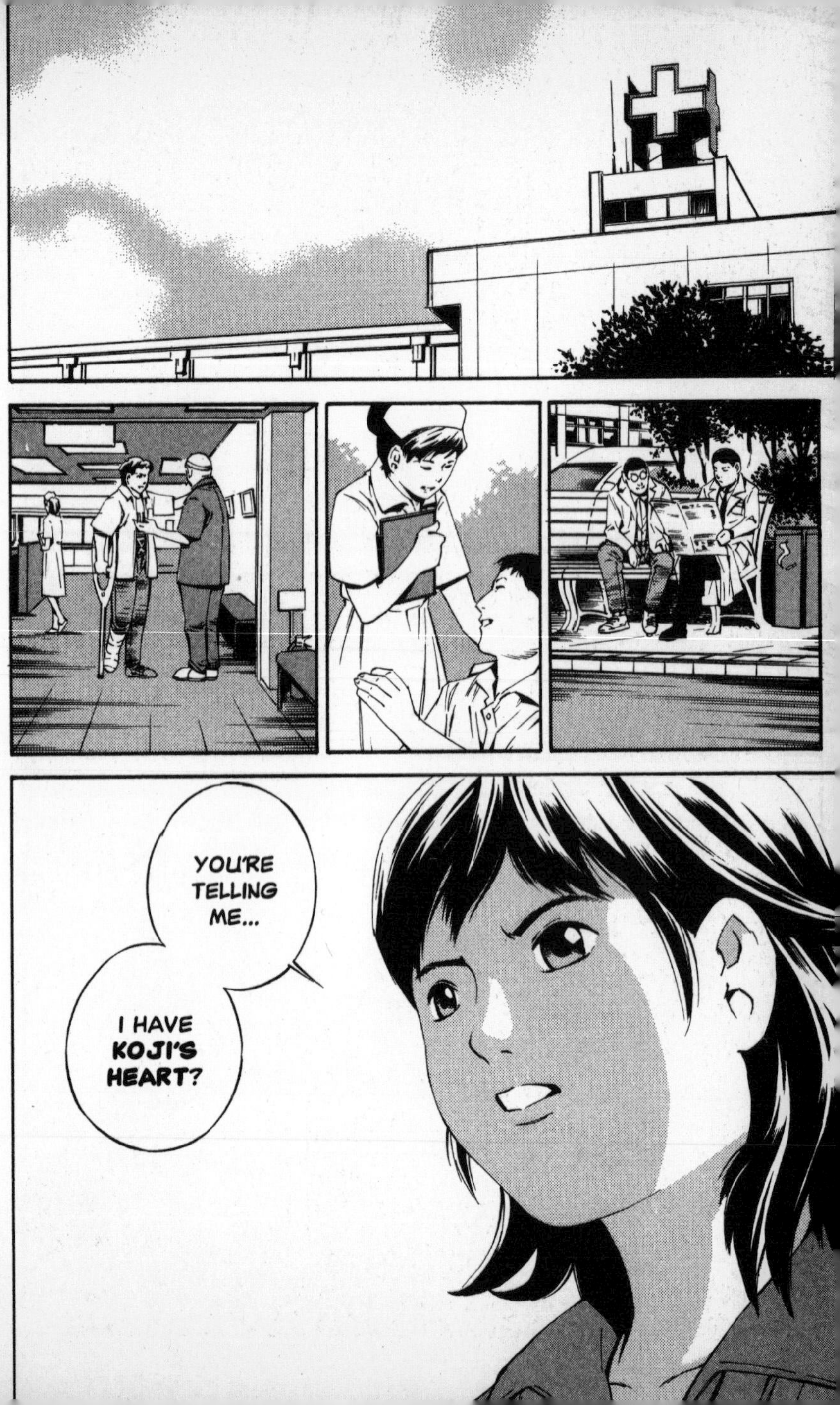
YOU'RE TELLING ME...
I HAVE KOJI'S HEART?

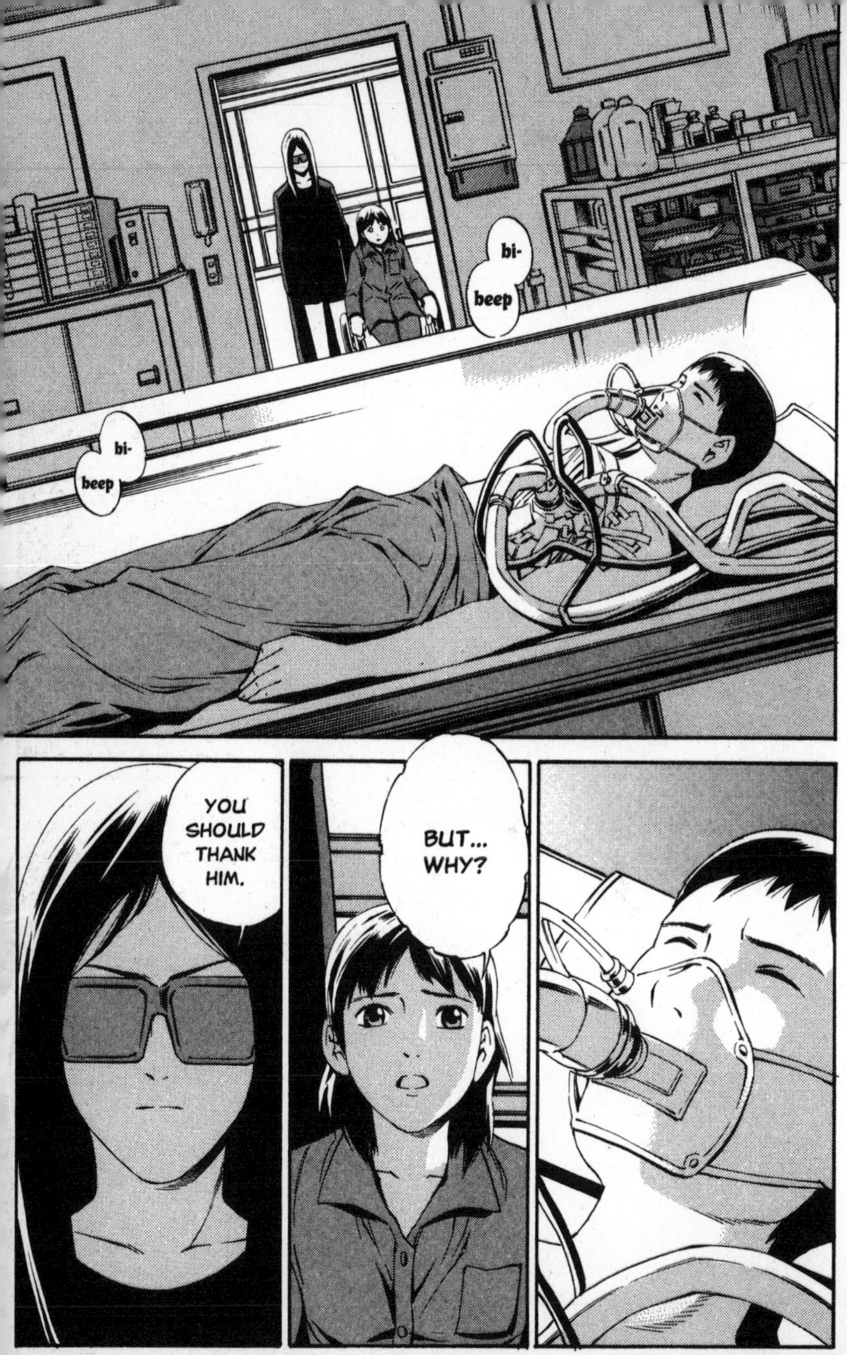
bi-
beep
bi-
beep
YOU SHOULD THANK HIM.
BUT... WHY?

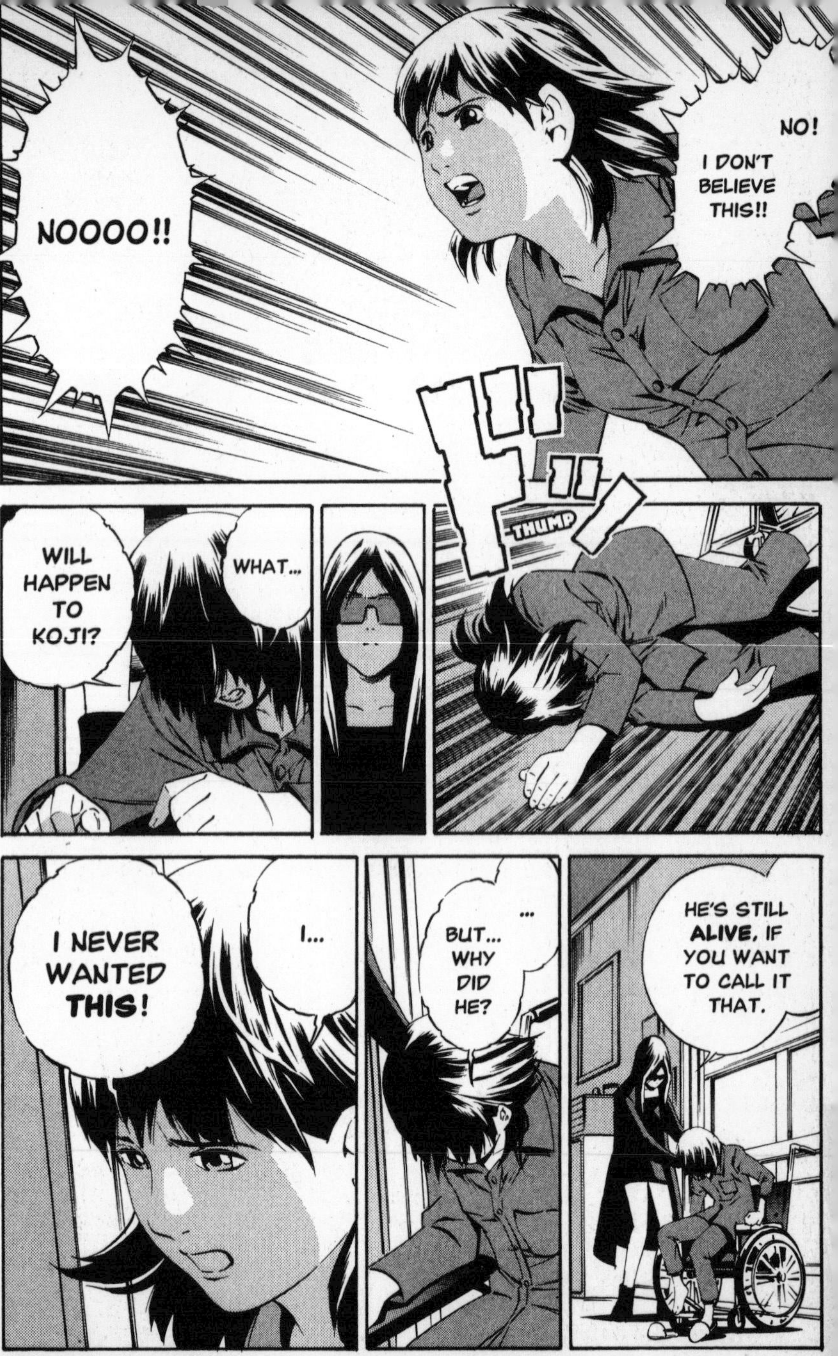
NO!
I DON'T BELIEVE THIS!!
NOOOO!!
THUMP
WHAT...
WILL HAPPEN TO KOJI?
HE'S STILL **ALIVE**, IF YOU WANT TO CALL IT THAT.
...
BUT... WHY DID HE?
I...
I NEVER WANTED **THIS**!

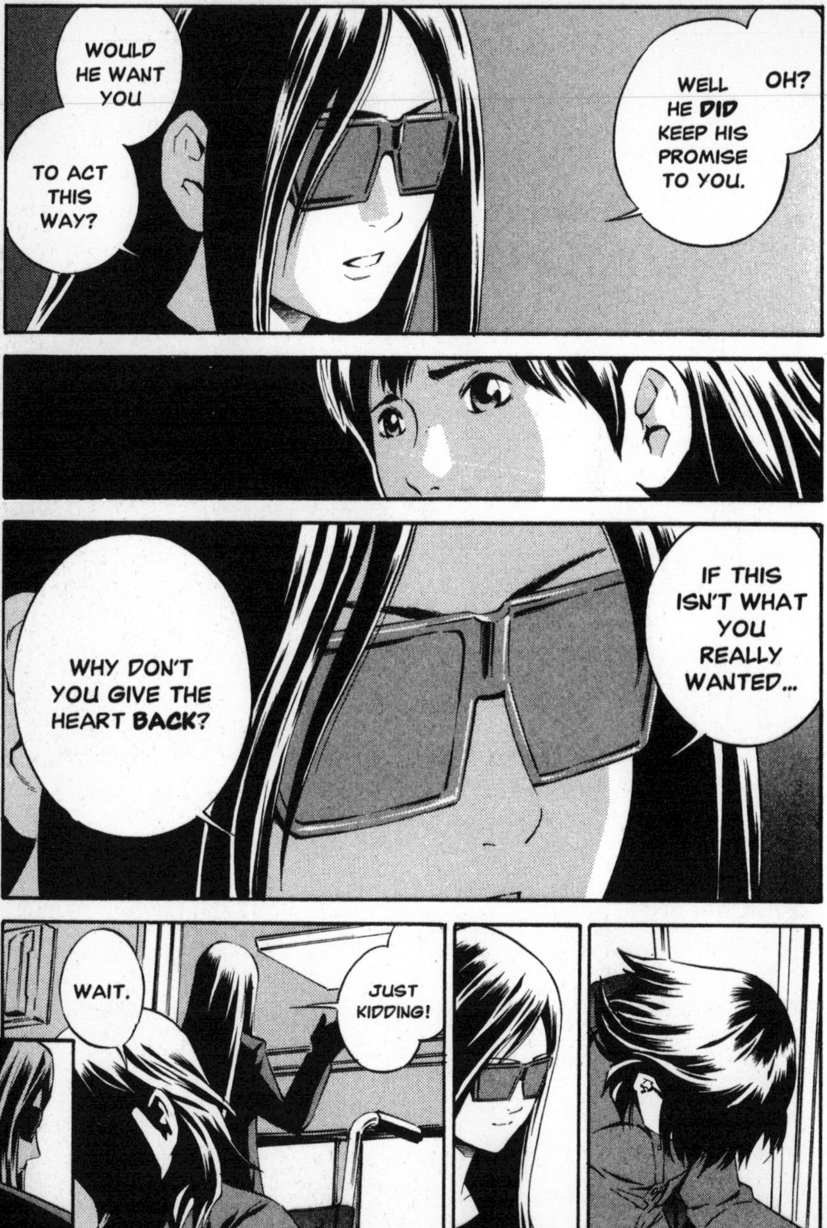
OH?
WELL HE **DID** KEEP HIS PROMISE TO YOU.
WOULD HE WANT YOU
TO ACT THIS WAY?
IF THIS ISN'T WHAT YOU REALLY WANTED...
WHY DON'T YOU GIVE THE HEART **BACK**?
JUST KIDDING!
WAIT.

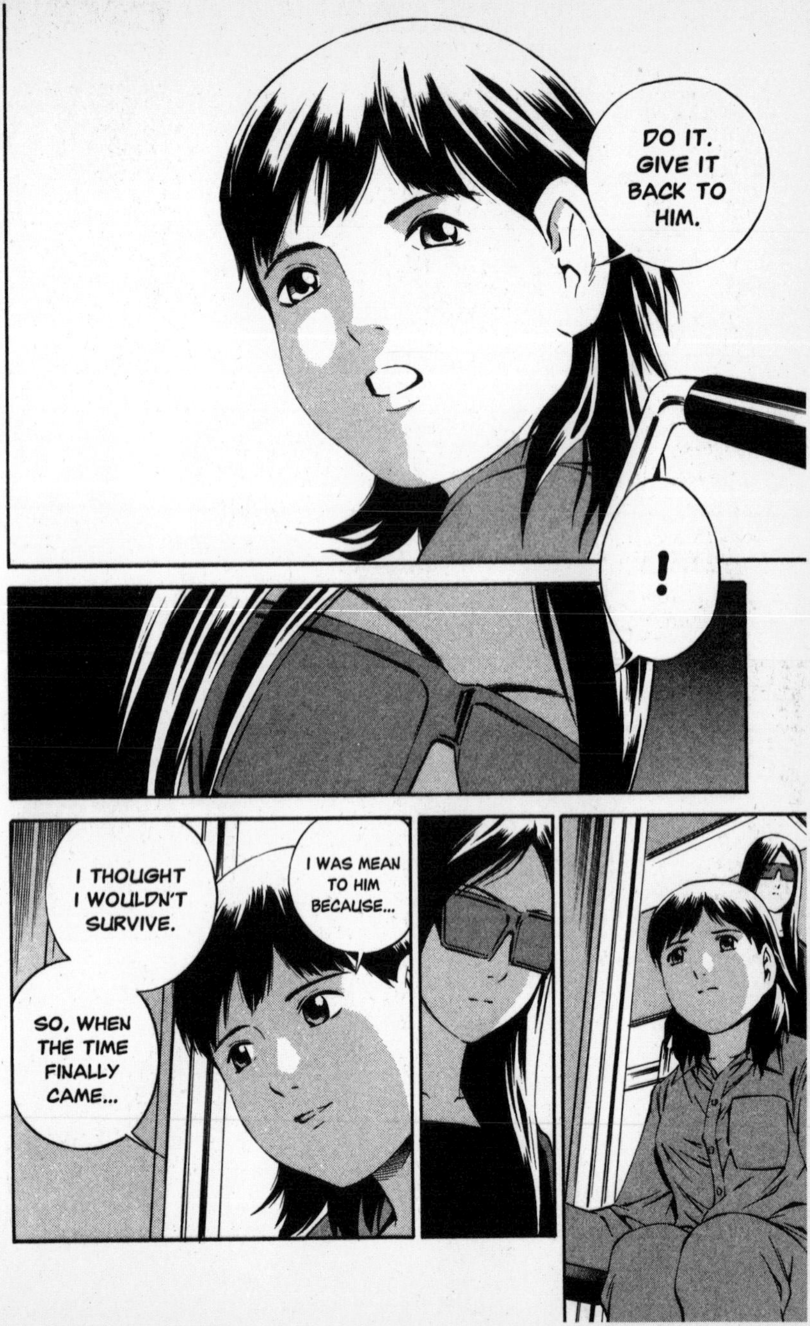
DO IT. GIVE IT BACK TO HIM.
!
I WAS MEAN TO HIM BECAUSE...
I THOUGHT I WOULDN'T SURVIVE.
SO, WHEN THE TIME FINALLY CAME...

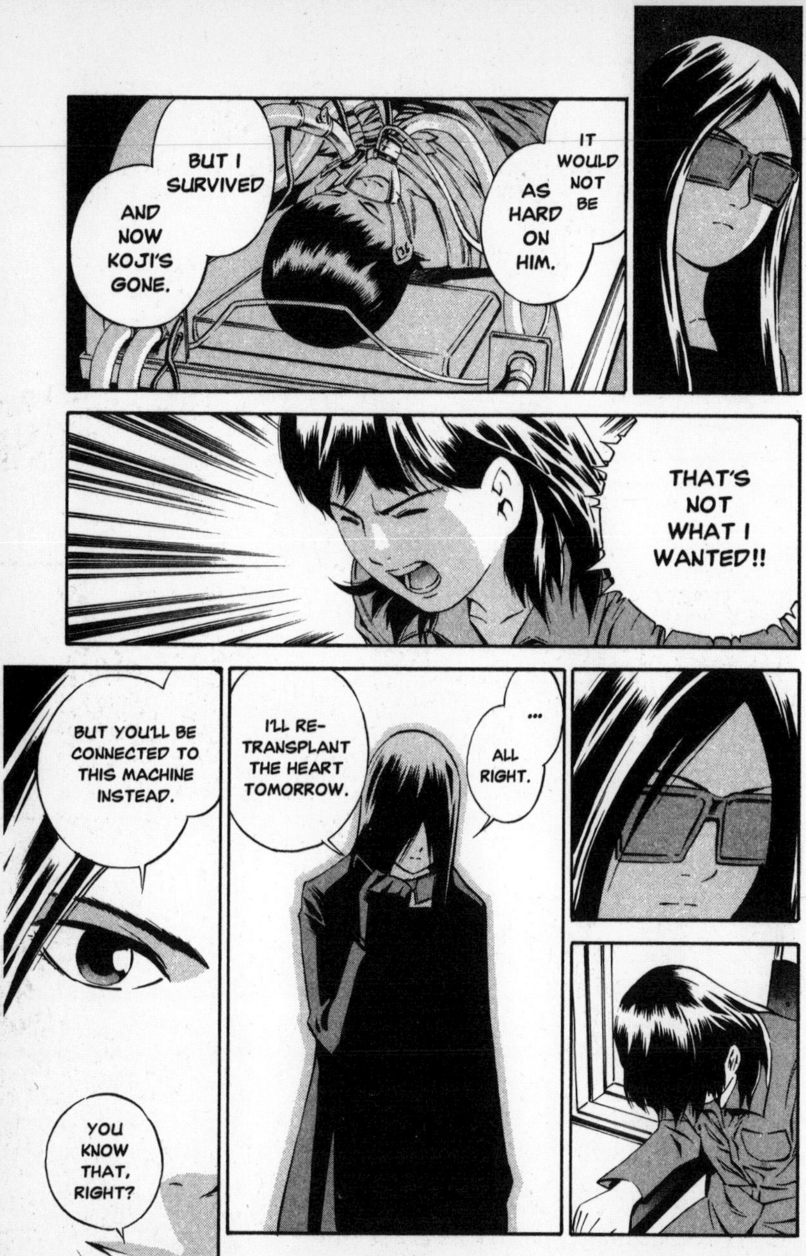
IT WOULD NOT BE AS HARD ON HIM.
BUT I SURVIVED AND NOW KOJI'S GONE.
THAT'S NOT WHAT I WANTED!!
...
ALL RIGHT.
I'LL RE-TRANSPLANT THE HEART TOMORROW.
BUT YOU'LL BE CONNECTED TO THIS MACHINE INSTEAD.
YOU KNOW THAT, RIGHT?

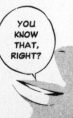

FINE.

NO, I JUST CAN'T SEE PEOPLE'S FEELINGS.

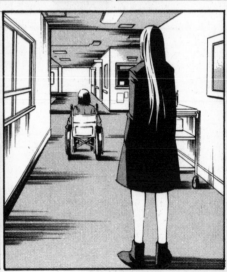

OPERATION IN PROGRESS

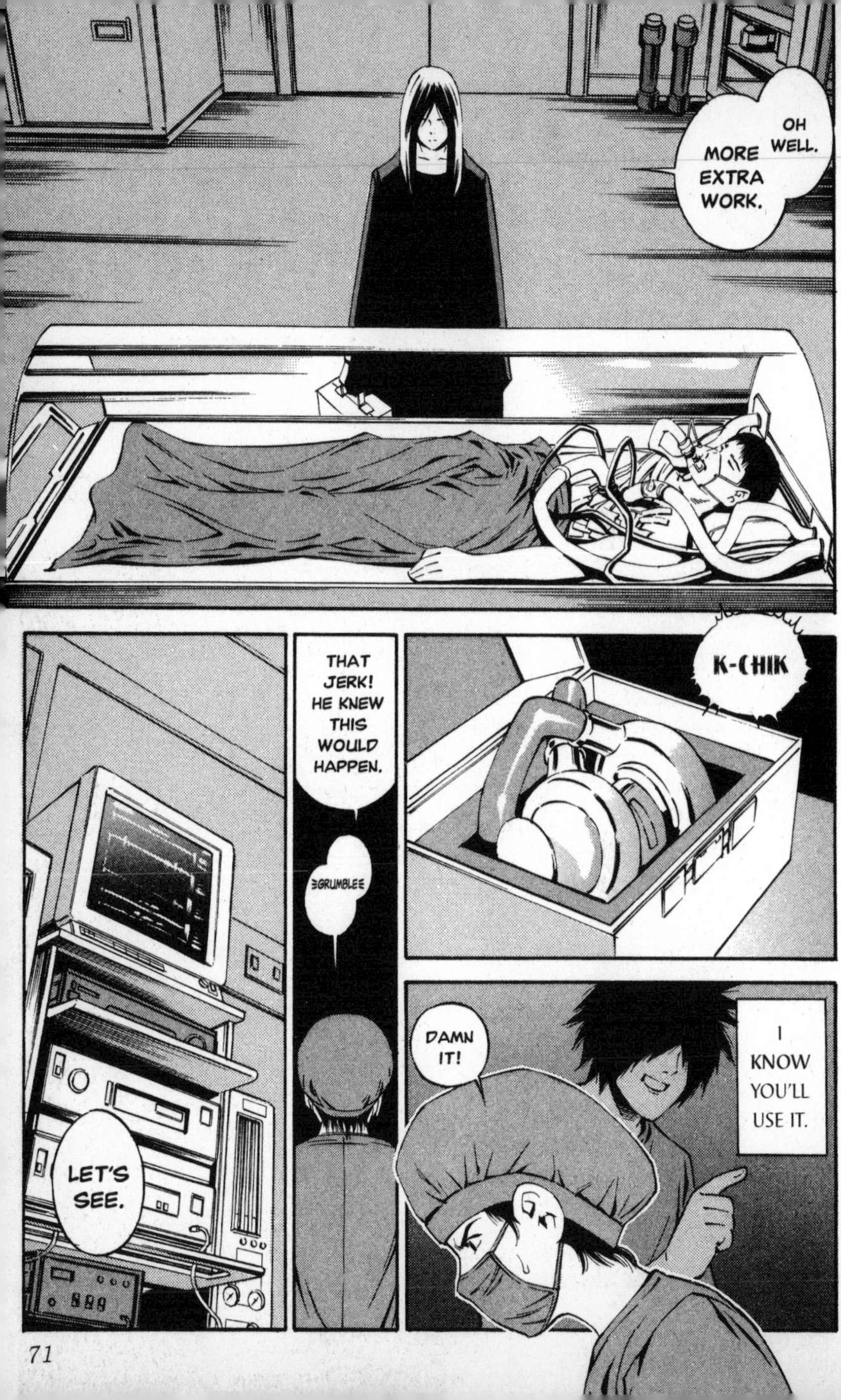
OH WELL.
MORE EXTRA WORK.
K-CHIK
THAT JERK! HE KNEW THIS WOULD HAPPEN.
GRUMBLE
LET'S SEE.
I KNOW YOU'LL USE IT.
DAMN IT!

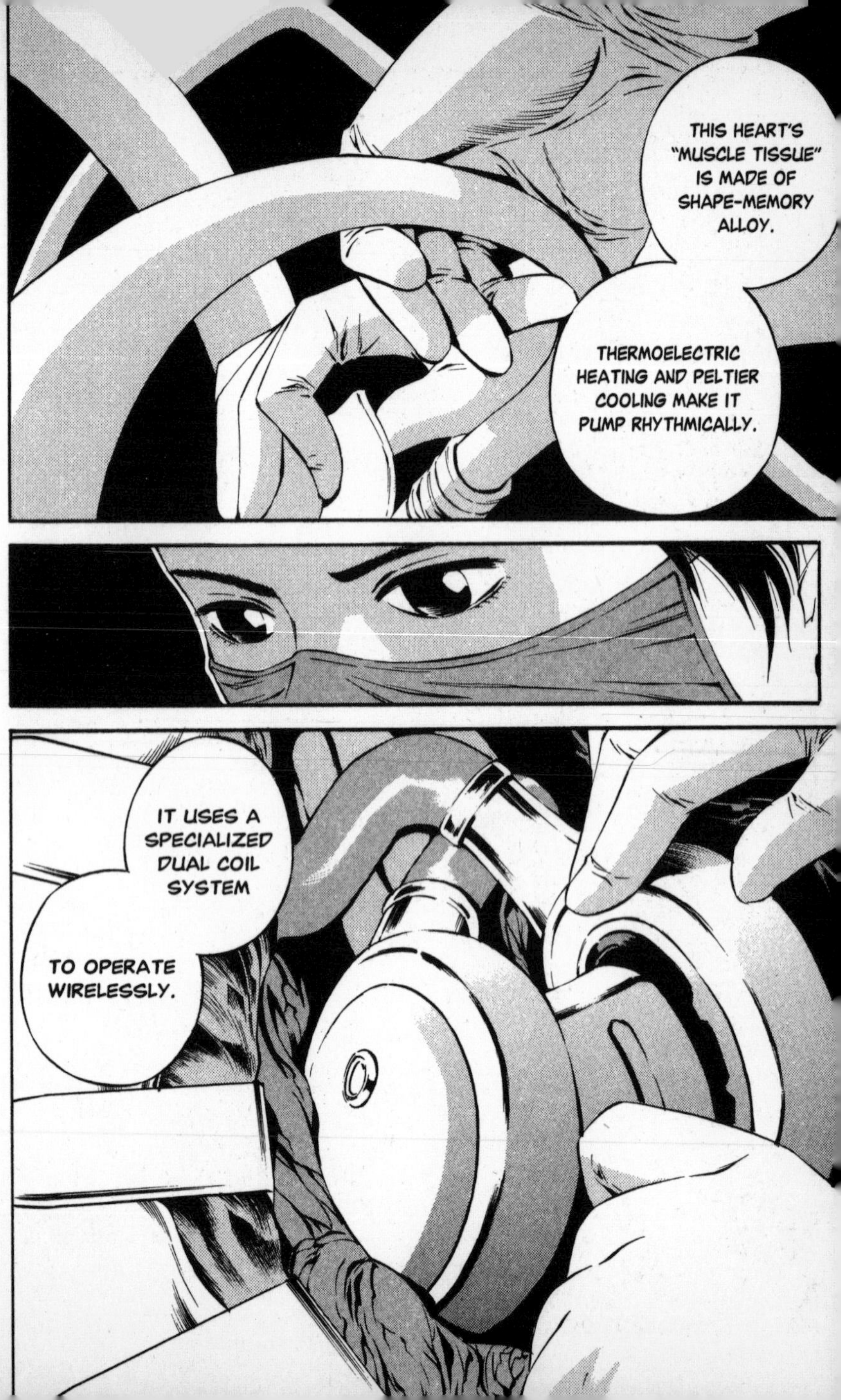
THIS HEART'S "MUSCLE TISSUE" IS MADE OF SHAPE-MEMORY ALLOY.
THERMOELECTRIC HEATING AND PELTIER COOLING MAKE IT PUMP RHYTHMICALLY.
IT USES A SPECIALIZED DUAL COIL SYSTEM
TO OPERATE WIRELESSLY.

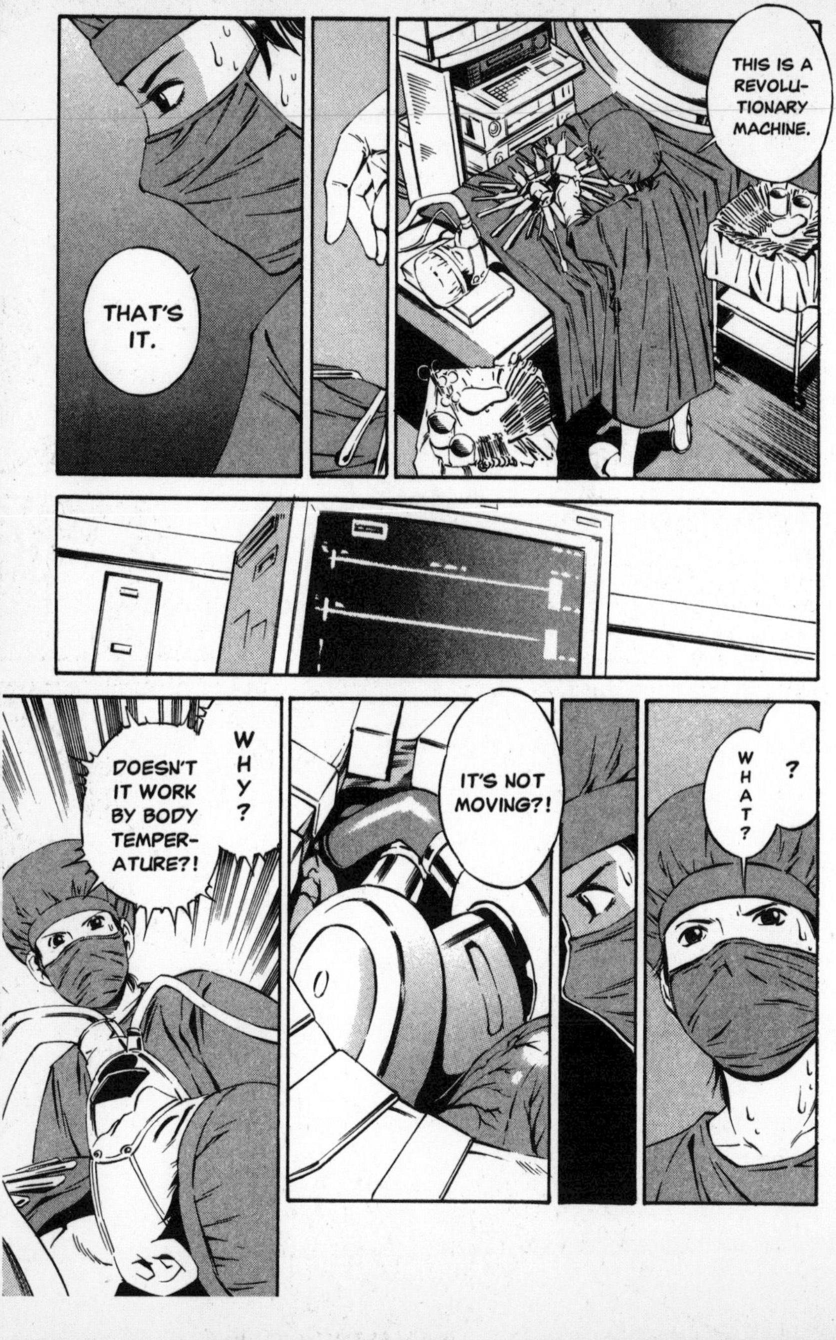
THIS IS A REVOLUTIONARY MACHINE.
THAT'S IT.
WHAT?
?
IT'S NOT MOVING?!
WHY?
DOESN'T IT WORK BY BODY TEMPERATURE?!

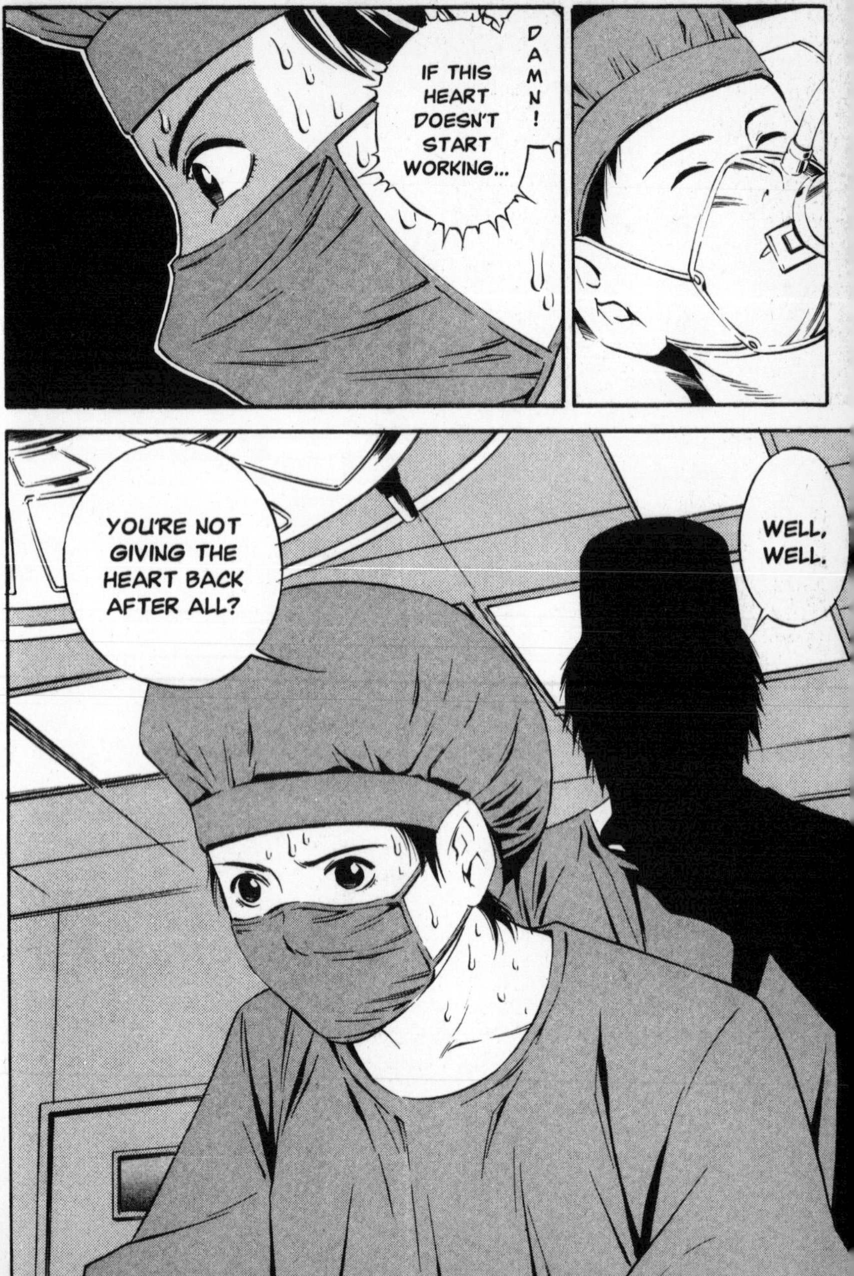
DAMN!
IF THIS HEART DOESN'T START WORKING...
WELL, WELL.
YOU'RE NOT GIVING THE HEART BACK AFTER ALL?

I TOLD YOU YOU'D NEED ME.

SHINO-YAMA?

VWRR

CLICK

YOU'RE SUCH A JERK, SHINO-YAMA.

GOD.

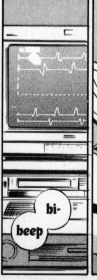

bi-beep

BA-DMP

BA-DMP

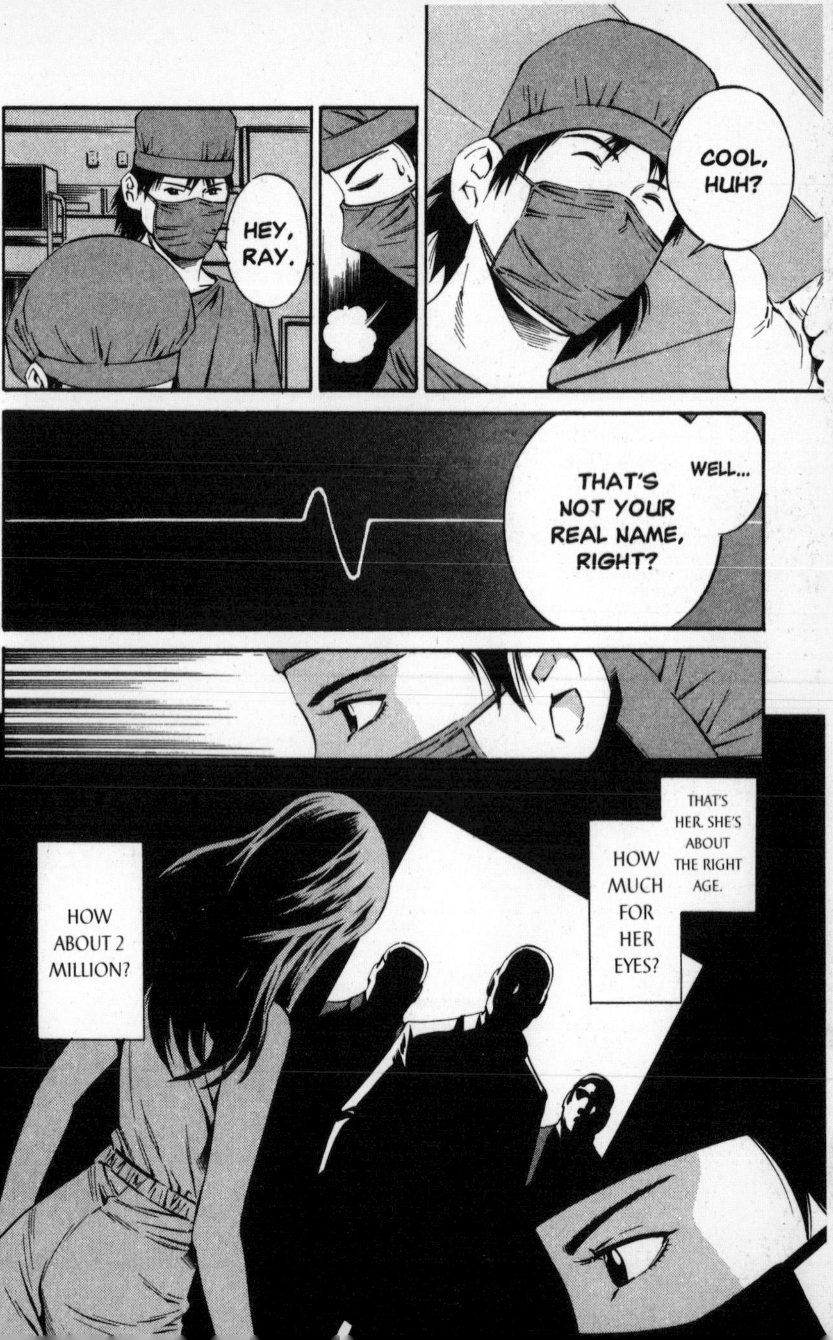
HEY, RAY.
COOL, HUH?
WELL...
THAT'S NOT YOUR REAL NAME, RIGHT?
THAT'S HER. SHE'S ABOUT THE RIGHT AGE.
HOW MUCH FOR HER EYES?
HOW ABOUT 2 MILLION?

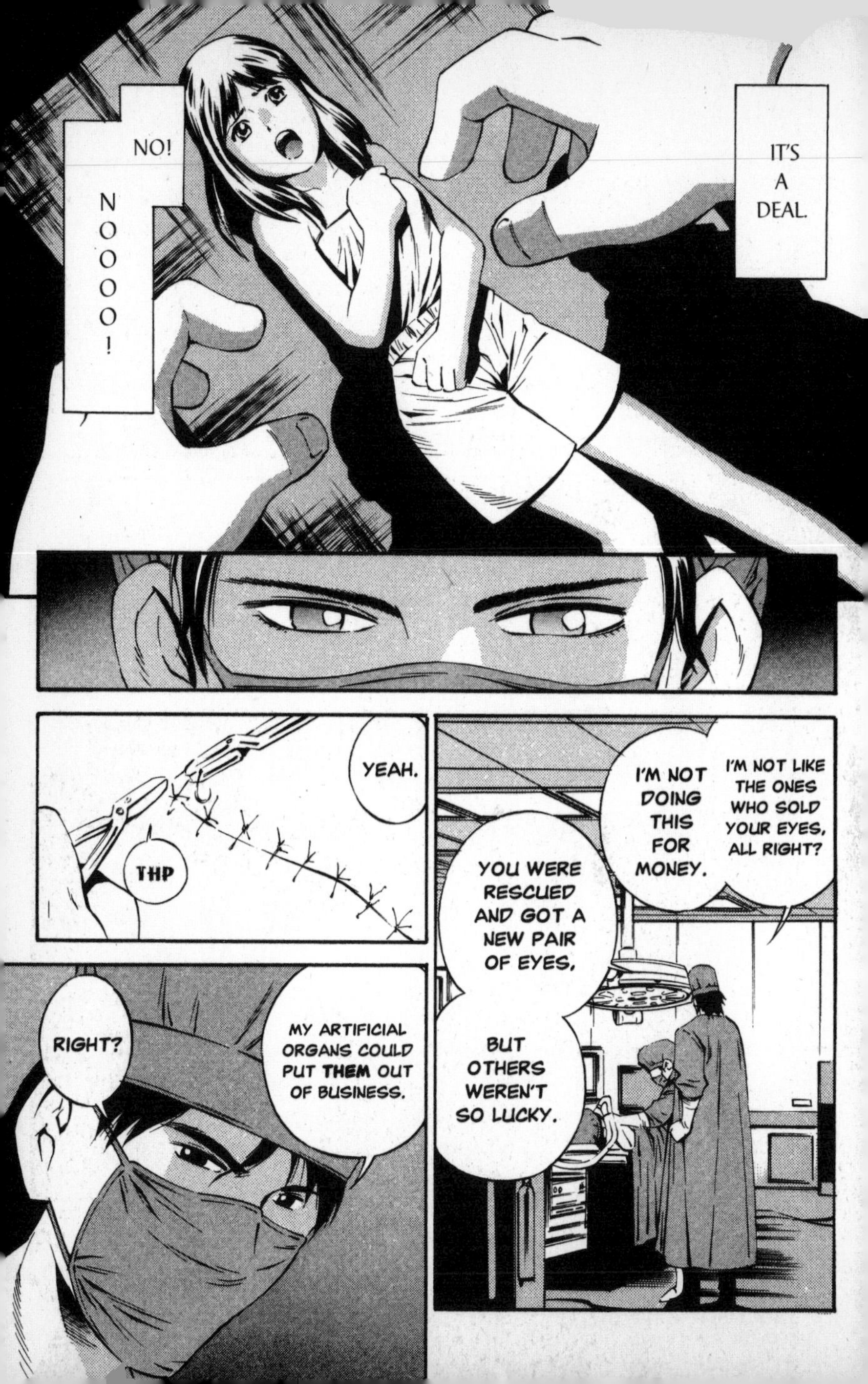
IT'S A DEAL.
NO! NOOOOO!
I'M NOT LIKE THE ONES WHO SOLD YOUR EYES, ALL RIGHT?
I'M NOT DOING THIS FOR MONEY.
YOU WERE RESCUED AND GOT A NEW PAIR OF EYES,
BUT OTHERS WEREN'T SO LUCKY.
YEAH.
THP
MY ARTIFICIAL ORGANS COULD PUT **THEM** OUT OF BUSINESS.
RIGHT?

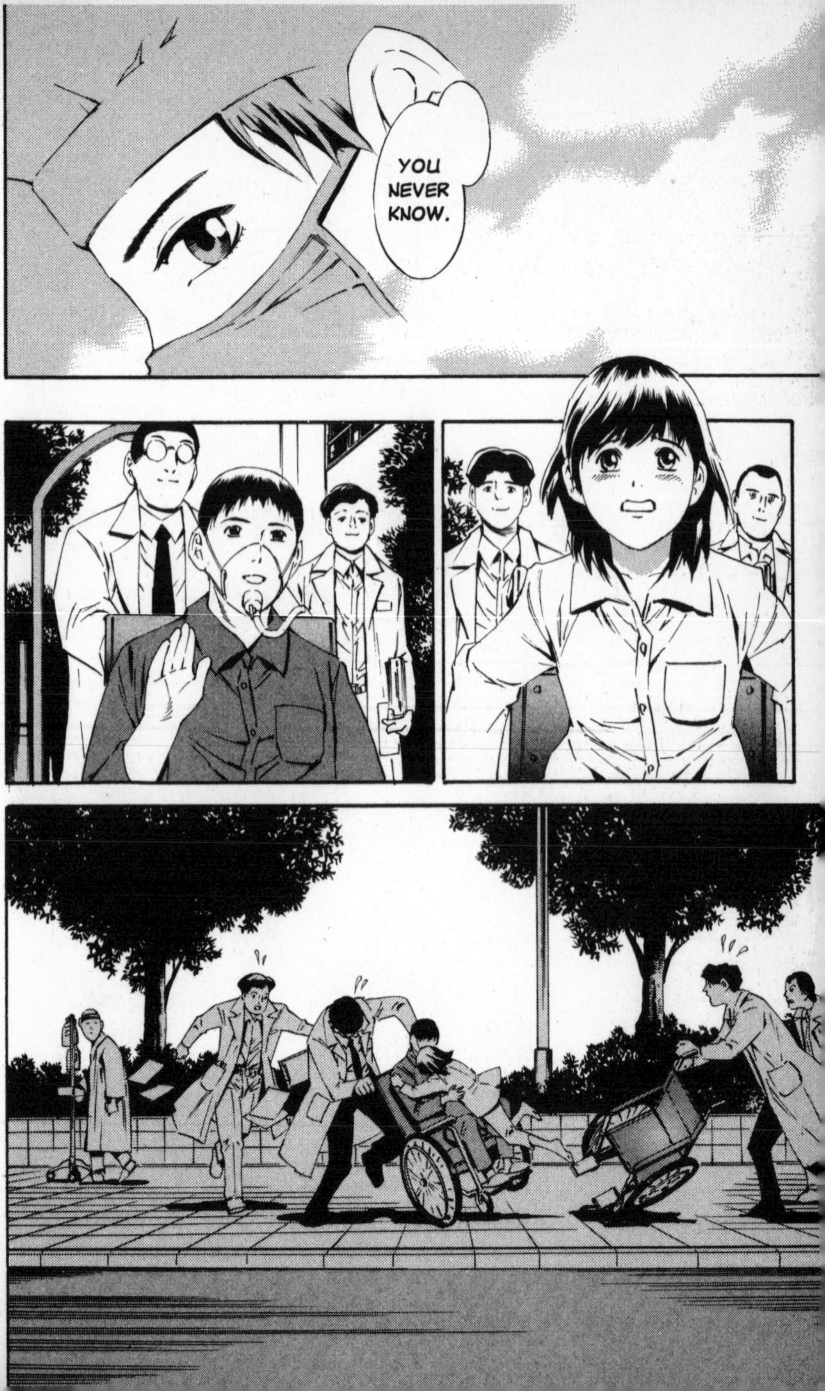
YOU NEVER KNOW.

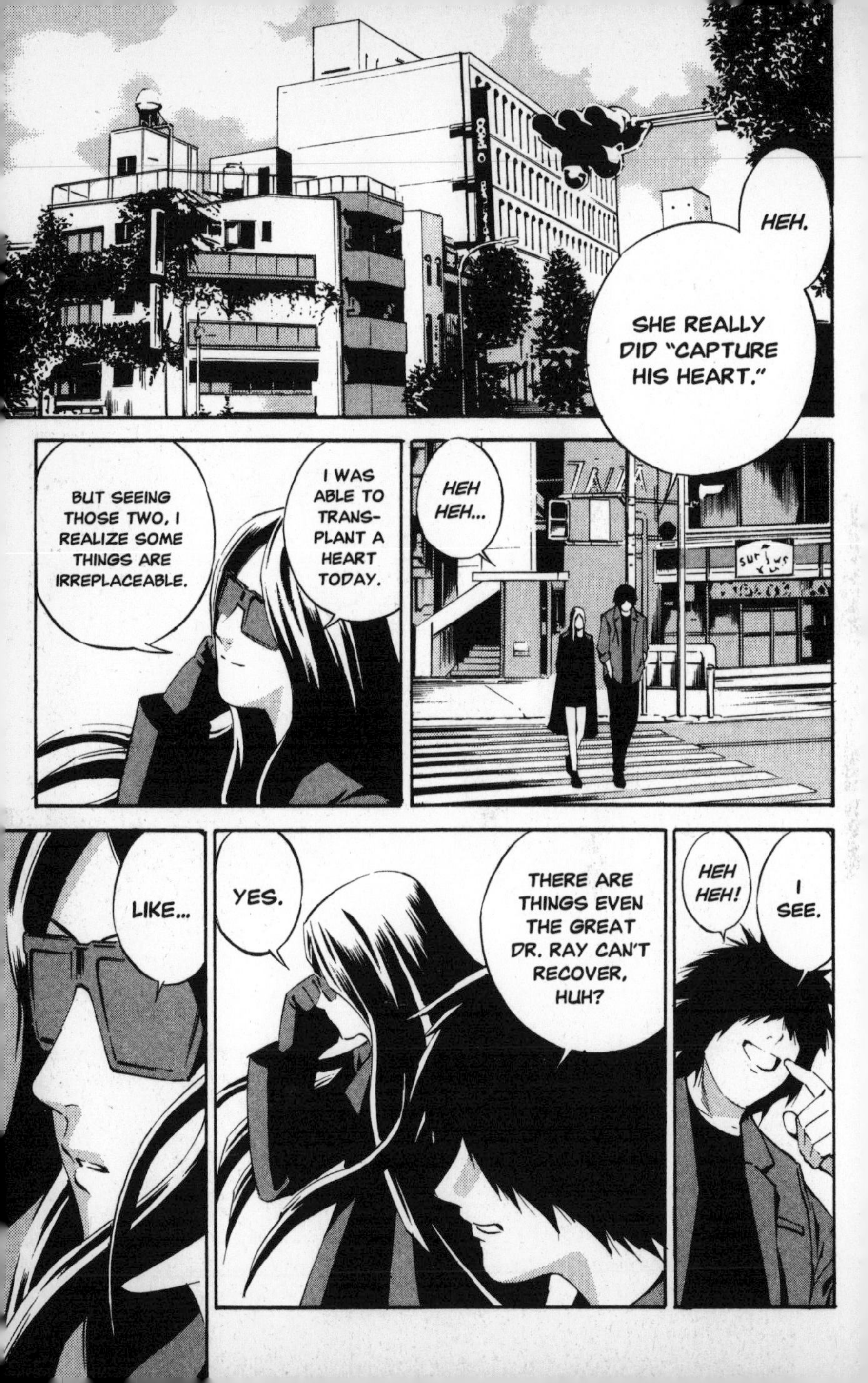
HEH.
SHE REALLY DID "CAPTURE HIS HEART."
HEH HEH...
I WAS ABLE TO TRANSPLANT A HEART TODAY.
BUT SEEING THOSE TWO, I REALIZE SOME THINGS ARE IRREPLACEABLE.
I SEE.
HEH HEH!
THERE ARE THINGS EVEN THE GREAT DR. RAY CAN'T RECOVER, HUH?
YES.
LIKE...

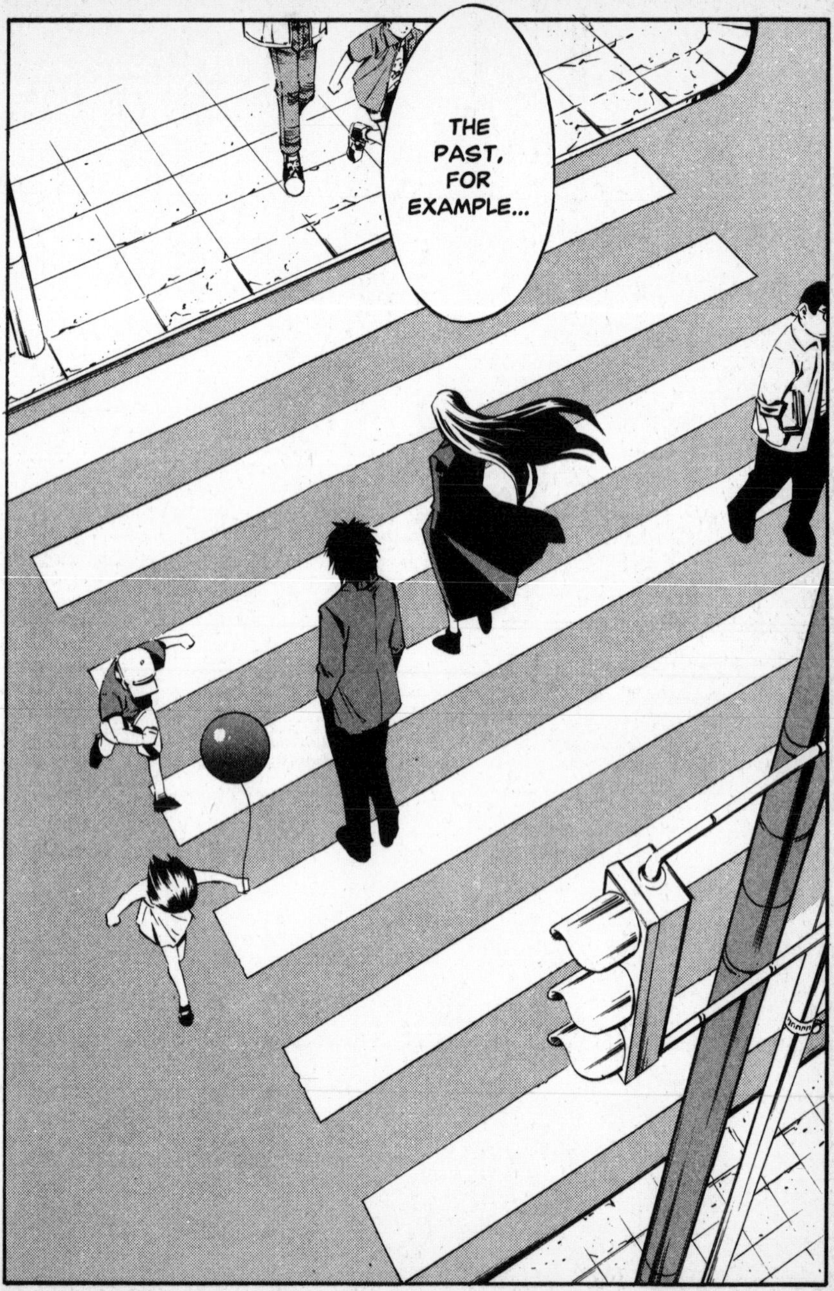
THE PAST, FOR EXAMPLE...

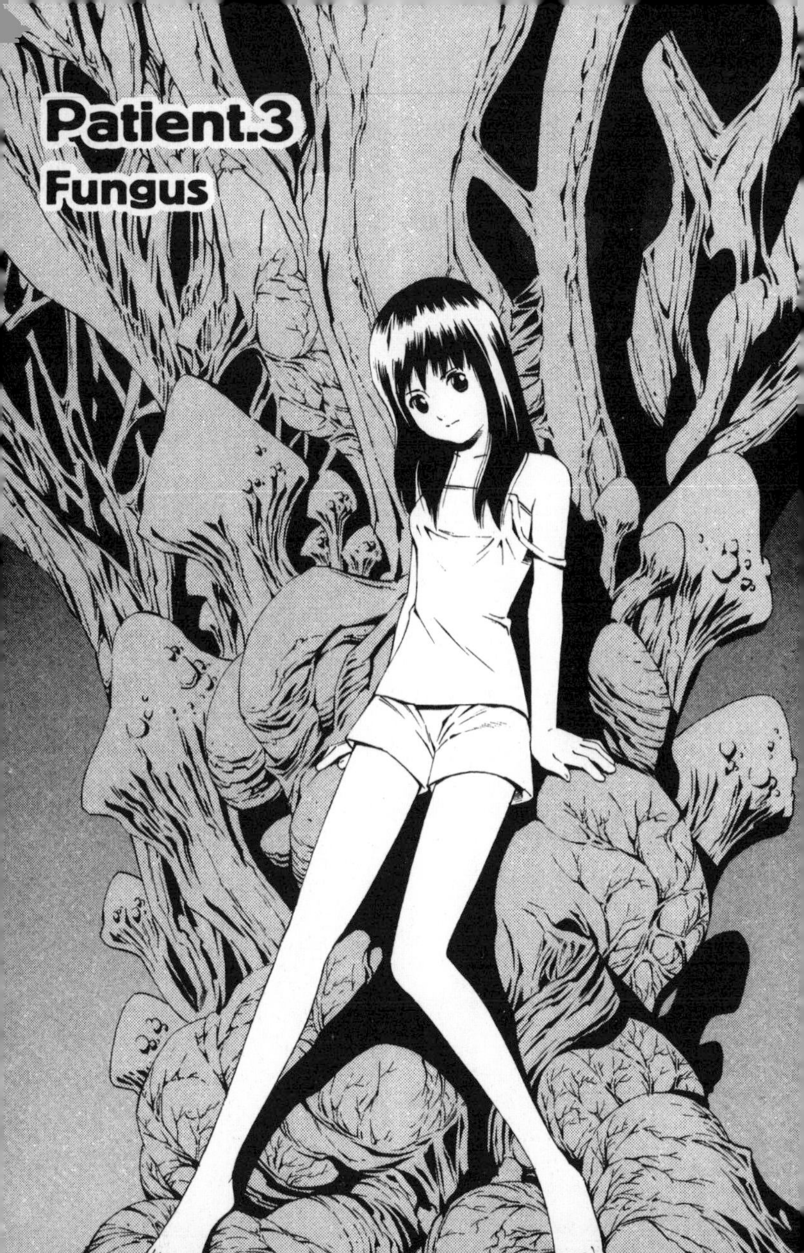
Patient.3
Fungus

WHAT'S YOUR SPECIAL TREASURE?

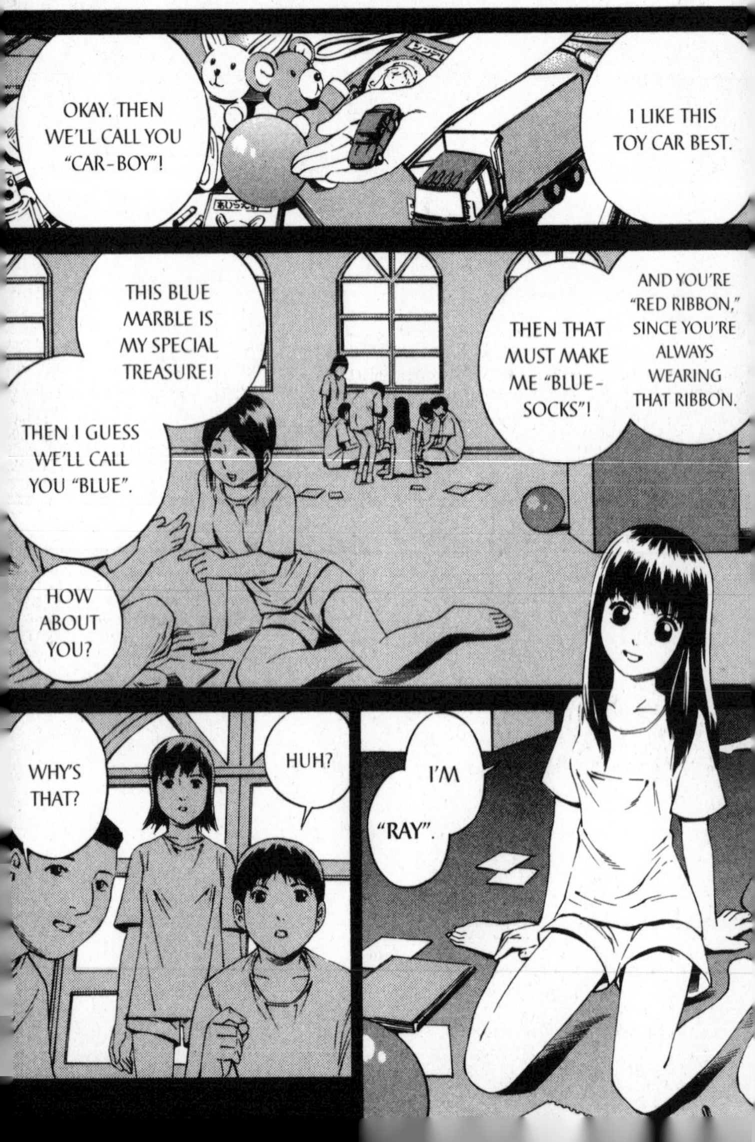
I LIKE THIS TOY CAR BEST.
OKAY. THEN WE'LL CALL YOU "CAR-BOY"!
THIS BLUE MARBLE IS MY SPECIAL TREASURE!
THEN I GUESS WE'LL CALL YOU "BLUE".
THEN THAT MUST MAKE ME "BLUE-SOCKS"!
AND YOU'RE "RED RIBBON," SINCE YOU'RE ALWAYS WEARING THAT RIBBON.
HOW ABOUT YOU?
I'M "RAY".
HUH?
WHY'S THAT?

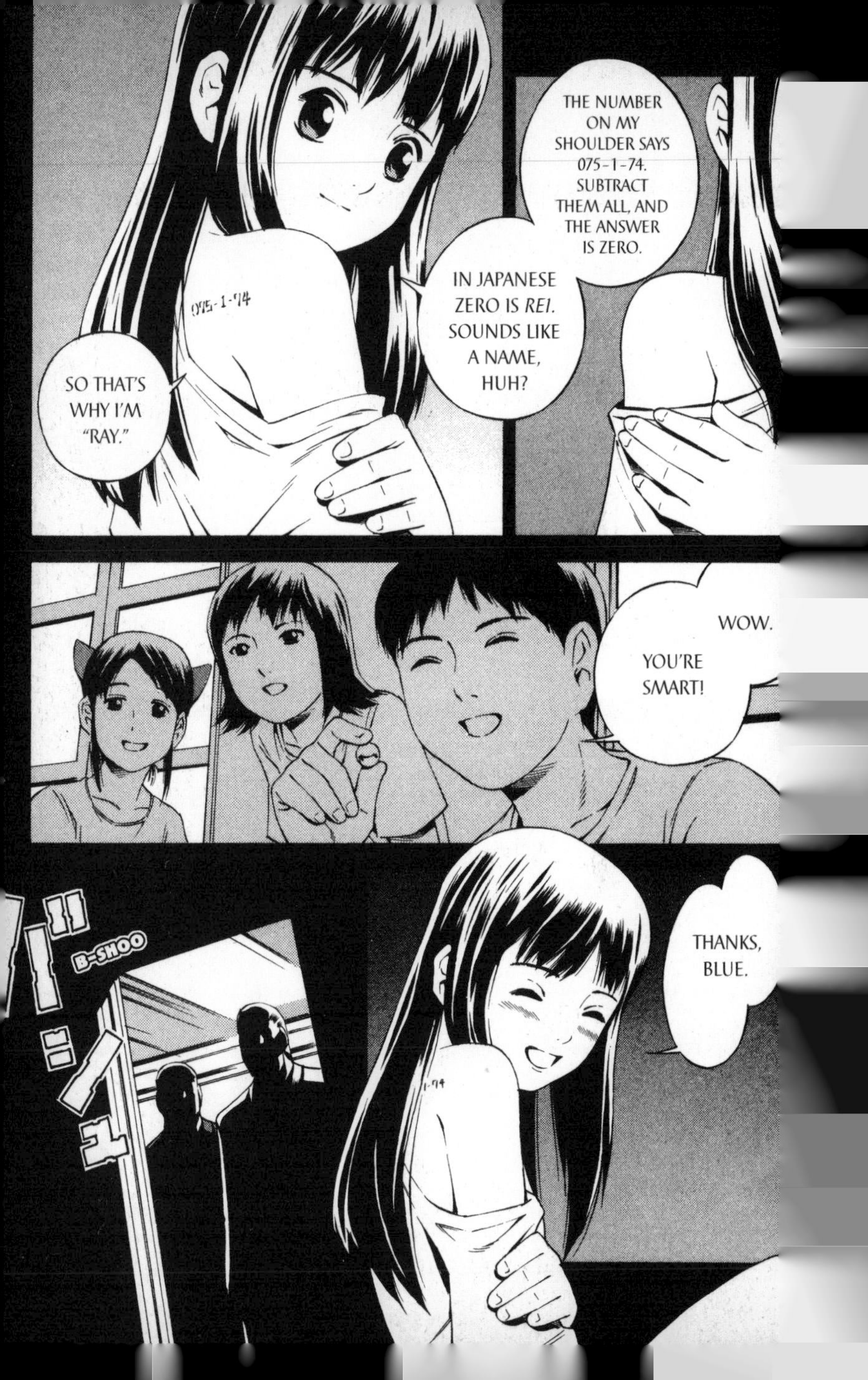
THE NUMBER ON MY SHOULDER SAYS 075-1-74. SUBTRACT THEM ALL, AND THE ANSWER IS ZERO.
IN JAPANESE ZERO IS *REI*. SOUNDS LIKE A NAME, HUH?
SO THAT'S WHY I'M "RAY."
075-1-74
WOW.
YOU'RE SMART!
THANKS, BLUE.
B-SHOO

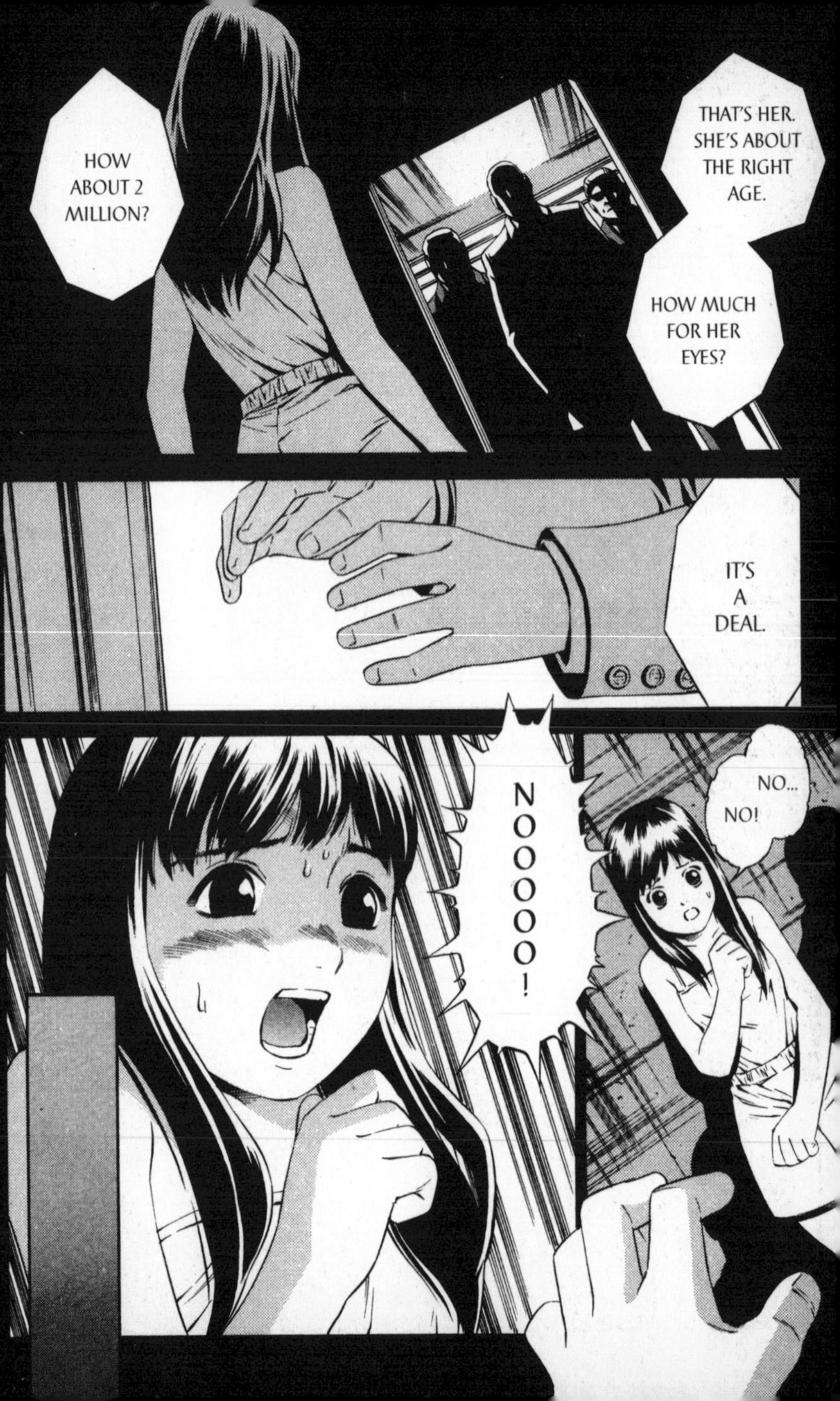
THAT'S HER. SHE'S ABOUT THE RIGHT AGE.
HOW MUCH FOR HER EYES?
HOW ABOUT 2 MILLION?
IT'S A DEAL.
NO... NO!
NOOOOOO!

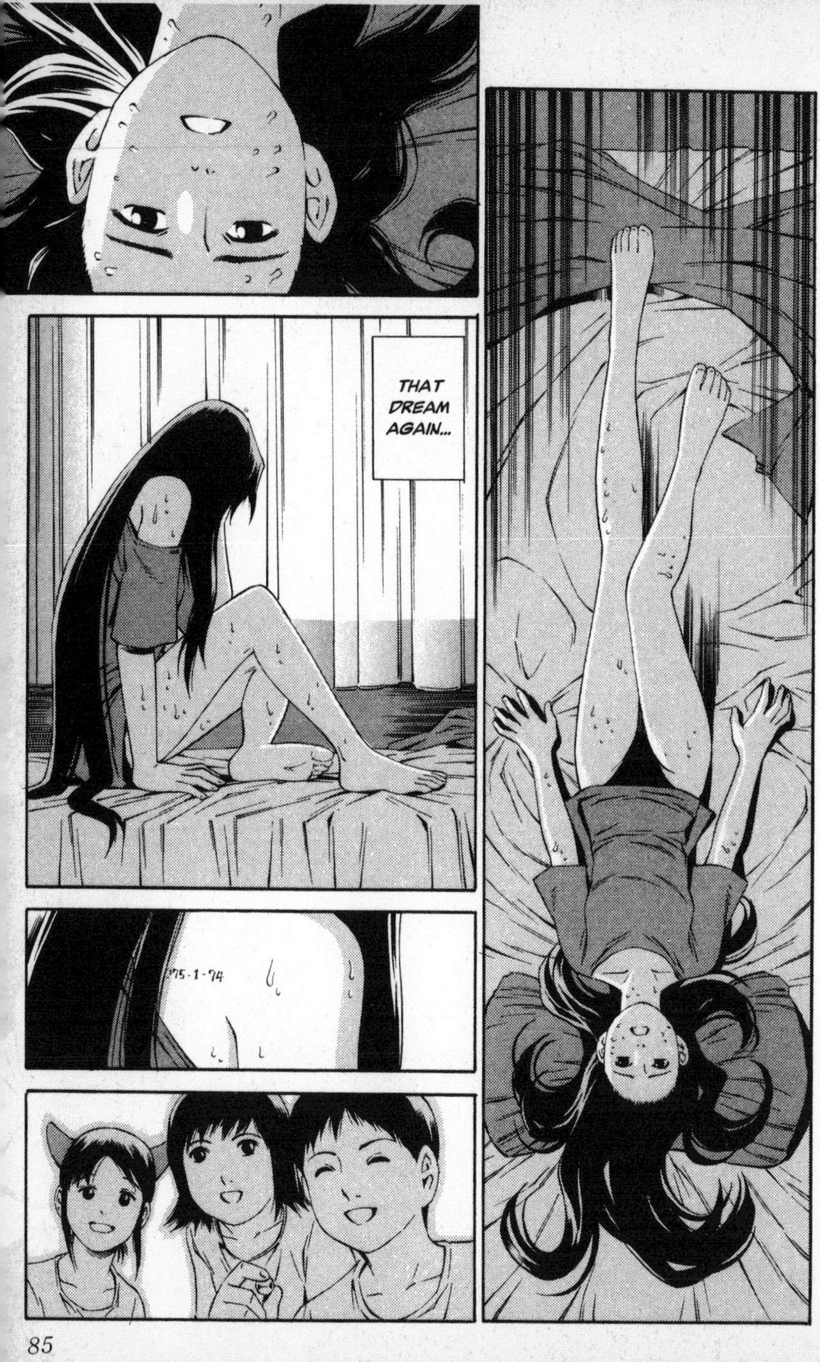
THAT DREAM AGAIN...
75-1-74

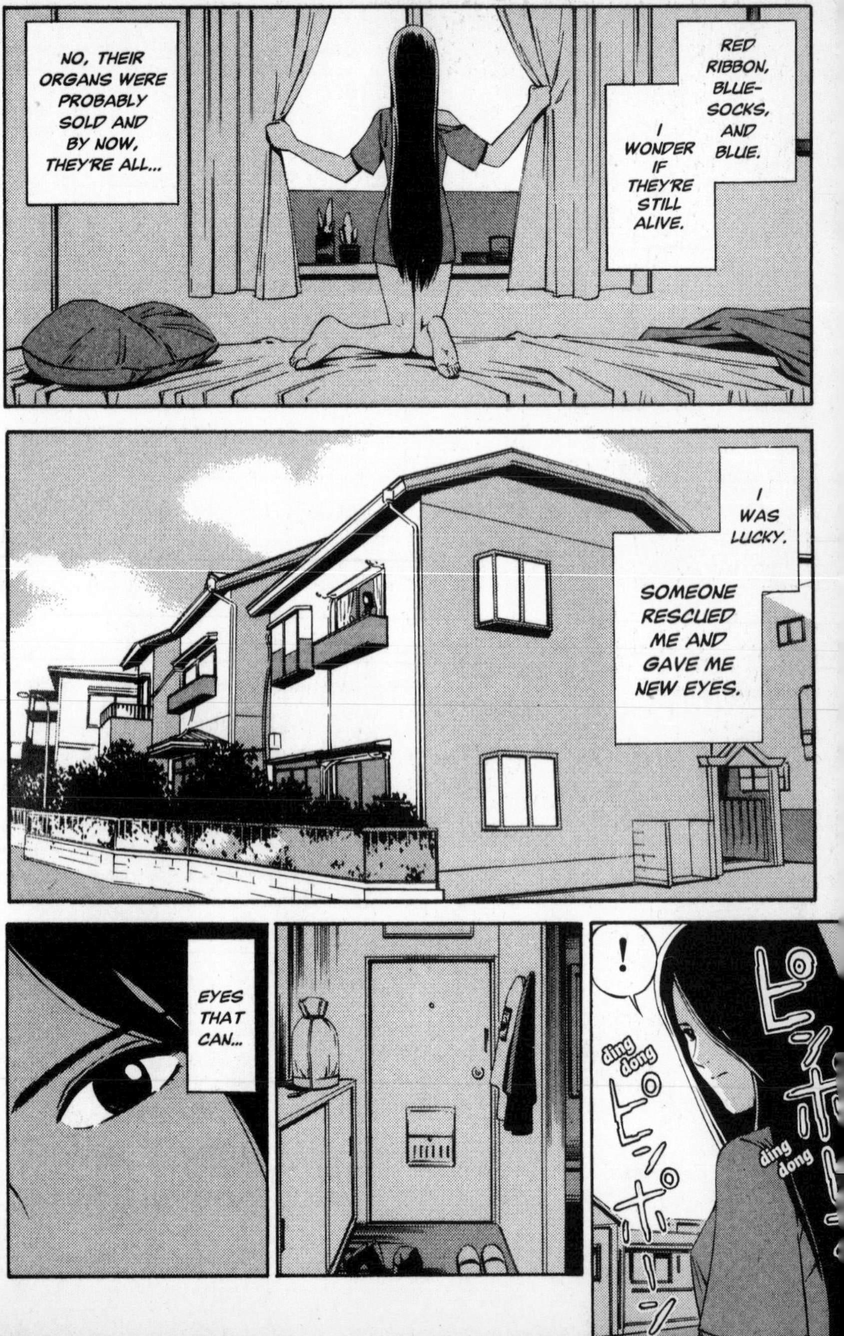
RED RIBBON, BLUE-SOCKS, AND BLUE.
I WONDER IF THEY'RE STILL ALIVE.
NO, THEIR ORGANS WERE PROBABLY SOLD AND BY NOW, THEY'RE ALL...
I WAS LUCKY.
SOMEONE RESCUED ME AND GAVE ME NEW EYES.
EYES THAT CAN...
ding dong
ding dong
!

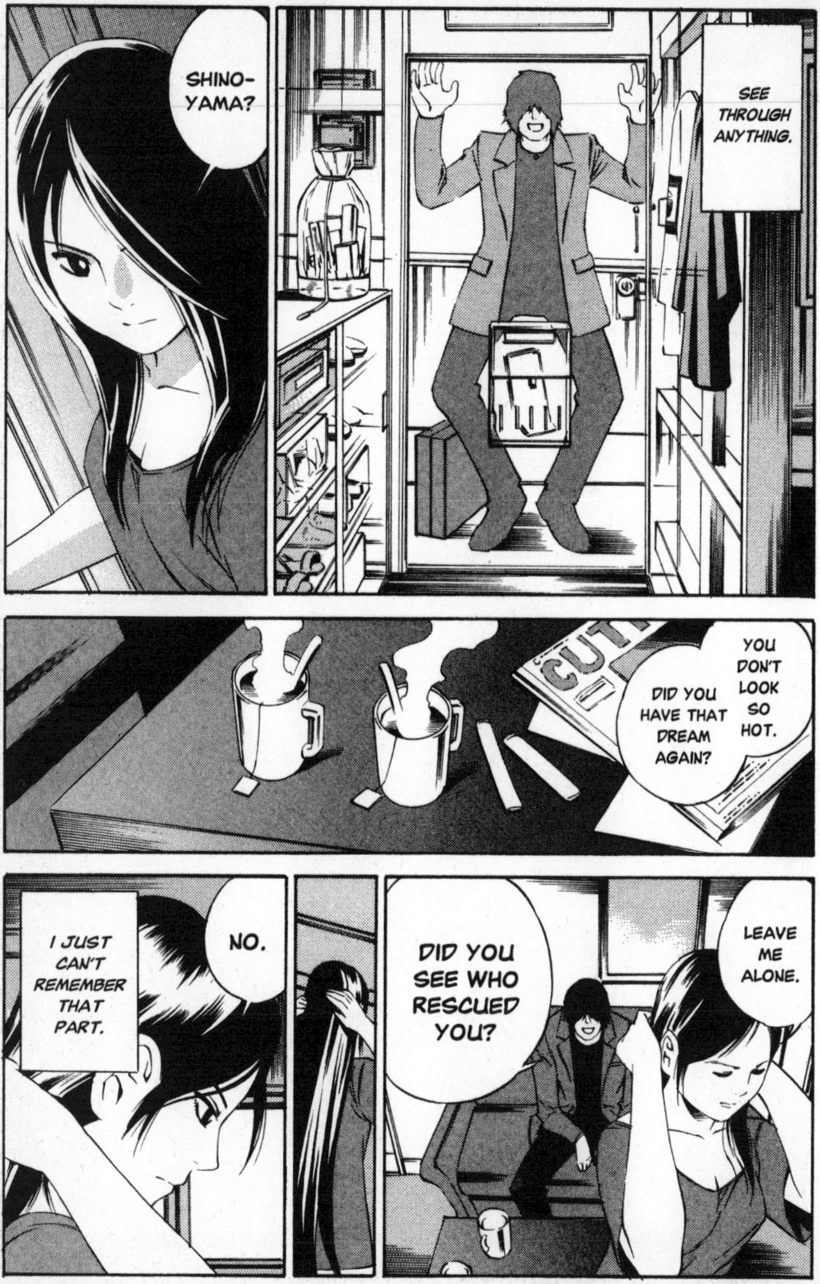
SEE THROUGH ANYTHING.
SHINO-YAMA?
YOU DON'T LOOK SO HOT.
DID YOU HAVE THAT DREAM AGAIN?
LEAVE ME ALONE.
DID YOU SEE WHO RESCUED YOU?
NO.
I JUST CAN'T REMEMBER THAT PART.

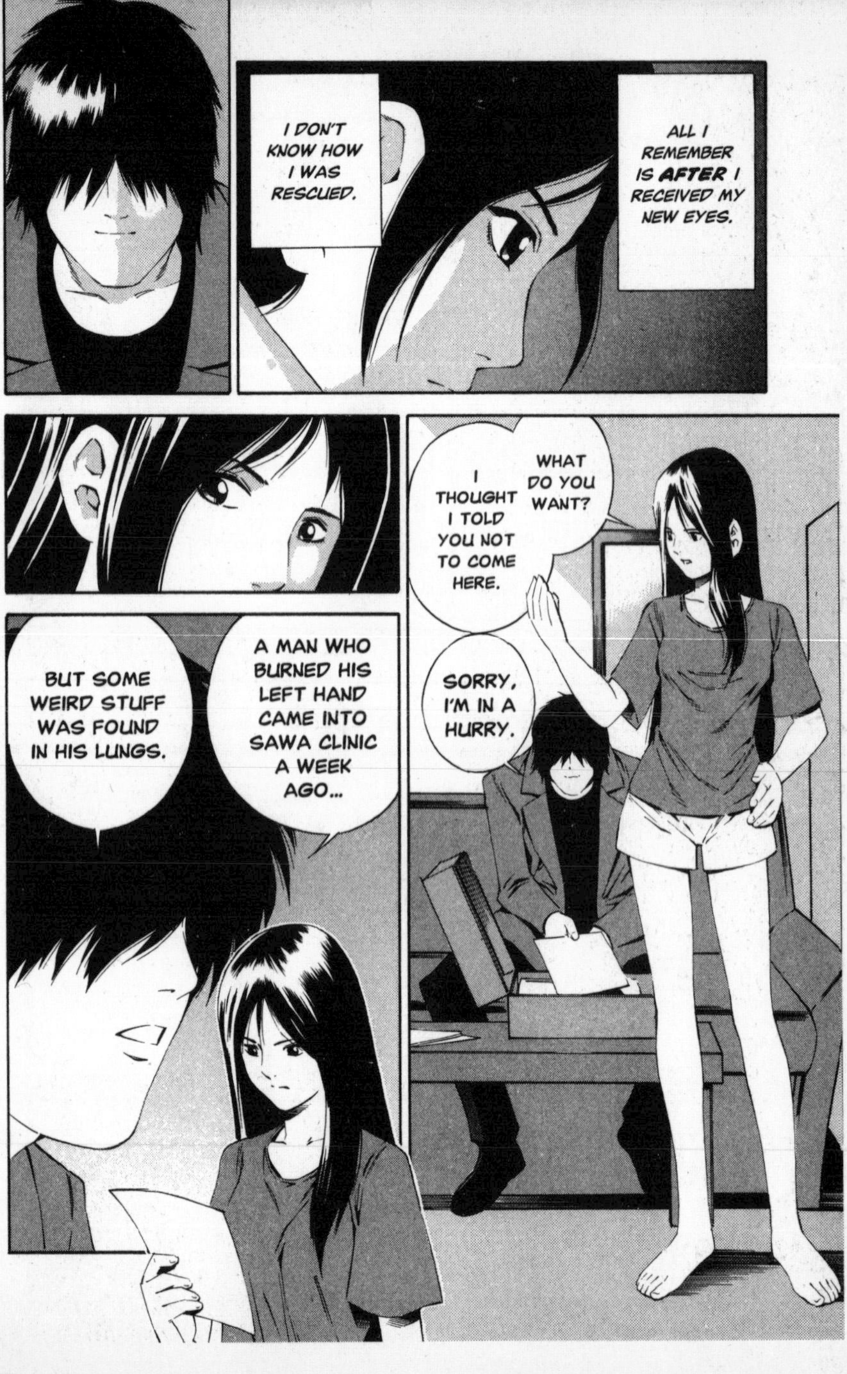
I DON'T KNOW HOW I WAS RESCUED.
ALL I REMEMBER IS **AFTER** I RECEIVED MY NEW EYES.
WHAT DO YOU WANT?
I THOUGHT I TOLD YOU NOT TO COME HERE.
SORRY, I'M IN A HURRY.
A MAN WHO BURNED HIS LEFT HAND CAME INTO SAWA CLINIC A WEEK AGO...
BUT SOME WEIRD STUFF WAS FOUND IN HIS LUNGS.

RIGHT. THERE'S A CERTAIN "LEONE FUNGUS," WHICH ONLY EXISTS IN AFRICA.

IT'S A FUNGUS.

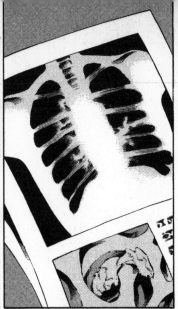

THE FIRST DOCUMENTATION OF THIS INFECTION WAS FROM BACK IN FEBRUARY OF 1970.

PEOPLE IN THE PARTY OF BRITISH BIOLOGIST LEONE BRYAN WERE INFECTED WHILE IN A REMOTE PART OF AFRICA.

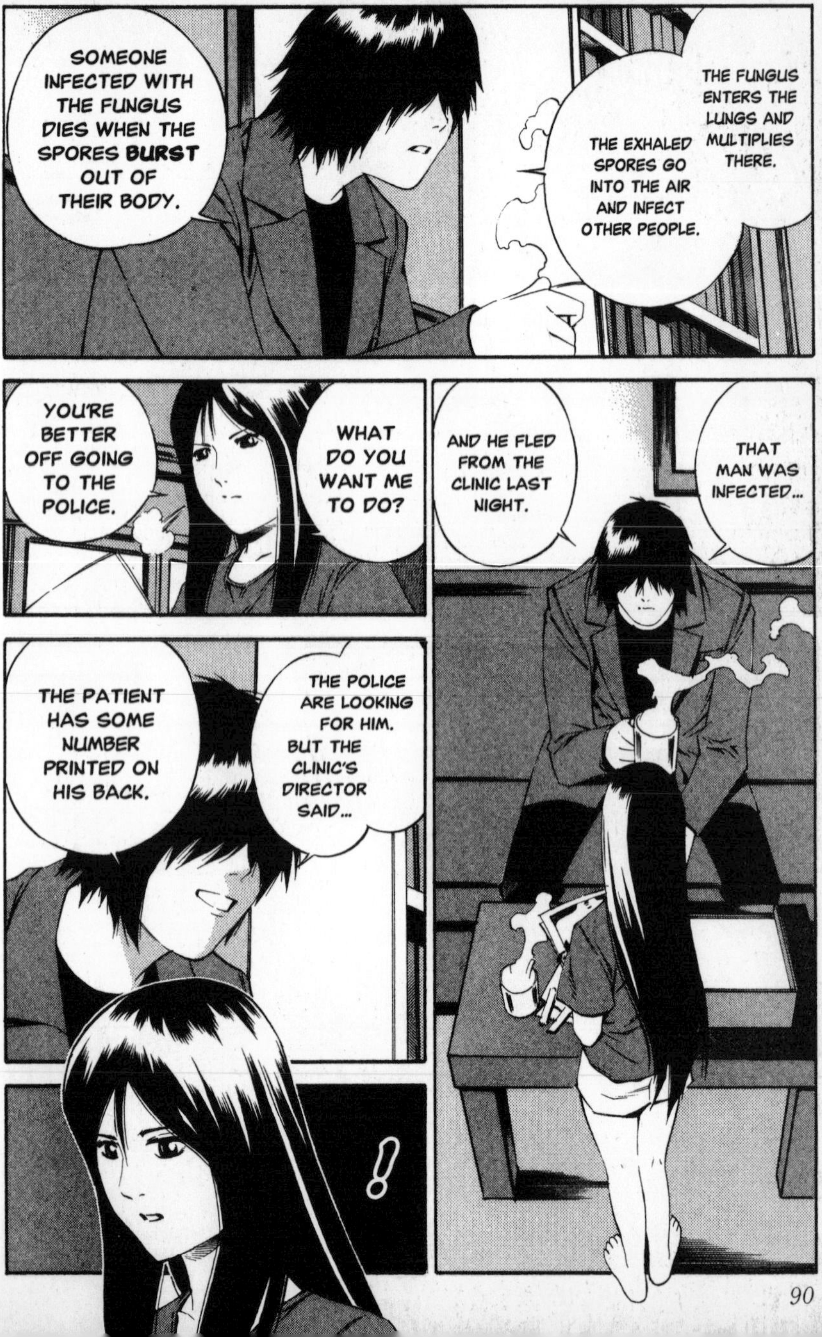
THE FUNGUS ENTERS THE LUNGS AND MULTIPLIES THERE.
THE EXHALED SPORES GO INTO THE AIR AND INFECT OTHER PEOPLE.
SOMEONE INFECTED WITH THE FUNGUS DIES WHEN THE SPORES **BURST** OUT OF THEIR BODY.
THAT MAN WAS INFECTED...
AND HE FLED FROM THE CLINIC LAST NIGHT.
WHAT DO YOU WANT ME TO DO?
YOU'RE BETTER OFF GOING TO THE POLICE.
THE POLICE ARE LOOKING FOR HIM. BUT THE CLINIC'S DIRECTOR SAID...
THE PATIENT HAS SOME NUMBER PRINTED ON HIS BACK.
!

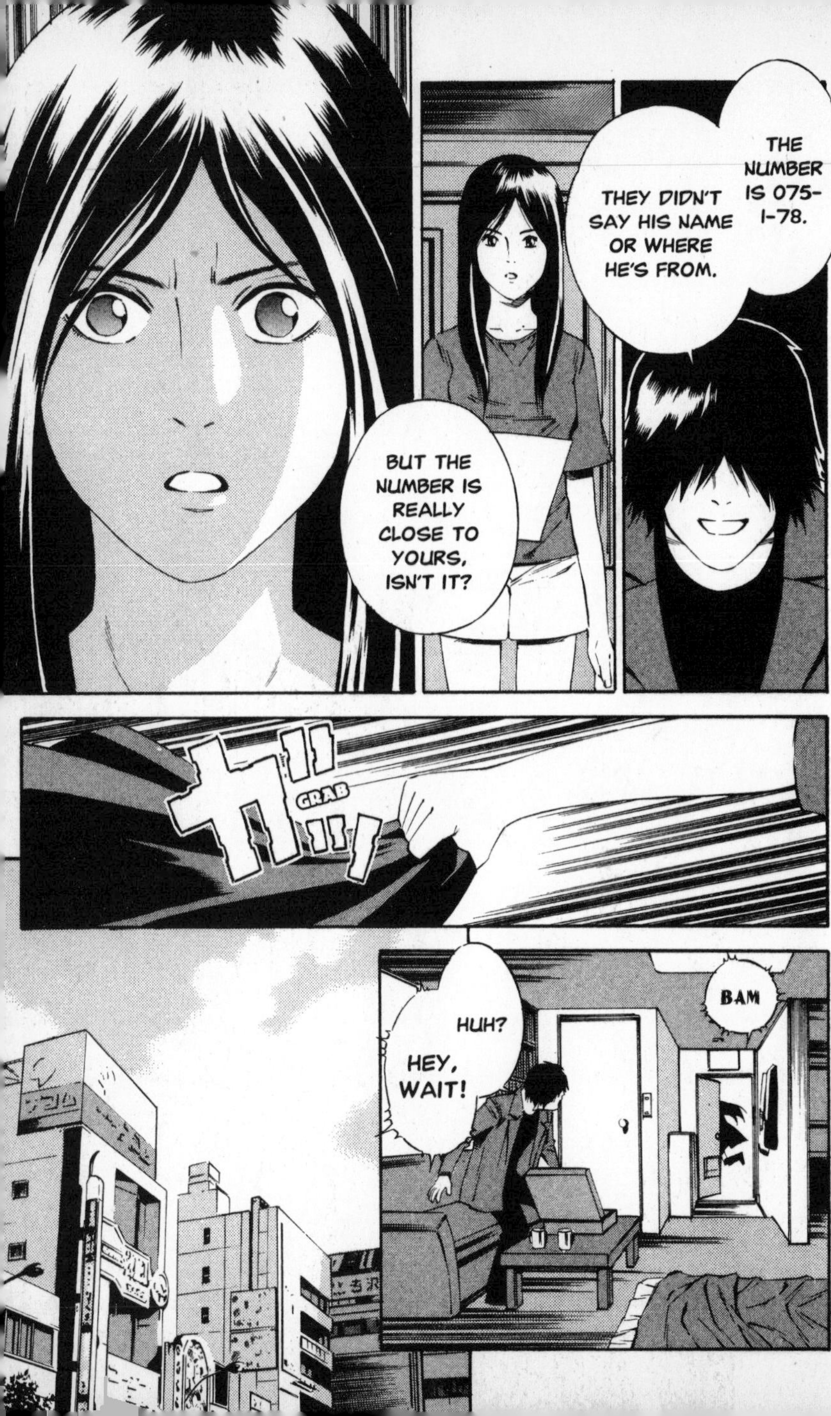
THE NUMBER IS 075-1-78.
THEY DIDN'T SAY HIS NAME OR WHERE HE'S FROM.
BUT THE NUMBER IS REALLY CLOSE TO YOURS, ISN'T IT?
GRAB
BAM
HUH?
HEY, WAIT!

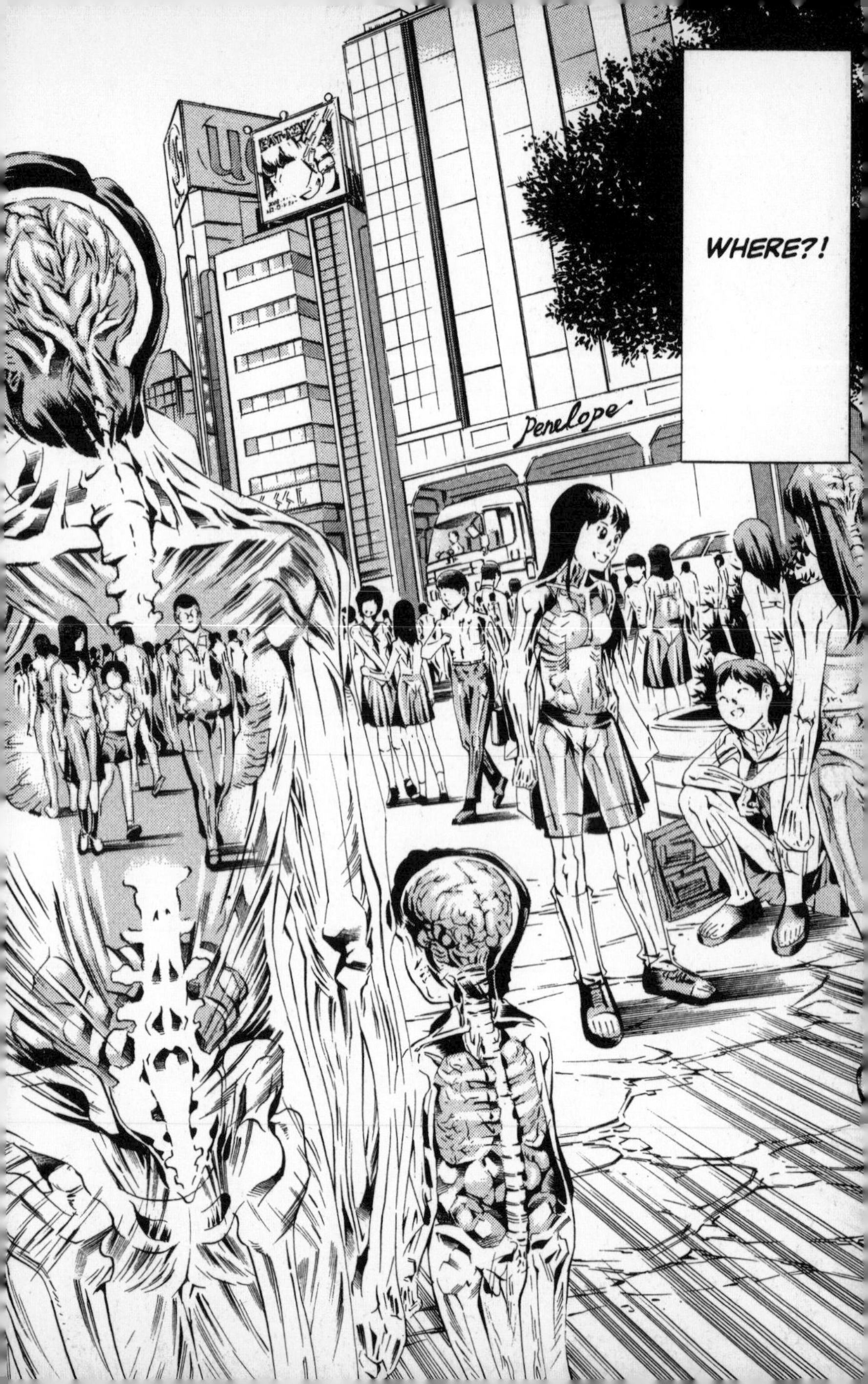
WHERE?!
Penelope

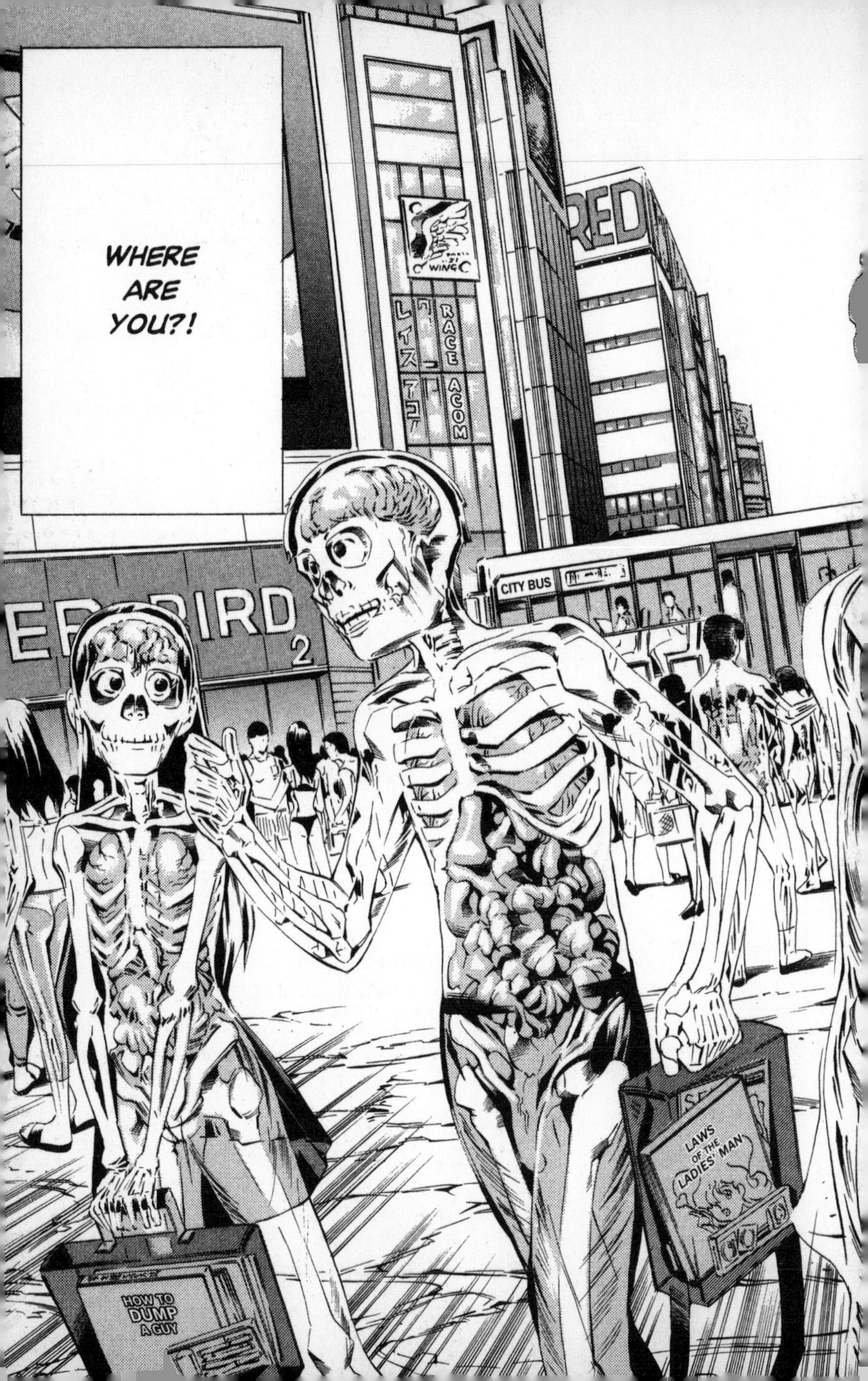
WHERE ARE YOU?!
WING
RACE ACOM
RED
CITY BUS
ER BIRD
2
HOW TO DUMP A GUY
LAWS OF THE LADIES' MAN

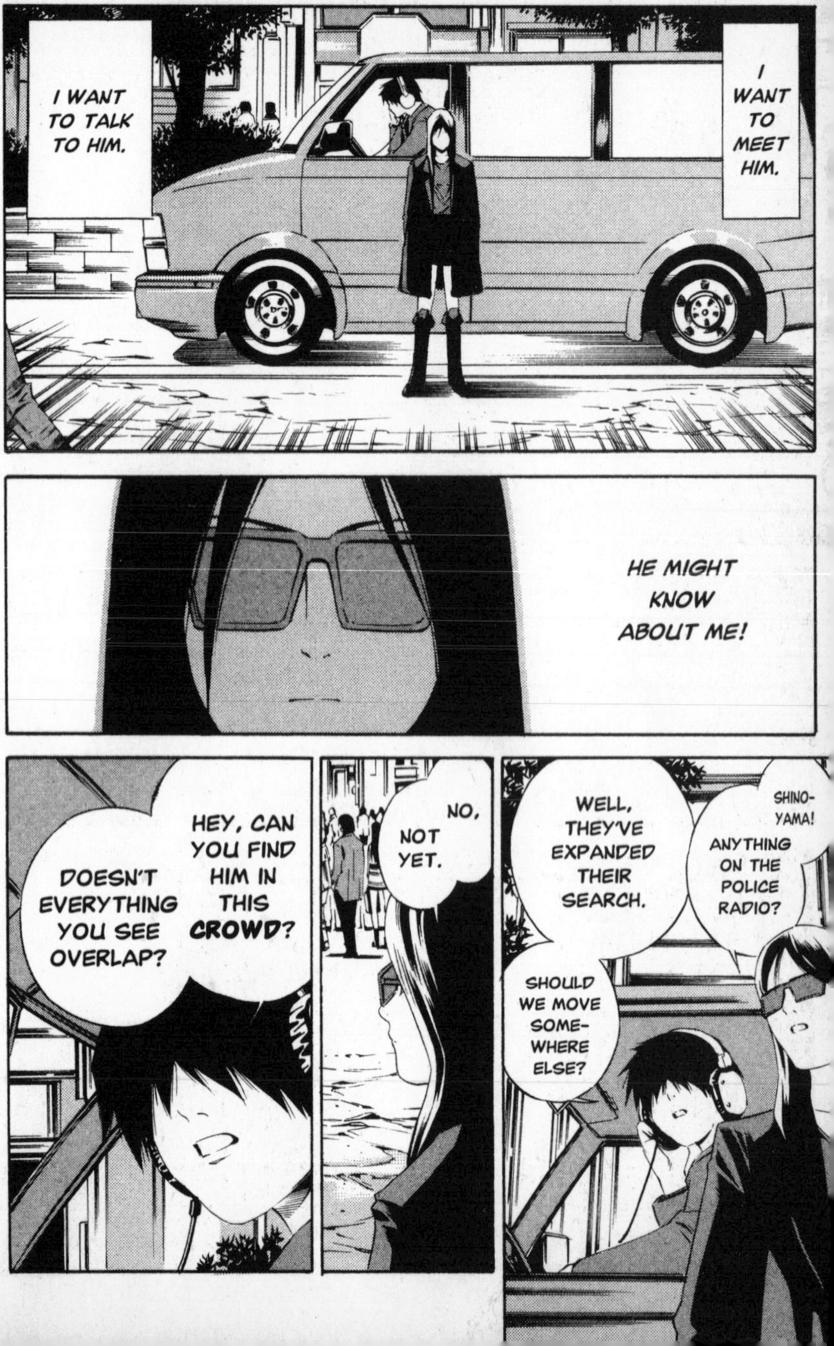
I WANT TO MEET HIM.
I WANT TO TALK TO HIM.
HE MIGHT KNOW ABOUT ME!
SHINO-YAMA! ANYTHING ON THE POLICE RADIO?
WELL, THEY'VE EXPANDED THEIR SEARCH.
SHOULD WE MOVE SOME-WHERE ELSE?
NO, NOT YET.
HEY, CAN YOU FIND HIM IN THIS **CROWD**?
DOESN'T EVERYTHING YOU SEE OVERLAP?

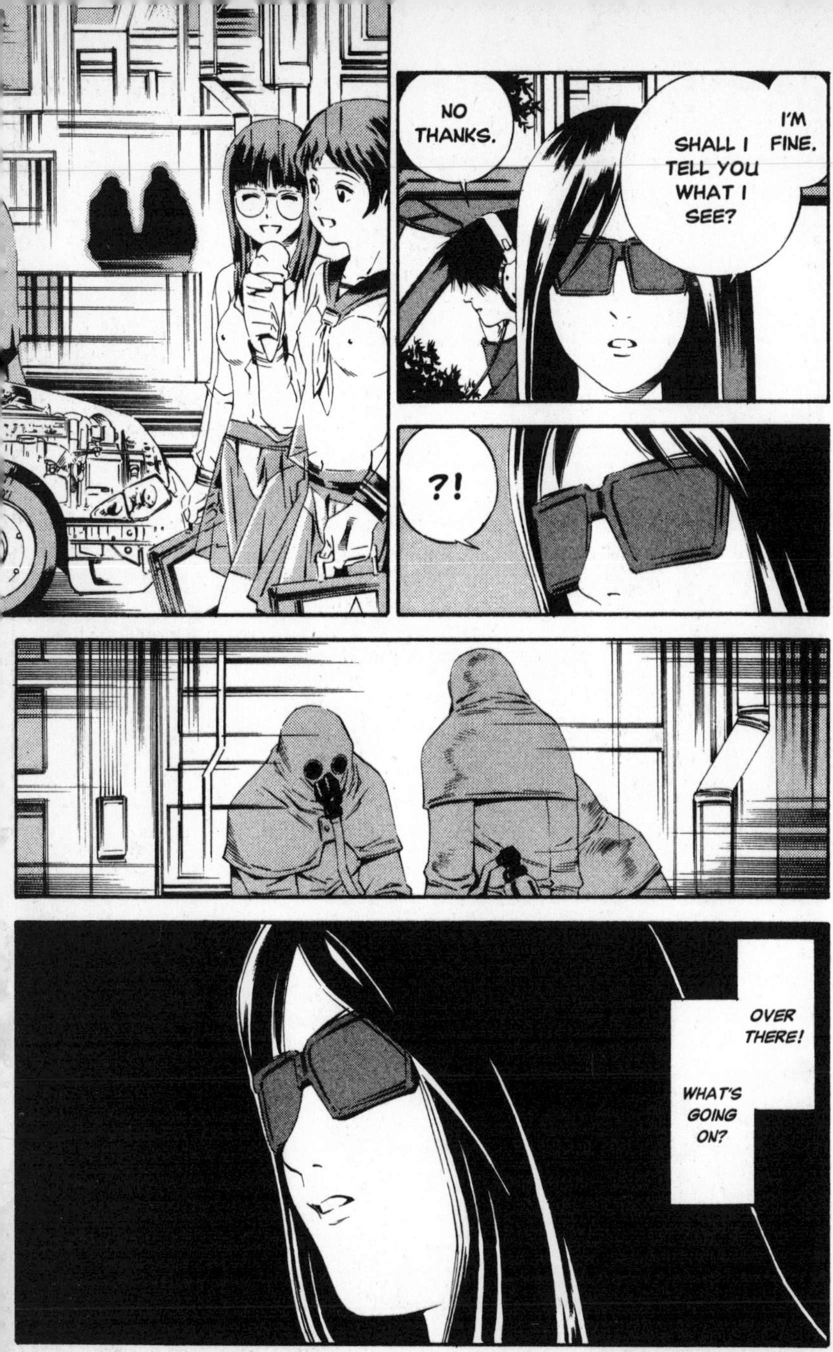
I'M FINE.
SHALL I TELL YOU WHAT I SEE?
NO THANKS.
?!
OVER THERE!
WHAT'S GOING ON?

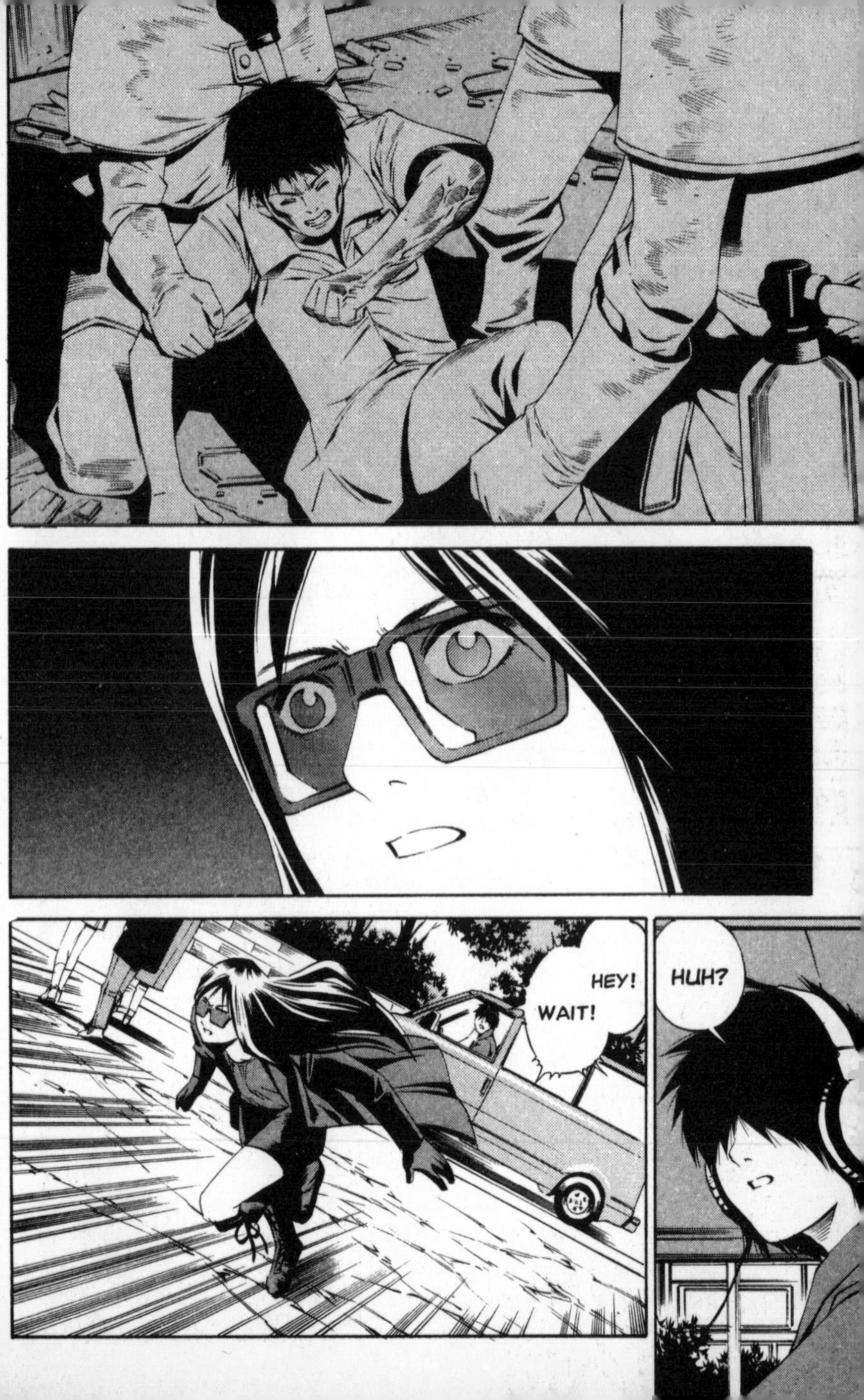
HUH?
HEY!
WAIT!

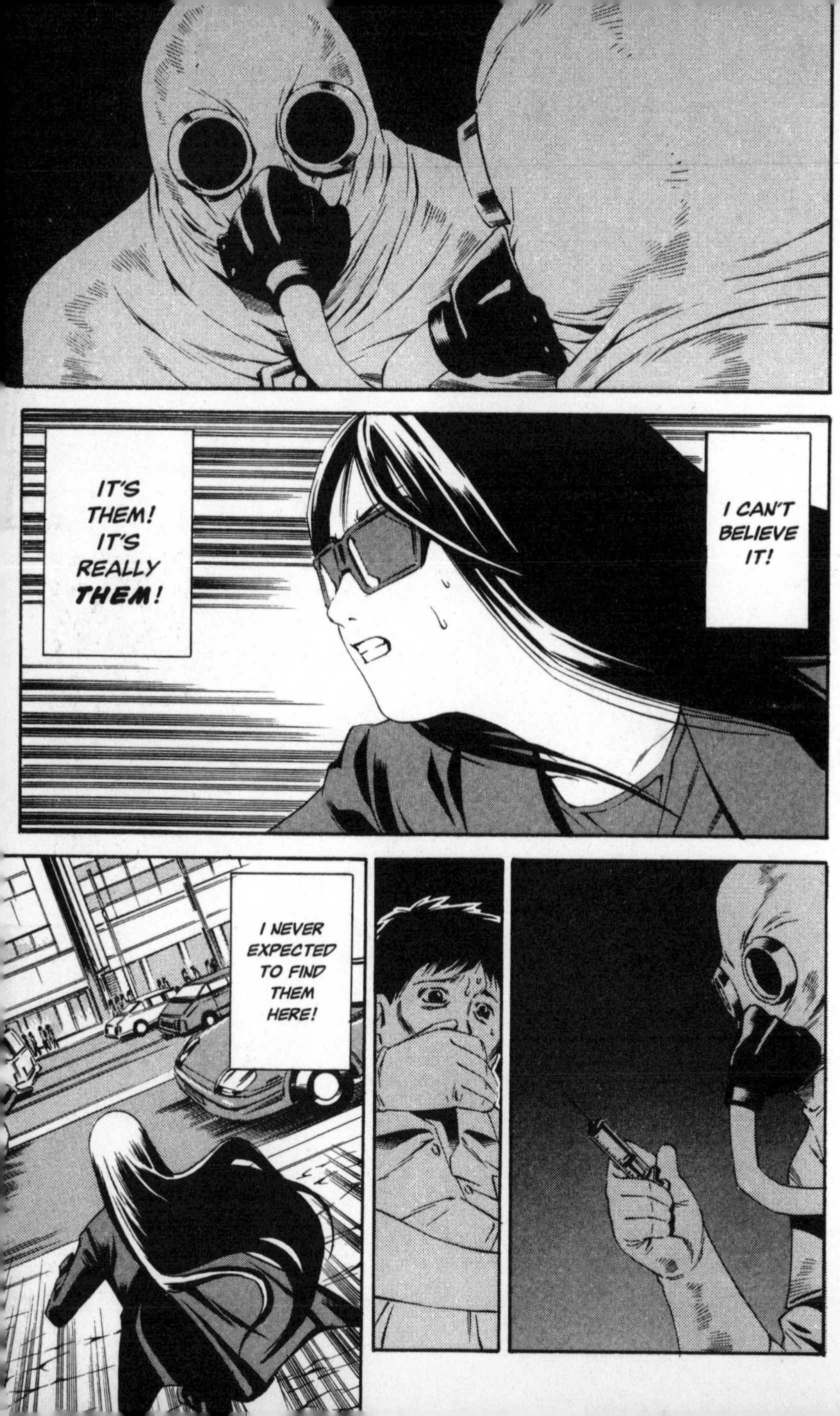
I CAN'T BELIEVE IT!
IT'S THEM! IT'S REALLY THEM!
I NEVER EXPECTED TO FIND THEM HERE!

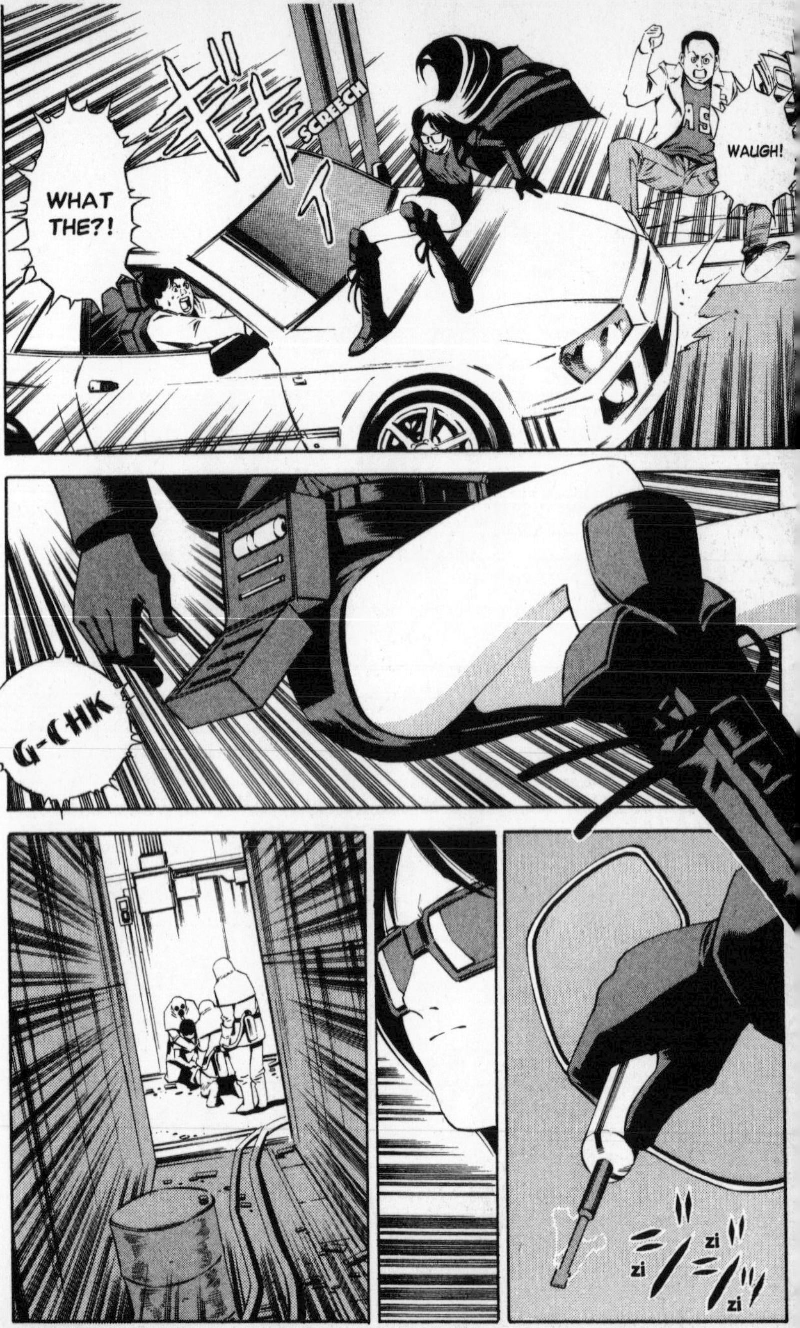
WAUGH!
SCREECH
WHAT THE?!
G-CHK
zi
zi
zi

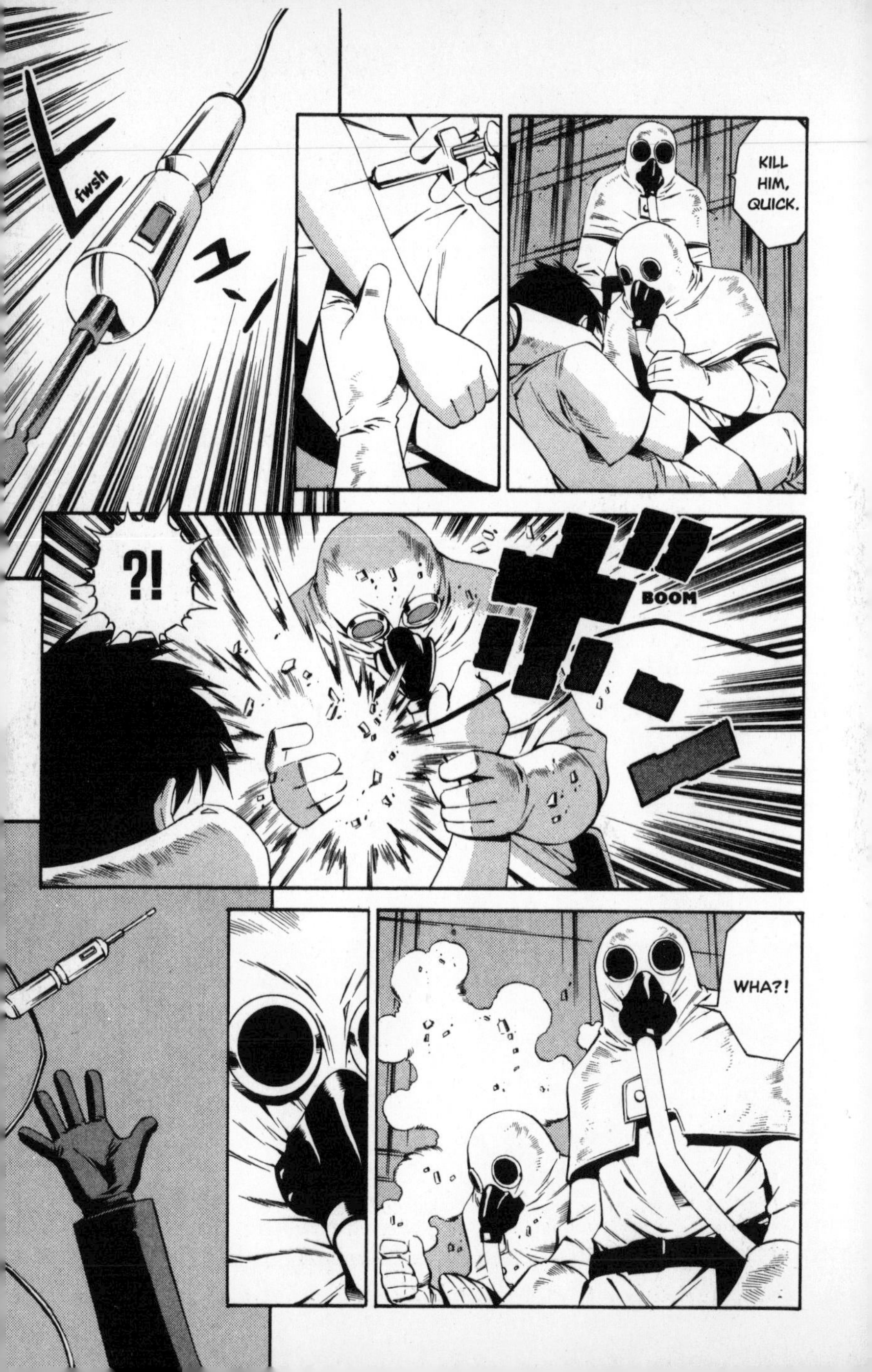
fwsh
KILL HIM, QUICK.
BOOM
?!
WHA?!

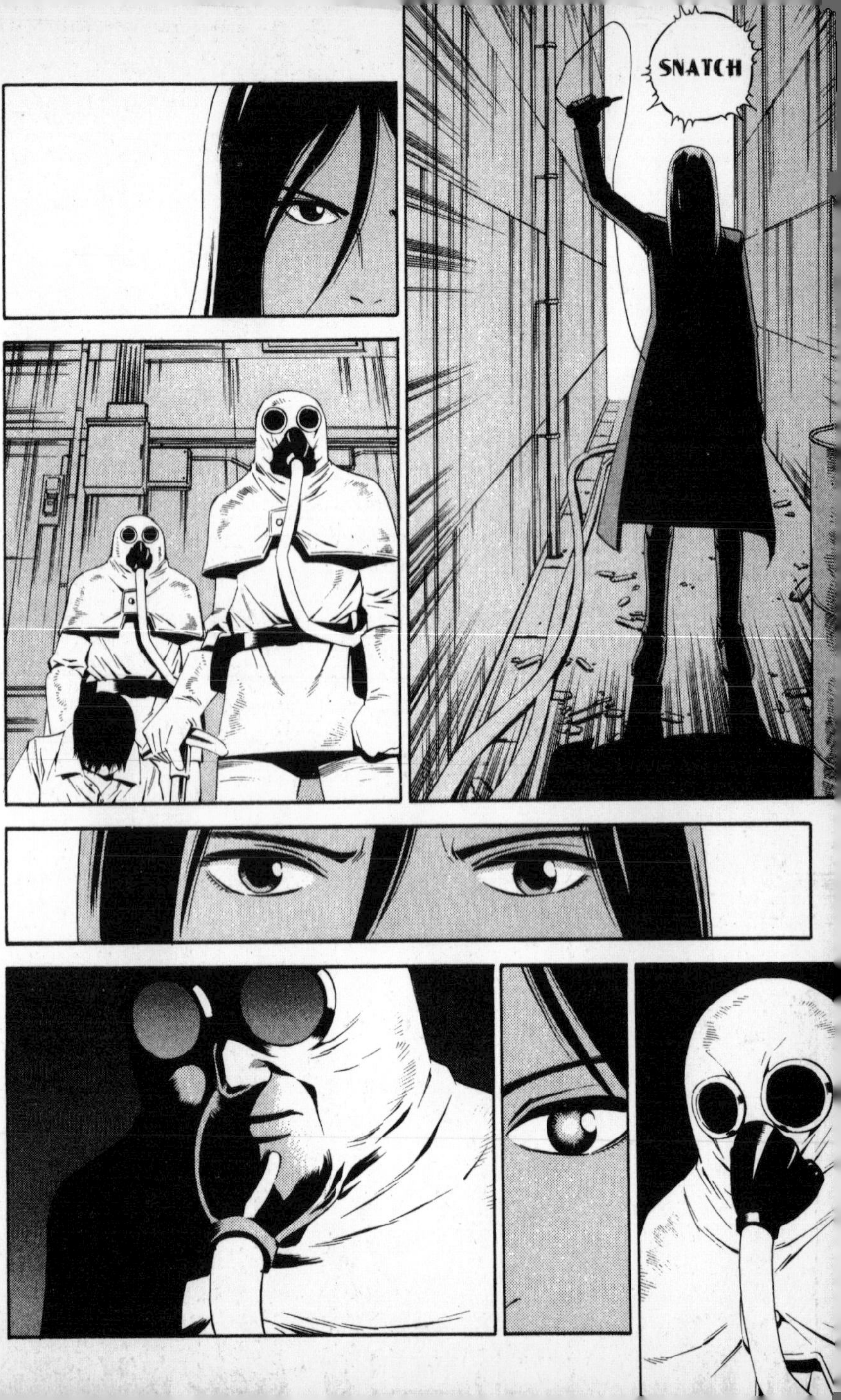
SNATCH

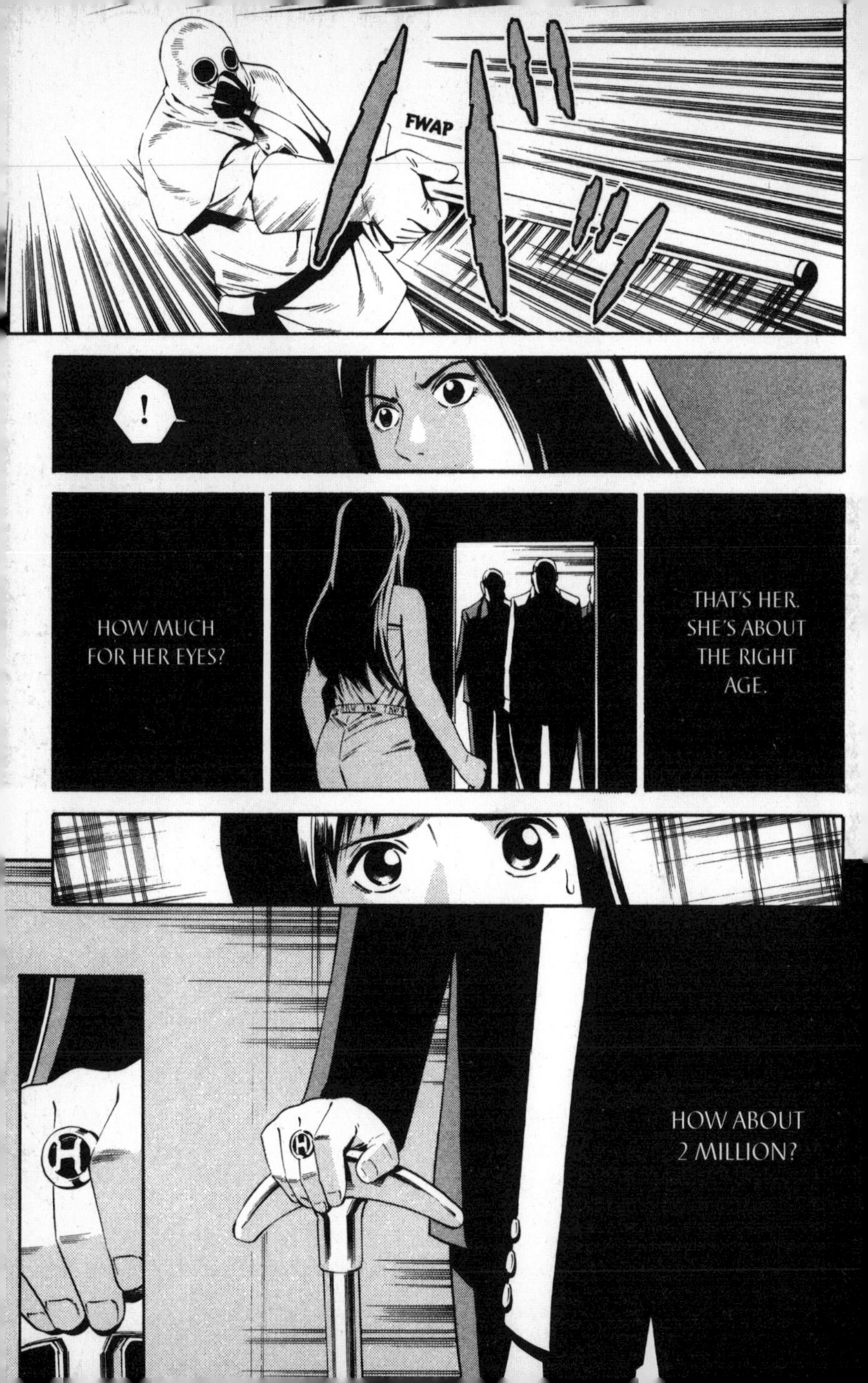
FWAP
!
THAT'S HER. SHE'S ABOUT THE RIGHT AGE.
HOW MUCH FOR HER EYES?
HOW ABOUT 2 MILLION?

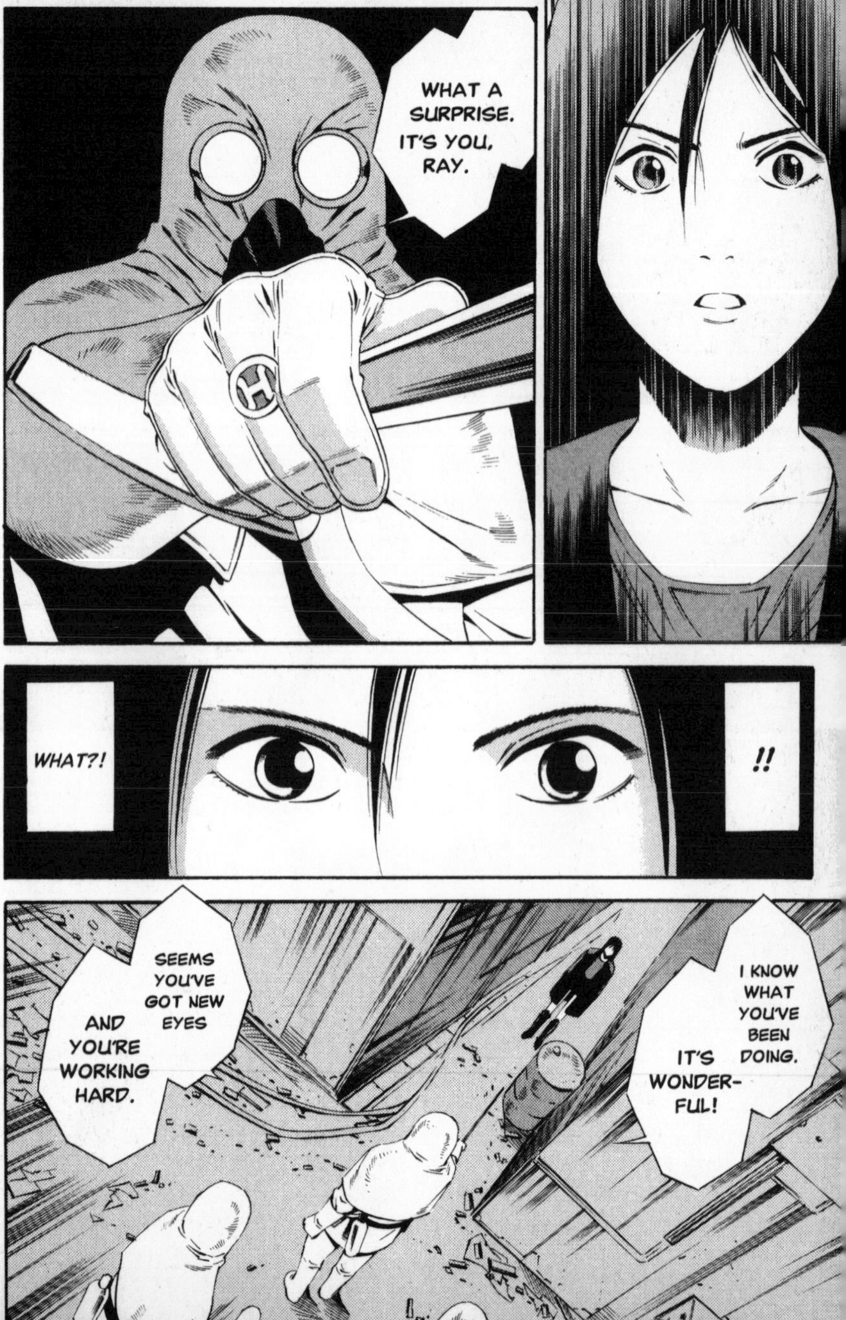
WHAT A SURPRISE. IT'S YOU, RAY.
WHAT?!
!!
I KNOW WHAT YOU'VE BEEN DOING. IT'S WONDER-FUL!
SEEMS YOU'VE GOT NEW EYES
AND YOU'RE WORKING HARD.

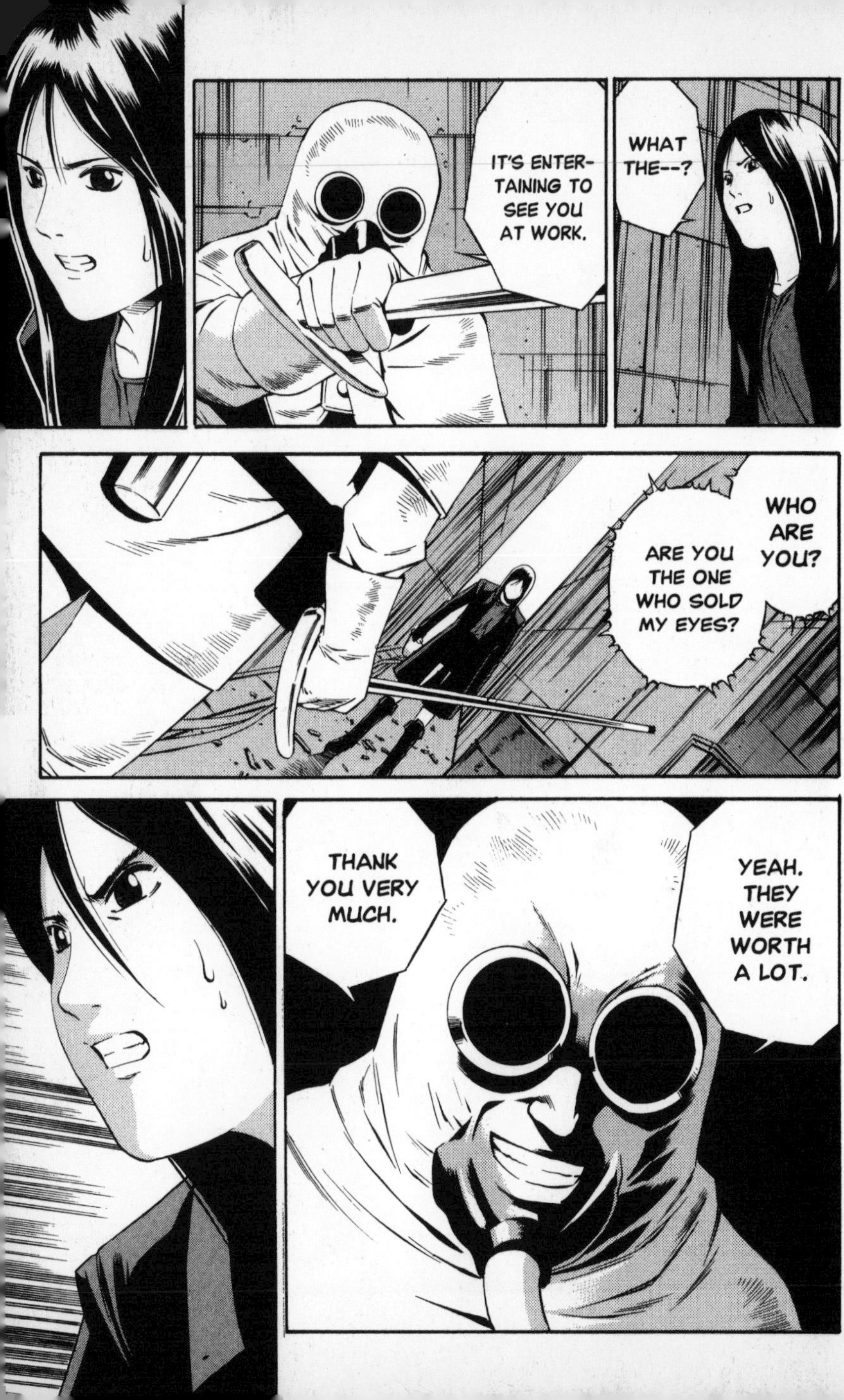
WHAT THE--?
IT'S ENTER-TAINING TO SEE YOU AT WORK.
WHO ARE YOU?
ARE YOU THE ONE WHO SOLD MY EYES?
YEAH. THEY WERE WORTH A LOT.
THANK YOU VERY MUCH.

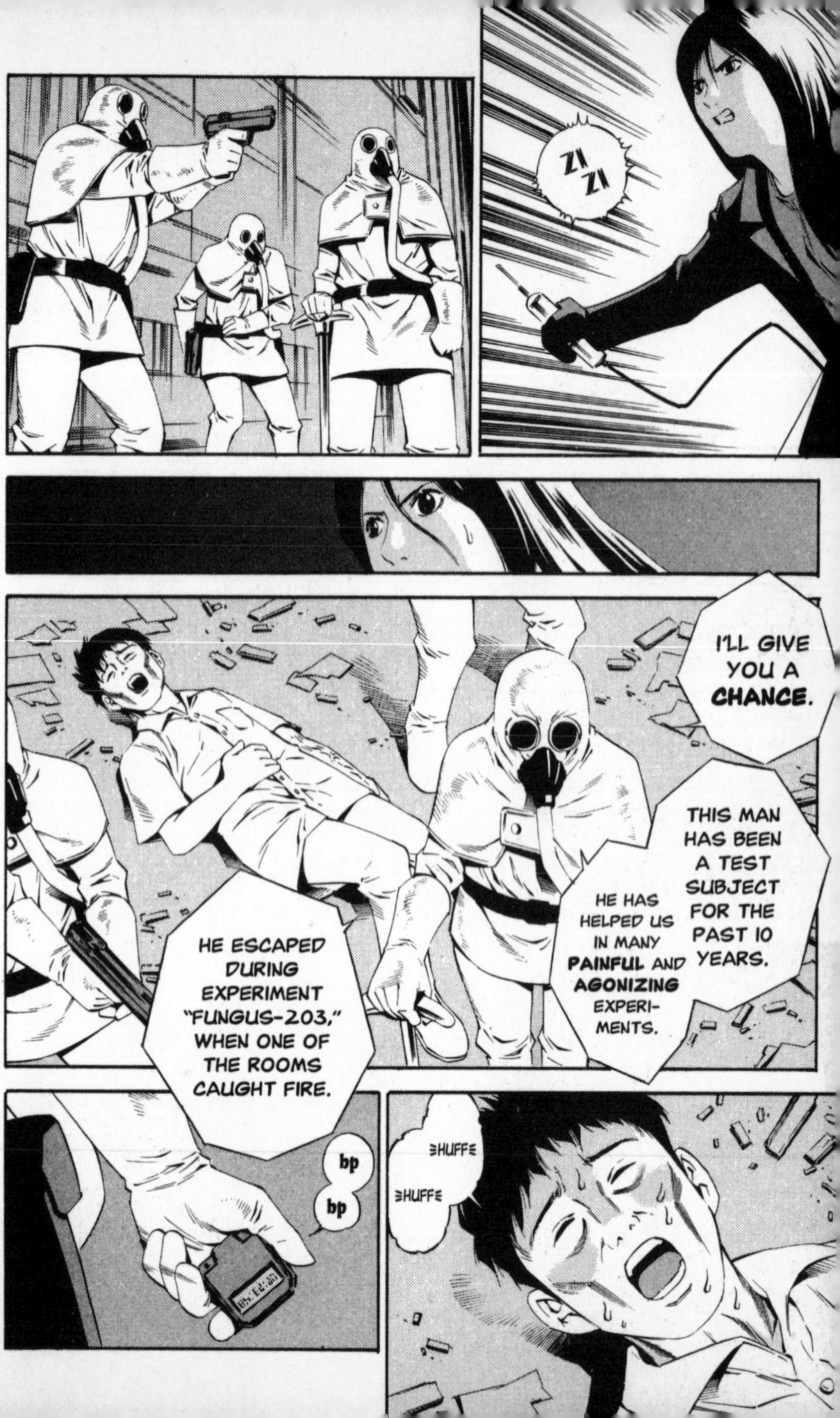
ZI ZI
I'LL GIVE YOU A CHANCE.
THIS MAN HAS BEEN A TEST SUBJECT FOR THE PAST 10 YEARS.
HE HAS HELPED US IN MANY PAINFUL AND AGONIZING EXPERI-MENTS.
HE ESCAPED DURING EXPERIMENT "FUNGUS-203," WHEN ONE OF THE ROOMS CAUGHT FIRE.
bp
bp
HUFF
HUFF

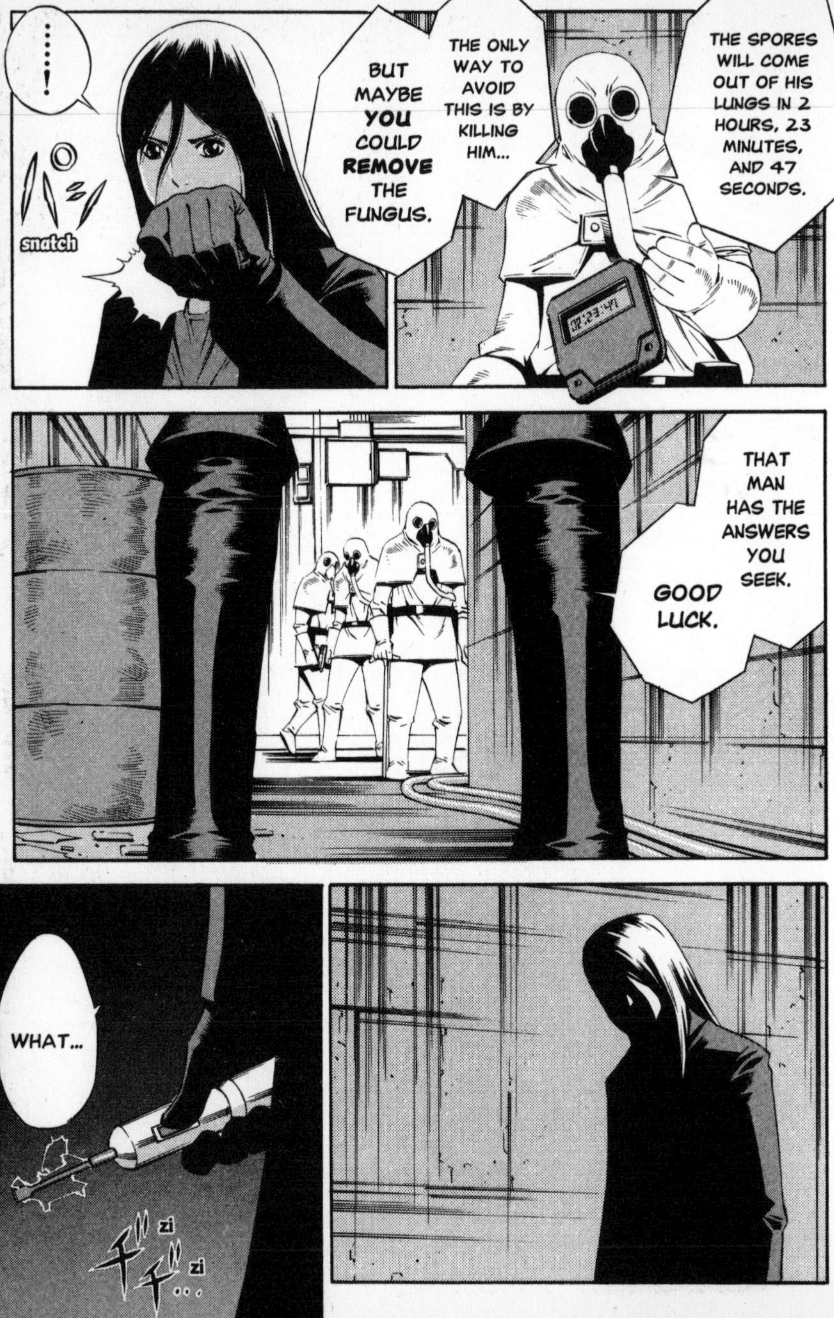
THE SPORES WILL COME OUT OF HIS LUNGS IN 2 HOURS, 23 MINUTES, AND 47 SECONDS.
THE ONLY WAY TO AVOID THIS IS BY KILLING HIM...
BUT MAYBE YOU COULD REMOVE THE FUNGUS.
.....!
snatch
THAT MAN HAS THE ANSWERS YOU SEEK.
GOOD LUCK.
WHAT...
zi
zi

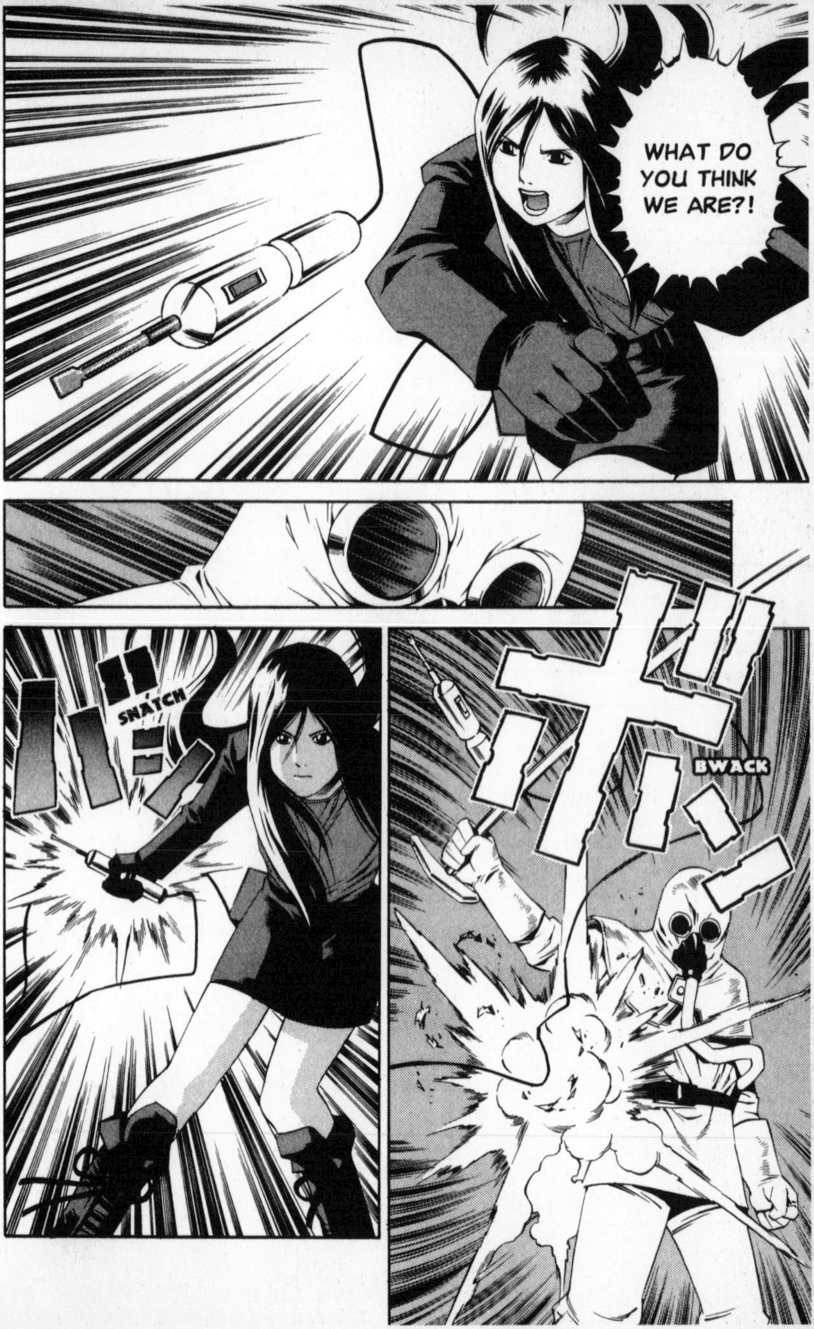
WHAT DO YOU THINK WE ARE?!
SNATCH
BWACK

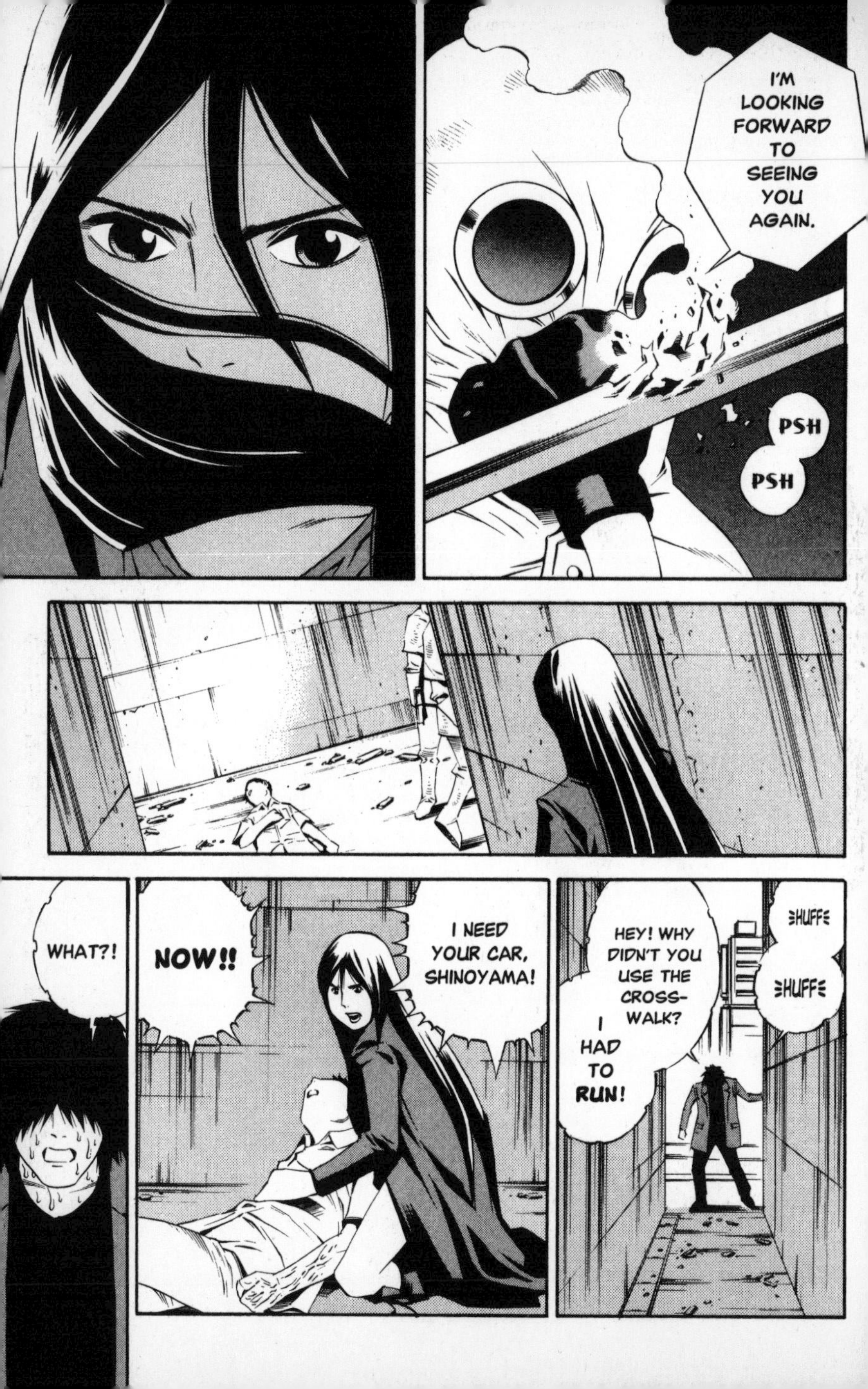
I'M LOOKING FORWARD TO SEEING YOU AGAIN.
PSH
PSH
HUFF
HUFF
HEY! WHY DIDN'T YOU USE THE CROSS-WALK?
I HAD TO RUN!
I NEED YOUR CAR, SHINOYAMA!
NOW!!
WHAT?!

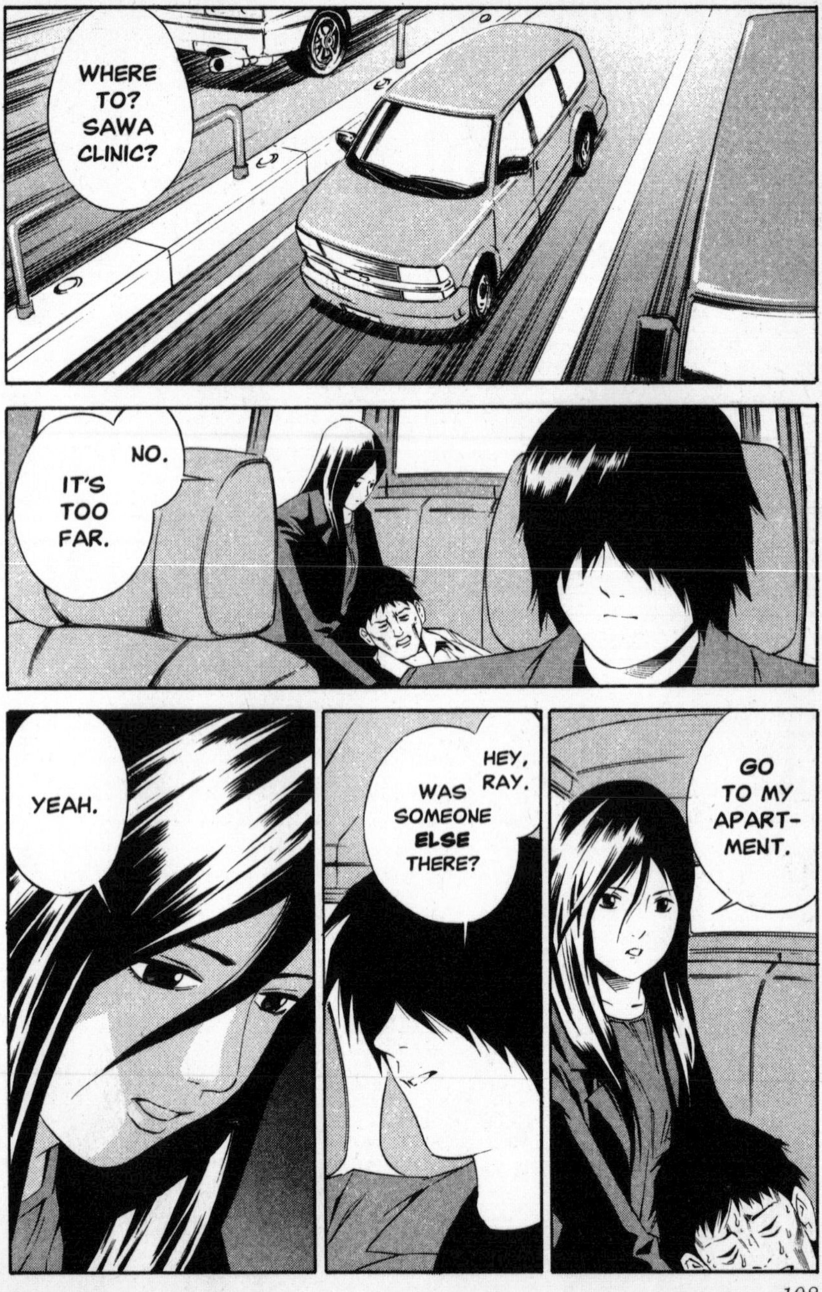
WHERE TO? SAWA CLINIC?
NO.
IT'S TOO FAR.
GO TO MY APART-MENT.
HEY, RAY.
WAS SOMEONE ELSE THERE?
YEAH.

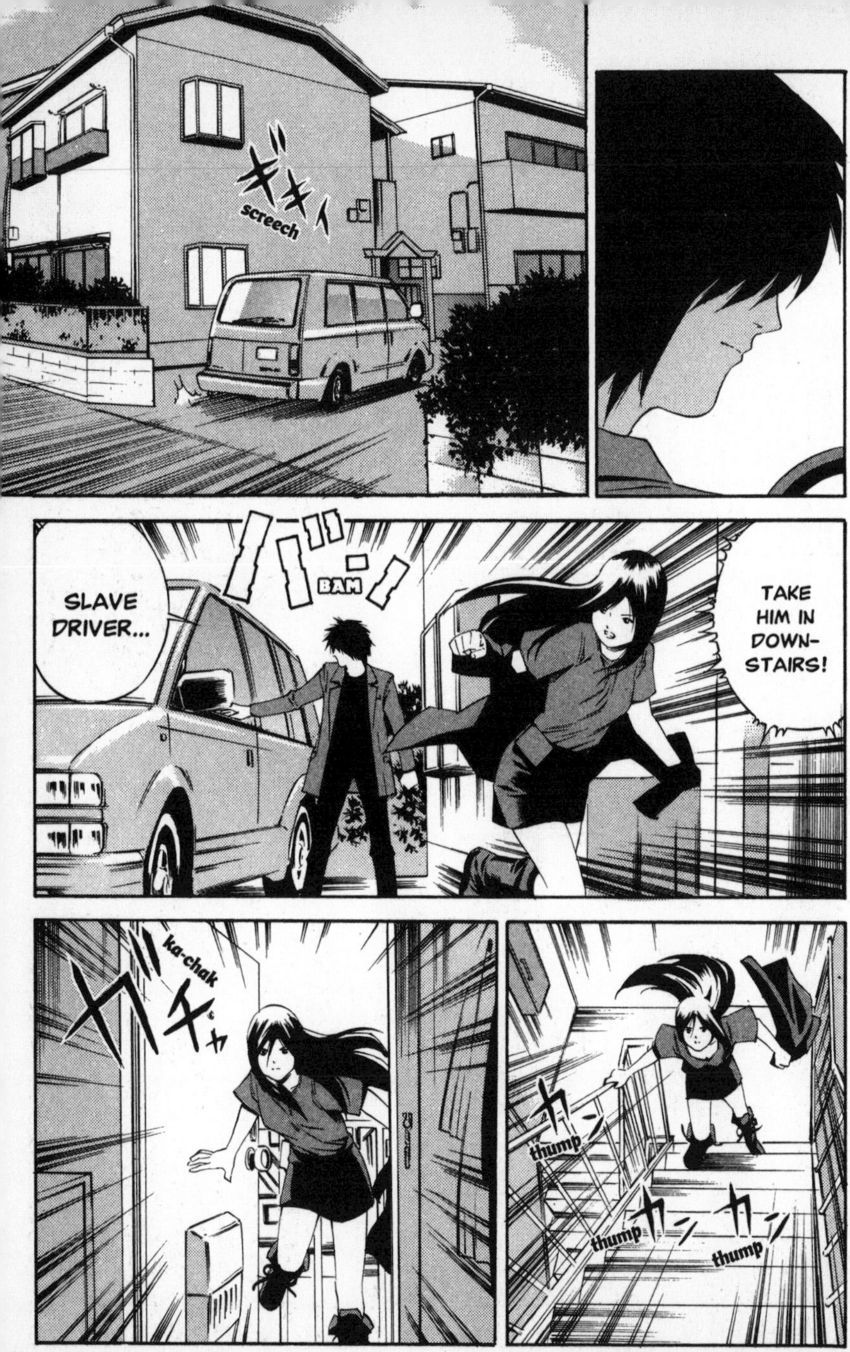
ギギィ
screech
バン
BAM
TAKE HIM IN DOWN-STAIRS!
SLAVE DRIVER...
ガチャ
ka-chak
カン
thump
カン
thump
カン
thump

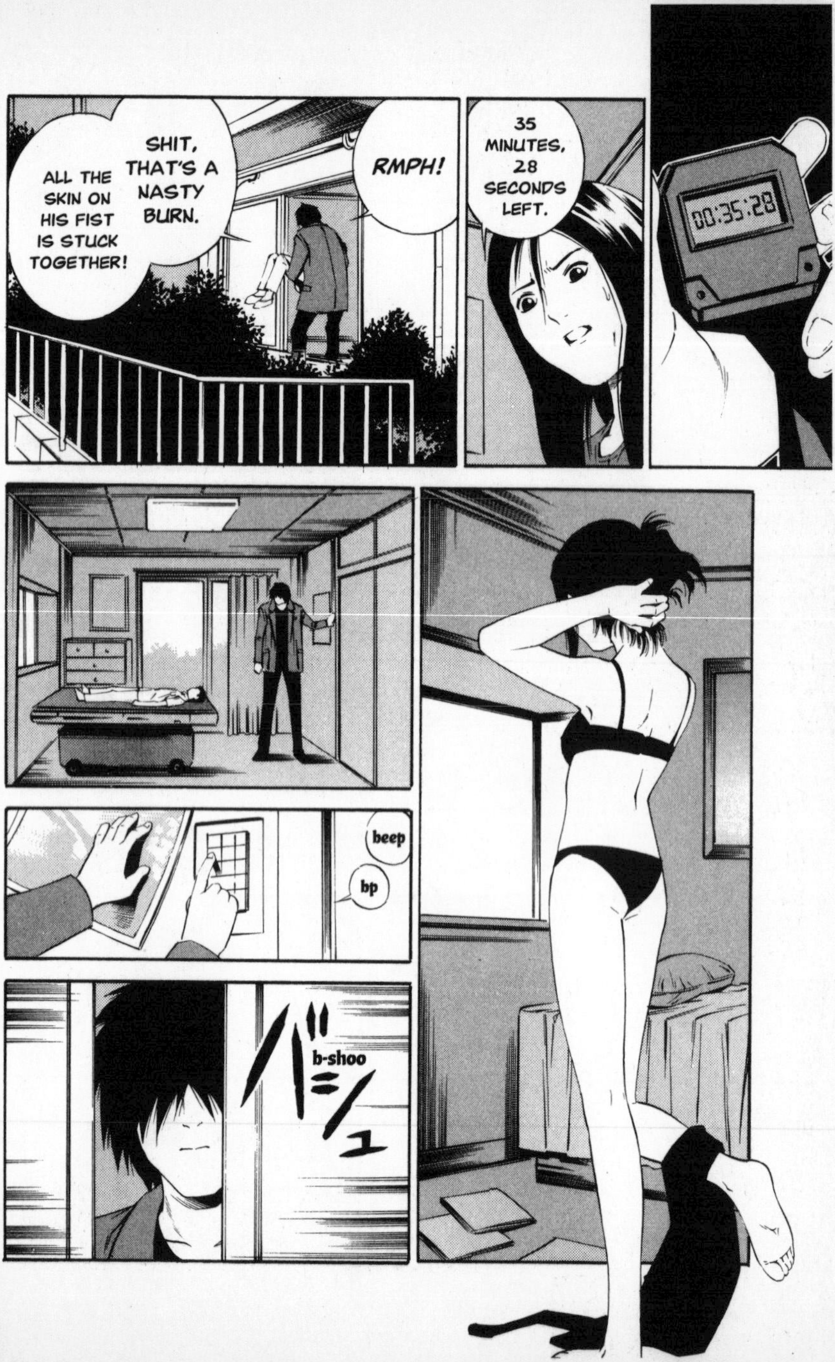
00:35:28
35 MINUTES, 28 SECONDS LEFT.
RMPH!
SHIT, THAT'S A NASTY BURN.
ALL THE SKIN ON HIS FIST IS STUCK TOGETHER!
beep
bp
b-shoo

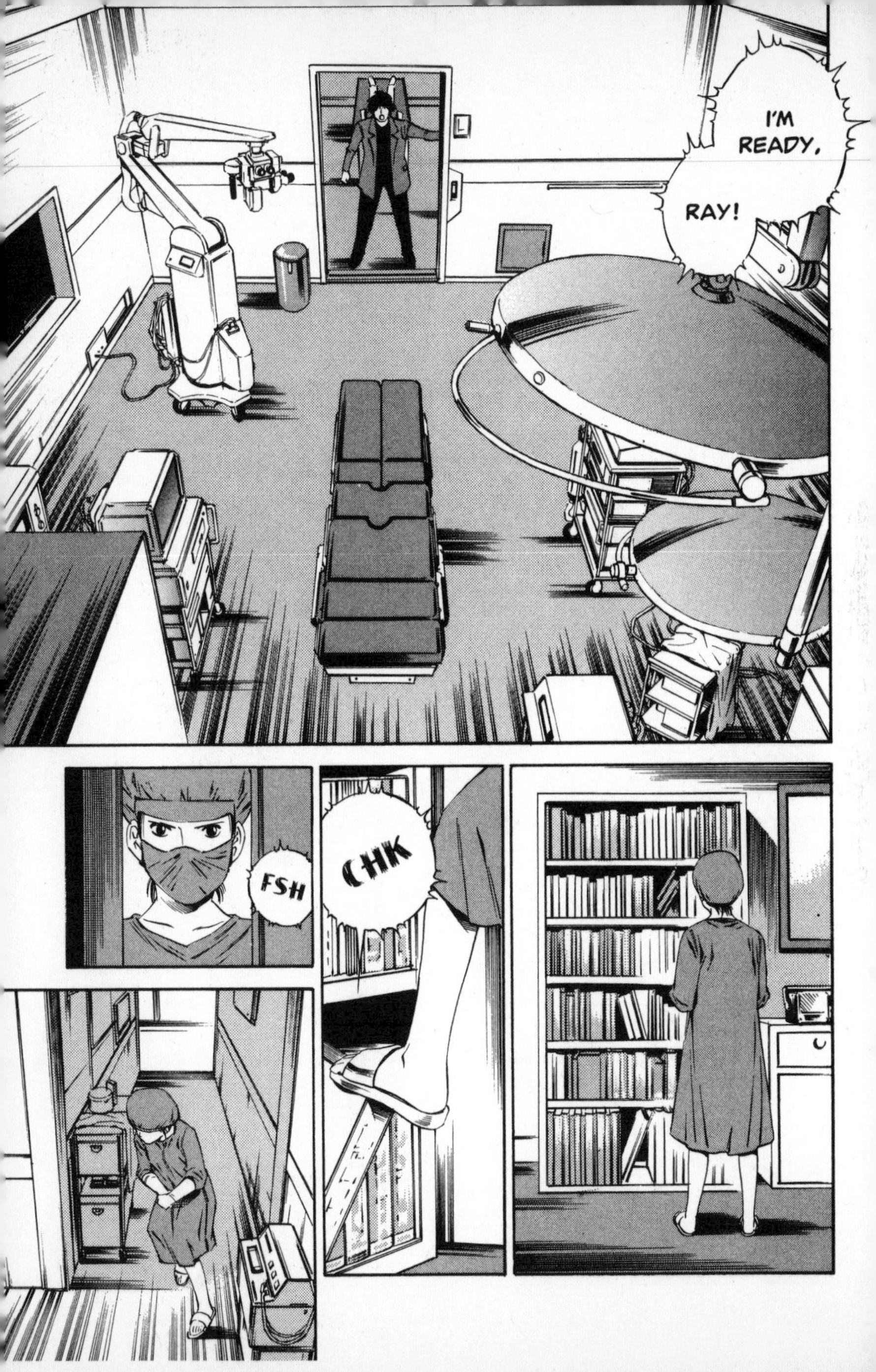
I'M READY, RAY!
FSH
CHK

THE ROOM IS DISINFECTED. YOU CAN GO INSIDE.

I'M READY NOW.

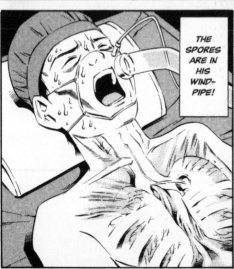

THE SPORES ARE IN HIS WIND-PIPE!

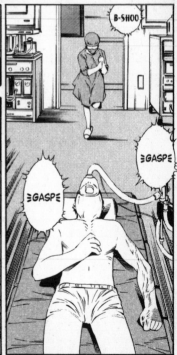

B-SHOO

≡GASP≡

≡GASP≡

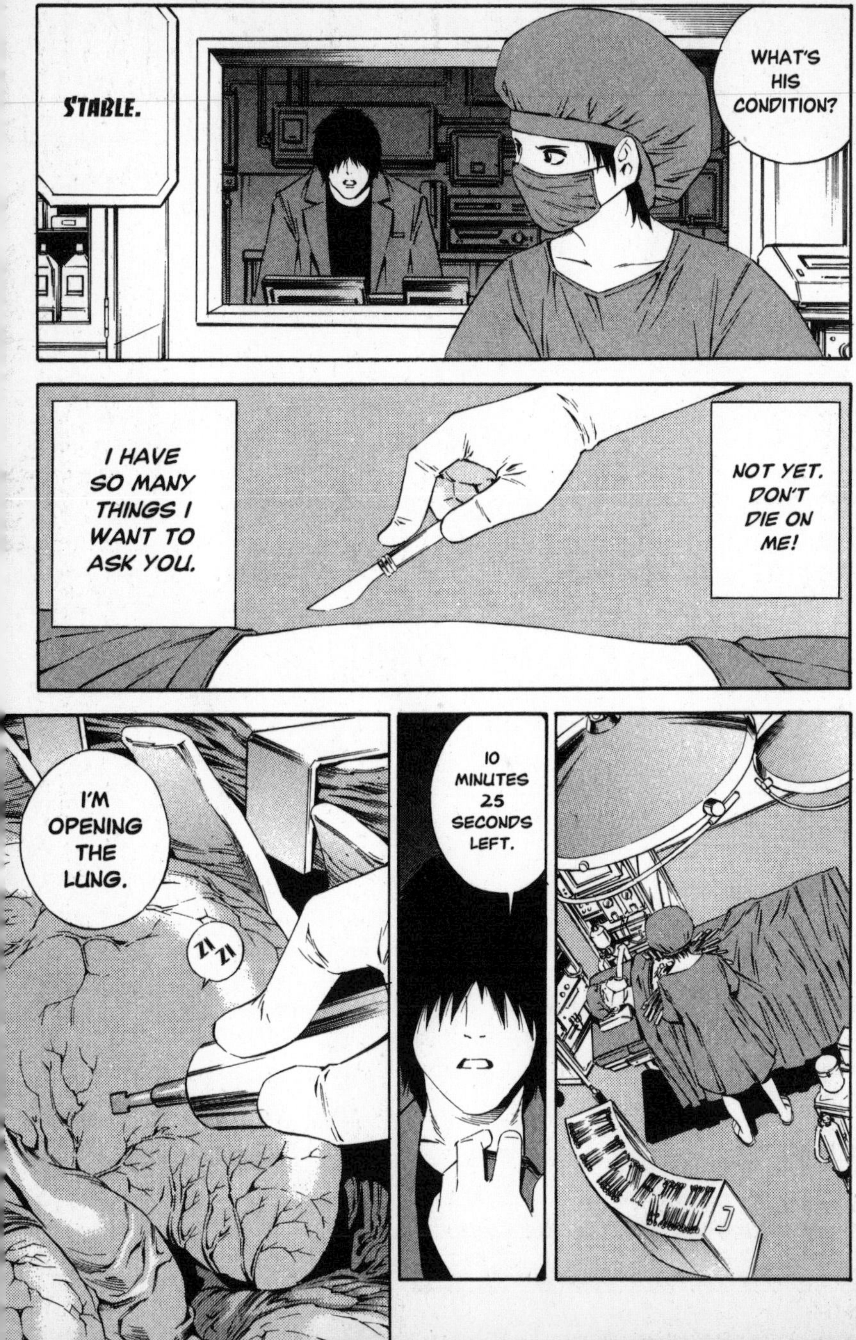
WHAT'S HIS CONDITION?
STABLE.
NOT YET. DON'T DIE ON ME!
I HAVE SO MANY THINGS I WANT TO ASK YOU.
10 MINUTES 25 SECONDS LEFT.
I'M OPENING THE LUNG.
ZI ZI

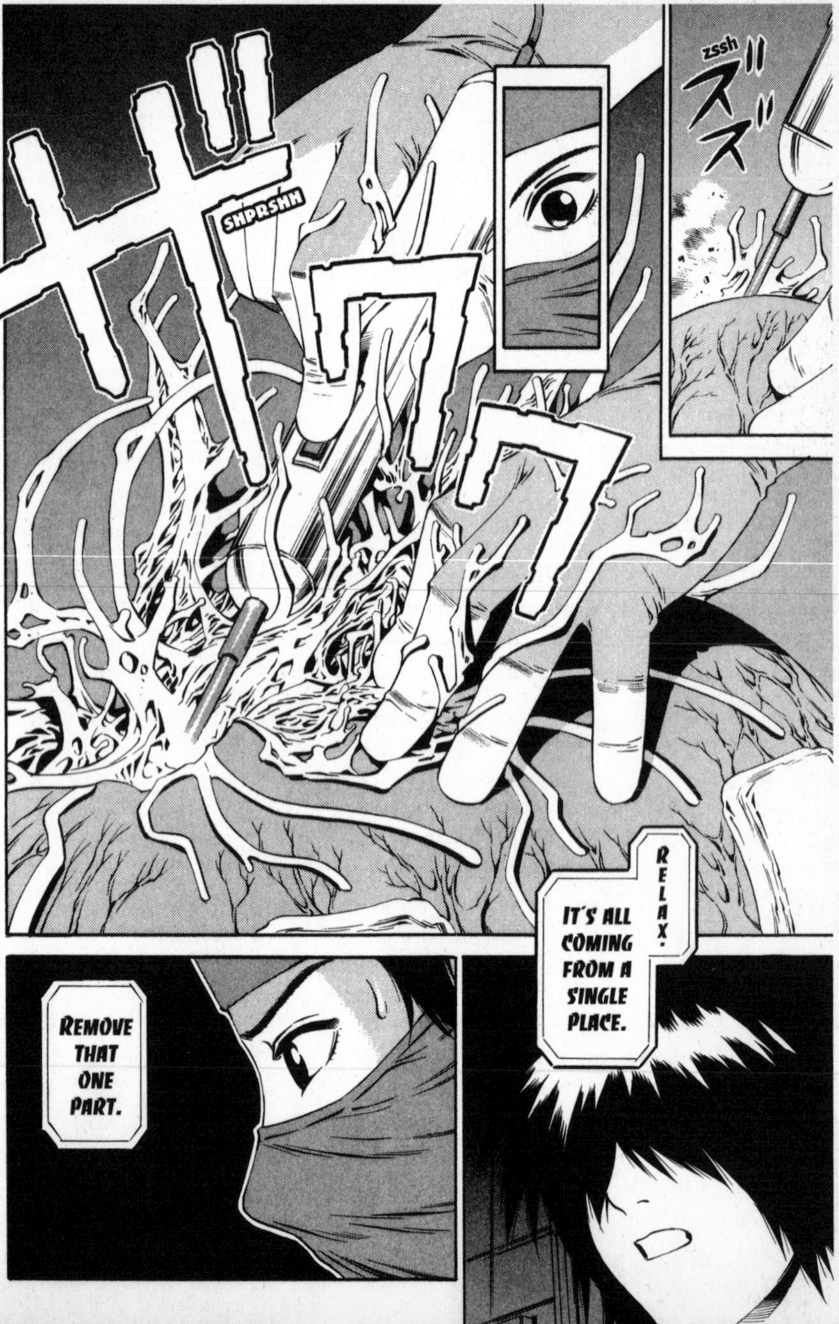
zssh
ズズ
SHPRSHH
ザワワ
RELAX.
IT'S ALL COMING FROM A SINGLE PLACE.
REMOVE THAT ONE PART.

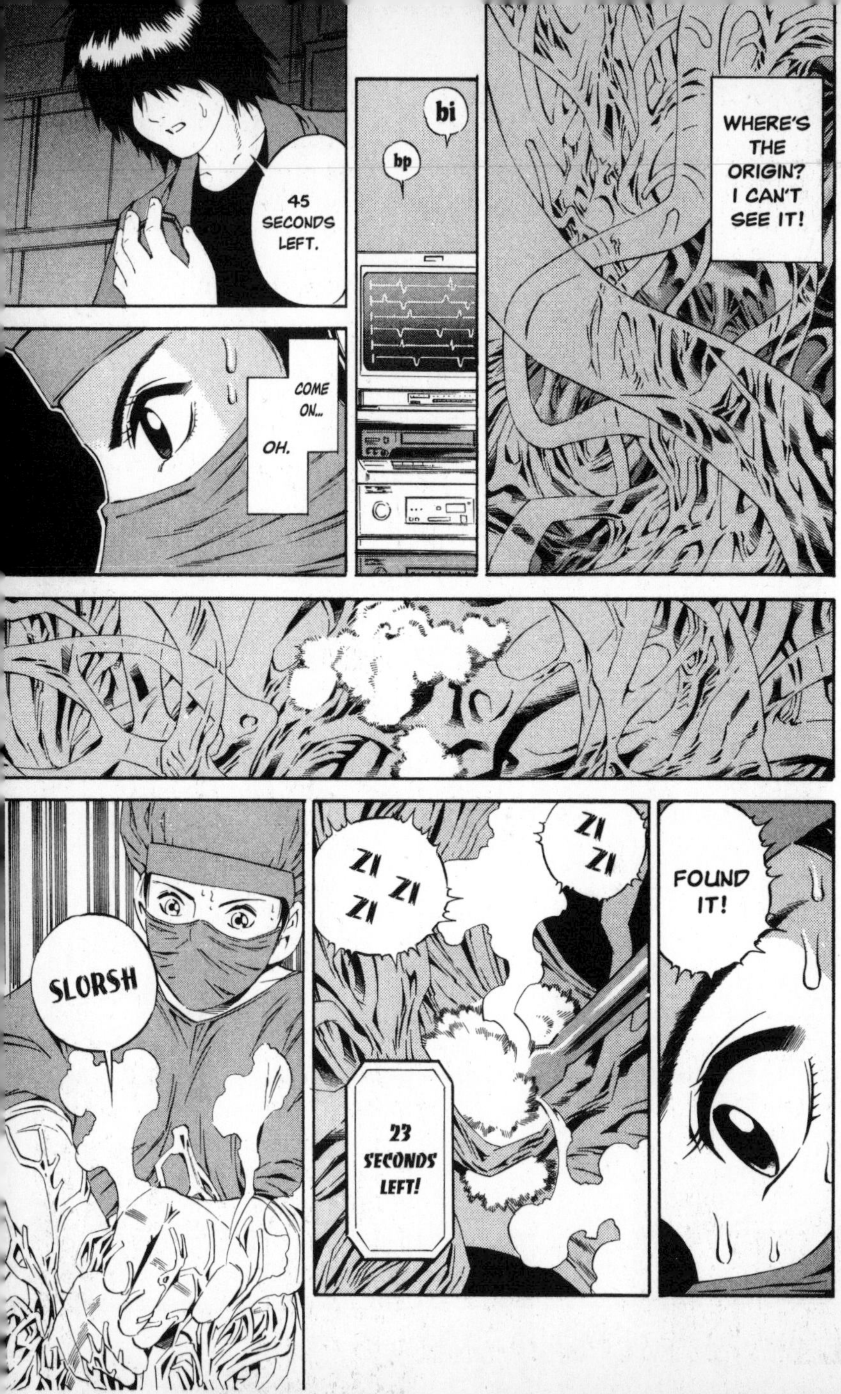
45 SECONDS LEFT.
bi
bp
WHERE'S THE ORIGIN? I CAN'T SEE IT!
COME ON...
OH.
SLORSH
ZI ZI ZI
ZI ZI
23 SECONDS LEFT!
FOUND IT!

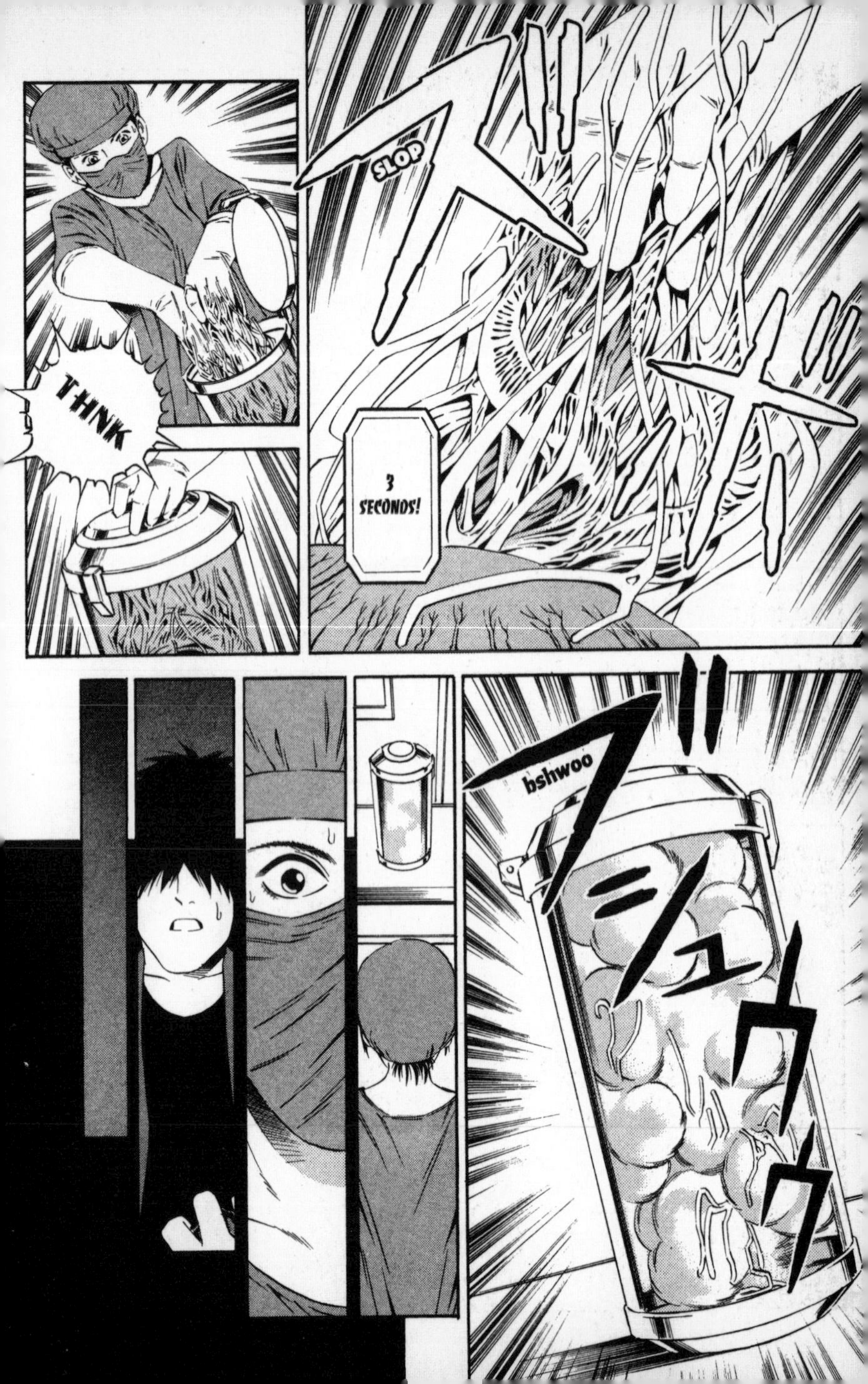
SLOP
3 SECONDS!
THNK
bshwoo

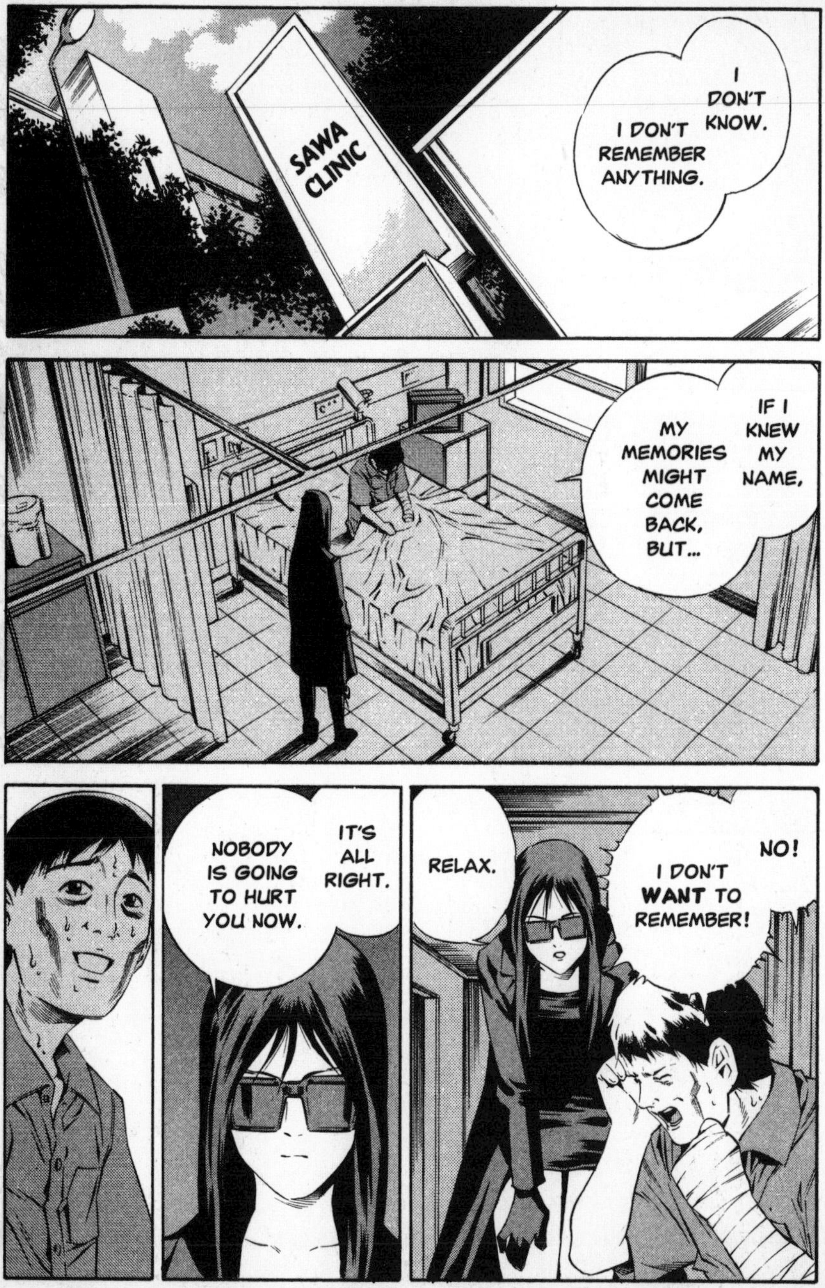
SAWA CLINIC
I DON'T KNOW.
I DON'T REMEMBER ANYTHING.
IF I KNEW MY NAME,
MY MEMORIES MIGHT COME BACK, BUT...
NO!
I DON'T WANT TO REMEMBER!
RELAX.
IT'S ALL RIGHT.
NOBODY IS GOING TO HURT YOU NOW.

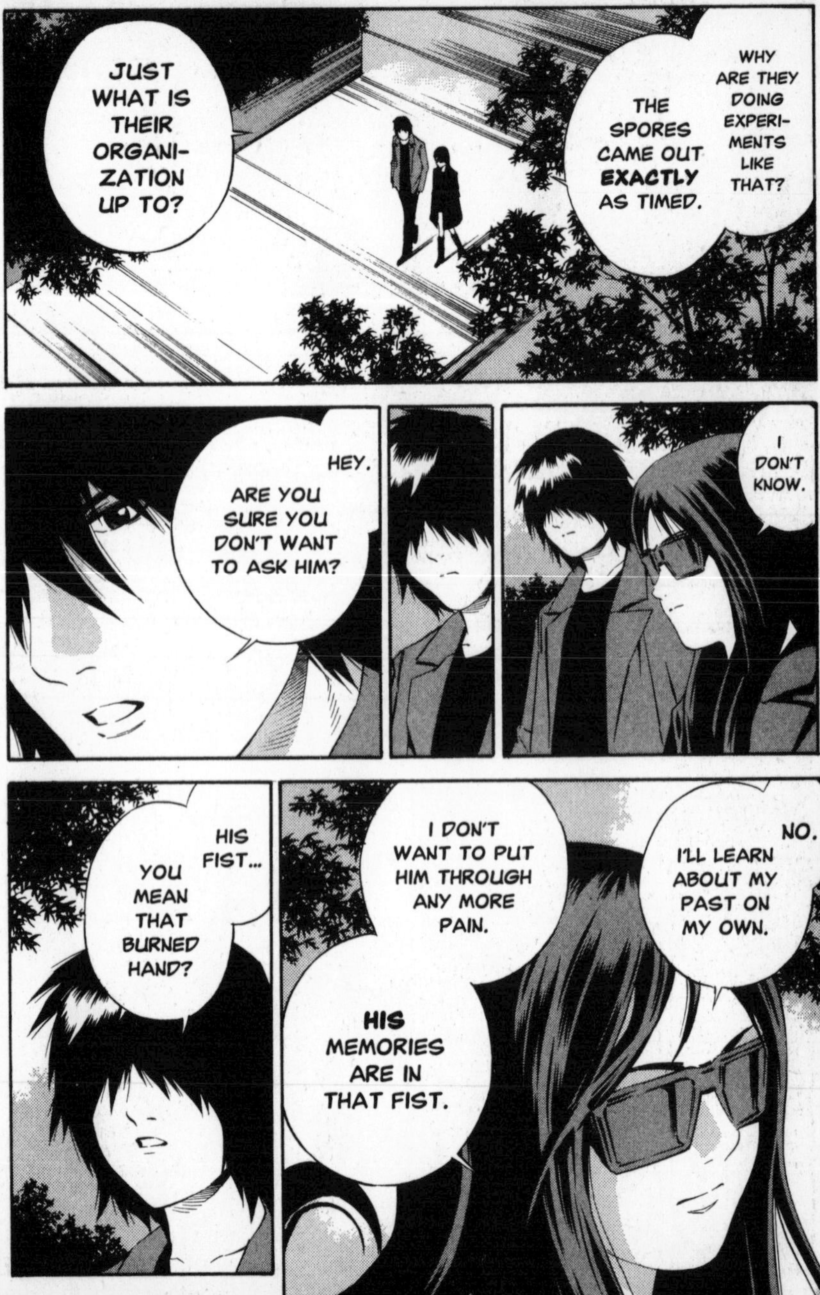
WHY ARE THEY DOING EXPERI-MENTS LIKE THAT?
THE SPORES CAME OUT **EXACTLY** AS TIMED.
JUST WHAT IS THEIR ORGANI-ZATION UP TO?
I DON'T KNOW.
HEY.
ARE YOU SURE YOU DON'T WANT TO ASK HIM?
NO.
I'LL LEARN ABOUT MY PAST ON MY OWN.
I DON'T WANT TO PUT HIM THROUGH ANY MORE PAIN.
HIS MEMORIES ARE IN THAT FIST.
HIS FIST...
YOU MEAN THAT BURNED HAND?

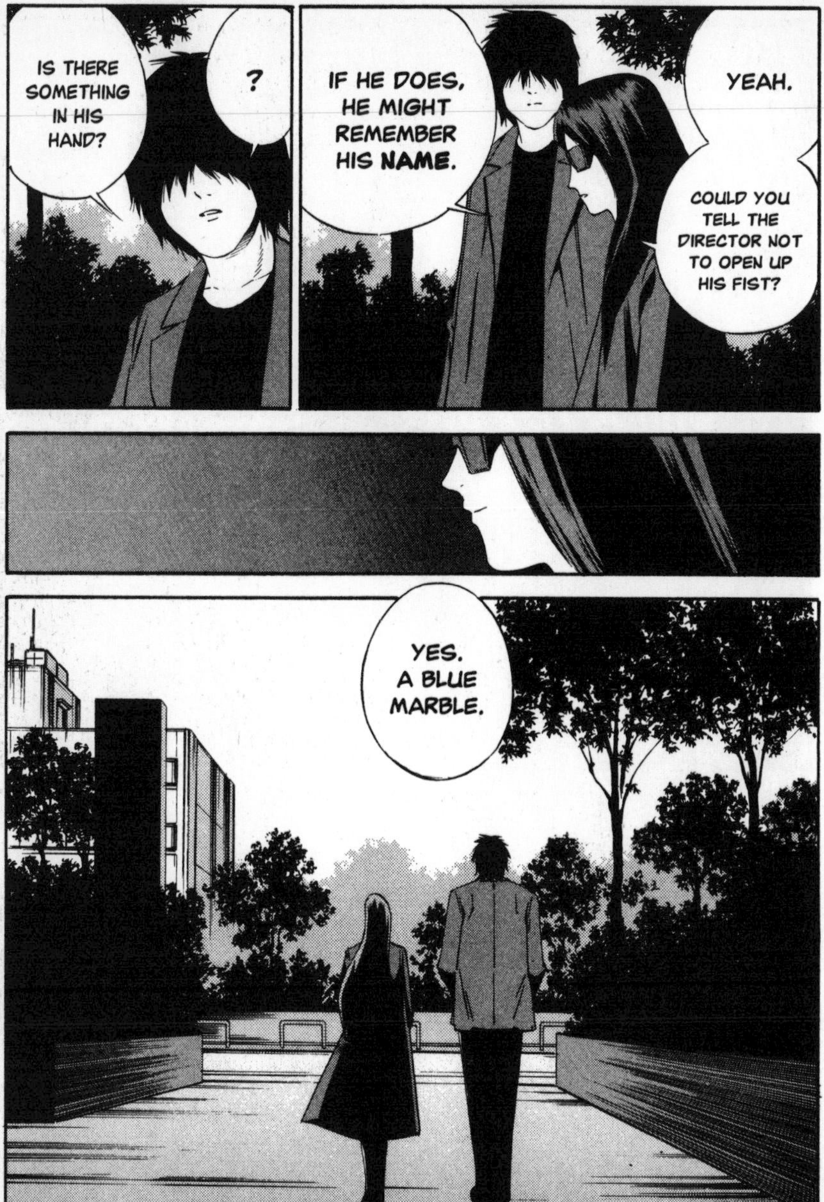
YEAH.
COULD YOU TELL THE DIRECTOR NOT TO OPEN UP HIS FIST?
IF HE DOES, HE MIGHT REMEMBER HIS NAME.
?
IS THERE SOMETHING IN HIS HAND?
YES. A BLUE MARBLE.

RAY

No.075-1-74

The surgeon

with X-ray eyes.

RAY···It's her name.

Patient.4
Dr. Sawa's Clinic

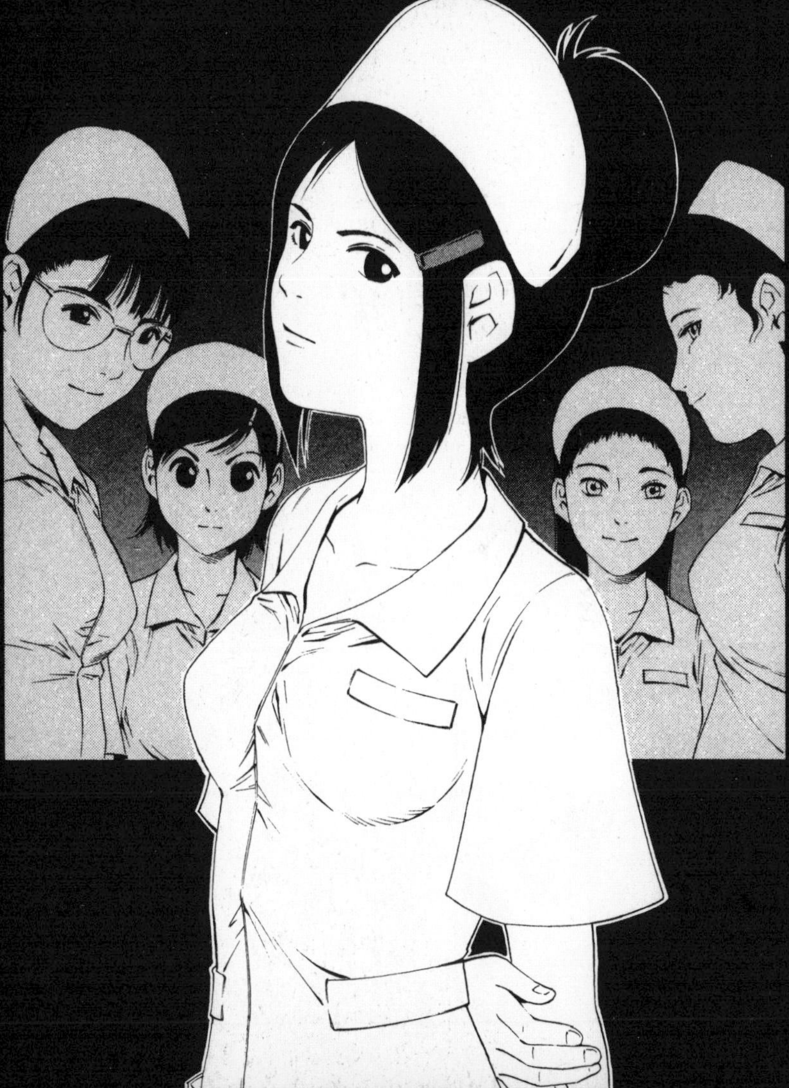

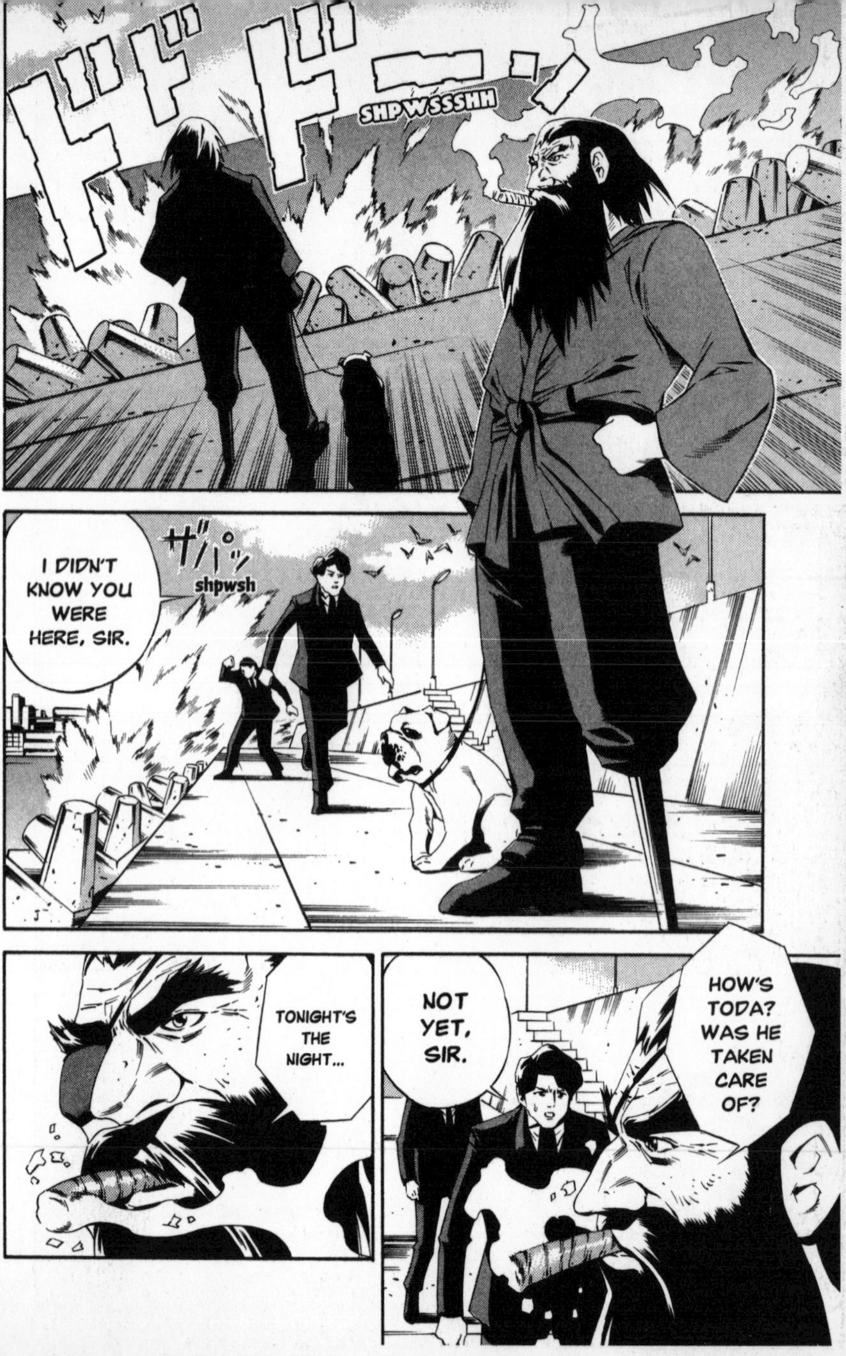
ドドドーーン
SHPWSSSHH
ザパッ
shpwsh
I DIDN'T KNOW YOU WERE HERE, SIR.
HOW'S TODA? WAS HE TAKEN CARE OF?
NOT YET, SIR.
TONIGHT'S THE NIGHT...

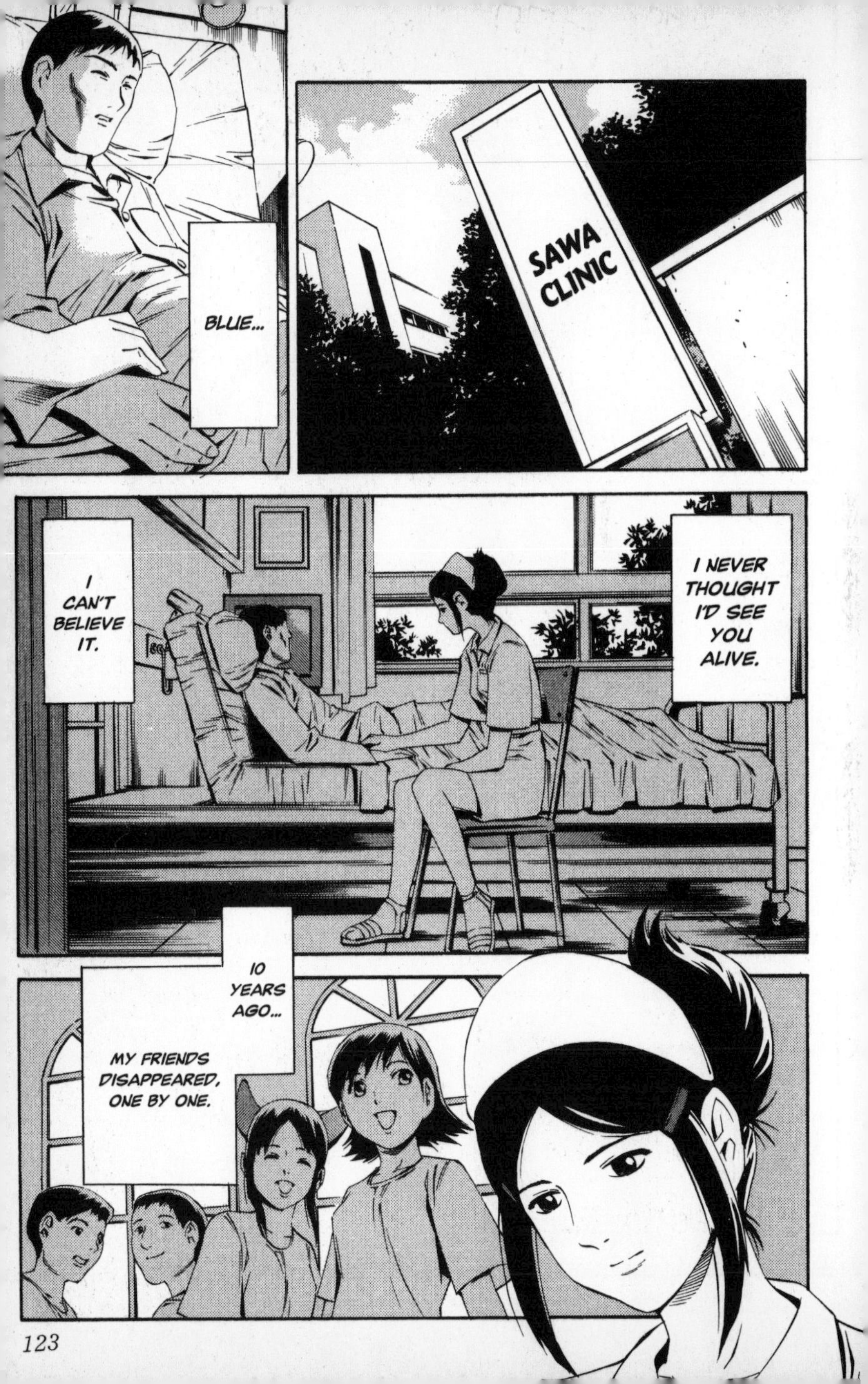
SAWA CLINIC
BLUE...
I NEVER THOUGHT I'D SEE YOU ALIVE.
I CAN'T BELIEVE IT.
10 YEARS AGO...
MY FRIENDS DISAPPEARED, ONE BY ONE.

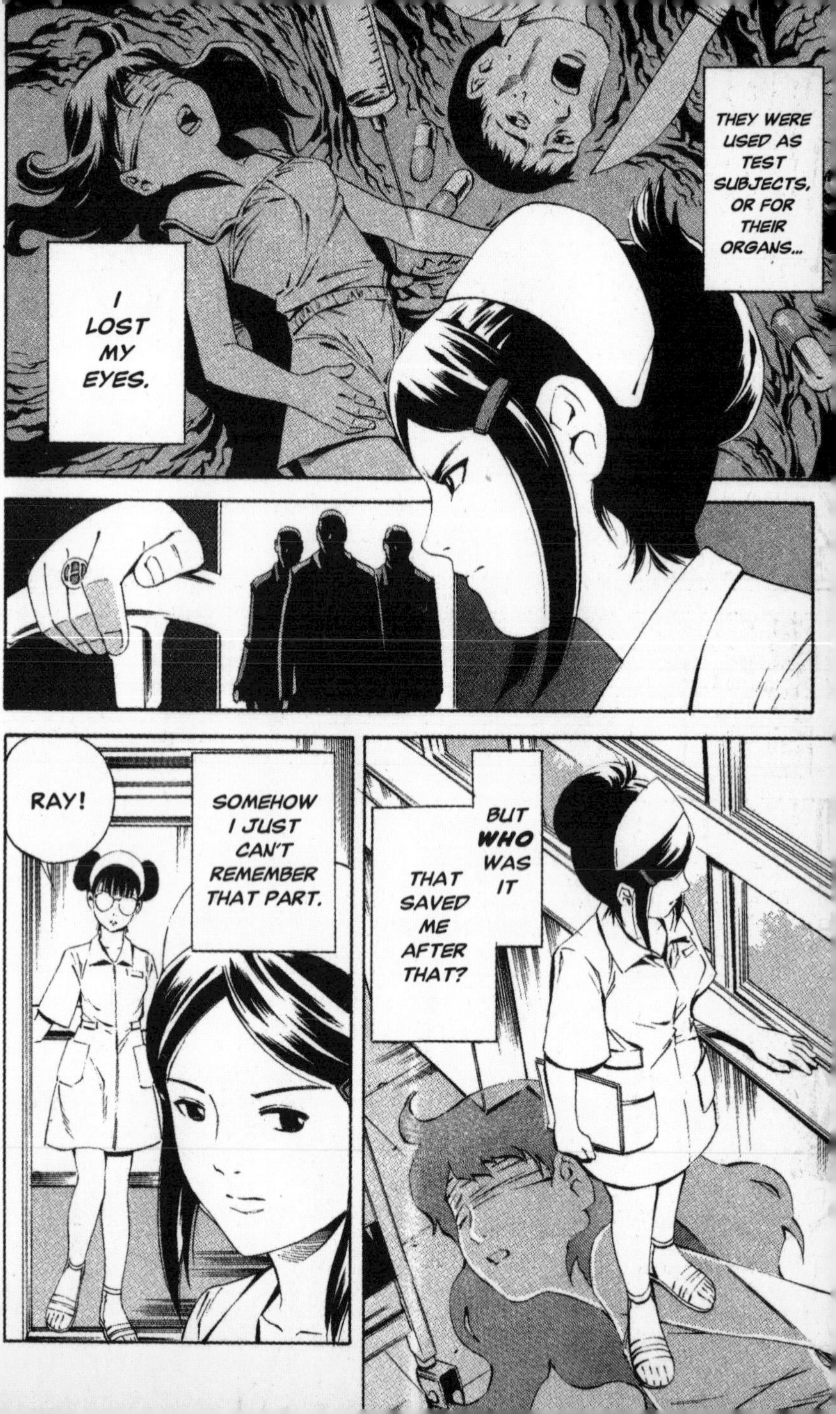
THEY WERE USED AS TEST SUBJECTS, OR FOR THEIR ORGANS...
I LOST MY EYES.
BUT WHO WAS IT
THAT SAVED ME AFTER THAT?
SOMEHOW I JUST CAN'T REMEMBER THAT PART.
RAY!

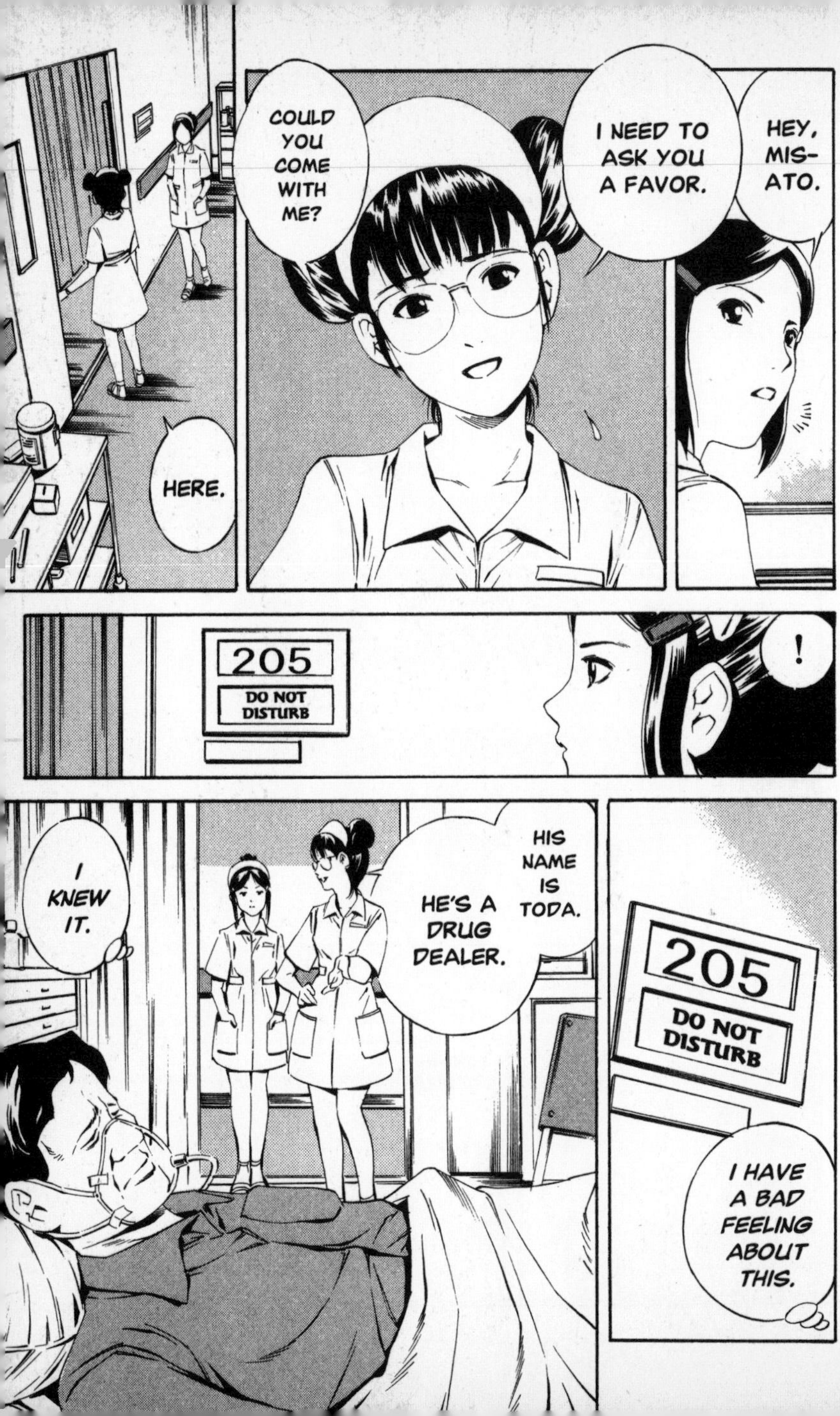
HEY, MIS-ATO.
I NEED TO ASK YOU A FAVOR.
COULD YOU COME WITH ME?
HERE.
!
I HAVE A BAD FEELING ABOUT THIS.
205
DO NOT DISTURB
HIS NAME IS TODA.
HE'S A DRUG DEALER.
I KNEW IT.

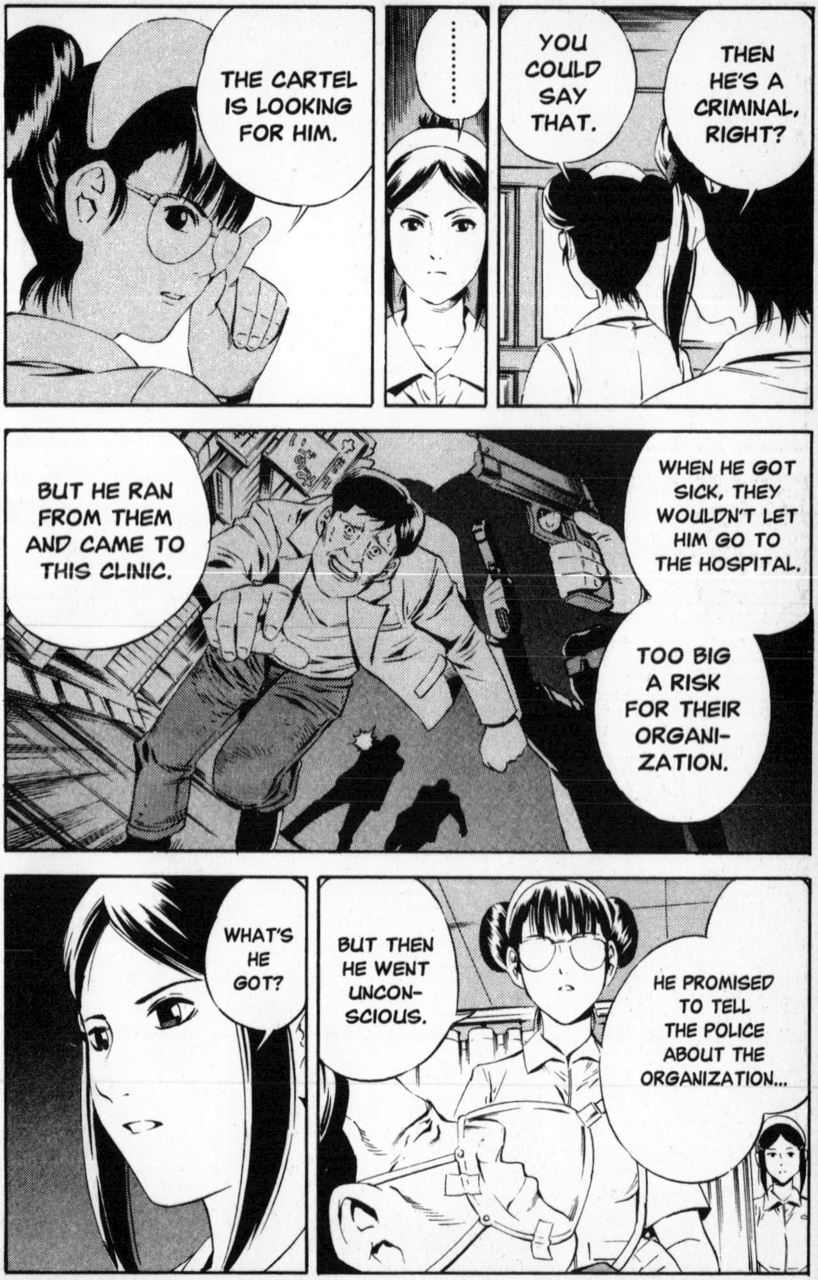

THEN HE'S A CRIMINAL, RIGHT?
YOU COULD SAY THAT.
......
THE CARTEL IS LOOKING FOR HIM.
WHEN HE GOT SICK, THEY WOULDN'T LET HIM GO TO THE HOSPITAL.
TOO BIG A RISK FOR THEIR ORGANI-ZATION.
BUT HE RAN FROM THEM AND CAME TO THIS CLINIC.
HE PROMISED TO TELL THE POLICE ABOUT THE ORGANIZATION...
BUT THEN HE WENT UNCON-SCIOUS.
WHAT'S HE GOT?

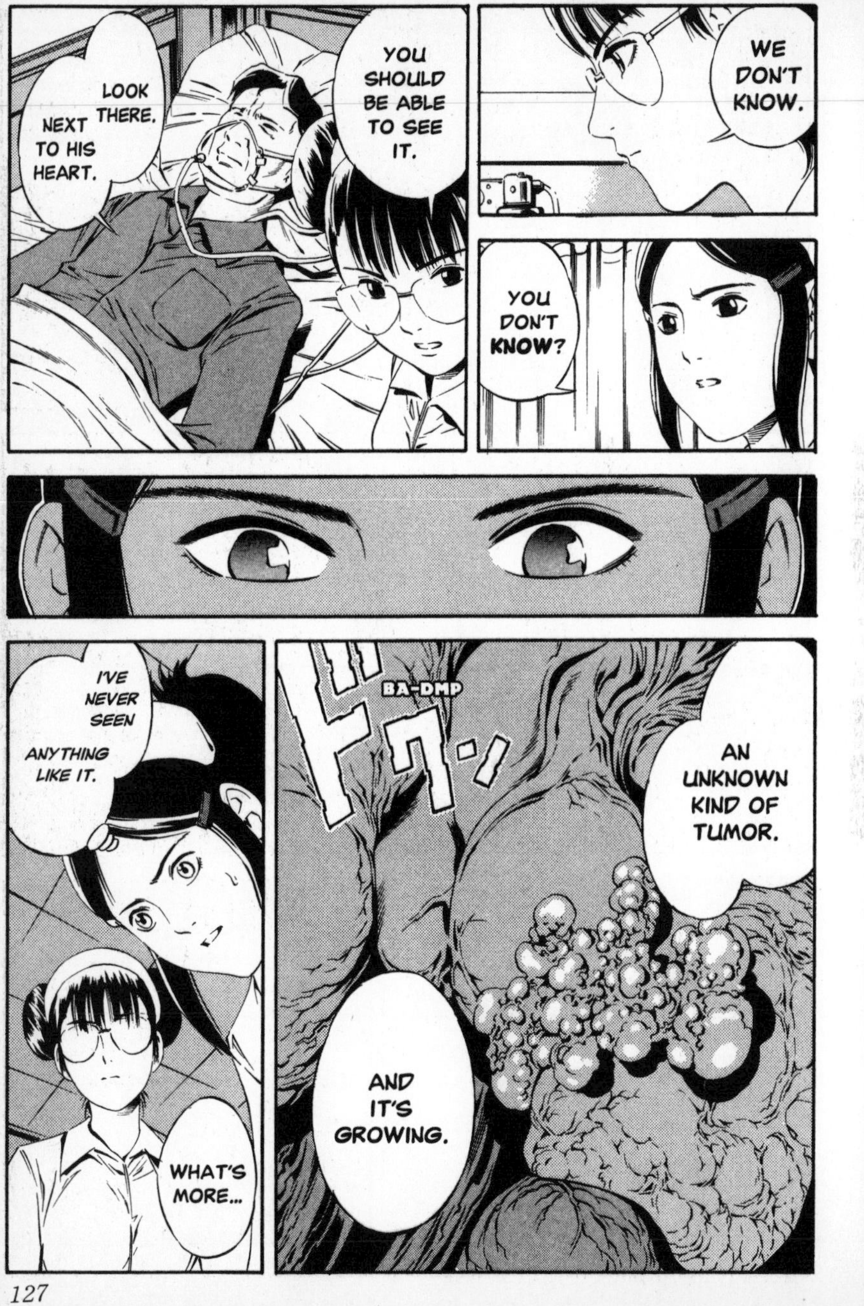
WE DON'T KNOW.
YOU SHOULD BE ABLE TO SEE IT.
LOOK THERE.
NEXT TO HIS HEART.
YOU DON'T KNOW?
BA-DMP
AN UNKNOWN KIND OF TUMOR.
I'VE NEVER SEEN ANYTHING LIKE IT.
WHAT'S MORE...
AND IT'S GROWING.

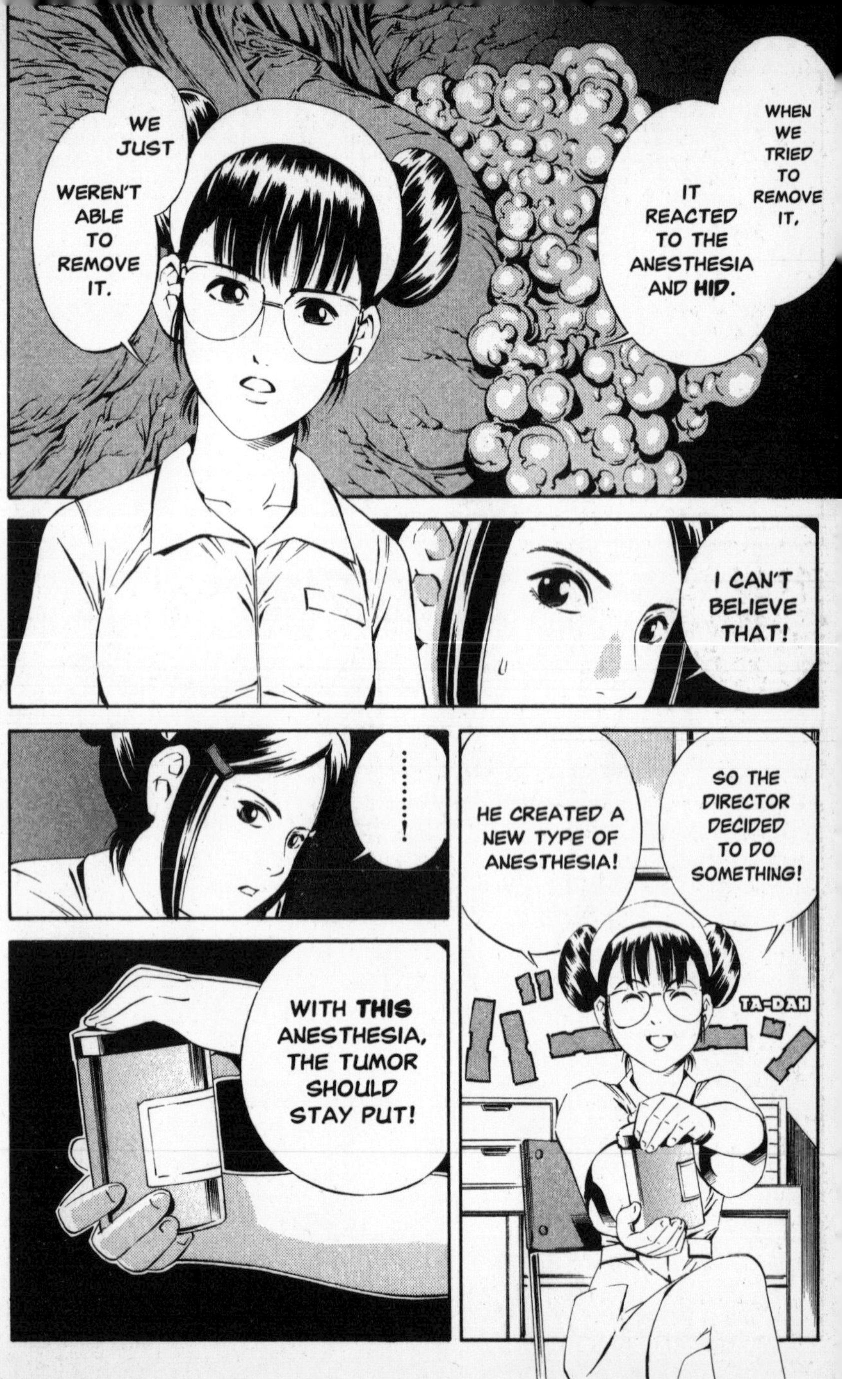
WHEN WE TRIED TO REMOVE IT,
IT REACTED TO THE ANESTHESIA AND **HID**.
WE JUST WEREN'T ABLE TO REMOVE IT.
I CAN'T BELIEVE THAT!
SO THE DIRECTOR DECIDED TO DO SOMETHING!
HE CREATED A NEW TYPE OF ANESTHESIA!
TA-DAH
......!
WITH **THIS** ANESTHESIA, THE TUMOR SHOULD STAY PUT!

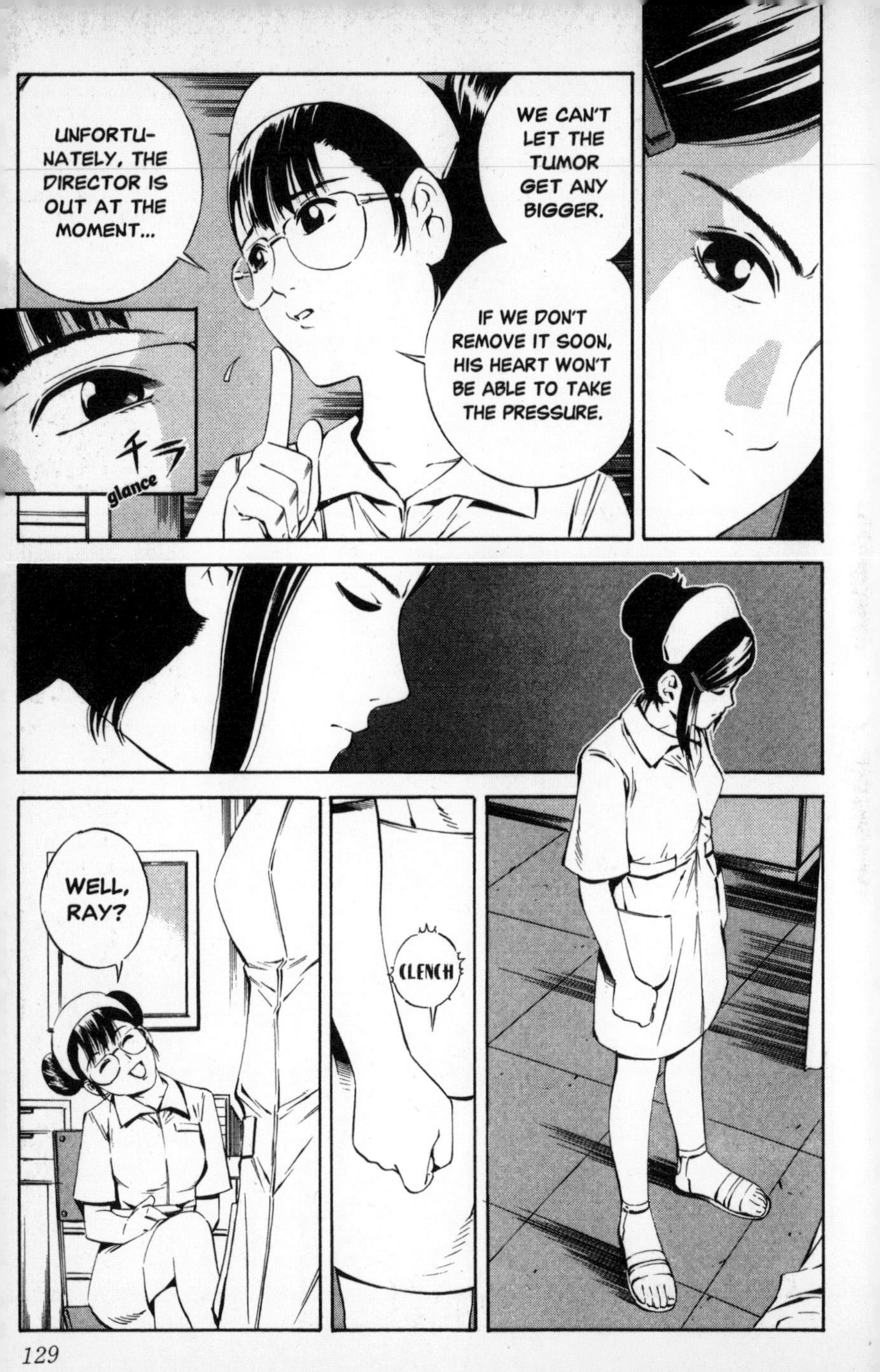
WE CAN'T LET THE TUMOR GET ANY BIGGER.
IF WE DON'T REMOVE IT SOON, HIS HEART WON'T BE ABLE TO TAKE THE PRESSURE.
UNFORTUNATELY, THE DIRECTOR IS OUT AT THE MOMENT...
チラ
glance
CLENCH
WELL, RAY?

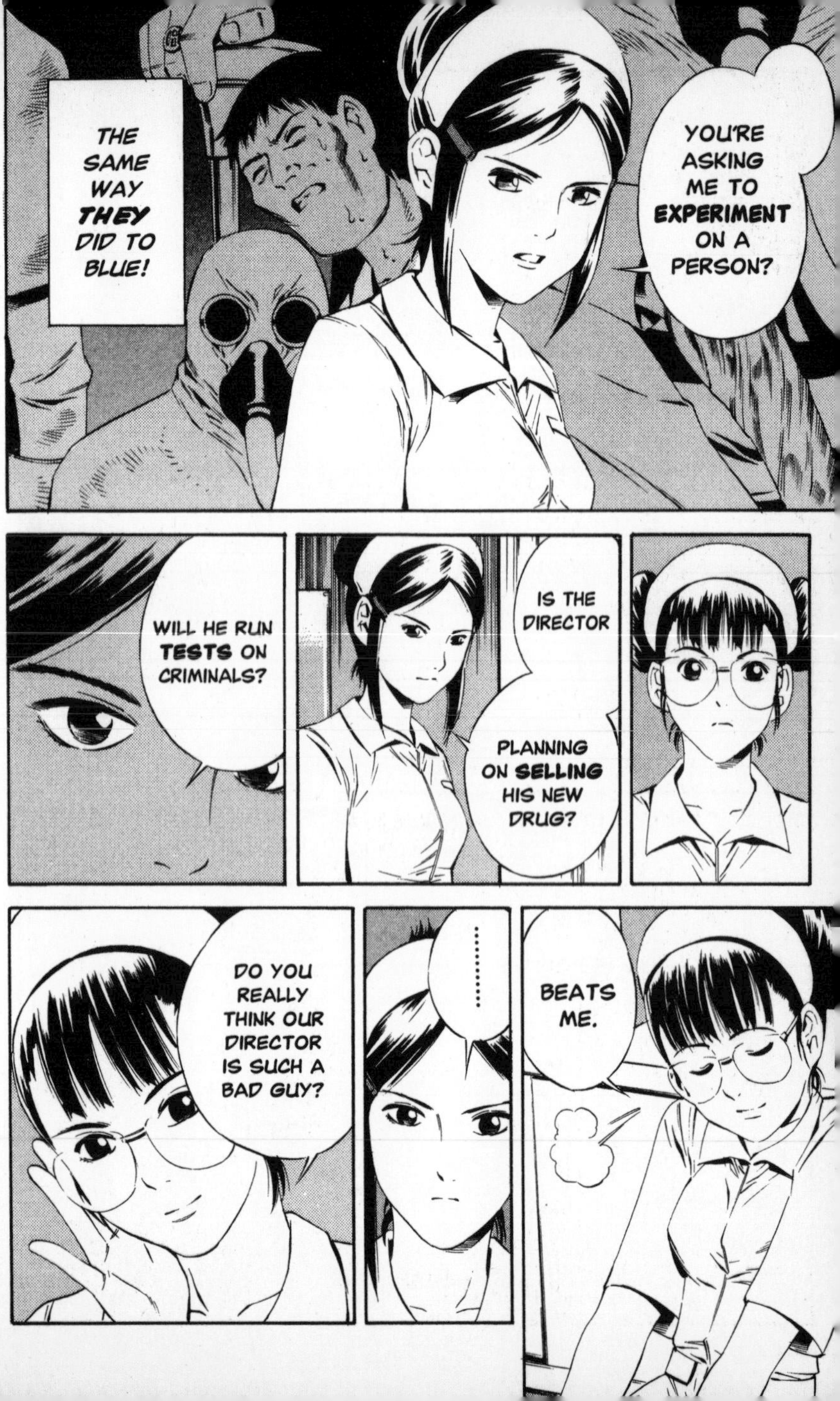
YOU'RE ASKING ME TO EXPERIMENT ON A PERSON?
THE SAME WAY THEY DID TO BLUE!
IS THE DIRECTOR PLANNING ON SELLING HIS NEW DRUG?
WILL HE RUN TESTS ON CRIMINALS?
BEATS ME.
......
DO YOU REALLY THINK OUR DIRECTOR IS SUCH A BAD GUY?

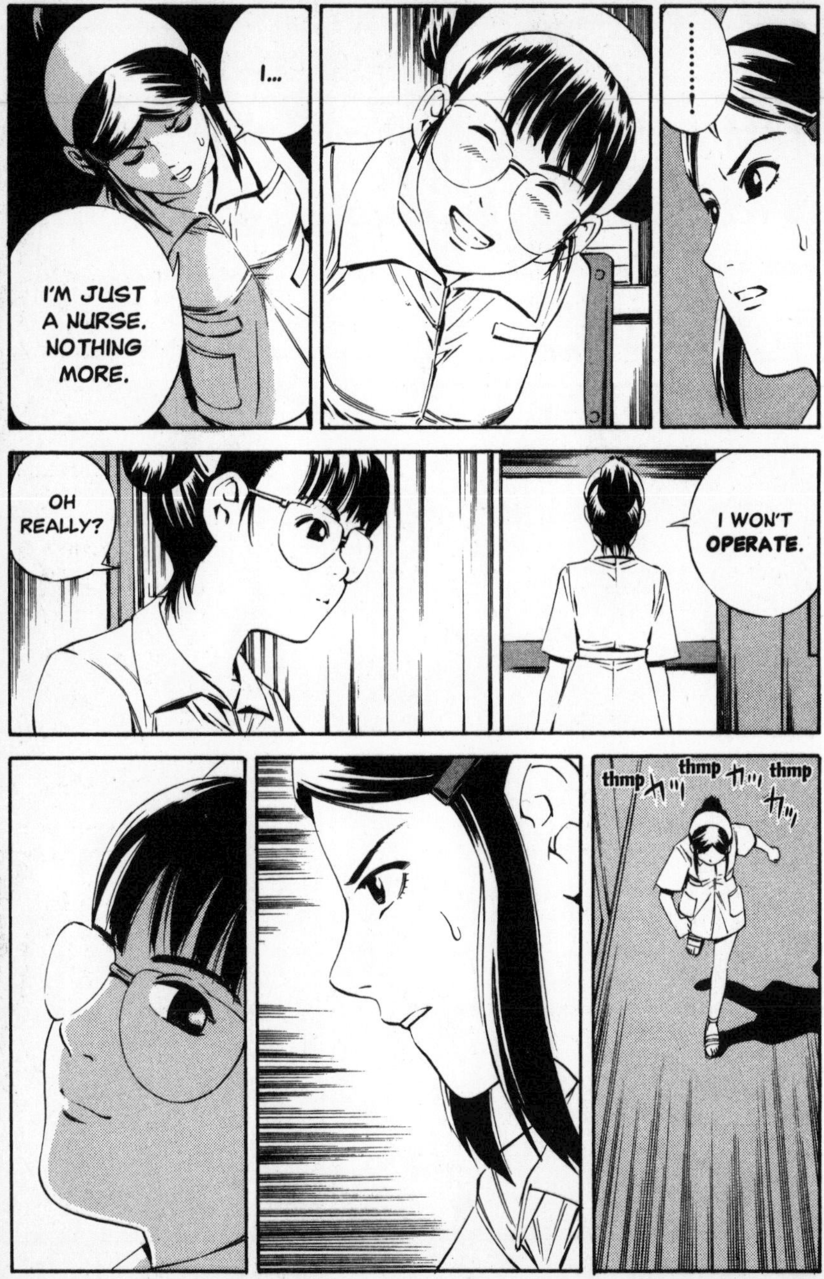
I...
I'M JUST A NURSE. NOTHING MORE.
......!
OH REALLY?
I WON'T OPERATE.
thmp カッ thmp カッ thmp カッ

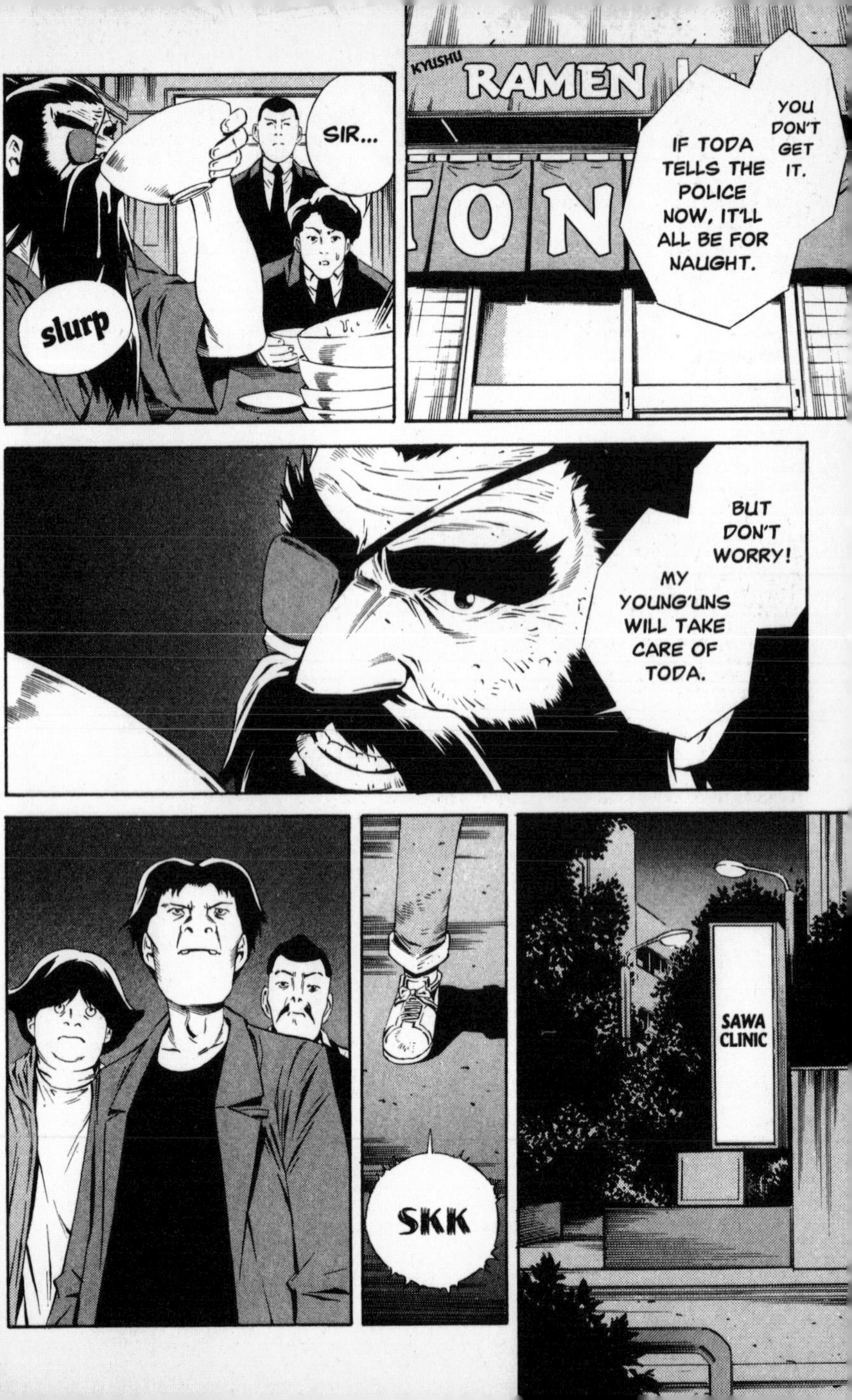
KYUSHU RAMEN
TON
YOU DON'T GET IT.
IF TODA TELLS THE POLICE NOW, IT'LL ALL BE FOR NAUGHT.
SIR...
slurp
BUT DON'T WORRY!
MY YOUNG'UNS WILL TAKE CARE OF TODA.
SAWA CLINIC
SKK

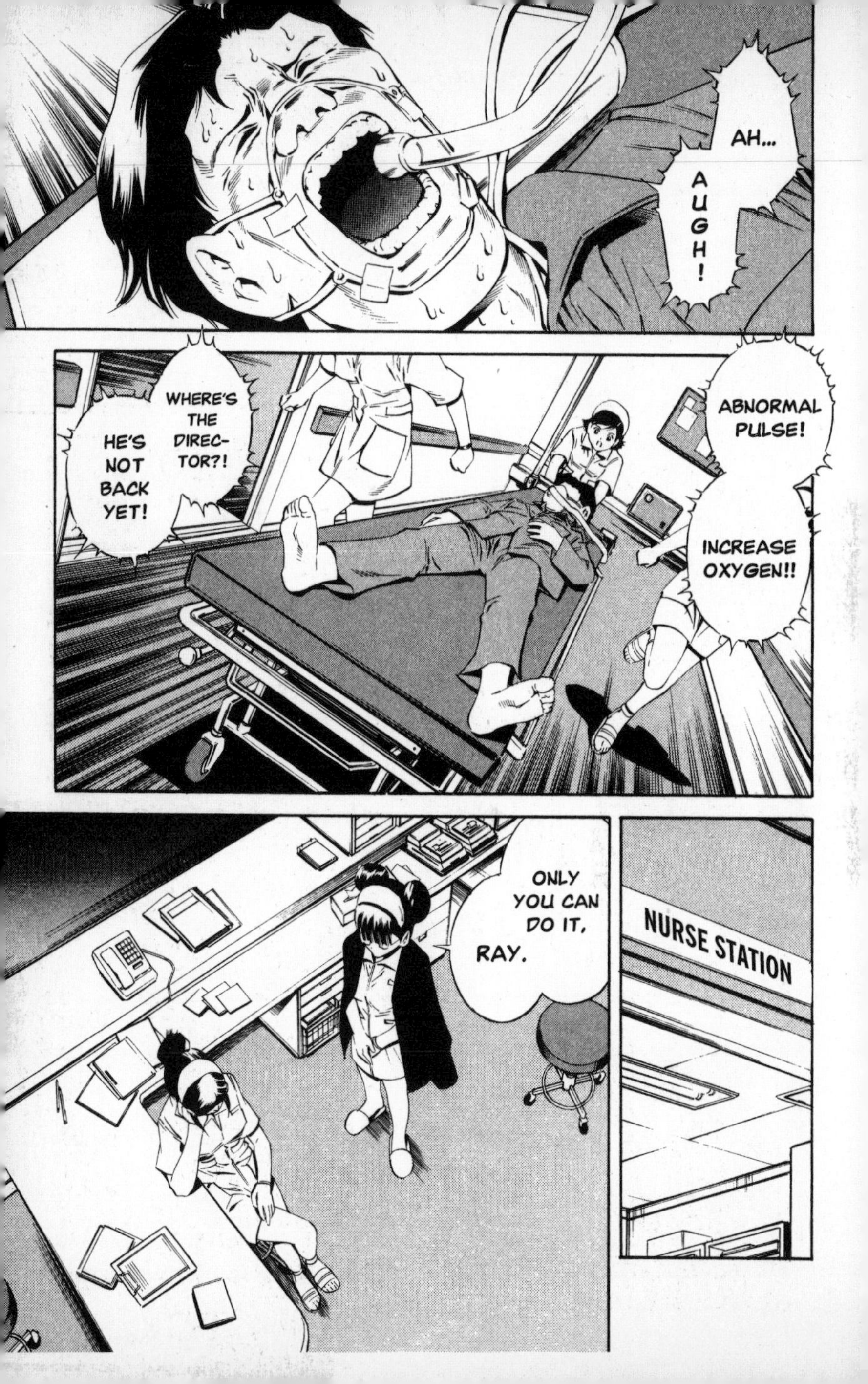
AH...
AUGH!
ABNORMAL PULSE!
INCREASE OXYGEN!!
WHERE'S THE DIREC-TOR?!
HE'S NOT BACK YET!
NURSE STATION
ONLY YOU CAN DO IT, RAY.

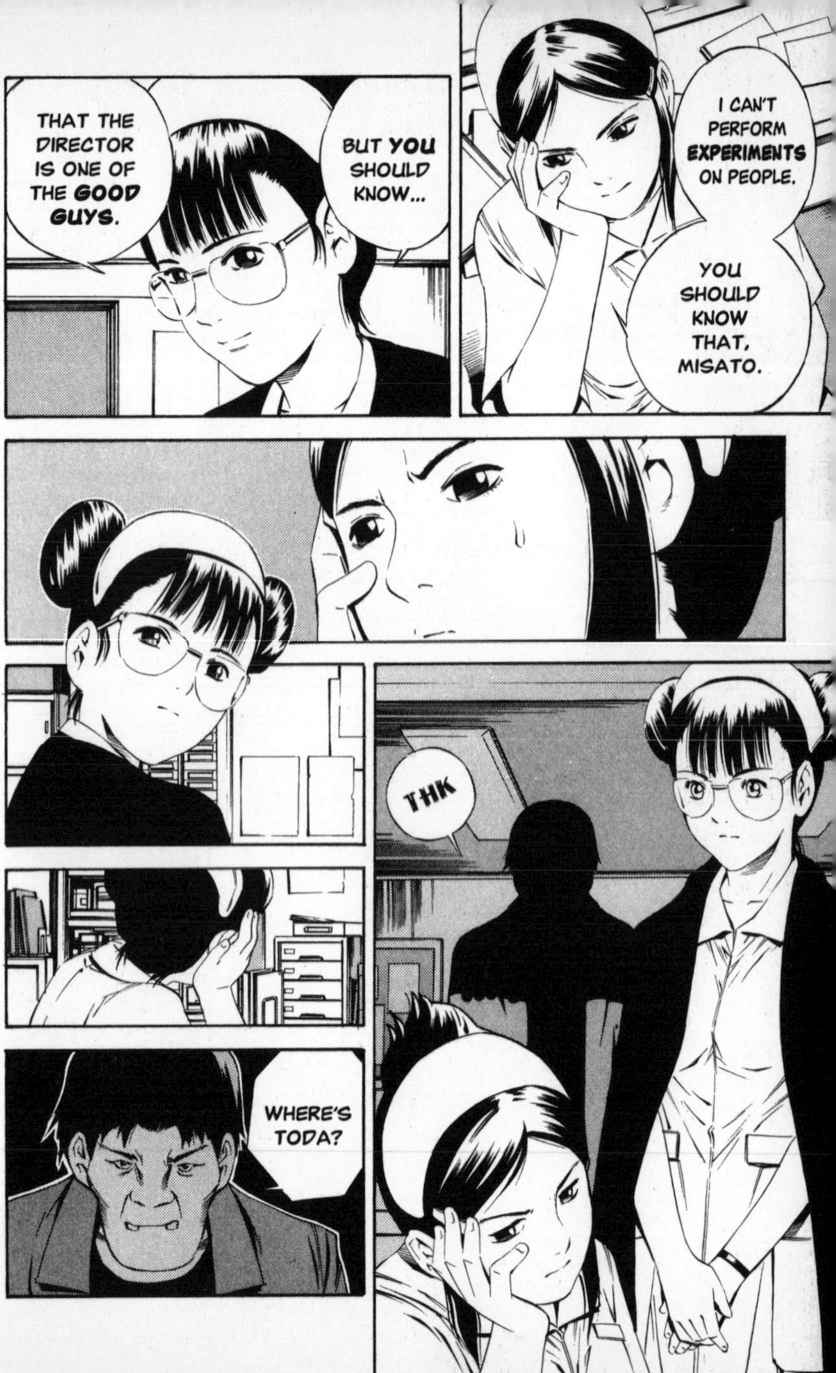
I CAN'T PERFORM EXPERIMENTS ON PEOPLE.
YOU SHOULD KNOW THAT, MISATO.
BUT YOU SHOULD KNOW...
THAT THE DIRECTOR IS ONE OF THE GOOD GUYS.
THK
WHERE'S TODA?

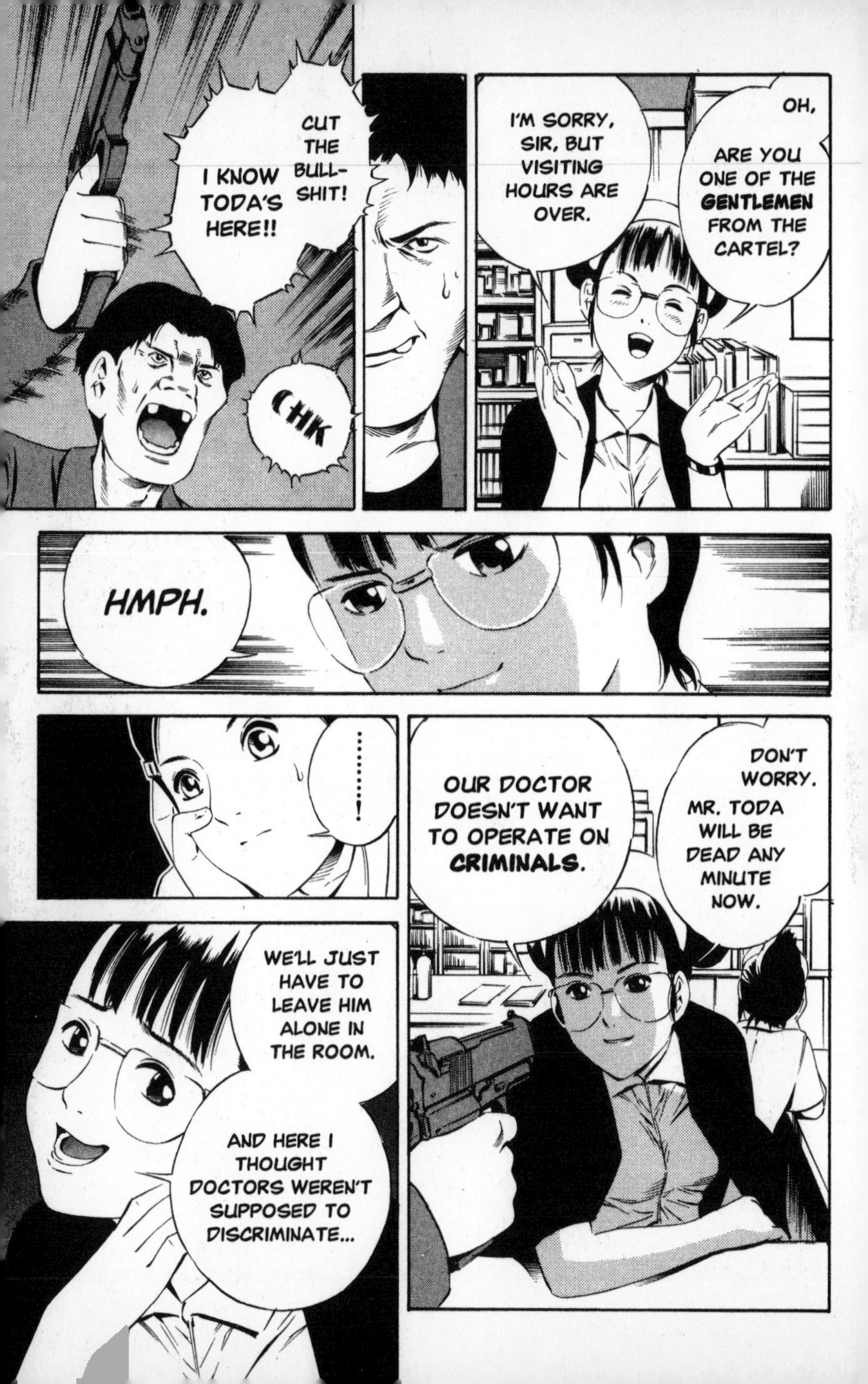

OH,
ARE YOU ONE OF THE GENTLEMEN FROM THE CARTEL?
I'M SORRY, SIR, BUT VISITING HOURS ARE OVER.
CUT THE BULL-SHIT!
I KNOW TODA'S HERE!!
CHK
HMPH.
DON'T WORRY.
MR. TODA WILL BE DEAD ANY MINUTE NOW.
OUR DOCTOR DOESN'T WANT TO OPERATE ON CRIMINALS.
......!
WE'LL JUST HAVE TO LEAVE HIM ALONE IN THE ROOM.
AND HERE I THOUGHT DOCTORS WEREN'T SUPPOSED TO DISCRIMINATE...

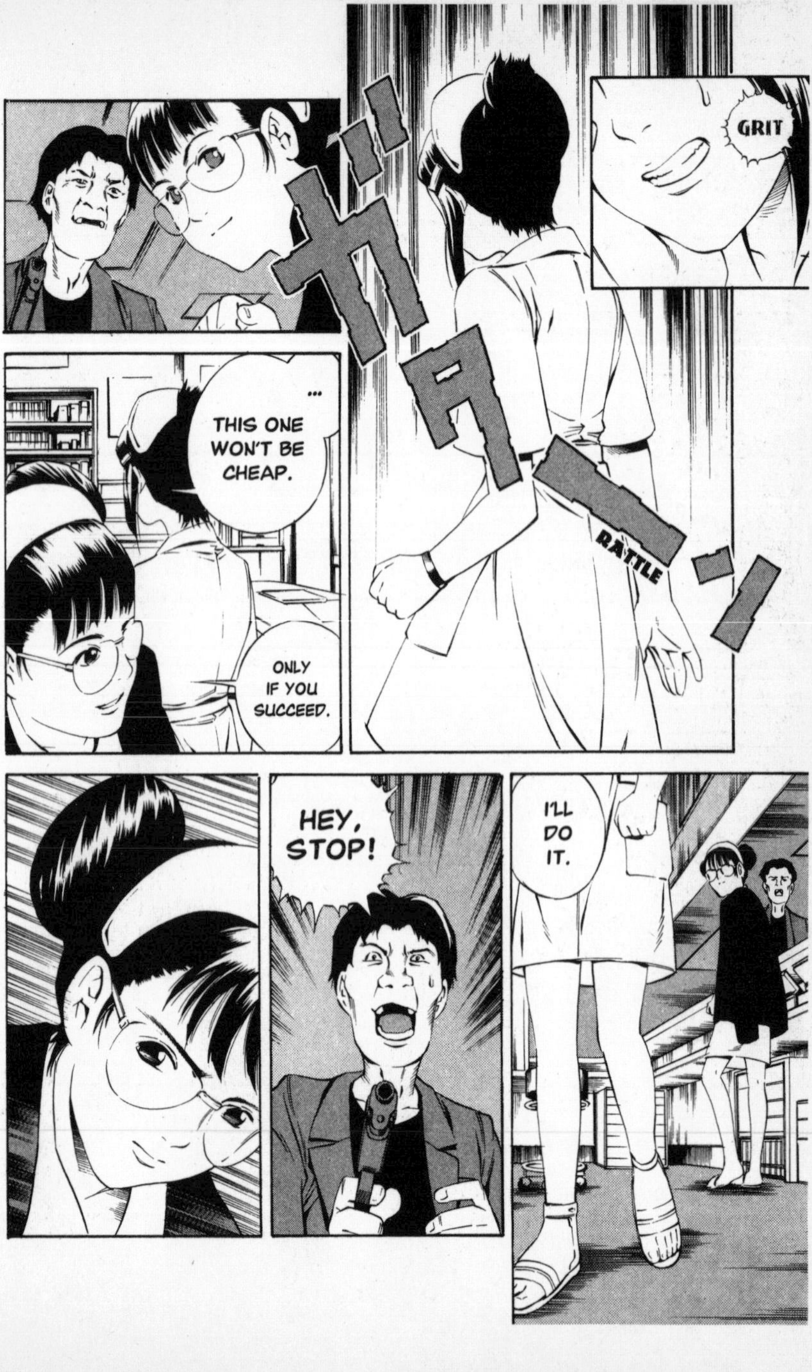
GRIT
ガターン
RATTLE
...
THIS ONE WON'T BE CHEAP.
ONLY IF YOU SUCCEED.
I'LL DO IT.
HEY, STOP!

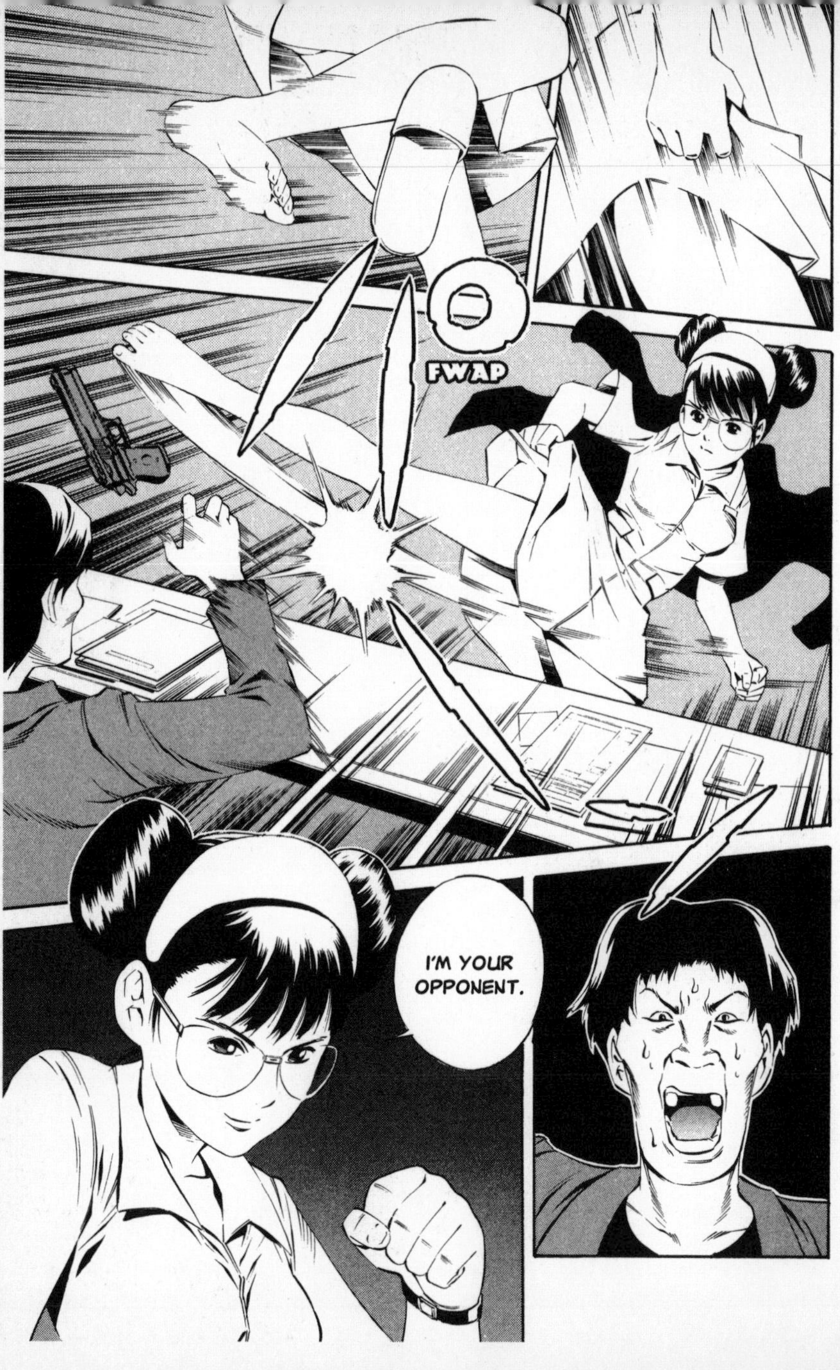
FWAP
I'M YOUR OPPONENT.

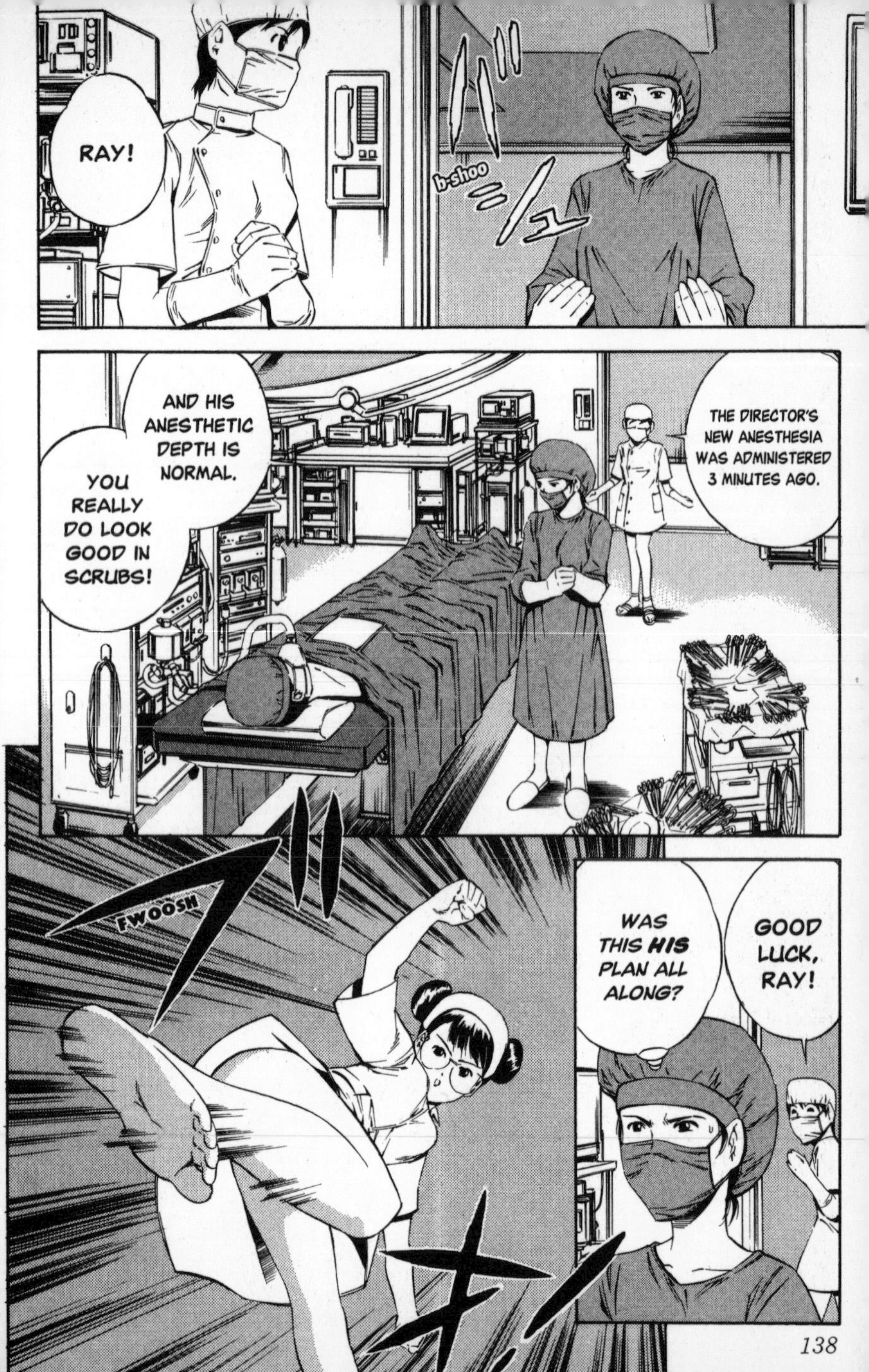
RAY!
b-shoo
THE DIRECTOR'S NEW ANESTHESIA WAS ADMINISTERED 3 MINUTES AGO.
AND HIS ANESTHETIC DEPTH IS NORMAL.
YOU REALLY DO LOOK GOOD IN SCRUBS!
FWOOSH
WAS THIS **HIS** PLAN ALL ALONG?
GOOD LUCK, RAY!

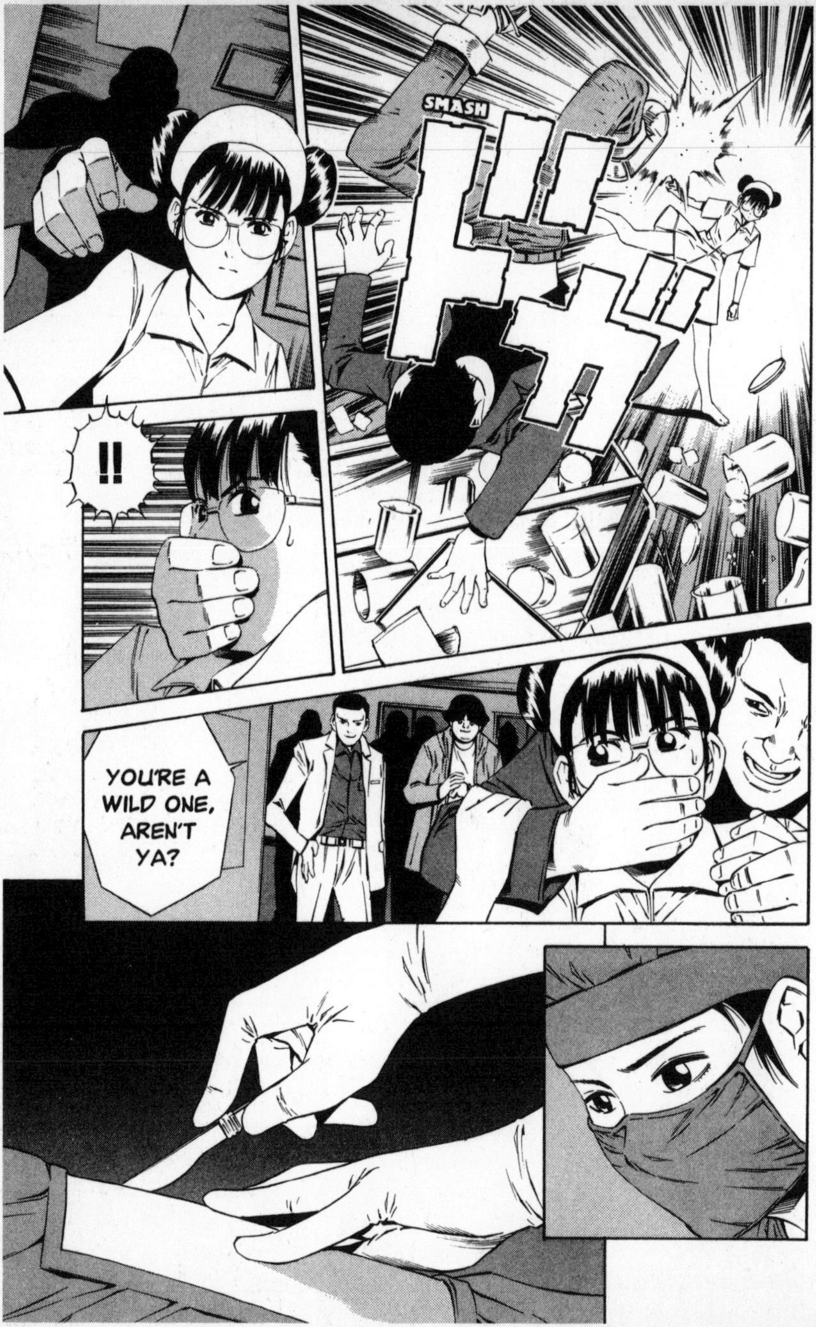
SMASH
!!
YOU'RE A WILD ONE, AREN'T YA?

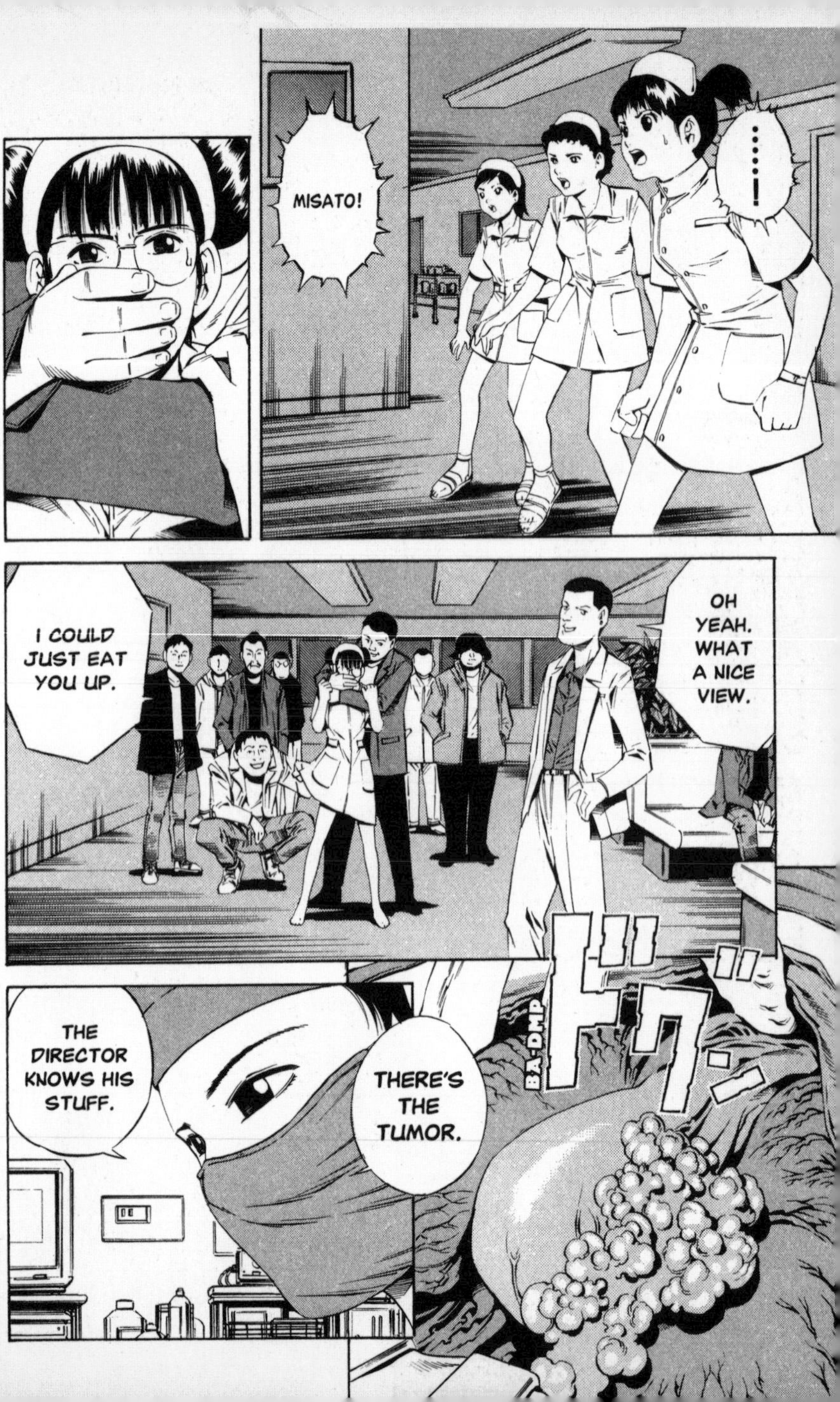
......!
MISATO!
OH YEAH. WHAT A NICE VIEW.
I COULD JUST EAT YOU UP.
BA-DMP
THERE'S THE TUMOR.
THE DIRECTOR KNOWS HIS STUFF.

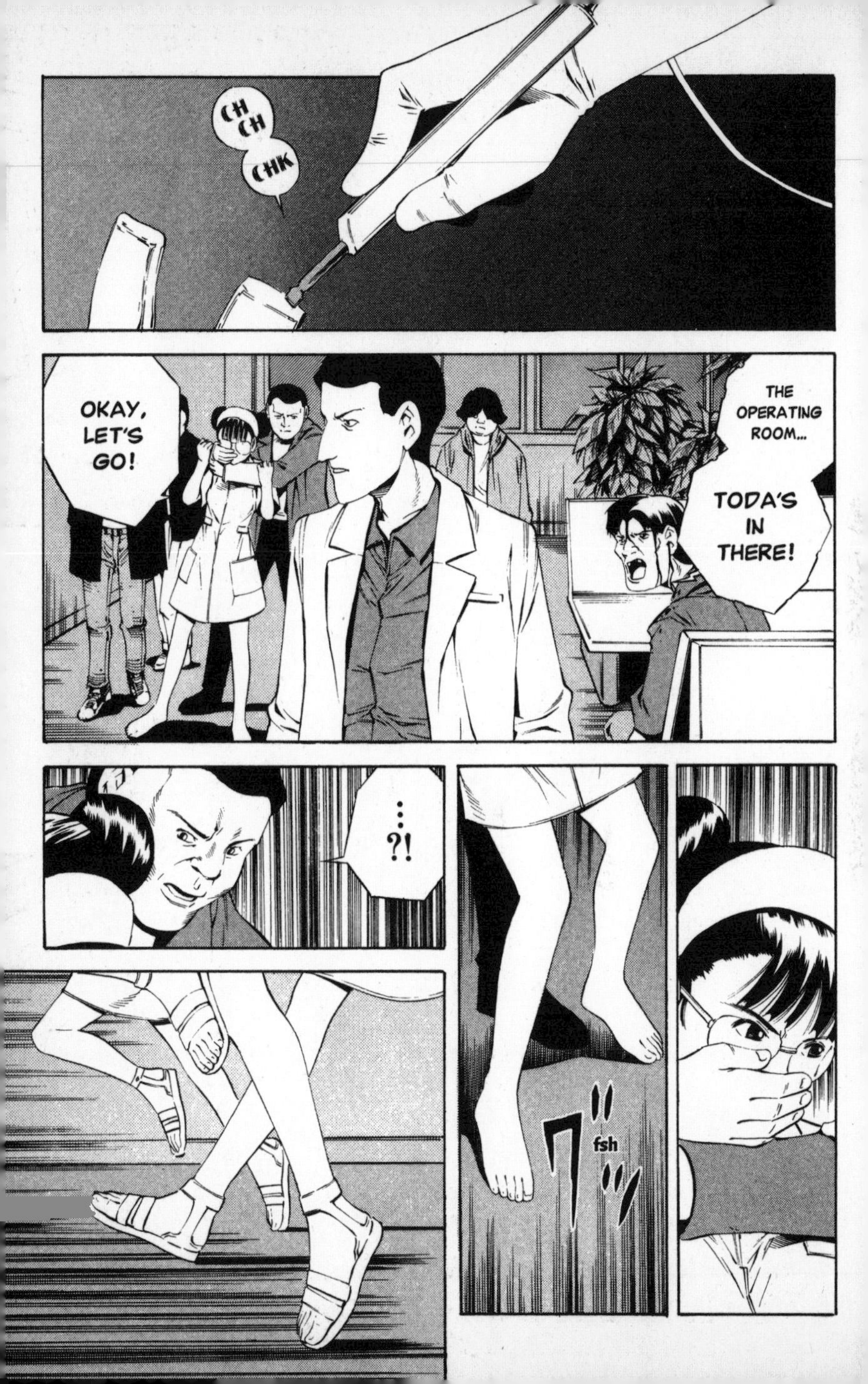
CH CH CHK
THE OPERATING ROOM...
TODA'S IN THERE!
OKAY, LET'S GO!
...?!
fsh

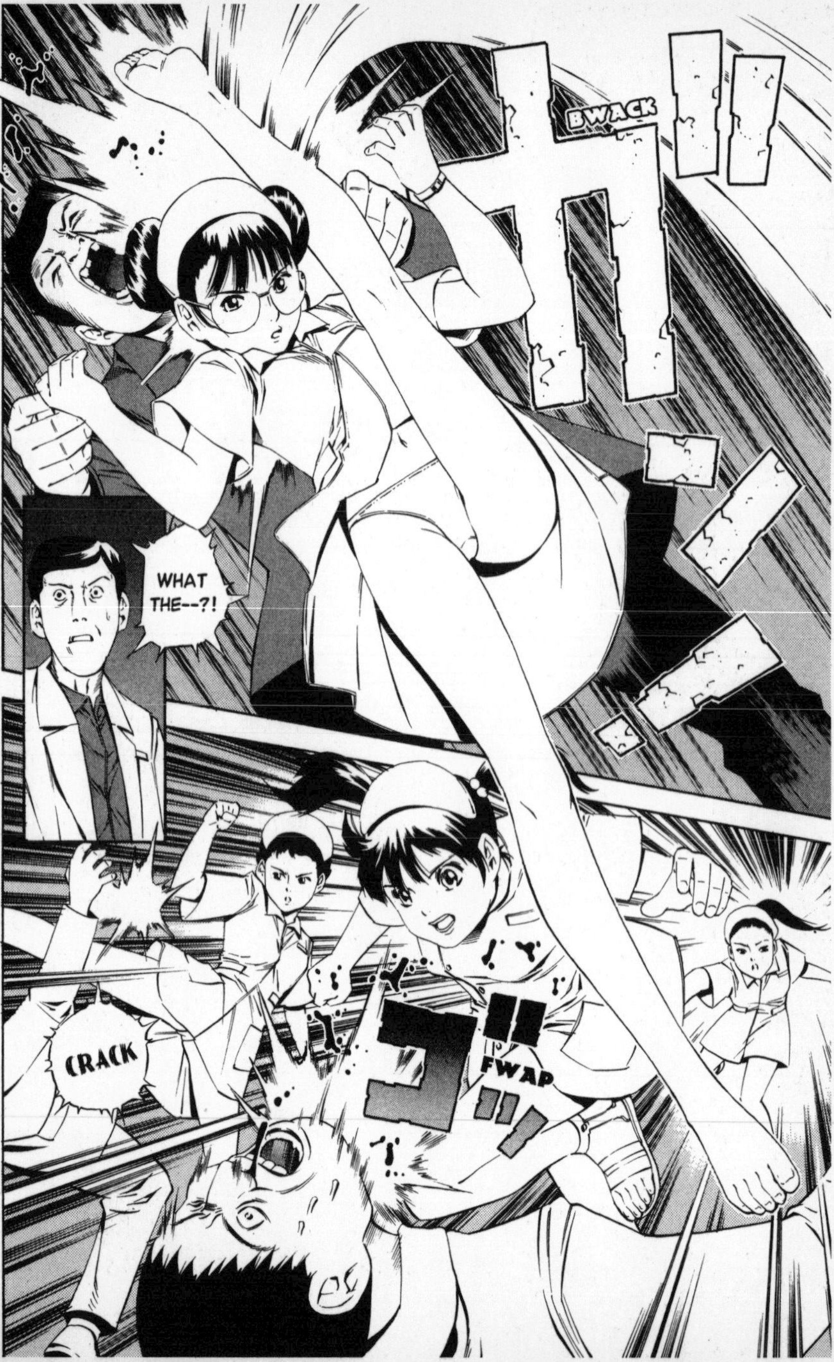
BWACK
WHAT THE--?!
FWAP
CRACK

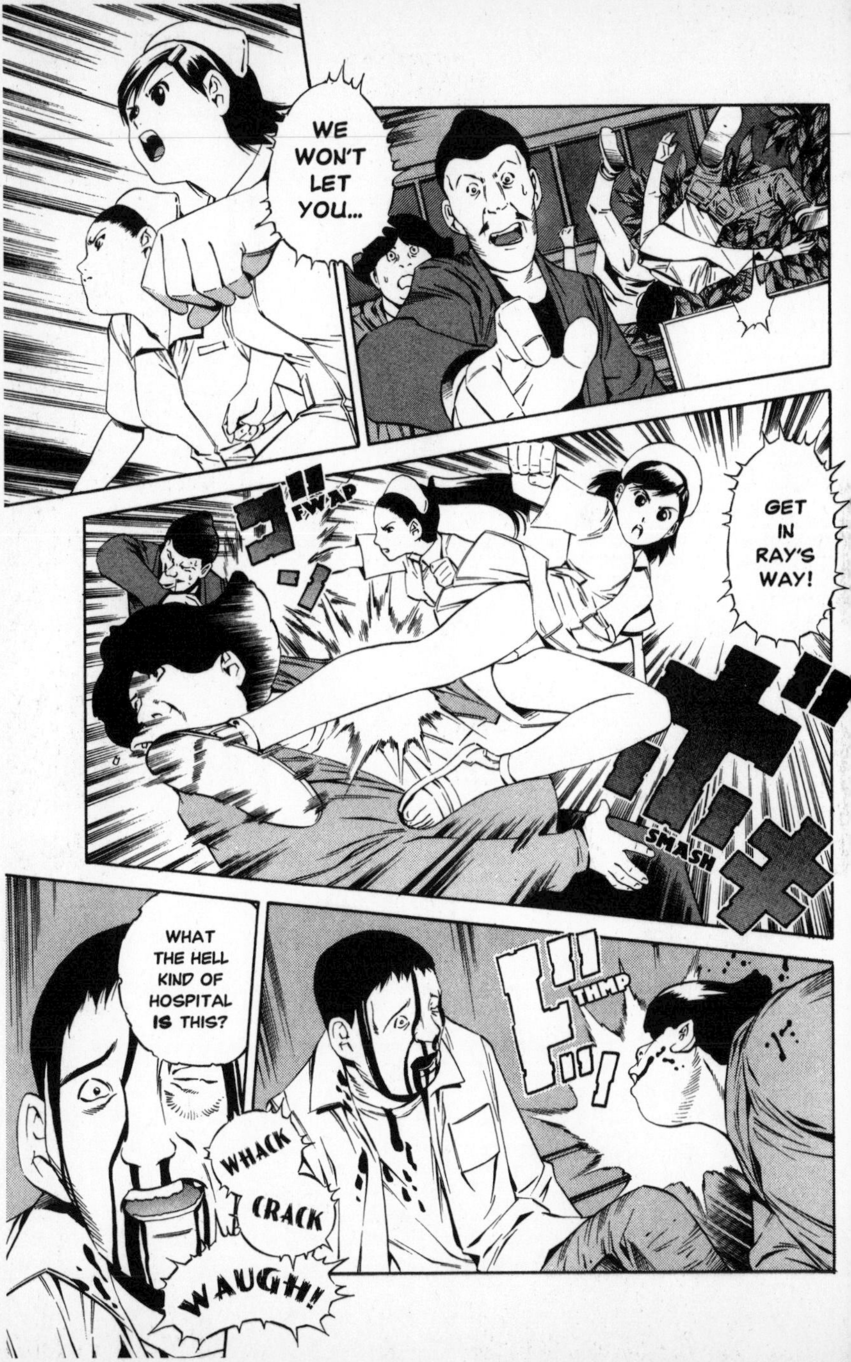

WE WON'T LET YOU...
GET IN RAY'S WAY!
FWAP
SMASH
WHAT THE HELL KIND OF HOSPITAL IS THIS?
THMP
WHACK
CRACK
WAUGH!

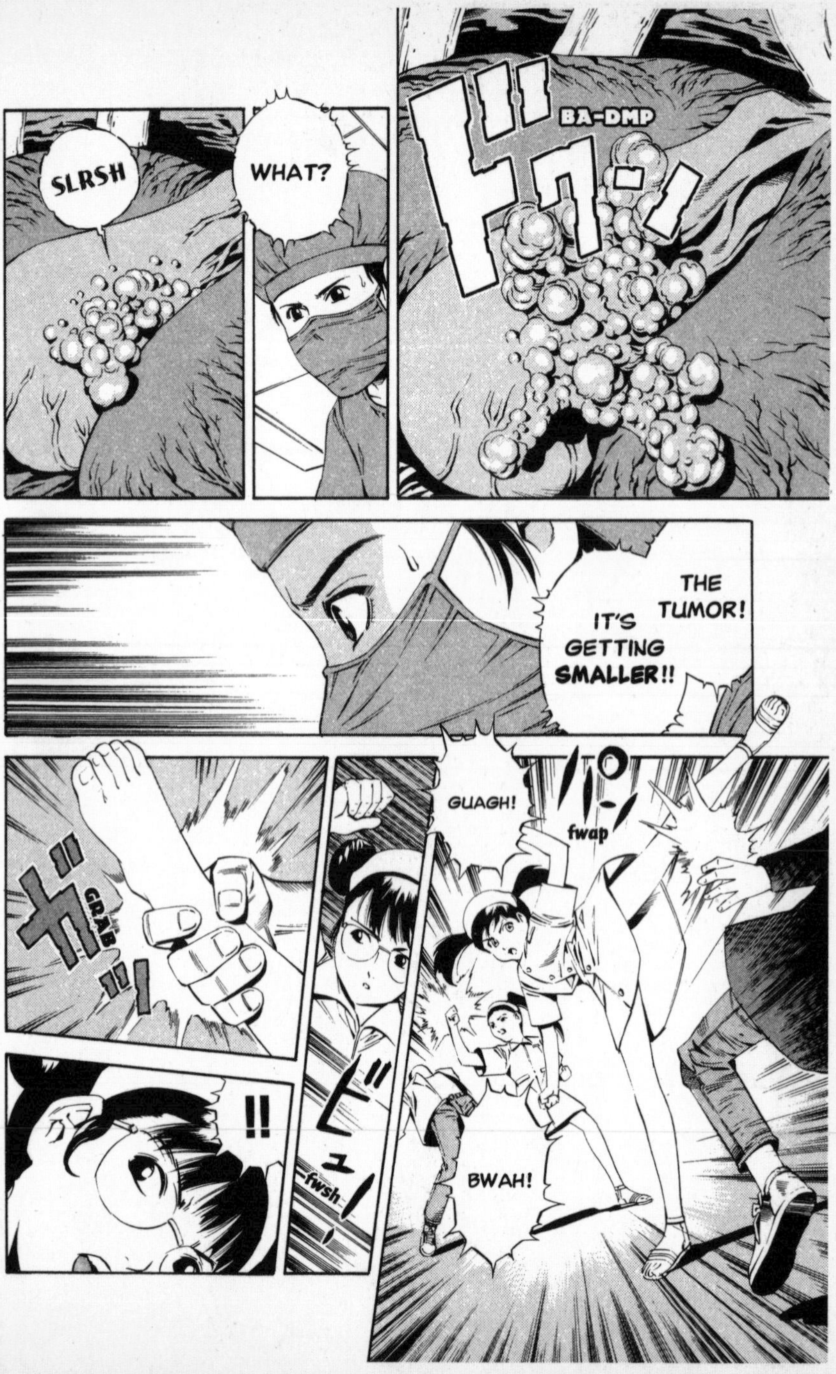
BA-DMP
WHAT?
SLRSH
THE TUMOR! IT'S GETTING SMALLER!!
GUAGH!
fwap
GRAB
fwsh
!!
BWAH!

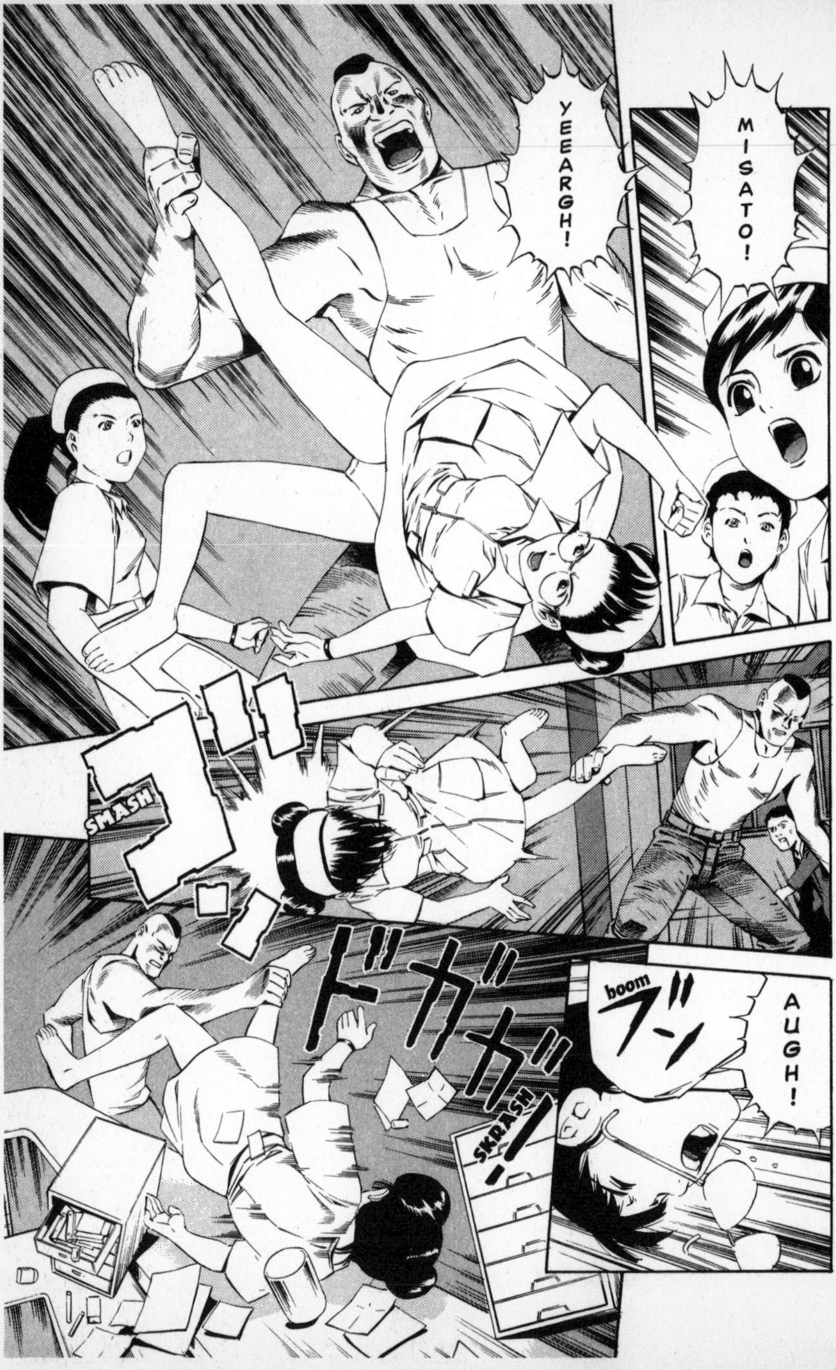
MISATO!
YEEARGH!
SMASH
boom
ブーン
AUGH!
SKRASH
ドガガッ

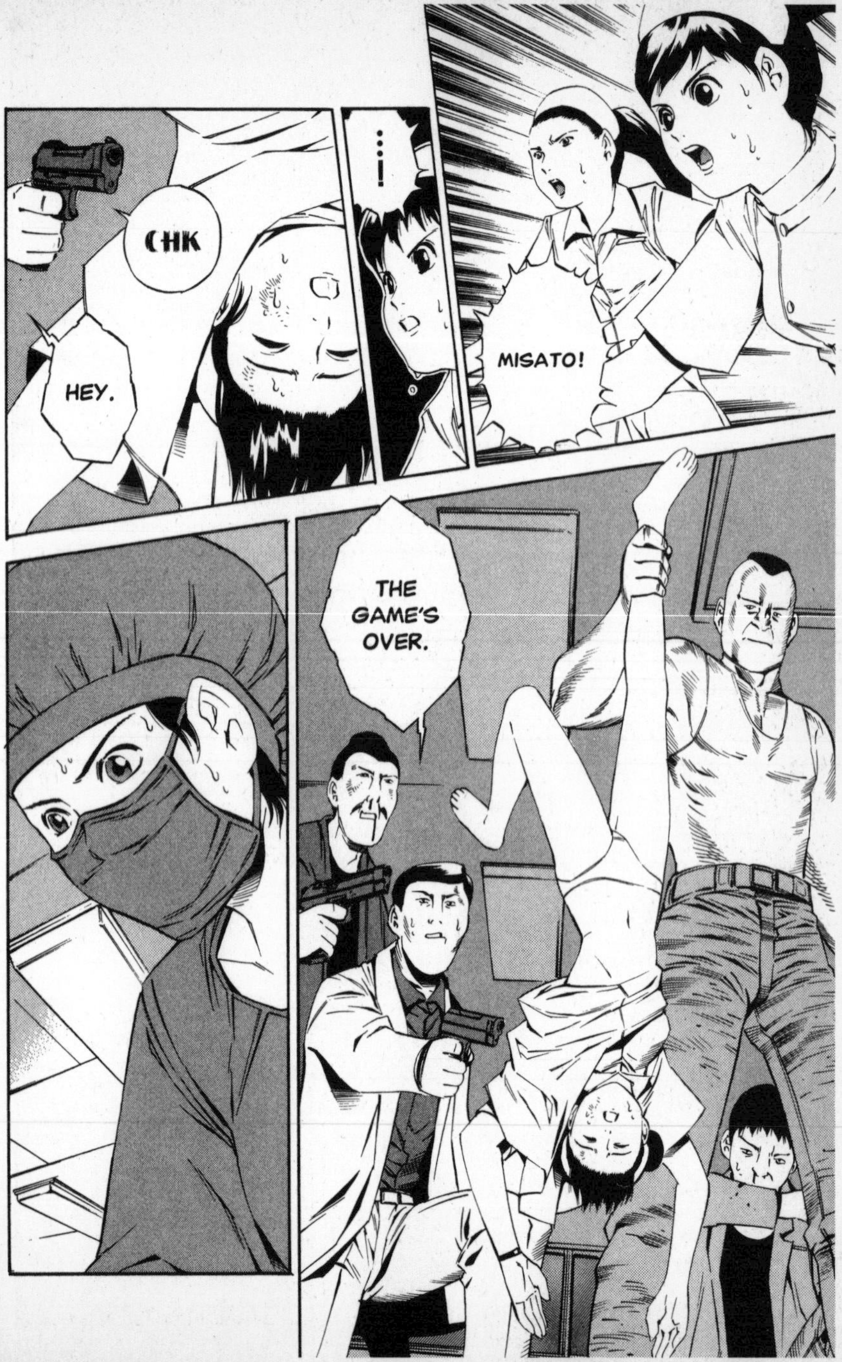
MISATO!
...!
CHK
HEY.
THE GAME'S OVER.

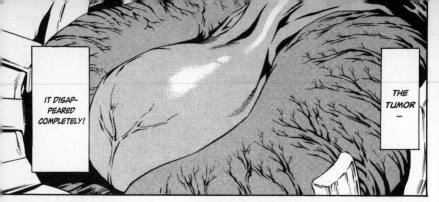

THE TUMOR ...
IT DISAPPEARED COMPLETELY!
THE ANESTHESIA ONLY HOLDS IT FOR A SHORT TIME!
WHAT DO I DO NOW? SHOULD I INJECT MORE ANESTHESIA?
NO. I CAN'T GIVE HIM ANY MORE. ANOTHER DOSE COULD BE FATAL.
WILL THE TUMOR APPEAR AGAIN AS THE ANESTHETIC WEARS OFF?
I DON'T KNOW...
I JUST DON'T KNOW WHAT WILL HAPPEN!
b-shoo

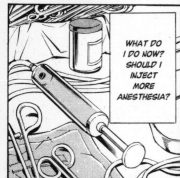

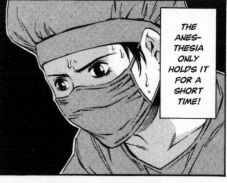

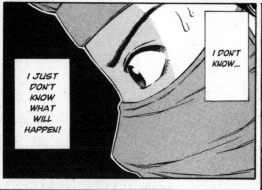

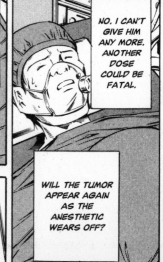

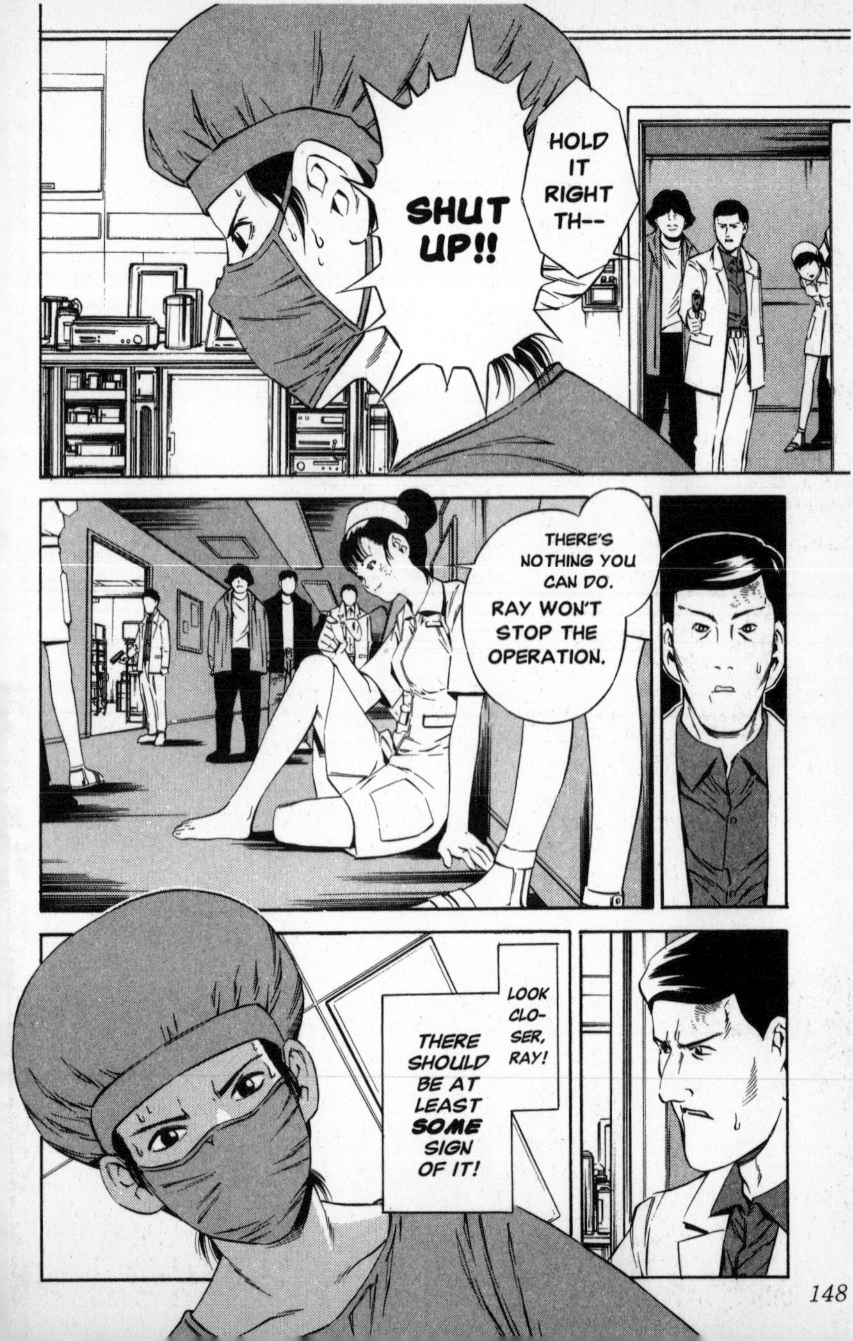
HOLD IT RIGHT TH--
SHUT UP!!
THERE'S NOTHING YOU CAN DO. RAY WON'T STOP THE OPERATION.
LOOK CLO- SER, RAY!
THERE SHOULD BE AT LEAST SOME SIGN OF IT!

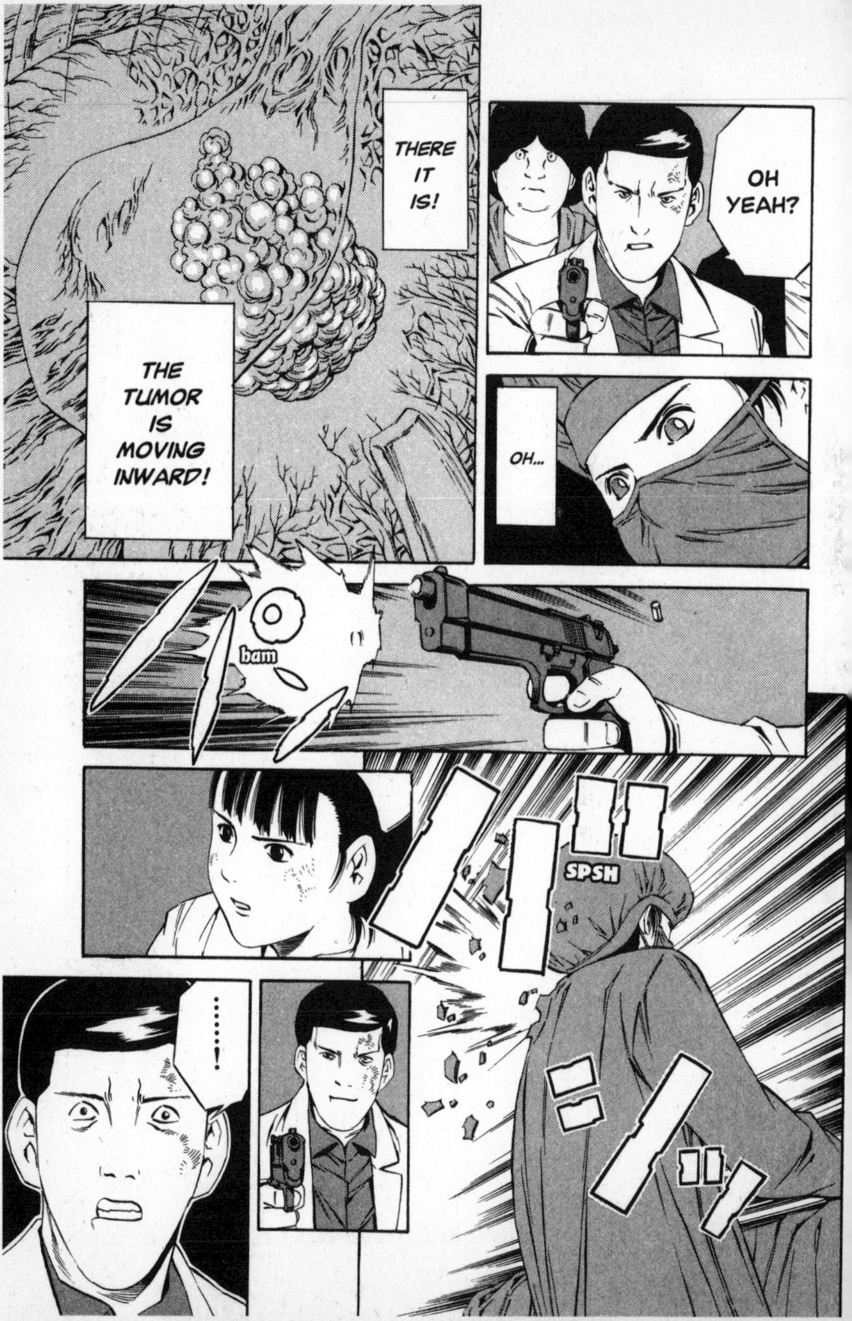
THERE IT IS!
THE TUMOR IS MOVING INWARD!
OH YEAH?
OH...
bam
SPSH
......!

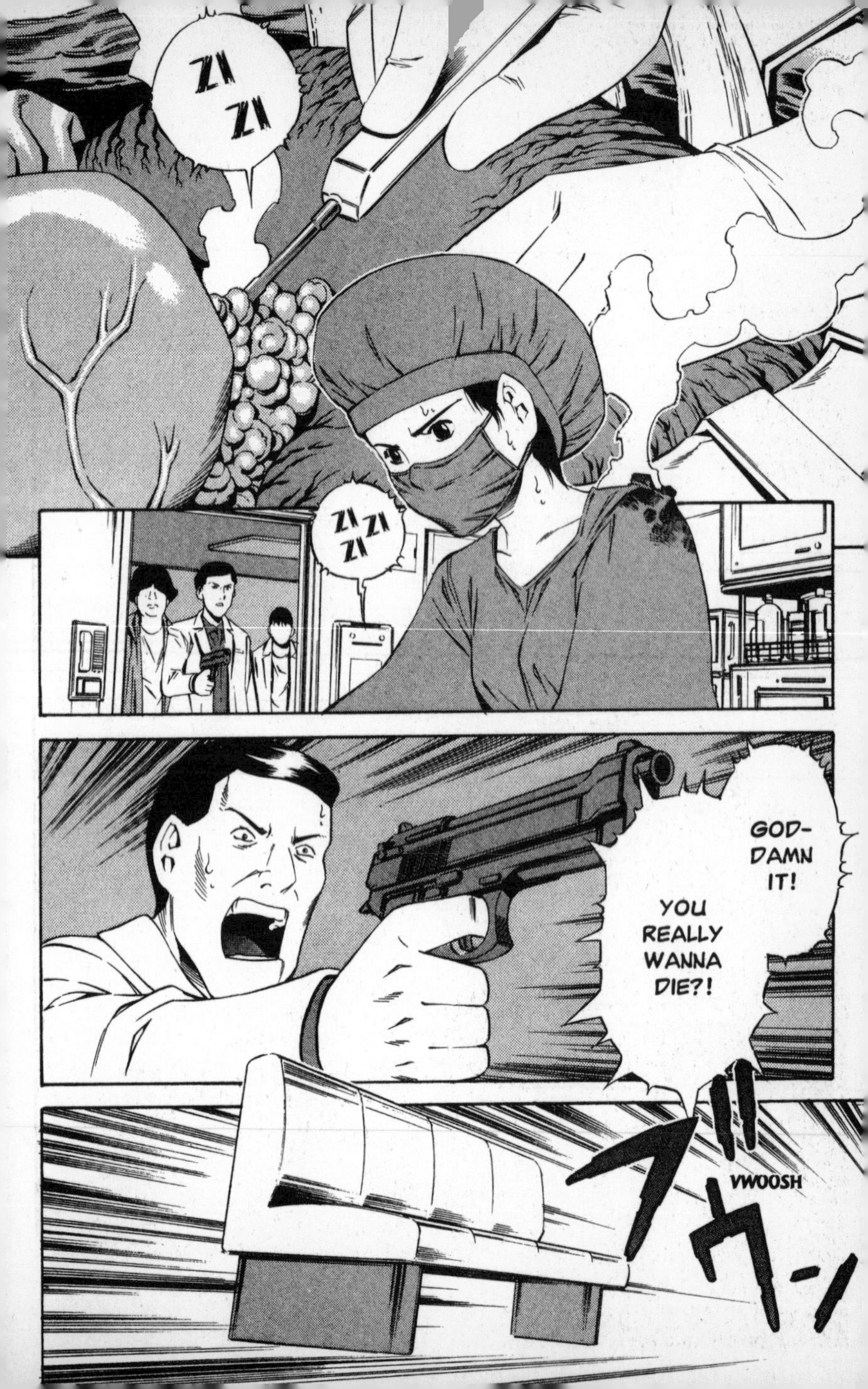
ZI ZI
ZI ZI ZI ZI
GOD-DAMN IT!
YOU REALLY WANNA DIE?!
VWOOSH

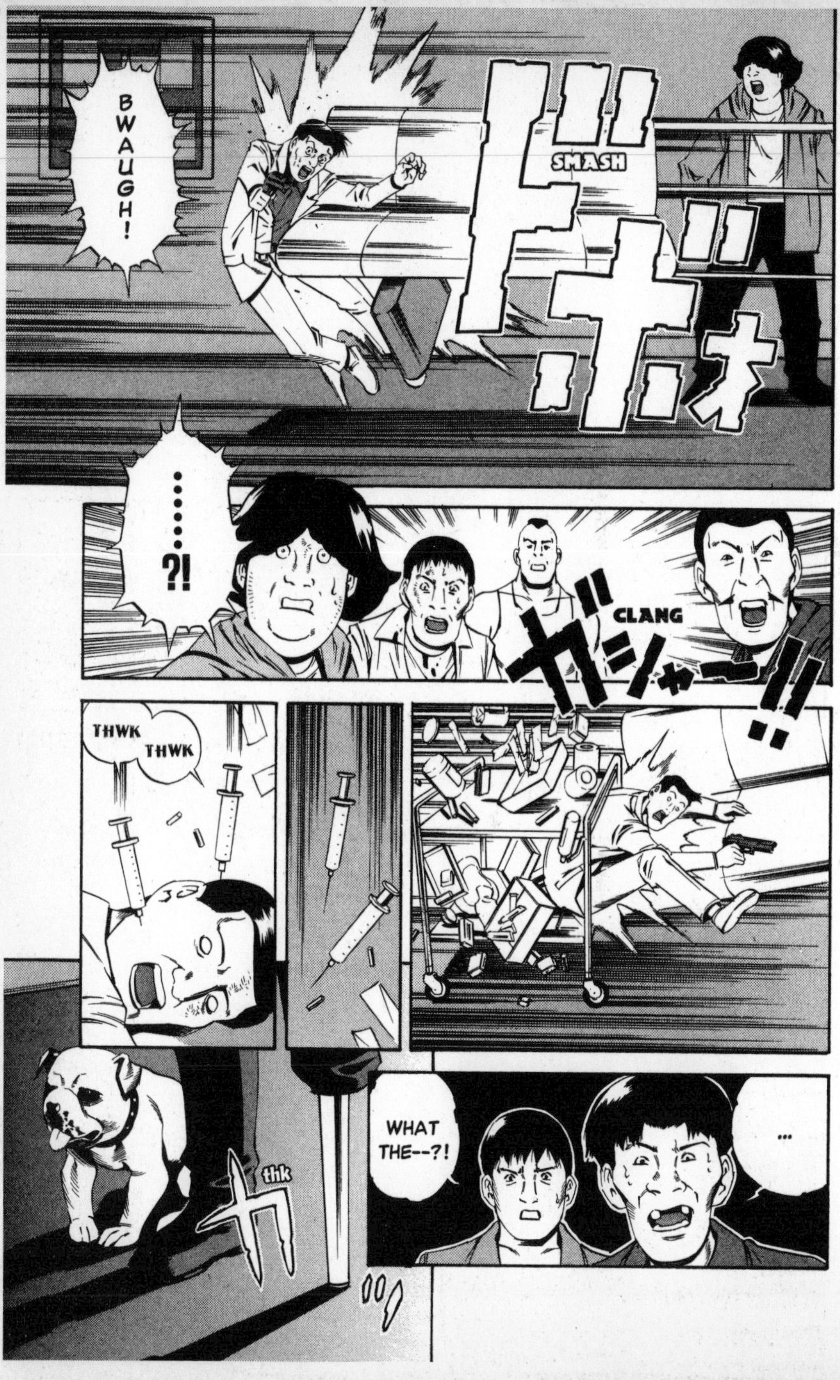
BWAUGH!
SMASH
......?!
CLANG
THWK THWK
WHAT THE--?!
...
thk

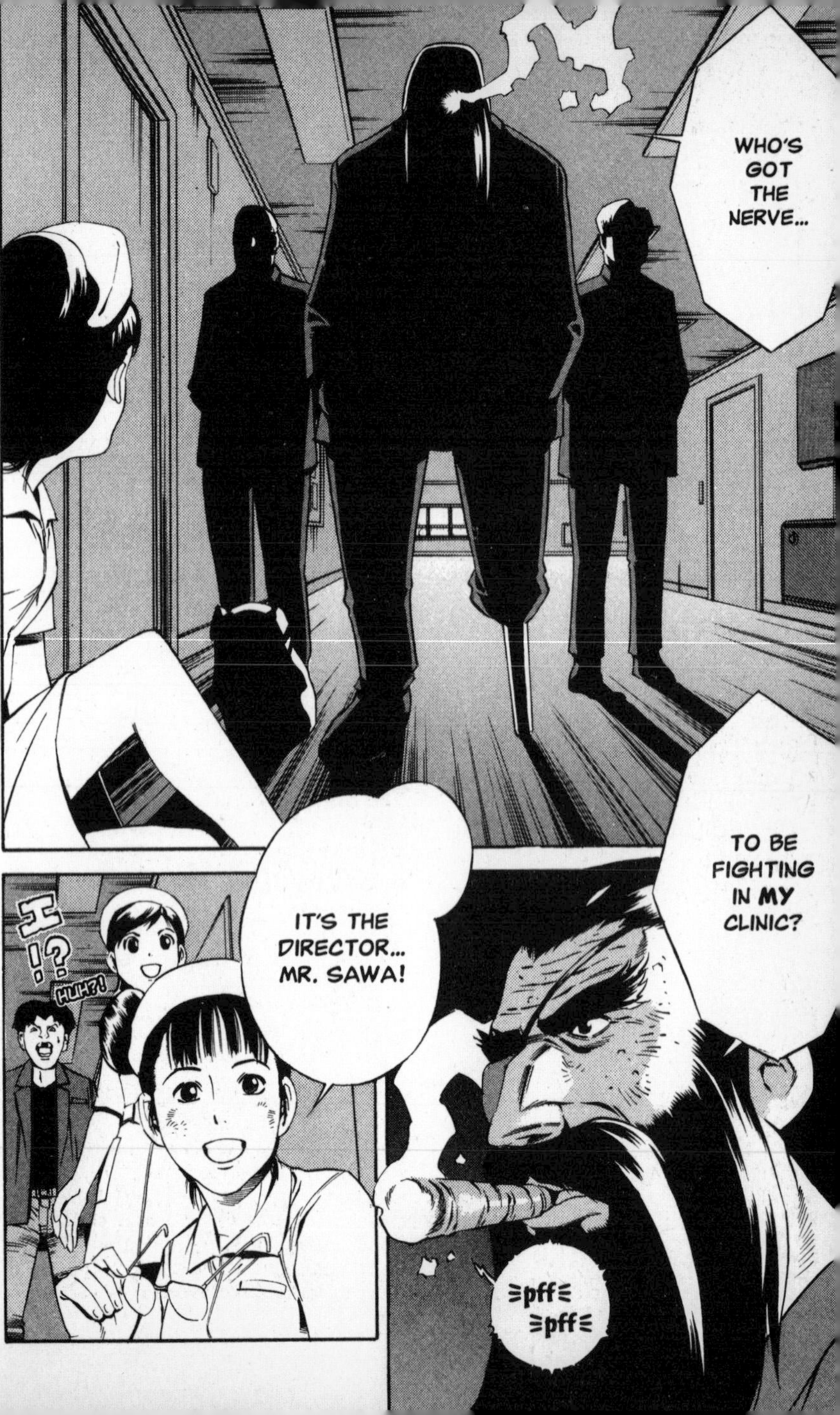

WHO'S GOT THE NERVE...
TO BE FIGHTING IN MY CLINIC?
IT'S THE DIRECTOR... MR. SAWA!
エ!?
HUH?!
pff
pff

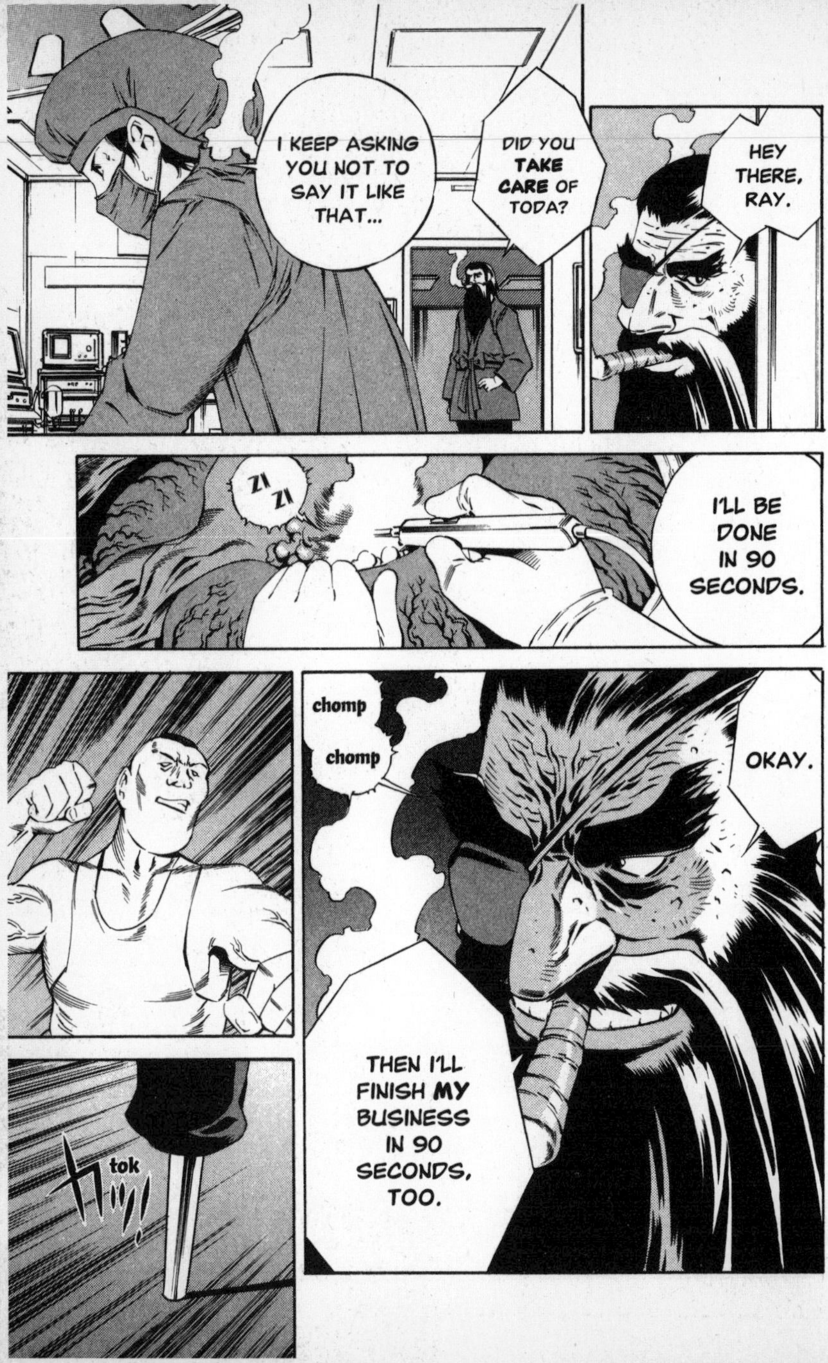
HEY THERE, RAY.
DID YOU TAKE CARE OF TODA?
I KEEP ASKING YOU NOT TO SAY IT LIKE THAT...
ZI ZI
I'LL BE DONE IN 90 SECONDS.
OKAY.
chomp
chomp
THEN I'LL FINISH MY BUSINESS IN 90 SECONDS, TOO.
tok

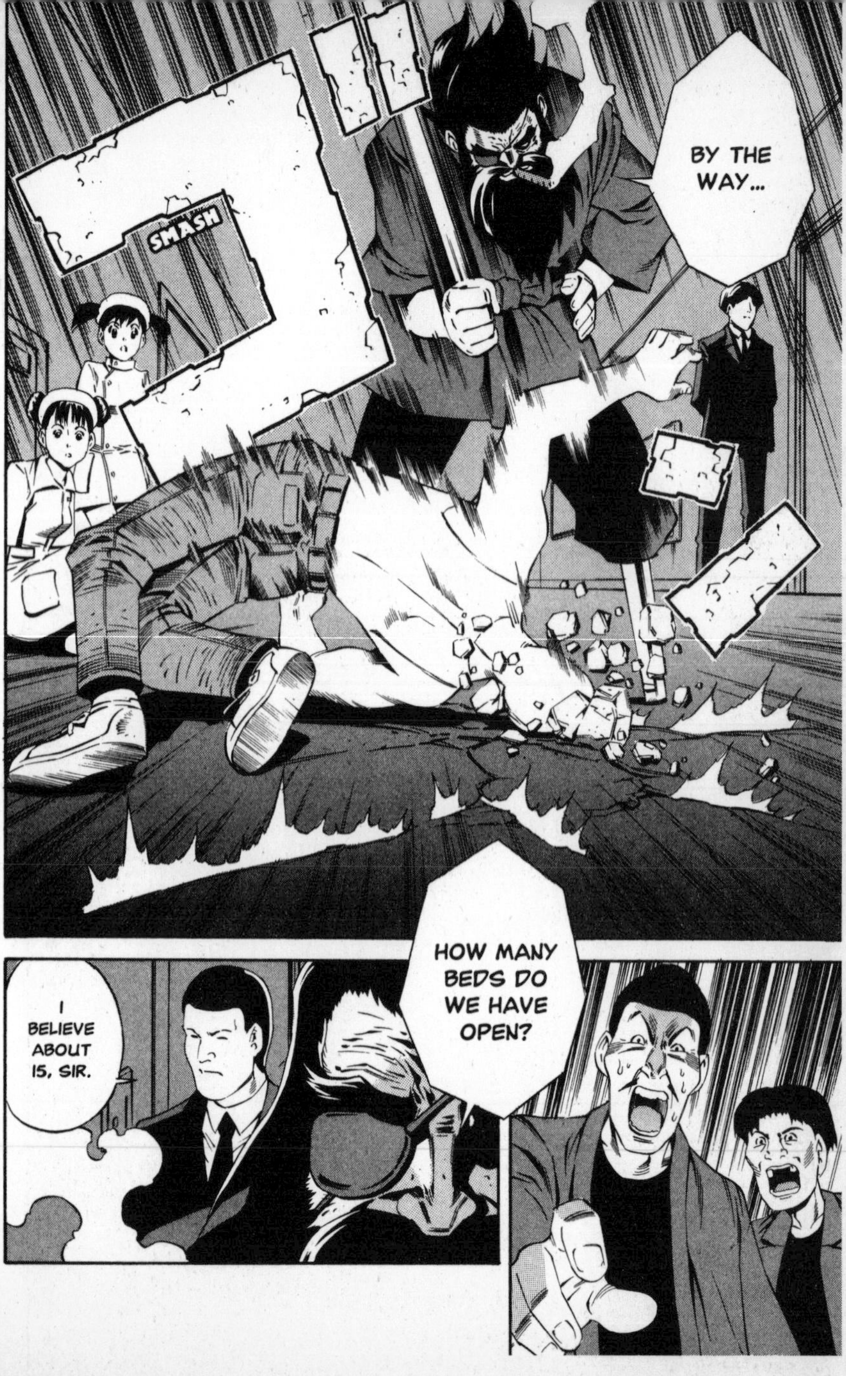
SMASH
BY THE WAY...
HOW MANY BEDS DO WE HAVE OPEN?
I BELIEVE ABOUT 15, SIR.

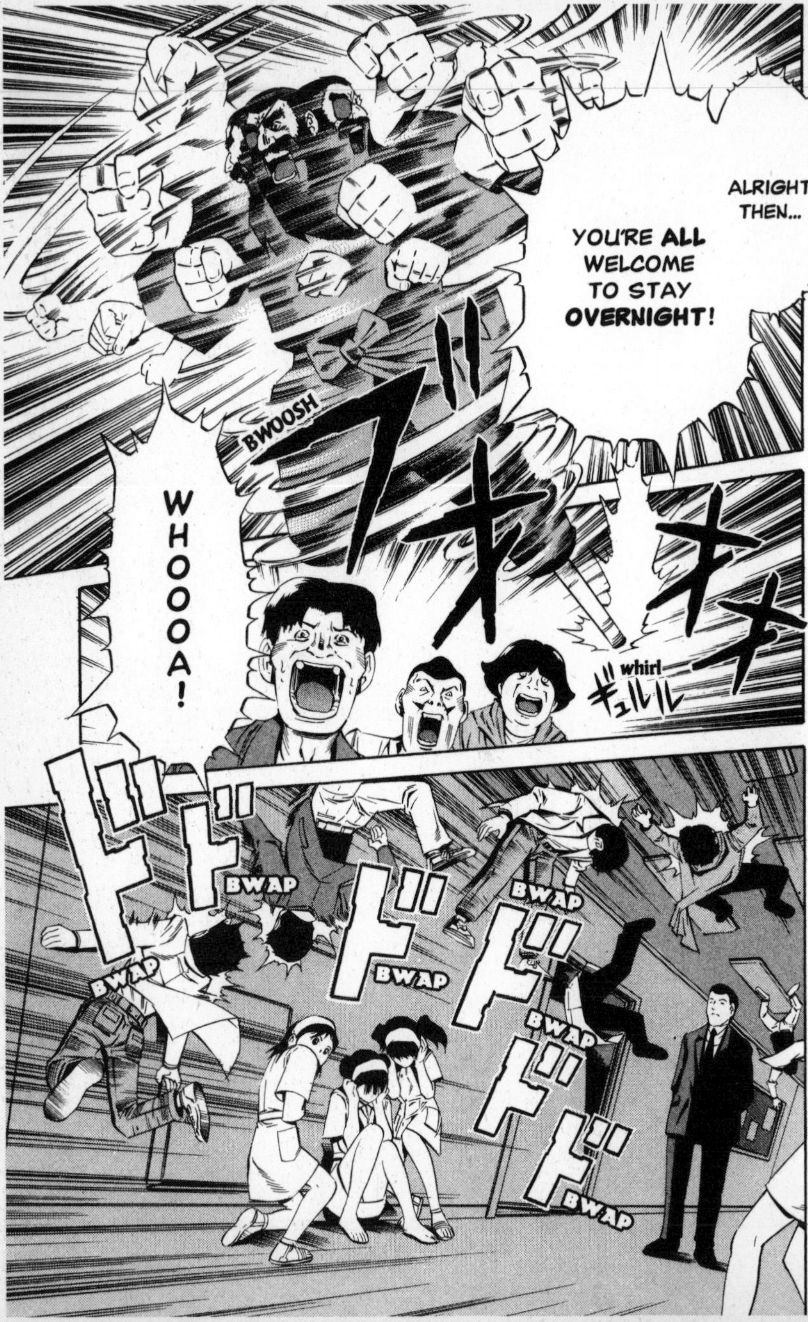
ALRIGHT THEN... YOU'RE ALL WELCOME TO STAY OVERNIGHT!
BWOOSH
ブォォォ
WHOOOOA!
whirl
ギュルル
BWAP
ドドドドドド
BWAP
BWAP
BWAP
BWAP
BWAP

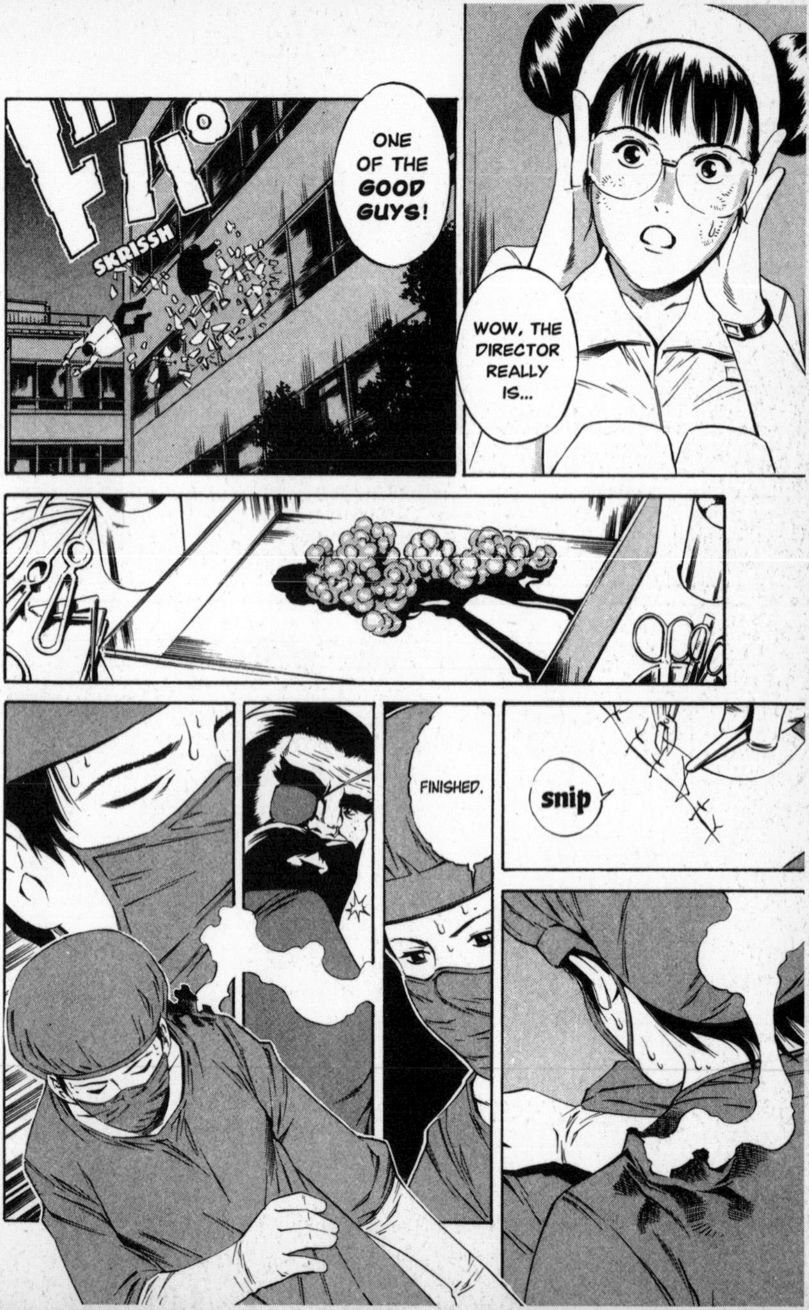
WOW, THE DIRECTOR REALLY IS...
ONE OF THE GOOD GUYS!
SKRISSH
snip
FINISHED.

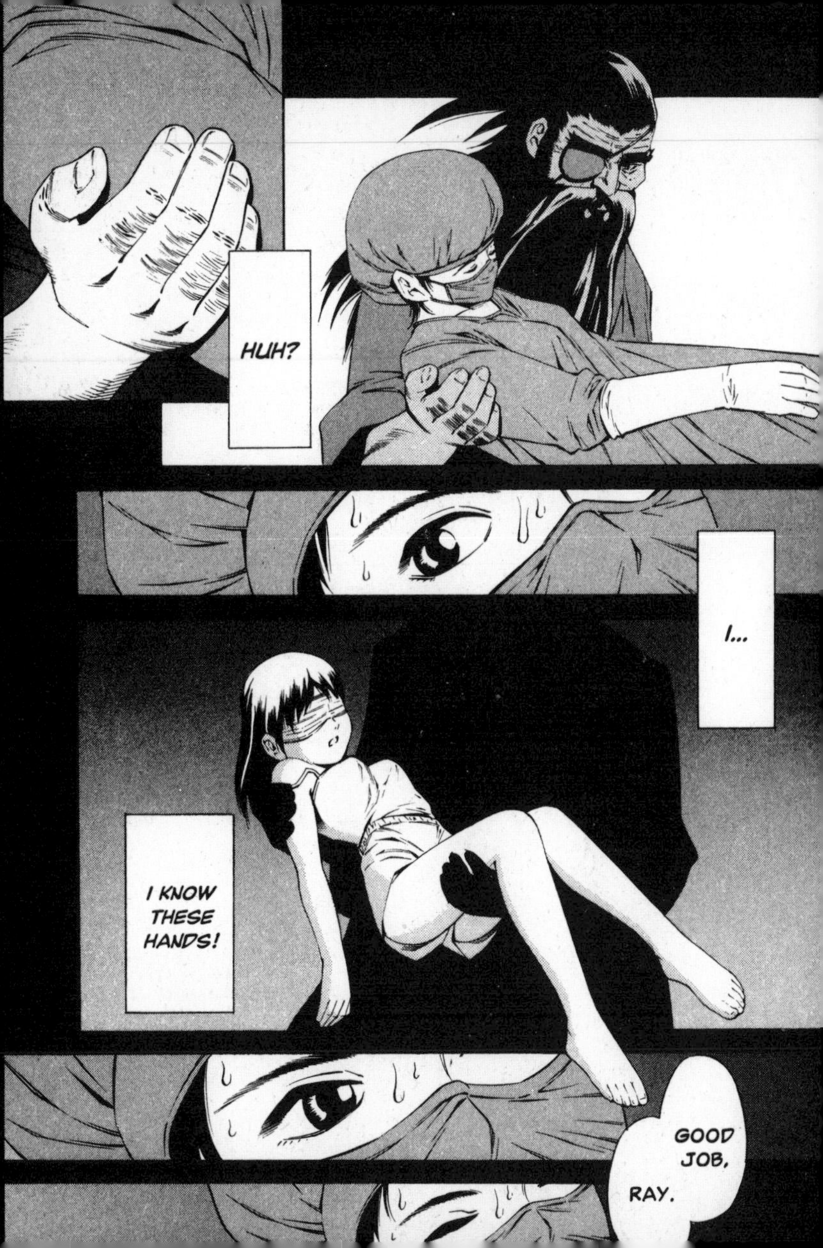
HUH?
I...
I KNOW THESE HANDS!
GOOD JOB, RAY.

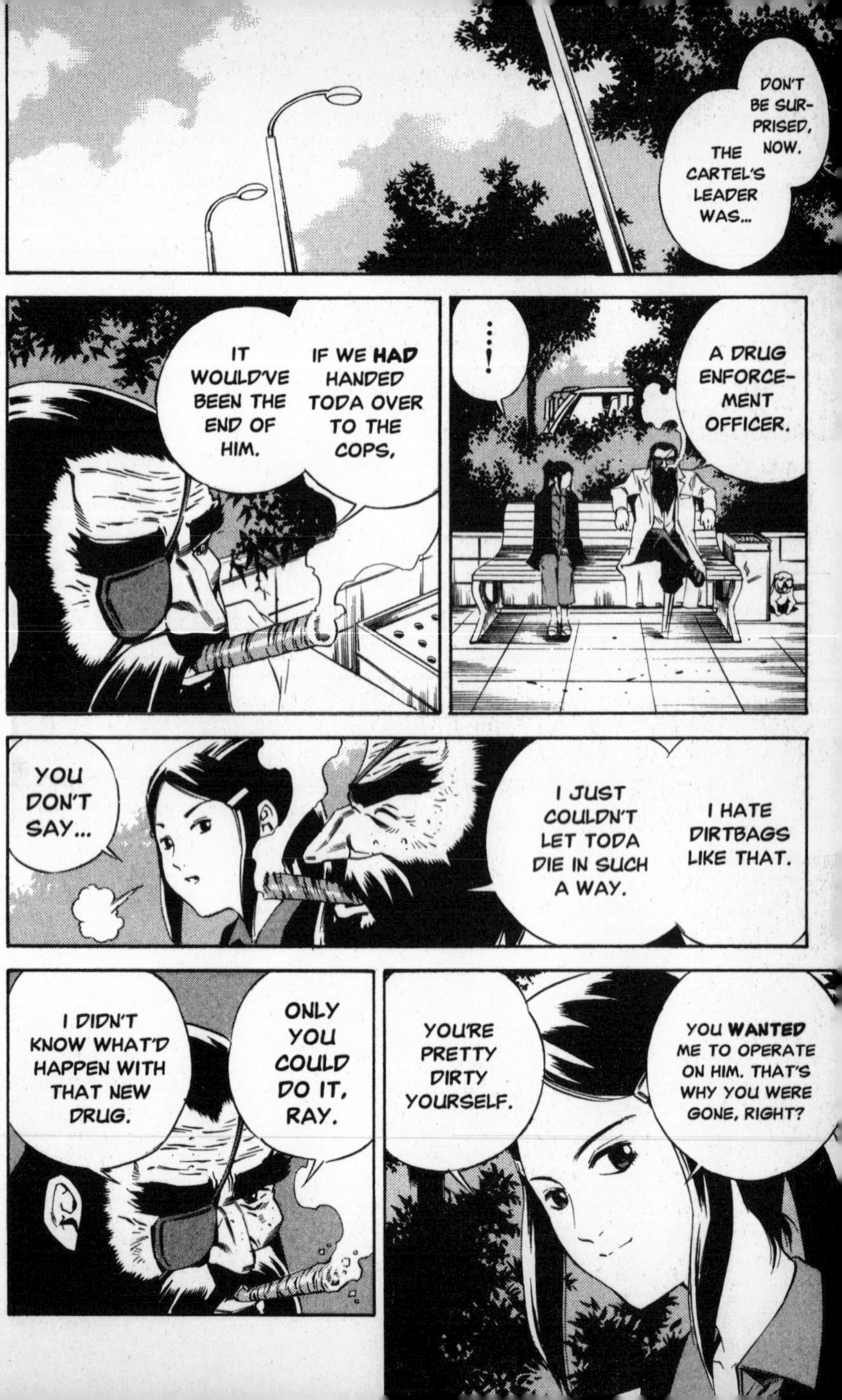
DON'T BE SURPRISED, NOW.
THE CARTEL'S LEADER WAS...
A DRUG ENFORCEMENT OFFICER.
...!
IF WE **HAD** HANDED TODA OVER TO THE COPS,
IT WOULD'VE BEEN THE END OF HIM.
I HATE DIRTBAGS LIKE THAT.
I JUST COULDN'T LET TODA DIE IN SUCH A WAY.
YOU DON'T SAY...
YOU **WANTED** ME TO OPERATE ON HIM. THAT'S WHY YOU WERE GONE, RIGHT?
YOU'RE PRETTY DIRTY YOURSELF.
ONLY YOU COULD DO IT, RAY.
I DIDN'T KNOW WHAT'D HAPPEN WITH THAT NEW DRUG.

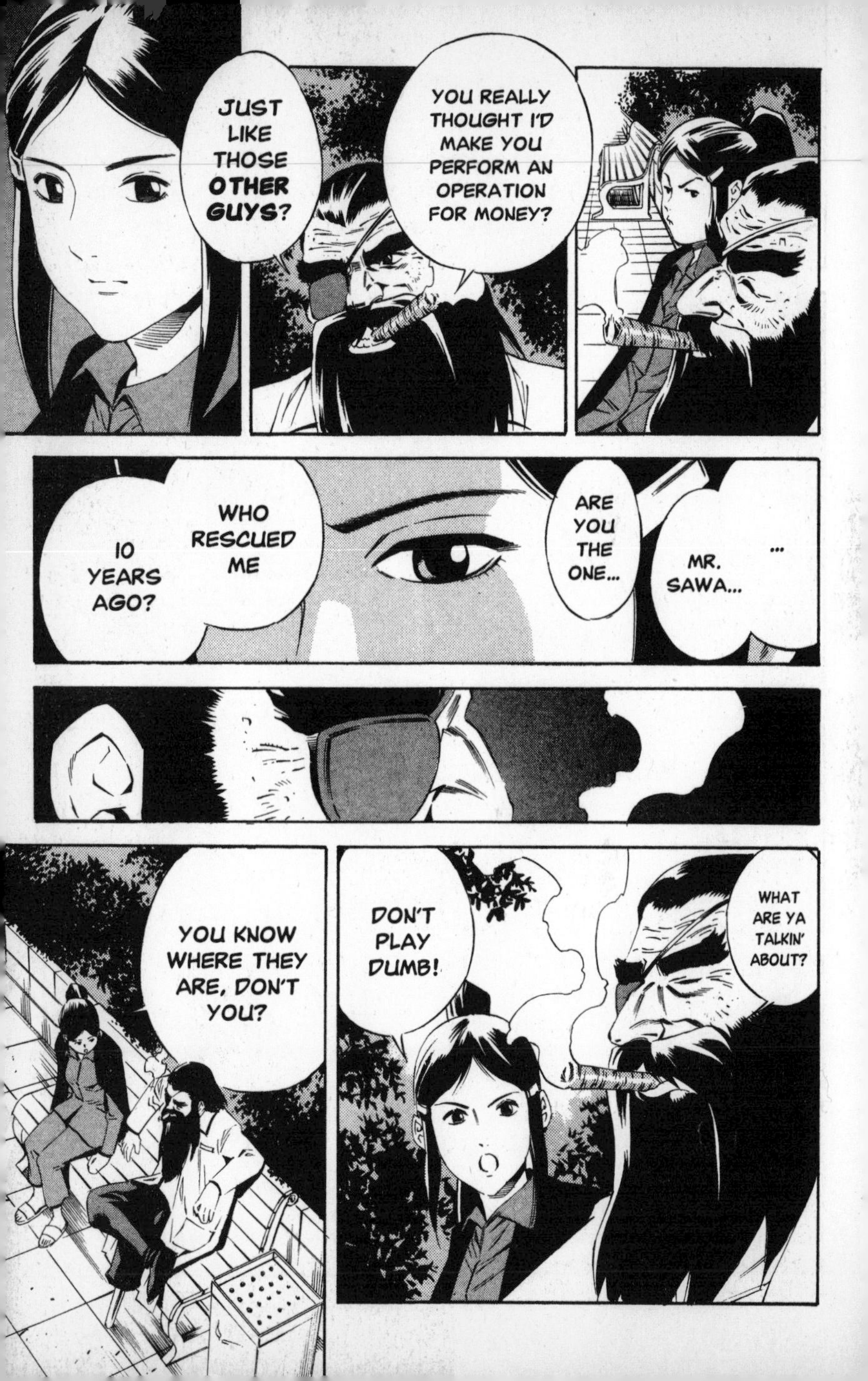
YOU REALLY THOUGHT I'D MAKE YOU PERFORM AN OPERATION FOR MONEY?
JUST LIKE THOSE OTHER GUYS?
...
MR. SAWA...
ARE YOU THE ONE...
WHO RESCUED ME
10 YEARS AGO?
WHAT ARE YA TALKIN' ABOUT?
DON'T PLAY DUMB!
YOU KNOW WHERE THEY ARE, DON'T YOU?

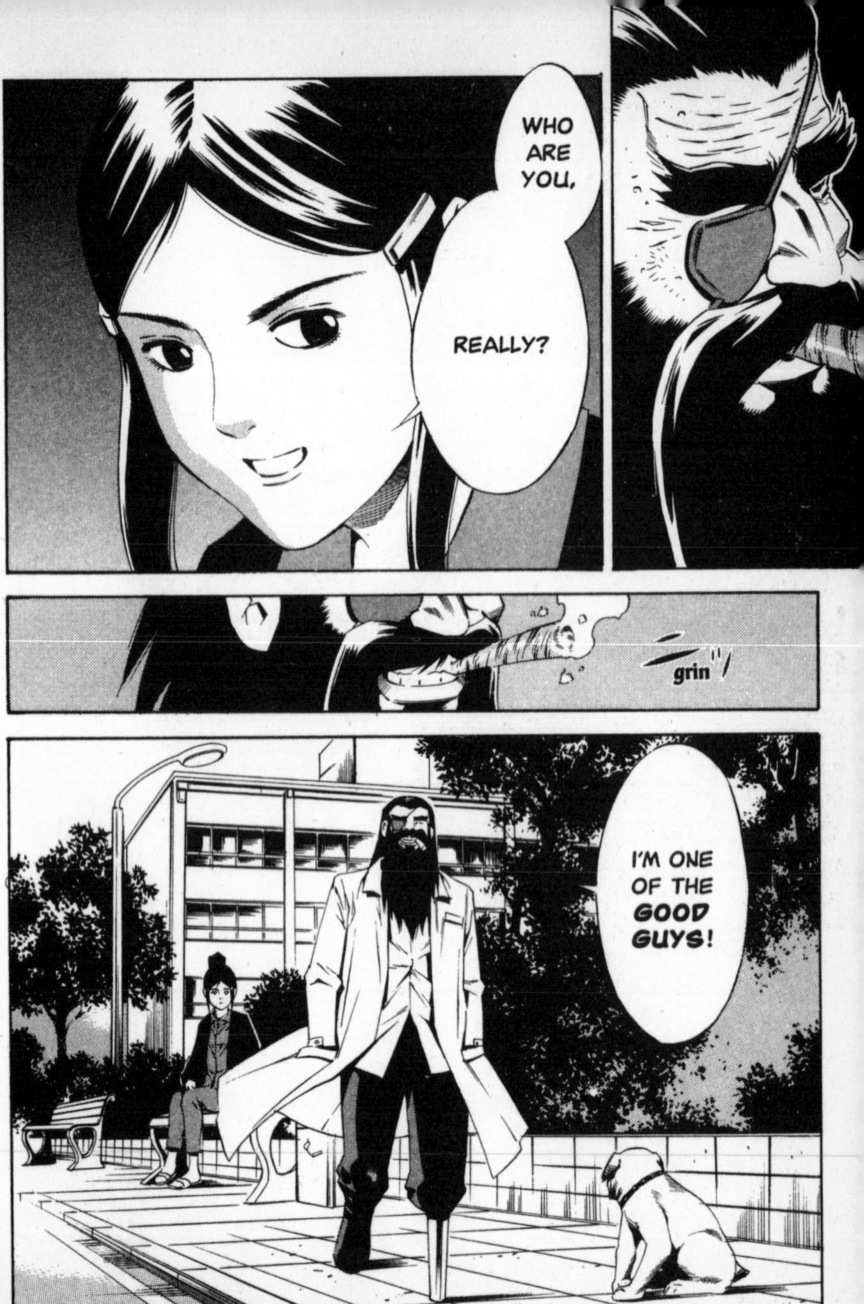
WHO ARE YOU,
REALLY?
grin
I'M ONE OF THE GOOD GUYS!

Patient.5

Passed Around

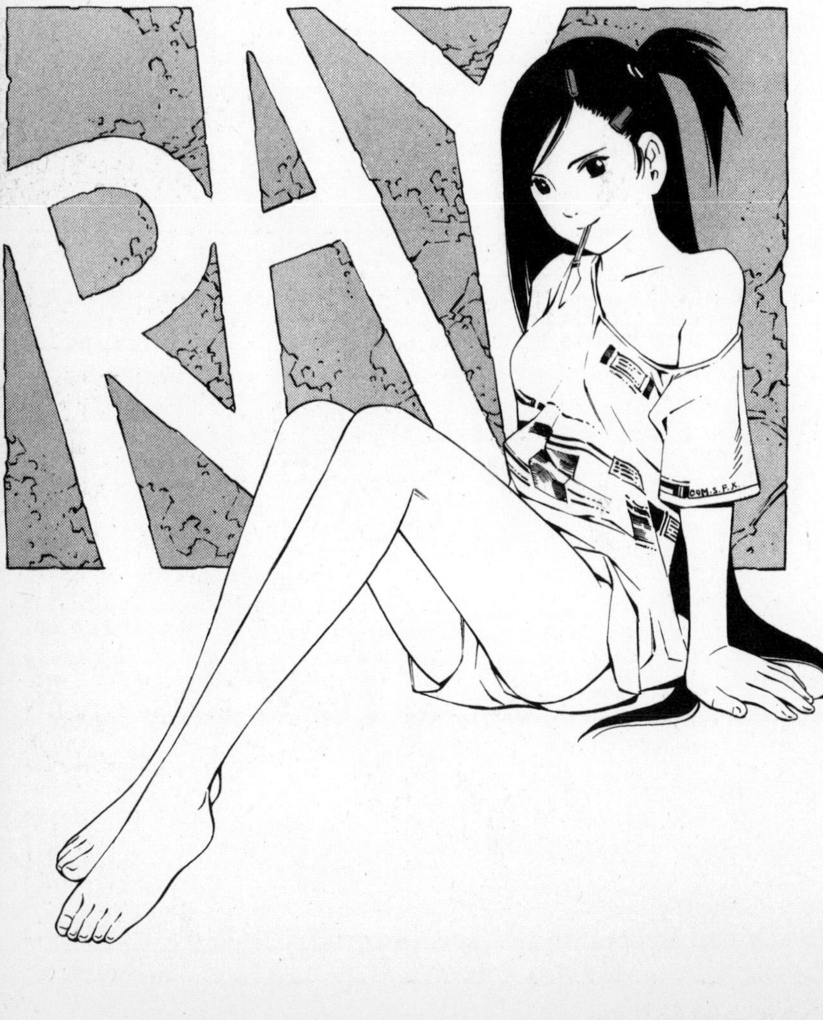
RAY

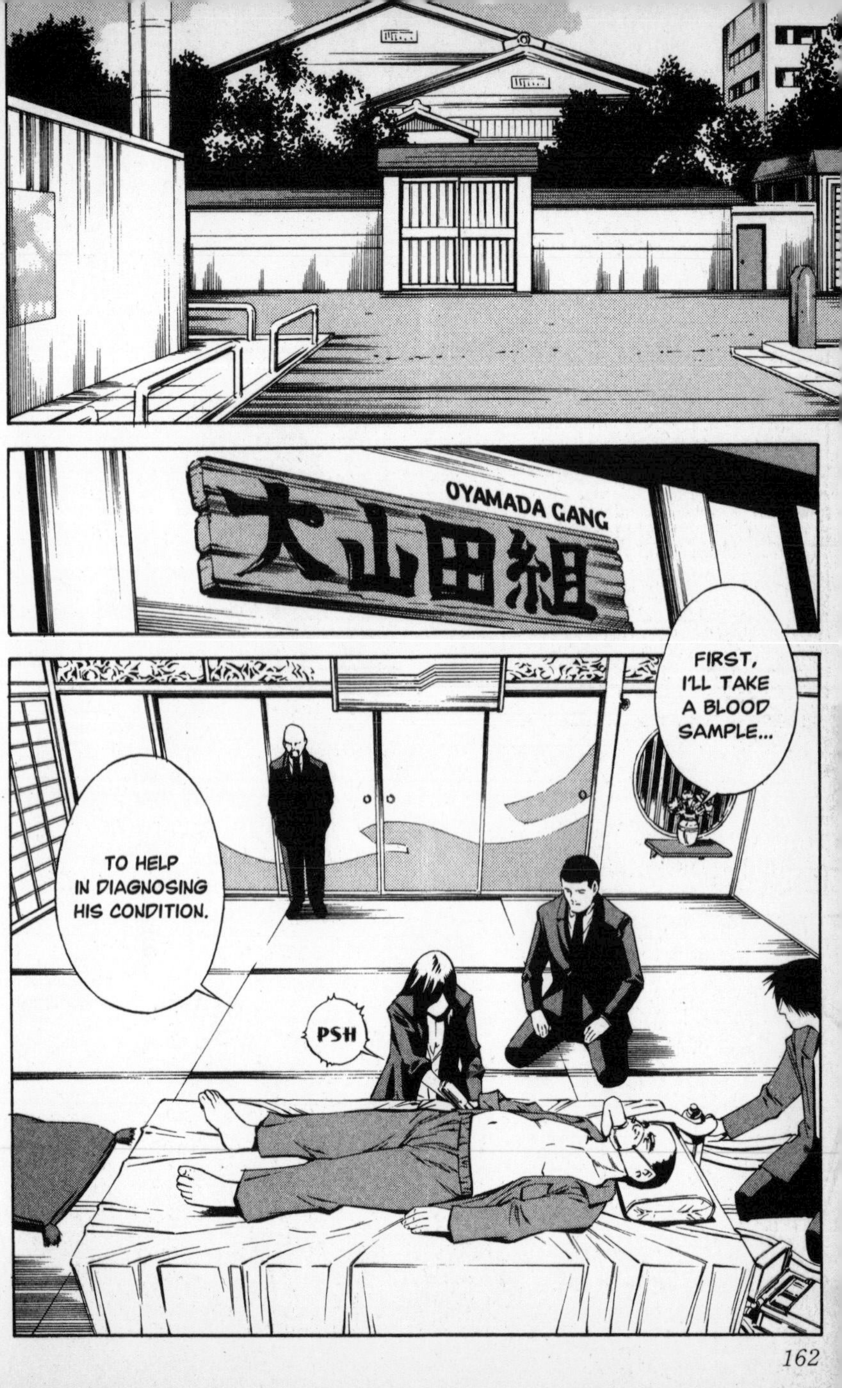

OYAMADA GANG
大山田組
FIRST, I'LL TAKE A BLOOD SAMPLE...
TO HELP IN DIAGNOSING HIS CONDITION.
PSH

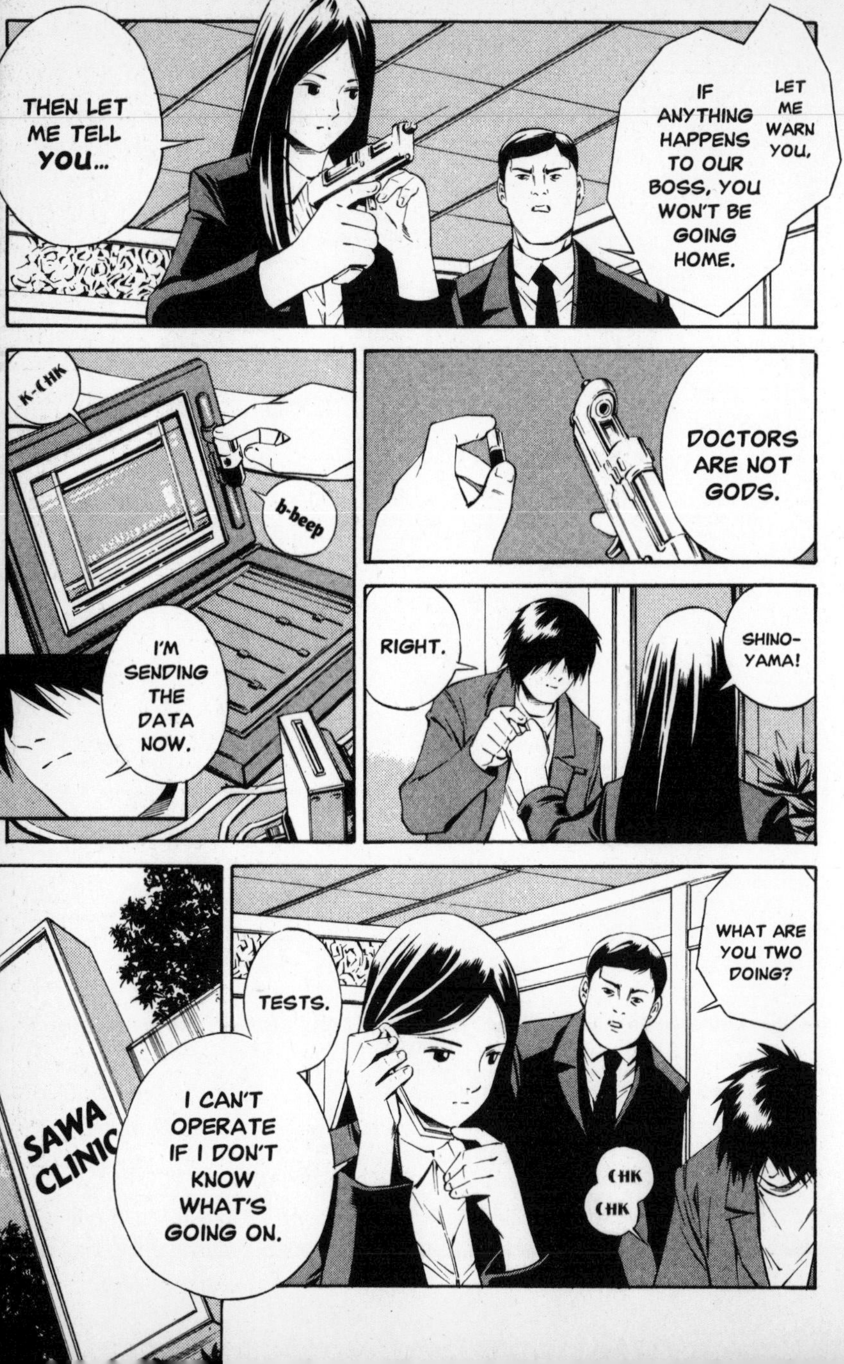
LET ME WARN YOU,
IF ANYTHING HAPPENS TO OUR BOSS, YOU WON'T BE GOING HOME.
THEN LET ME TELL **YOU**...
DOCTORS ARE NOT GODS.
SHINO-YAMA!
RIGHT.
K-CHK
b-beep
I'M SENDING THE DATA NOW.
WHAT ARE YOU TWO DOING?
TESTS.
I CAN'T OPERATE IF I DON'T KNOW WHAT'S GOING ON.
CHK
CHK
SAWA CLINIC

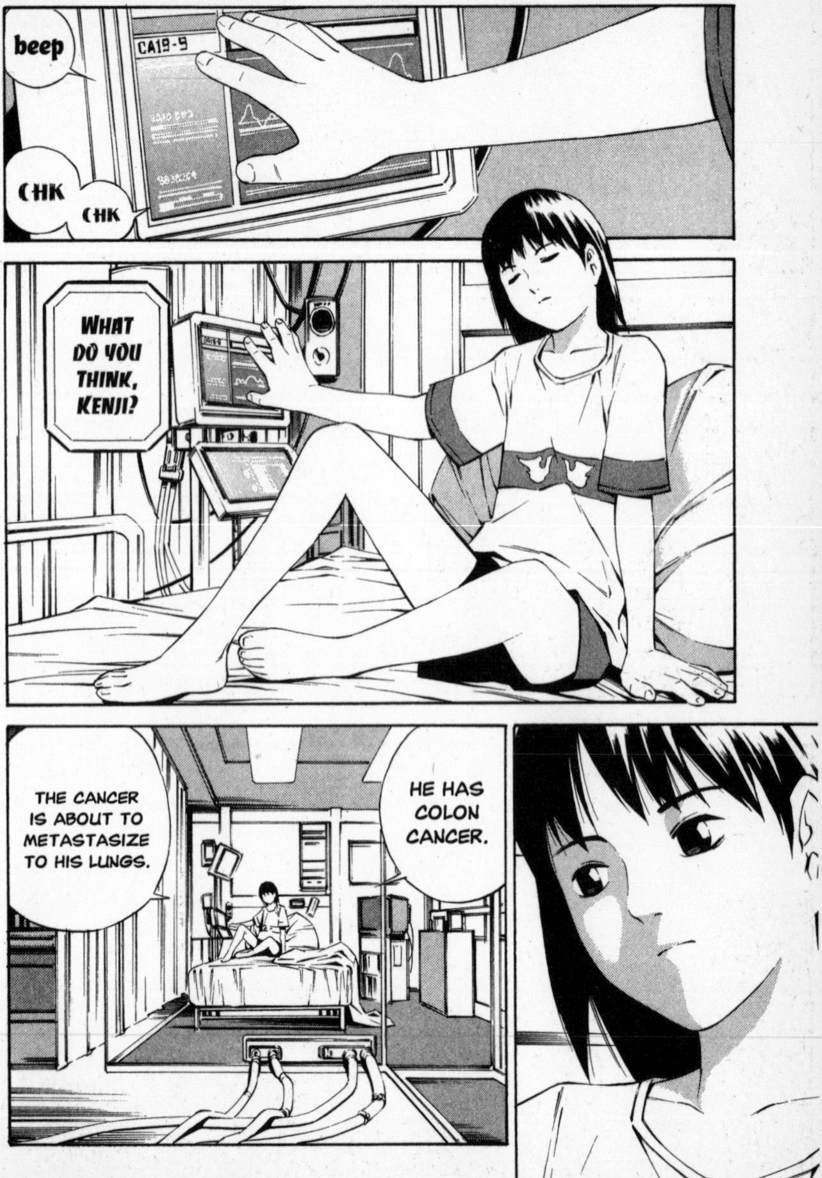

beep
CA19-9
CHK
CHK
WHAT DO YOU THINK, KENJI?
HE HAS COLON CANCER.
THE CANCER IS ABOUT TO METASTASIZE TO HIS LUNGS.

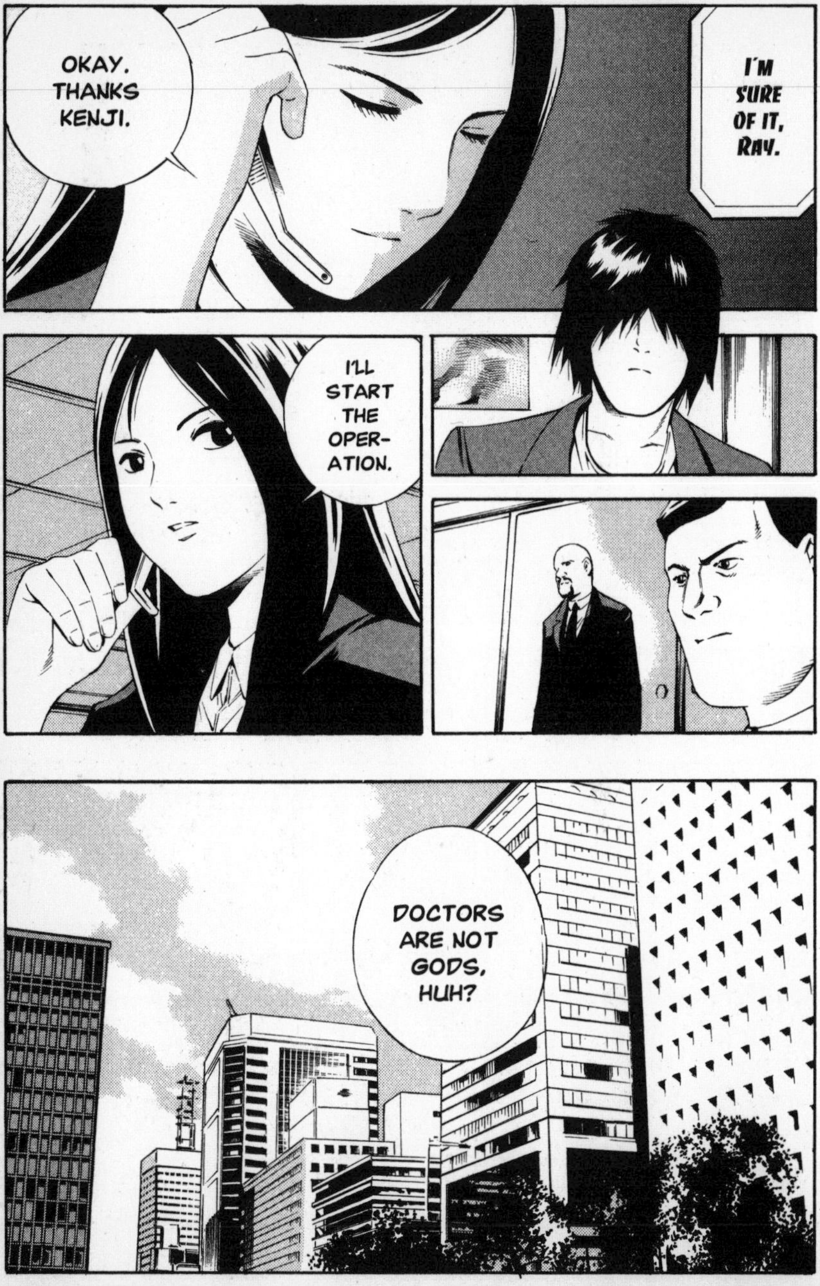
I'M SURE OF IT, RAY.
OKAY. THANKS KENJI.
I'LL START THE OPERATION.
DOCTORS ARE NOT GODS, HUH?

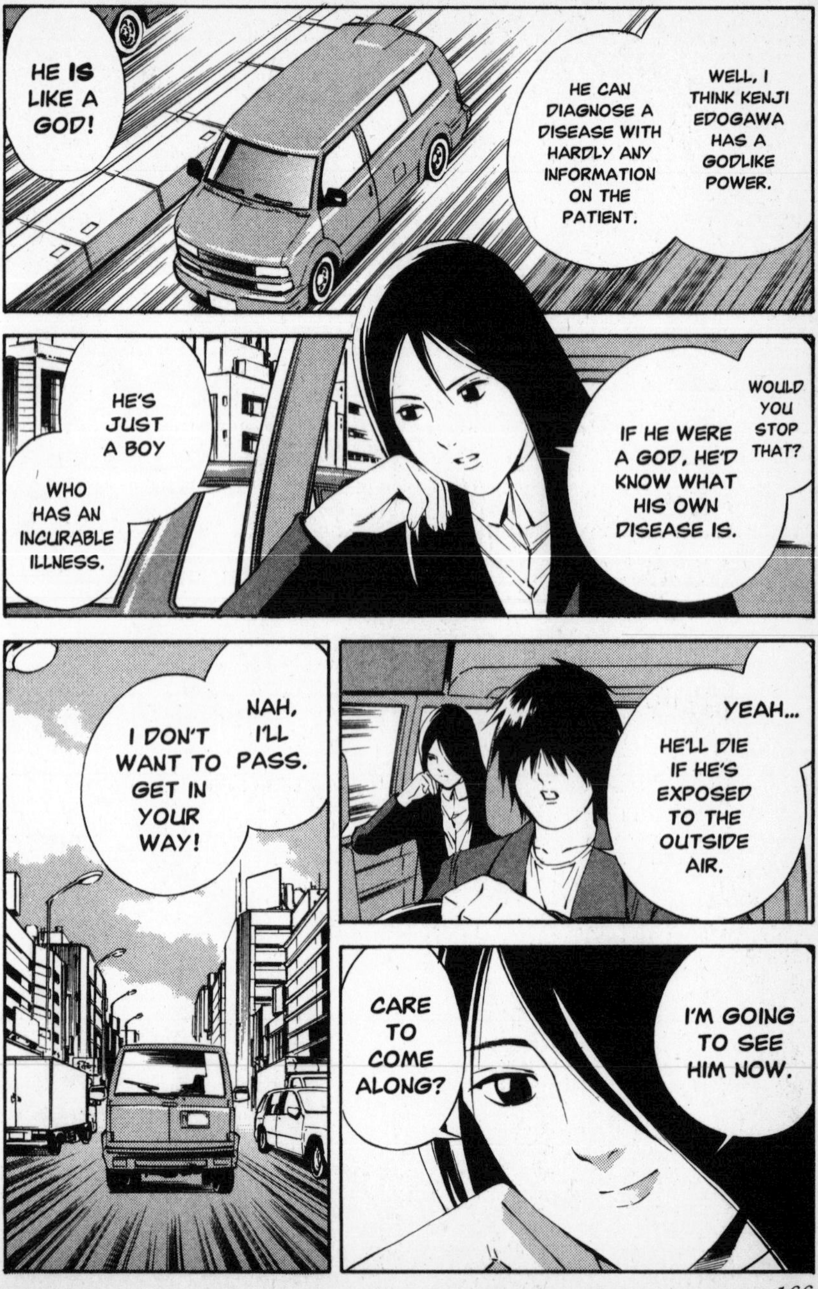
WELL, I THINK KENJI EDOGAWA HAS A GODLIKE POWER.
HE CAN DIAGNOSE A DISEASE WITH HARDLY ANY INFORMATION ON THE PATIENT.
HE **IS** LIKE A GOD!
WOULD YOU STOP THAT?
IF HE WERE A GOD, HE'D KNOW WHAT HIS OWN DISEASE IS.
HE'S JUST A BOY
WHO HAS AN INCURABLE ILLNESS.
YEAH...
HE'LL DIE IF HE'S EXPOSED TO THE OUTSIDE AIR.
I'M GOING TO SEE HIM NOW.
CARE TO COME ALONG?
NAH, I'LL PASS.
I DON'T WANT TO GET IN YOUR WAY!

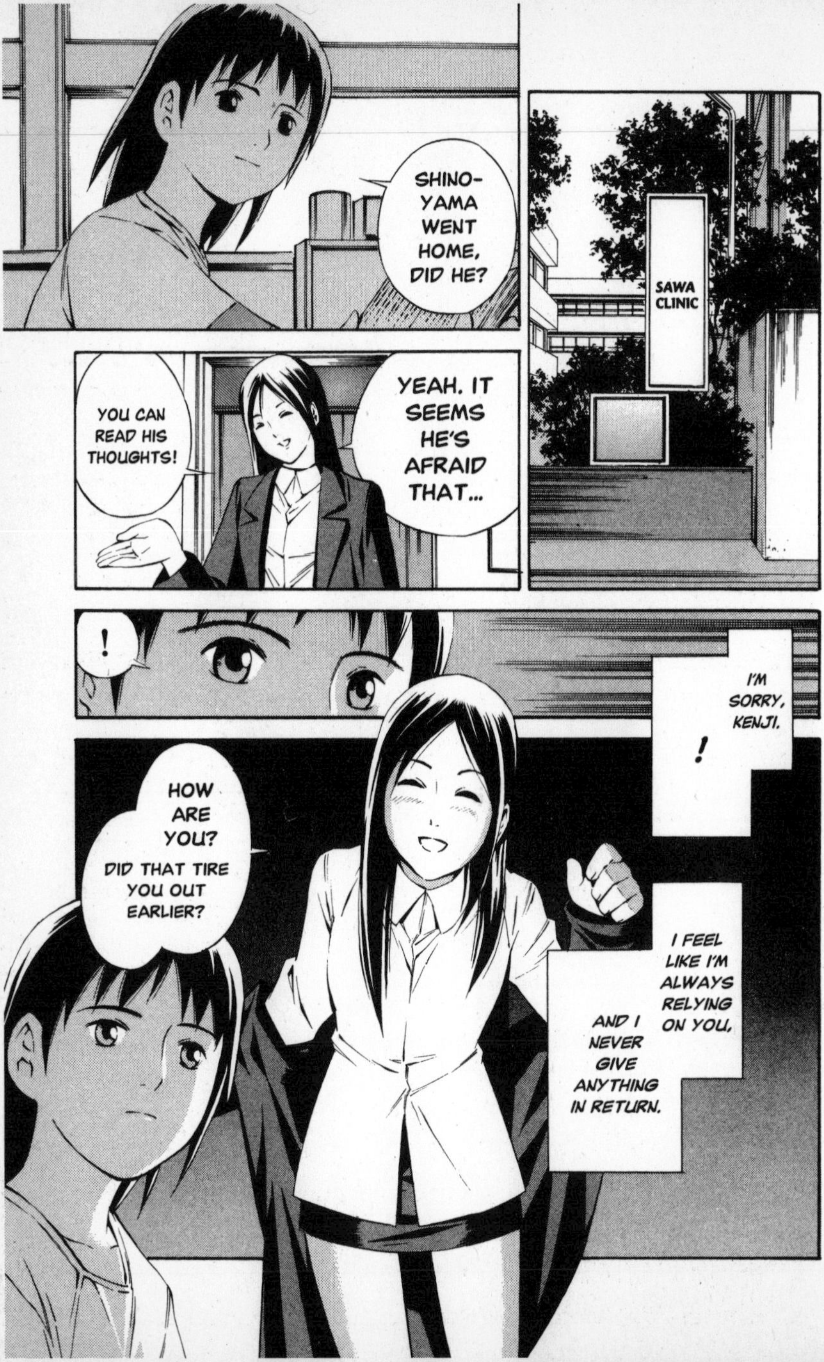
SAWA CLINIC
SHINO-YAMA WENT HOME, DID HE?
YEAH. IT SEEMS HE'S AFRAID THAT...
YOU CAN READ HIS THOUGHTS!
!
I'M SORRY, KENJI.
!
HOW ARE YOU?
DID THAT TIRE YOU OUT EARLIER?
I FEEL LIKE I'M ALWAYS RELYING ON YOU,
AND I NEVER GIVE ANYTHING IN RETURN.

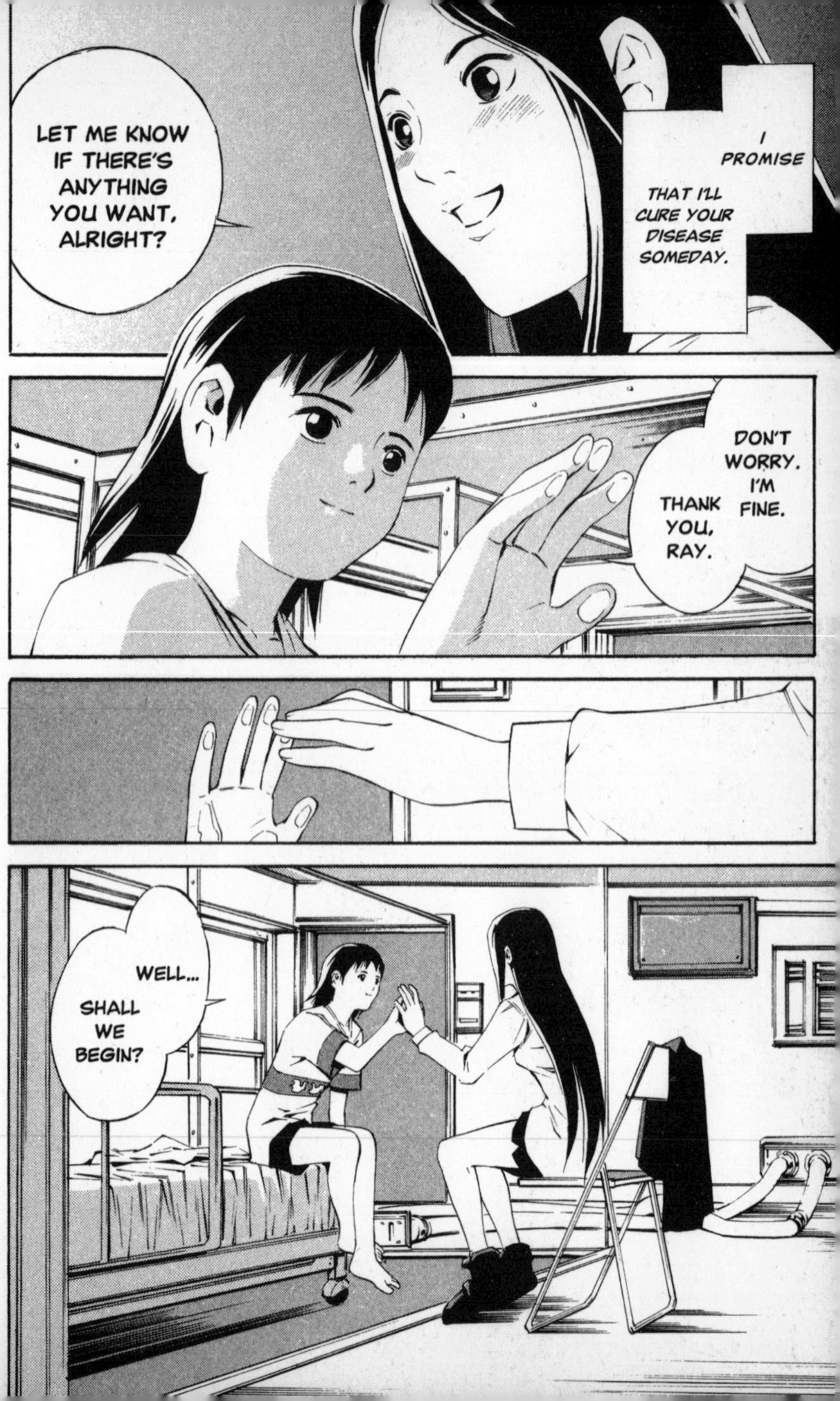
I PROMISE
THAT I'LL CURE YOUR DISEASE SOMEDAY.
LET ME KNOW IF THERE'S ANYTHING YOU WANT, ALRIGHT?
DON'T WORRY. I'M FINE.
THANK YOU, RAY.
WELL... SHALL WE BEGIN?

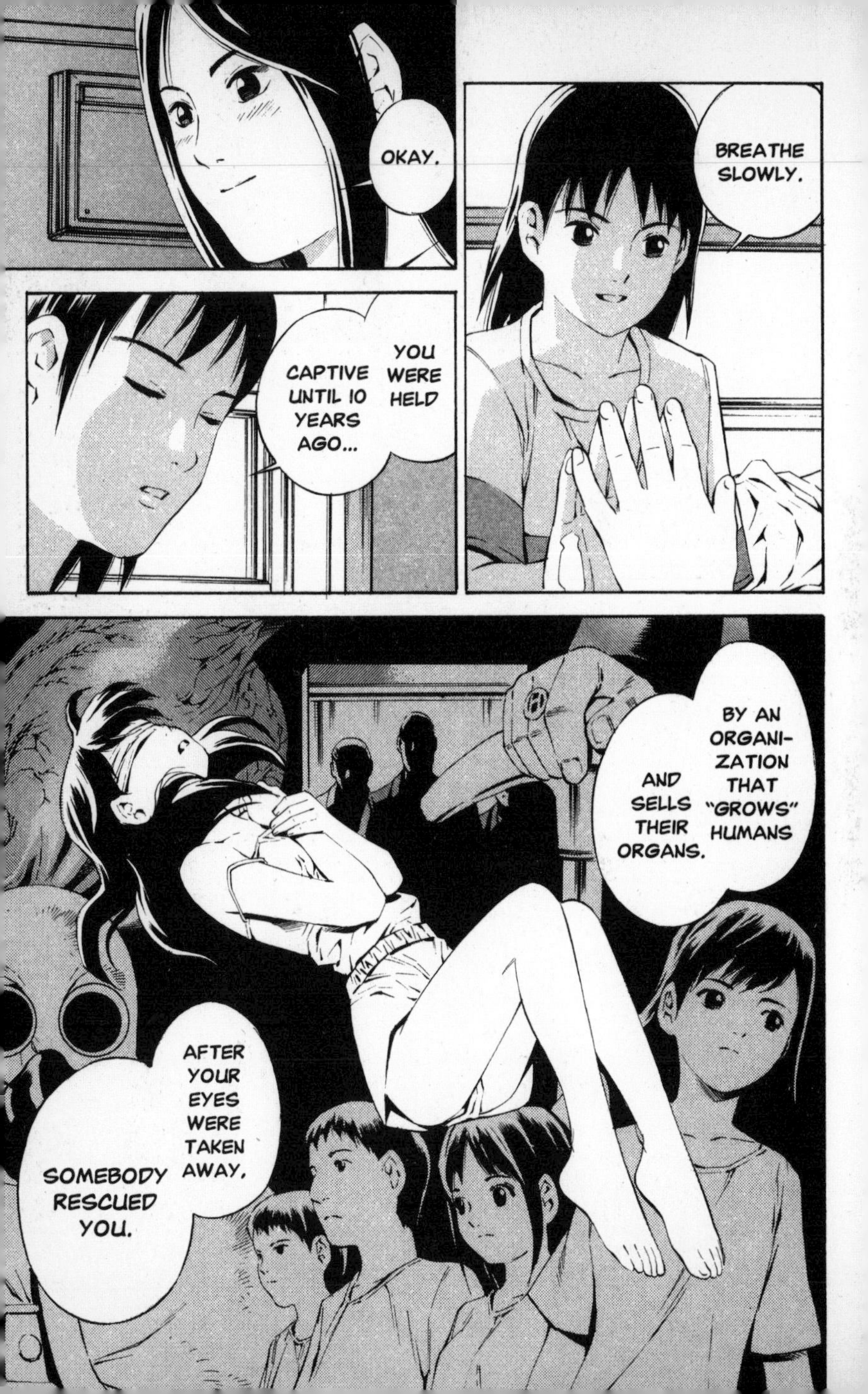
BREATHE SLOWLY.
OKAY.
YOU WERE HELD CAPTIVE UNTIL 10 YEARS AGO...
BY AN ORGANI-ZATION THAT "GROWS" HUMANS AND SELLS THEIR ORGANS.
AFTER YOUR EYES WERE TAKEN AWAY, SOMEBODY RESCUED YOU.

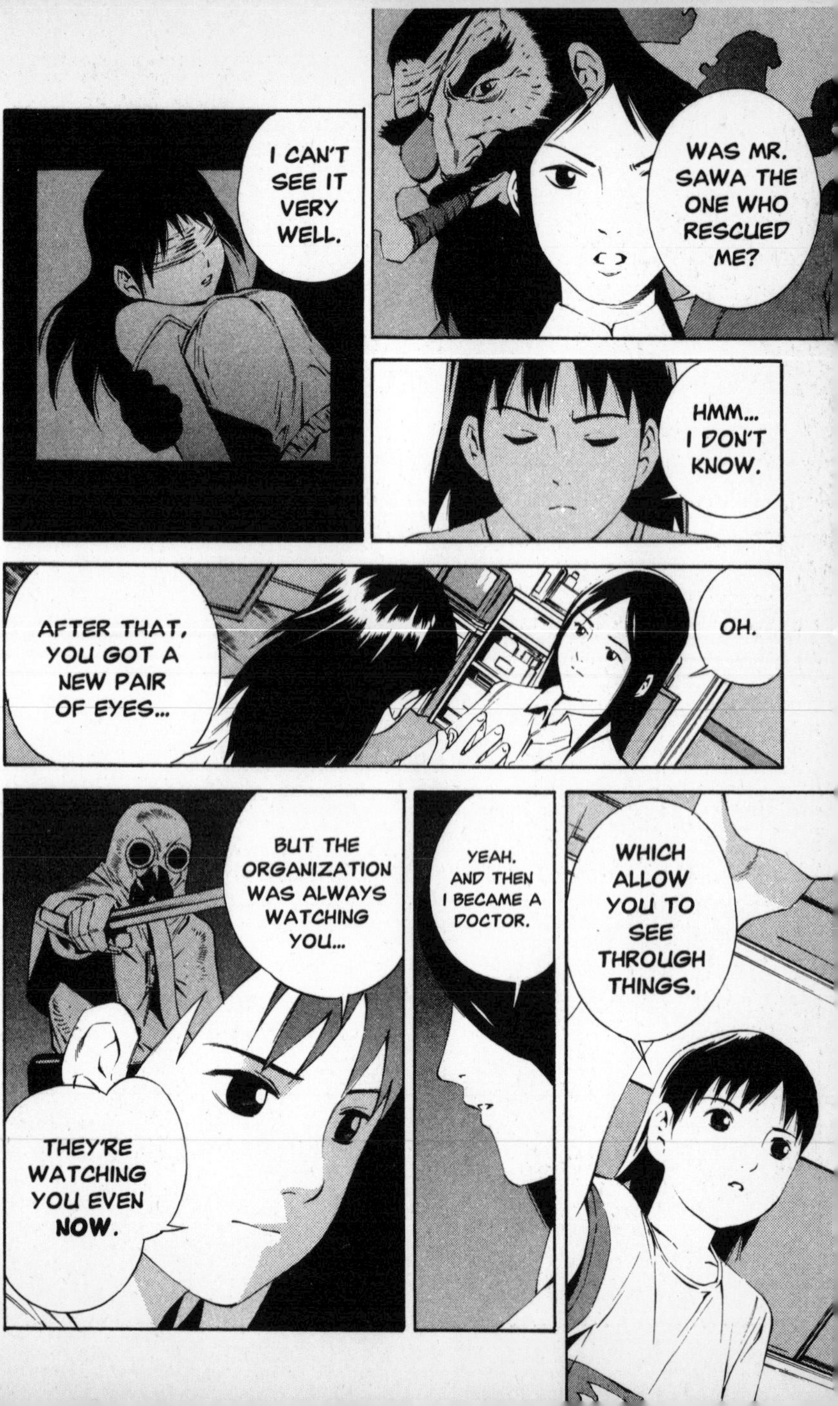
WAS MR. SAWA THE ONE WHO RESCUED ME?
HMM... I DON'T KNOW.
I CAN'T SEE IT VERY WELL.
OH.
AFTER THAT, YOU GOT A NEW PAIR OF EYES...
WHICH ALLOW YOU TO SEE THROUGH THINGS.
YEAH. AND THEN I BECAME A DOCTOR.
BUT THE ORGANIZATION WAS ALWAYS WATCHING YOU...
THEY'RE WATCHING YOU EVEN NOW.

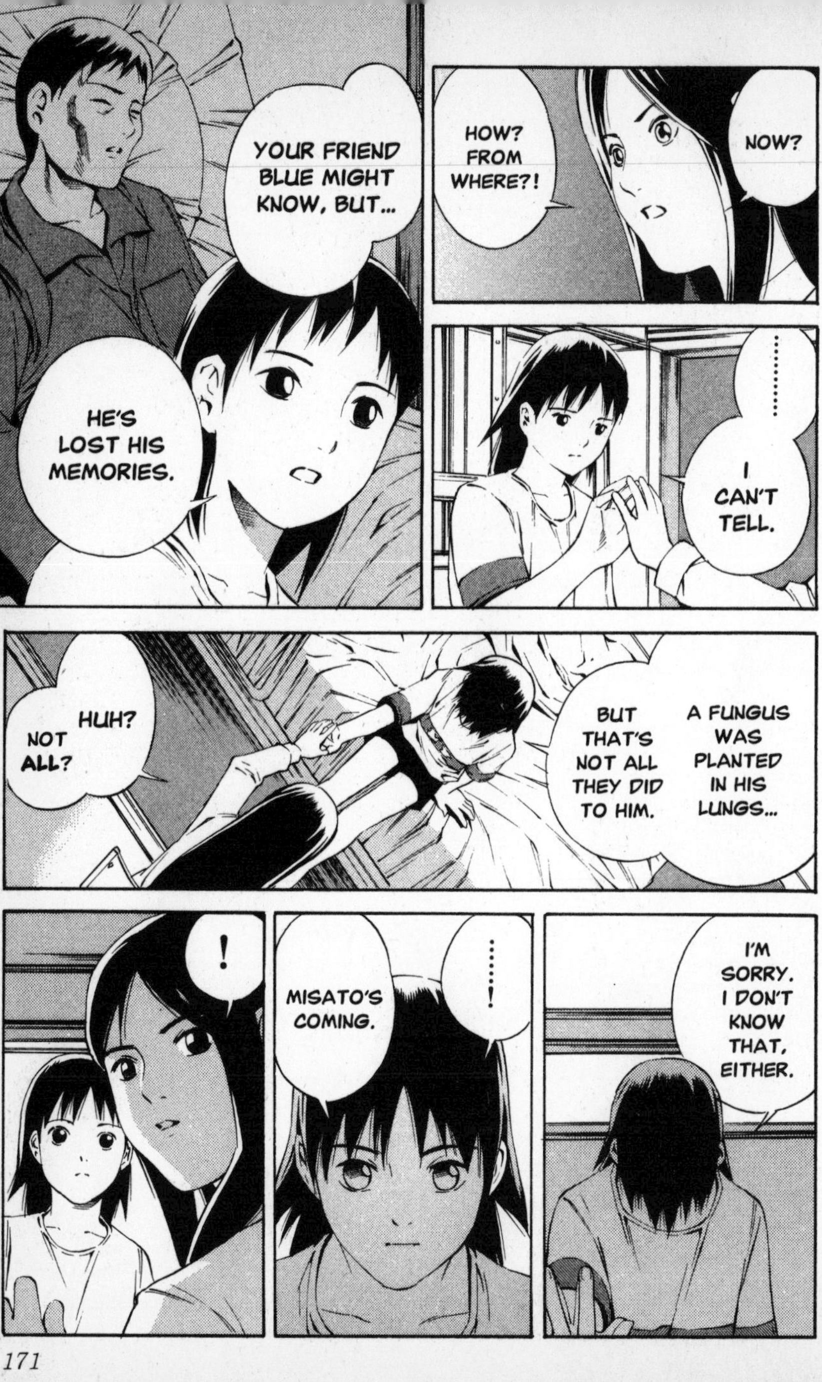
NOW?
HOW? FROM WHERE?!
...... I CAN'T TELL.
YOUR FRIEND BLUE MIGHT KNOW, BUT...
HE'S LOST HIS MEMORIES.
A FUNGUS WAS PLANTED IN HIS LUNGS...
BUT THAT'S NOT ALL THEY DID TO HIM.
HUH? NOT **ALL**?
I'M SORRY. I DON'T KNOW THAT, EITHER.
......!
MISATO'S COMING.
!

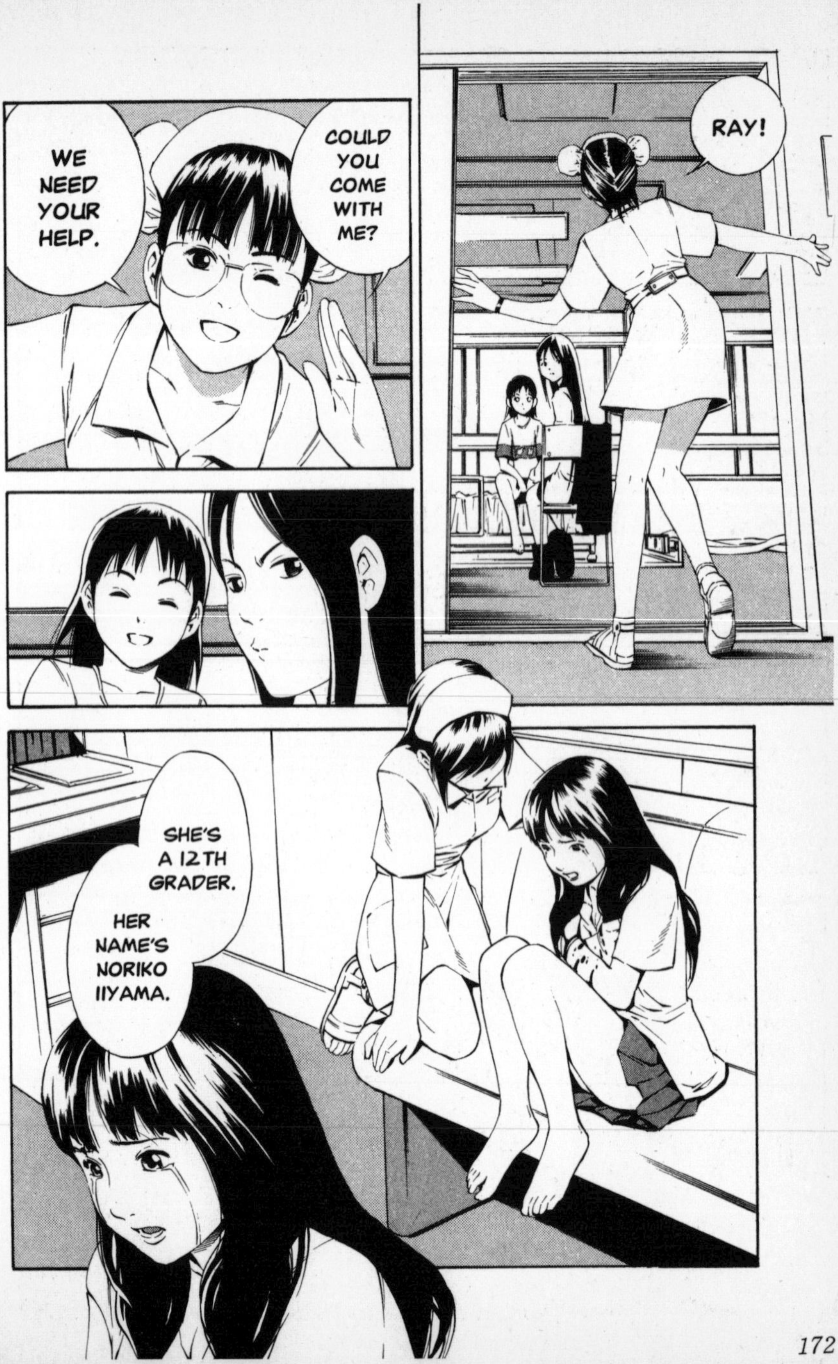
RAY!
COULD YOU COME WITH ME?
WE NEED YOUR HELP.
SHE'S A 12TH GRADER.
HER NAME'S NORIKO IIYAMA.

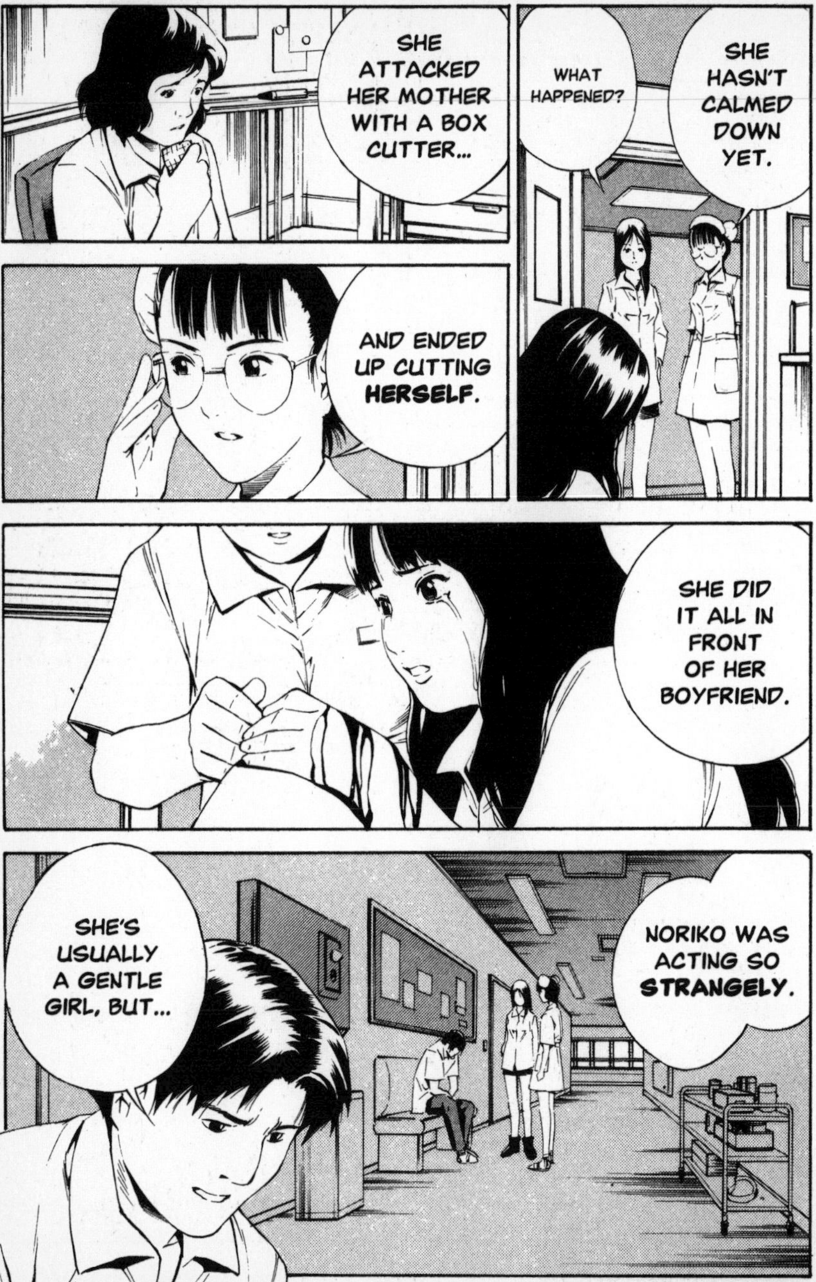
WHAT HAPPENED?
SHE HASN'T CALMED DOWN YET.
SHE ATTACKED HER MOTHER WITH A BOX CUTTER...
AND ENDED UP CUTTING HERSELF.
SHE DID IT ALL IN FRONT OF HER BOYFRIEND.
NORIKO WAS ACTING SO STRANGELY.
SHE'S USUALLY A GENTLE GIRL, BUT...

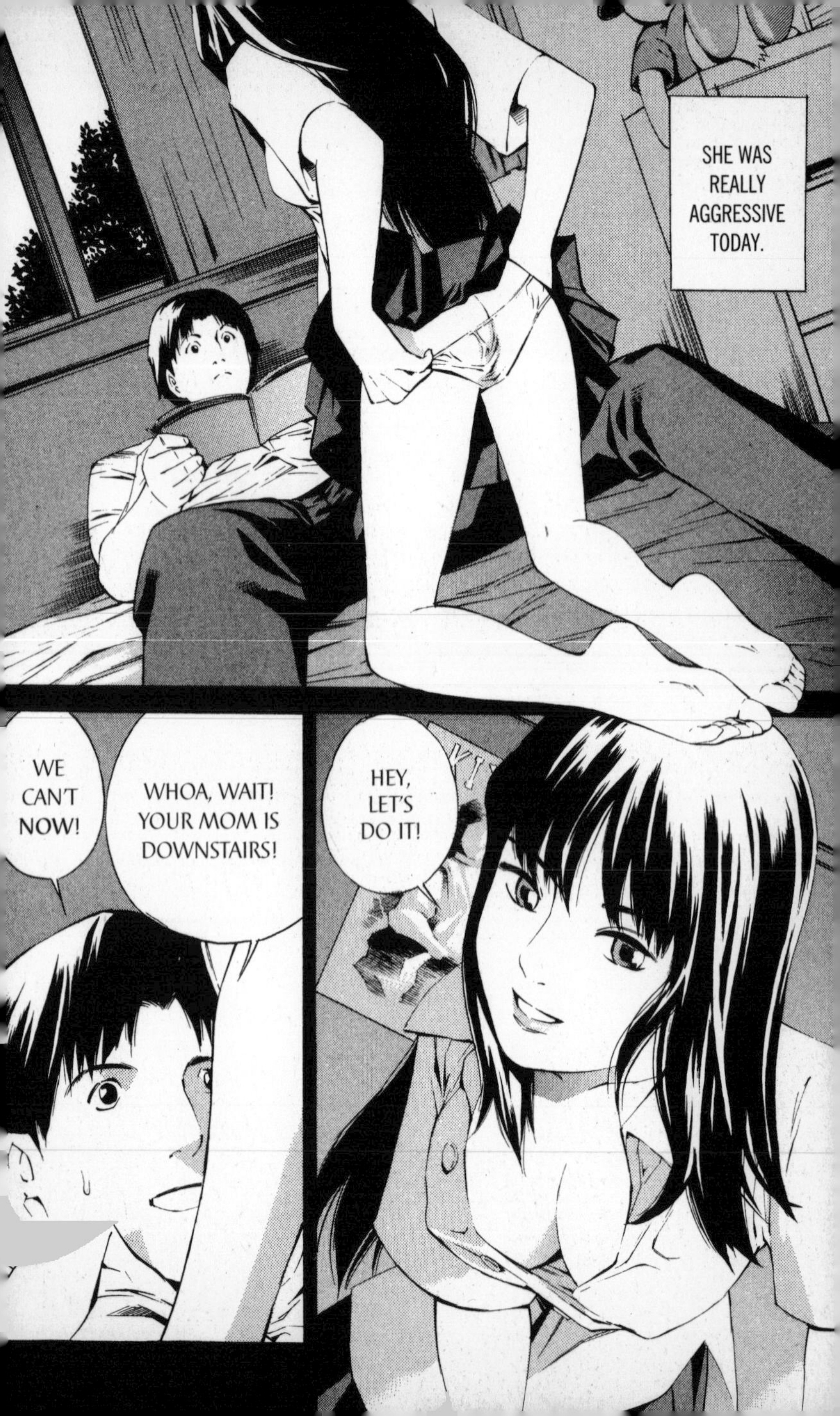
SHE WAS REALLY AGGRESSIVE TODAY.
HEY, LET'S DO IT!
WHOA, WAIT! YOUR MOM IS DOWNSTAIRS!
WE CAN'T NOW!

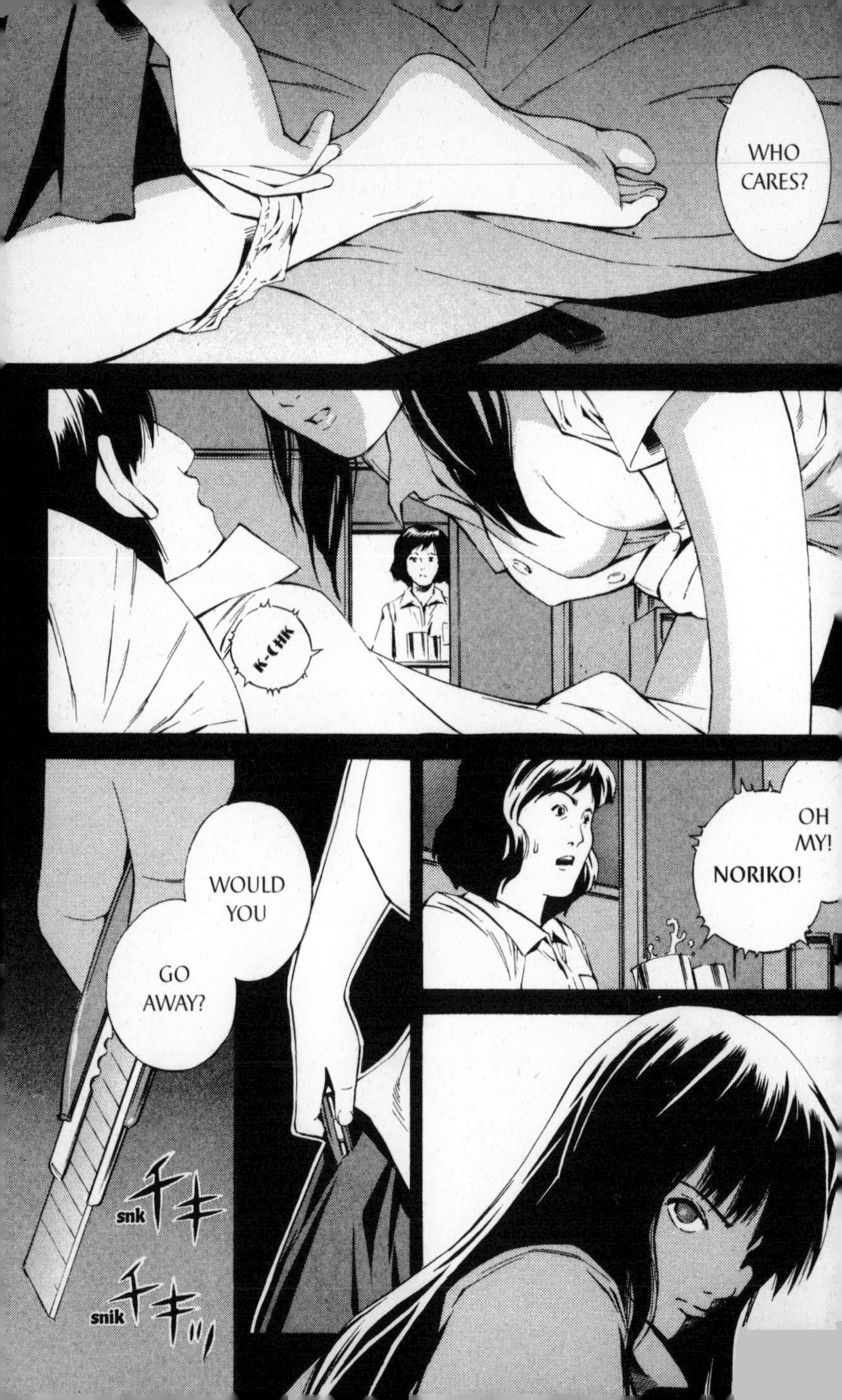
WHO CARES?
K-CHK
OH MY! NORIKO!
WOULD YOU GO AWAY?
snk チキ
snik チキッ

WELL, SHE'S AT THAT AWKWARD AGE...

I DIS-INFECTED THE CUT, RAY.

THAT WOUND NEEDS STITCHES.

I'M GIVING YOU AN ANESTHETIC, OKAY?

CALM DOWN, NORIKO!

N-NO!!

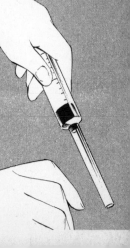

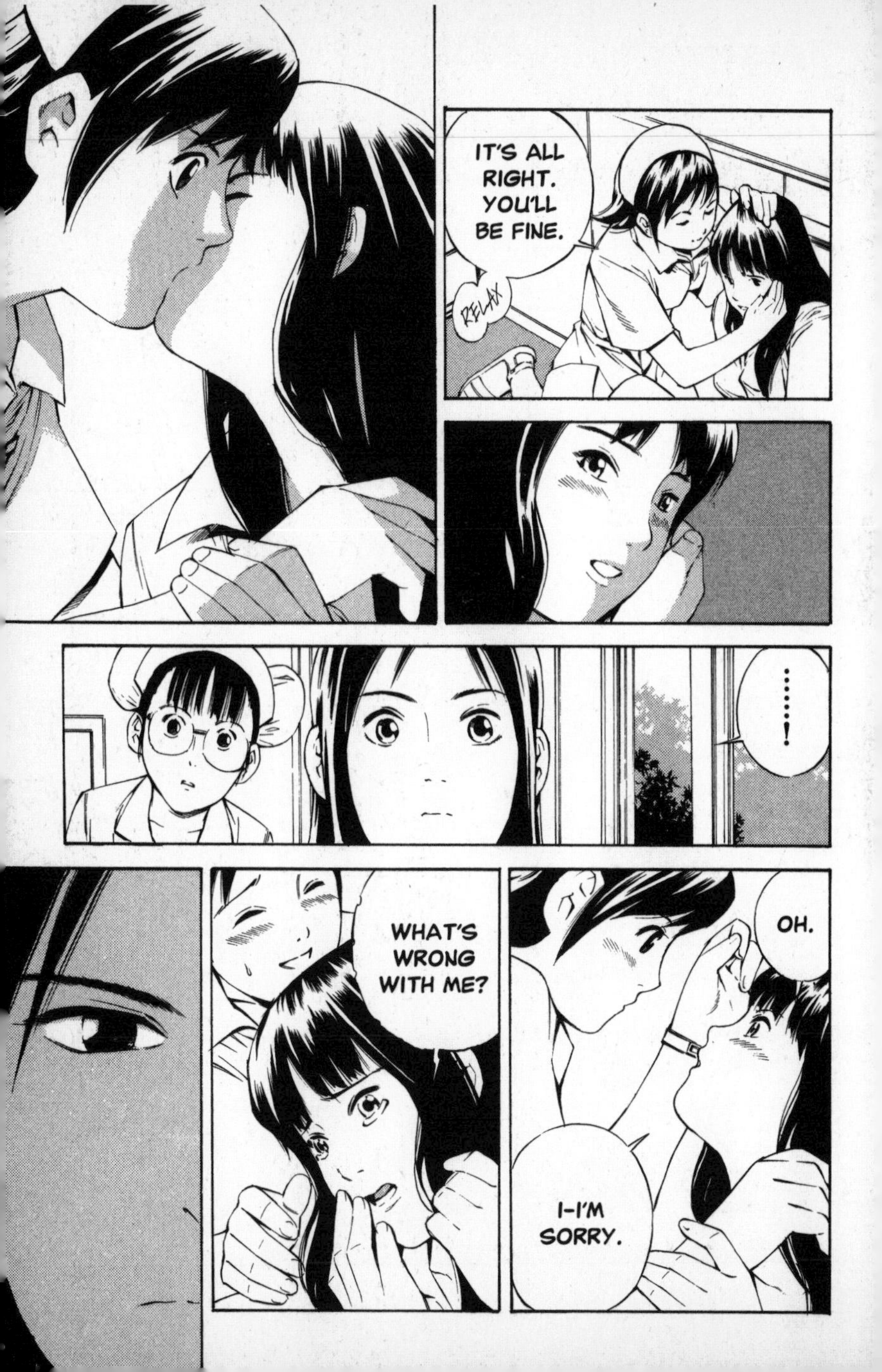
IT'S ALL RIGHT. YOU'LL BE FINE.
RELAX
......!
OH.
I-I'M SORRY.
WHAT'S WRONG WITH ME?

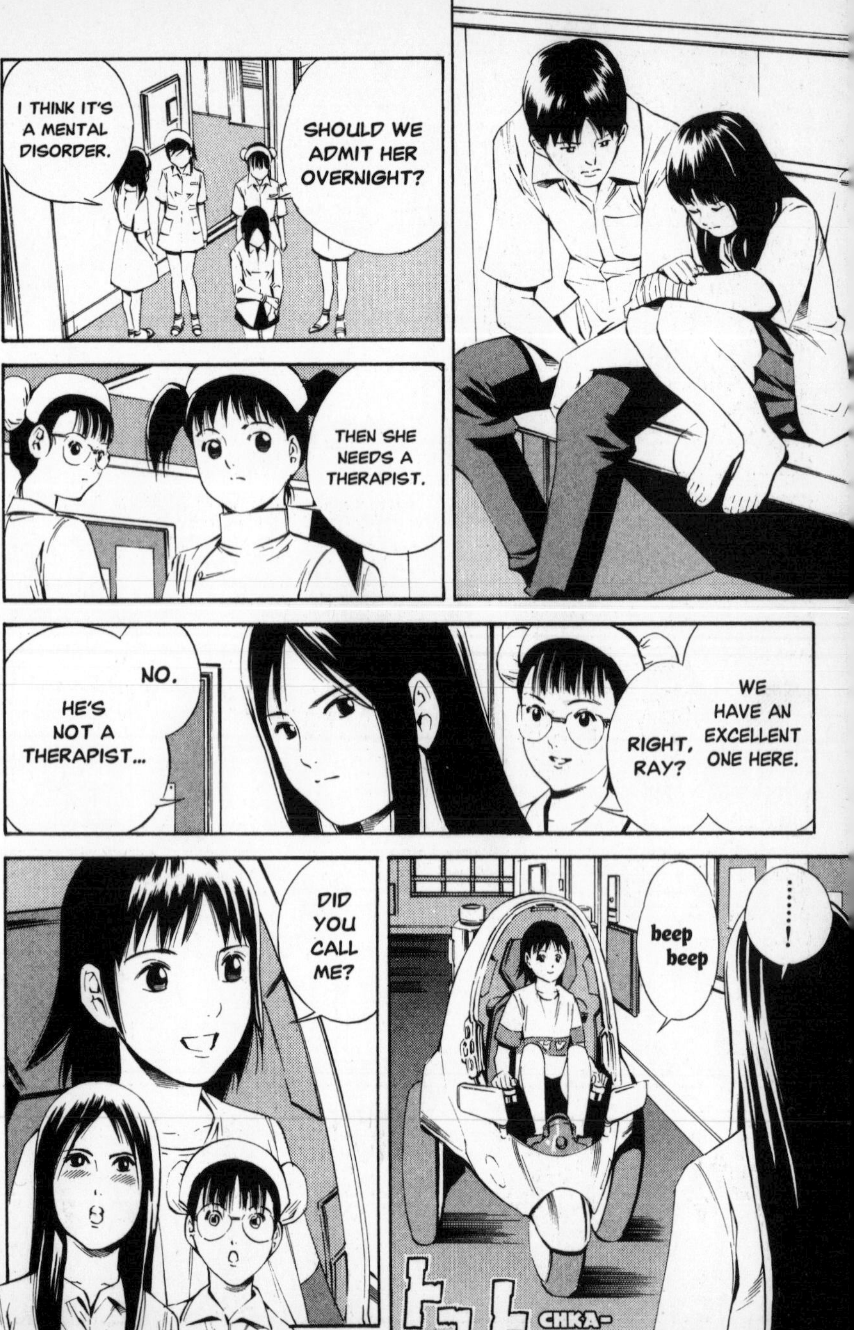

SHOULD WE ADMIT HER OVERNIGHT?
I THINK IT'S A MENTAL DISORDER.
THEN SHE NEEDS A THERAPIST.
WE HAVE AN EXCELLENT ONE HERE.
RIGHT, RAY?
NO.
HE'S NOT A THERAPIST...
......!
beep beep
CHKA-CHKA
DID YOU CALL ME?

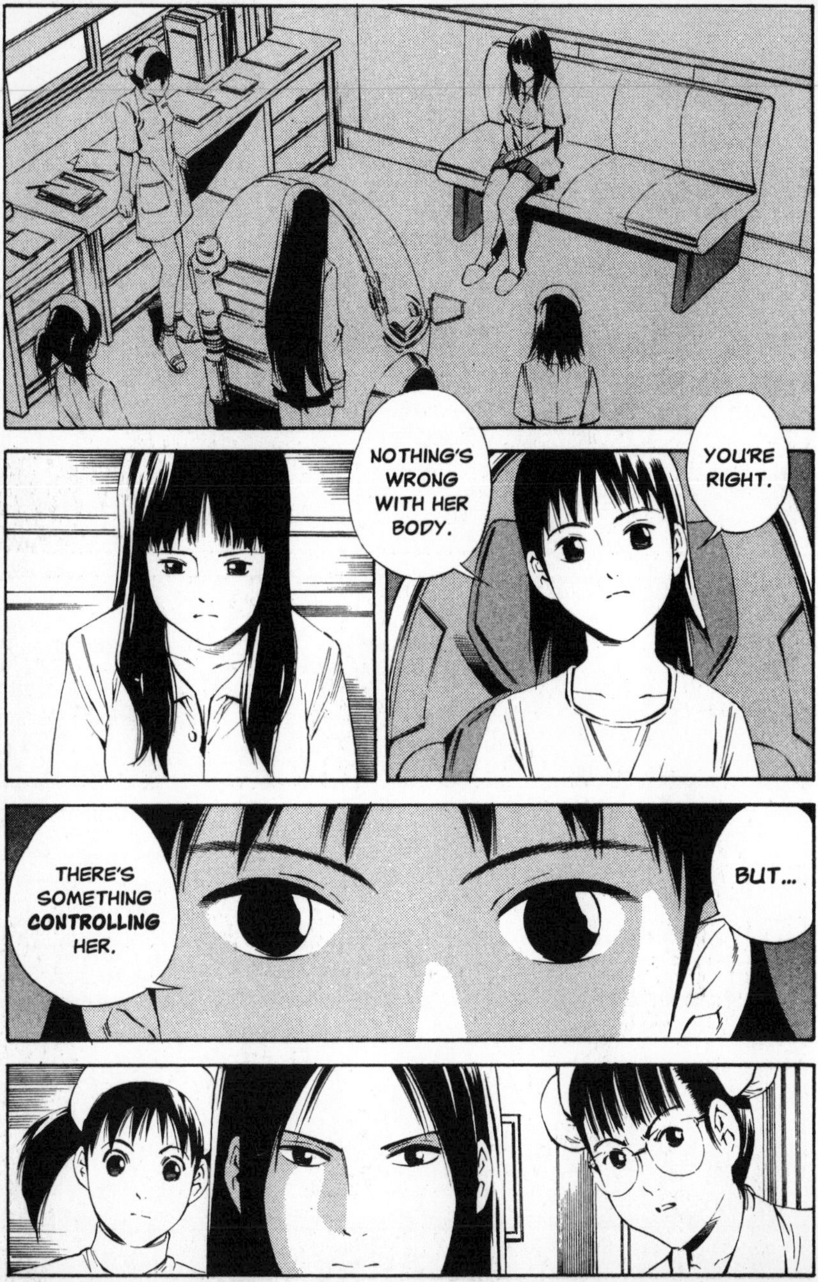
YOU'RE RIGHT.
NOTHING'S WRONG WITH HER BODY.
BUT...
THERE'S SOMETHING CONTROLLING HER.

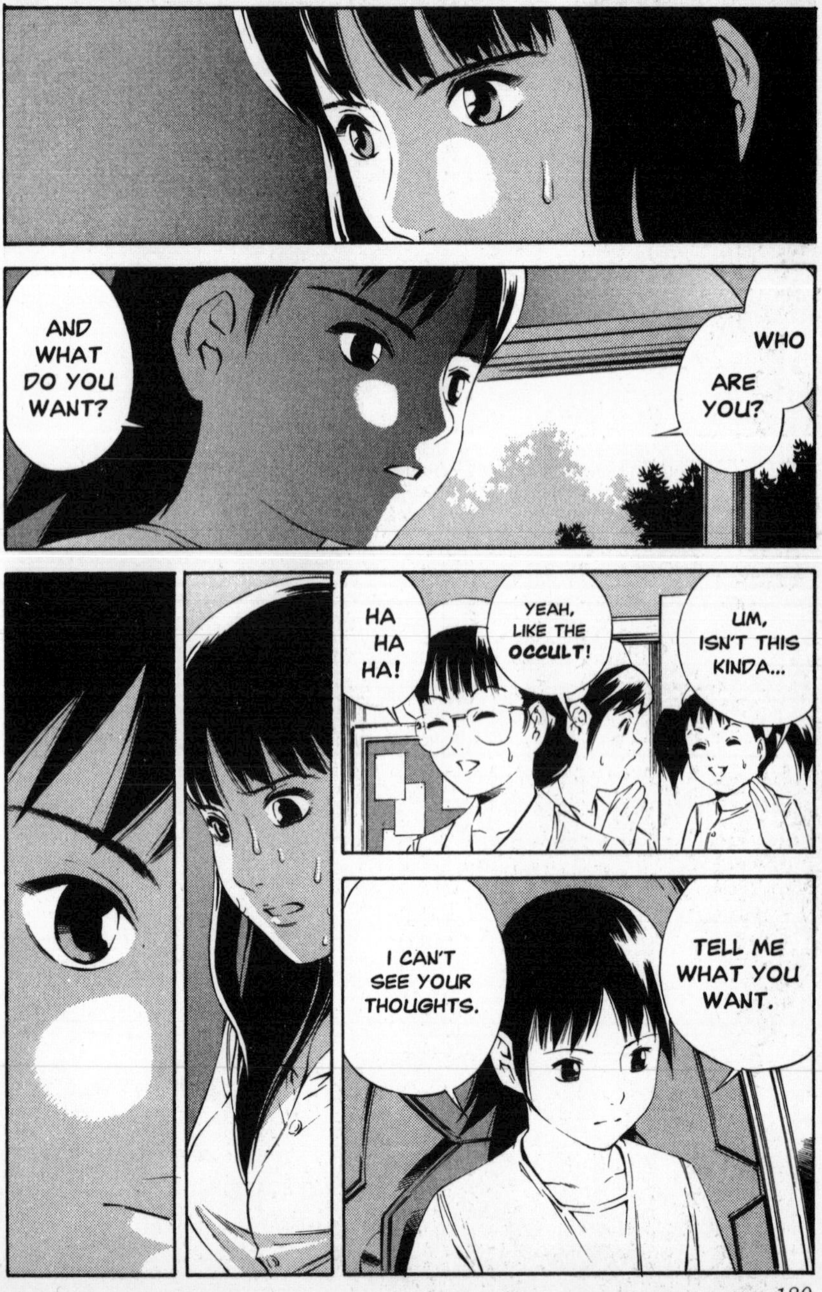
WHO ARE YOU?
AND WHAT DO YOU WANT?
UM, ISN'T THIS KINDA...
YEAH, LIKE THE OCCULT!
HA HA HA!
TELL ME WHAT YOU WANT.
I CAN'T SEE YOUR THOUGHTS.

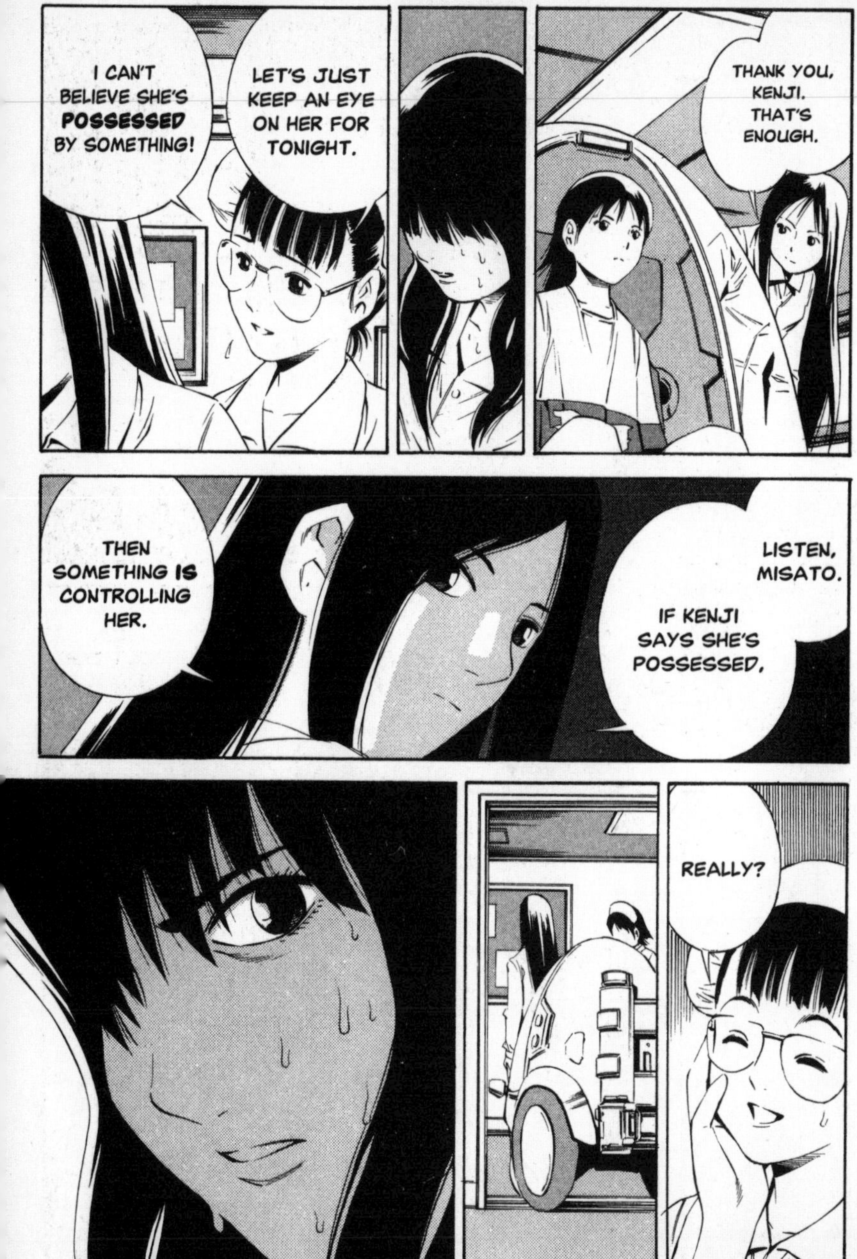

THANK YOU, KENJI. THAT'S ENOUGH.
LET'S JUST KEEP AN EYE ON HER FOR TONIGHT.
I CAN'T BELIEVE SHE'S **POSSESSED** BY SOMETHING!
LISTEN, MISATO.
IF KENJI SAYS SHE'S POSSESSED,
THEN SOMETHING **IS** CONTROLLING HER.
REALLY?

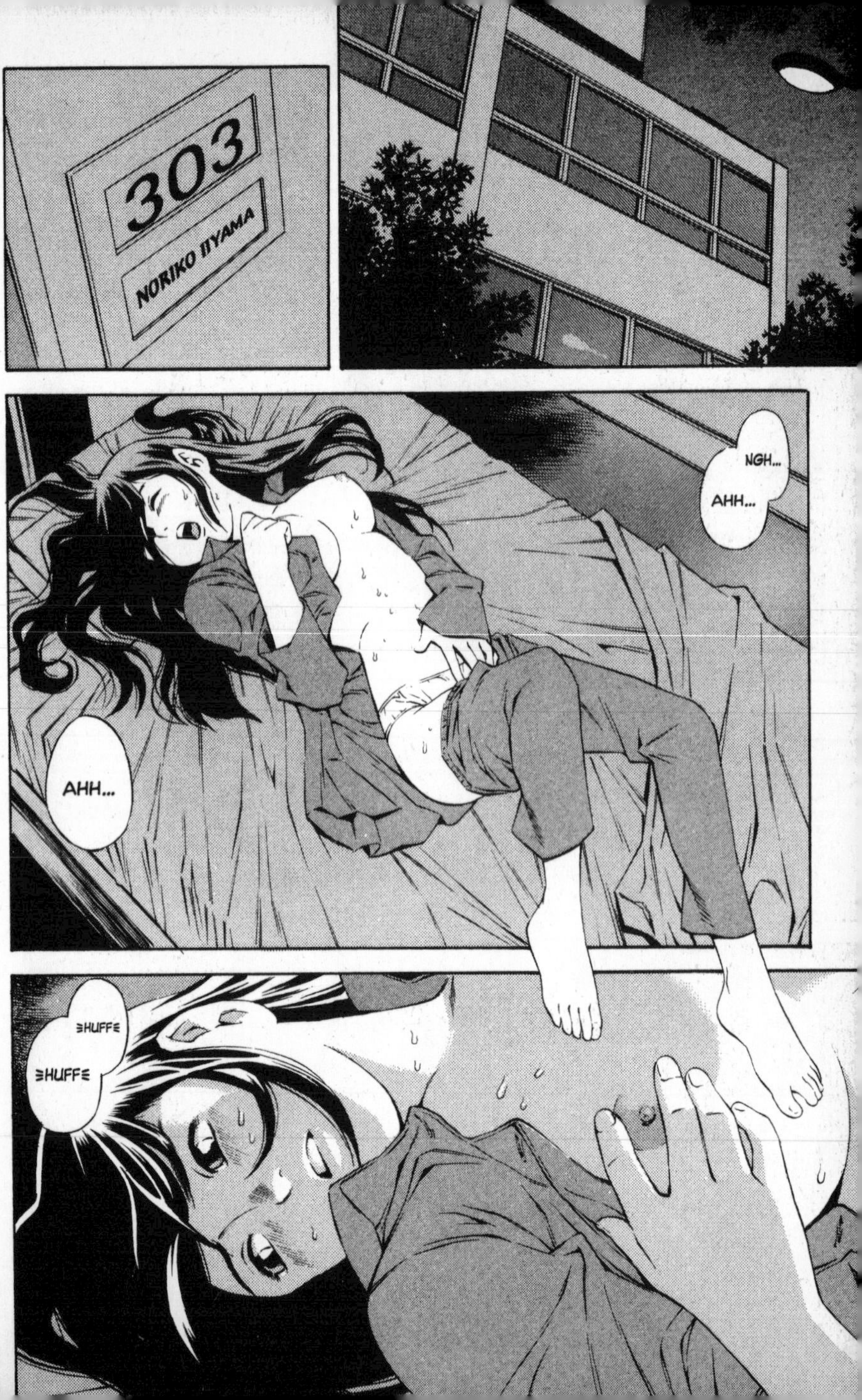
303
NORIKO IIYAMA
NGH...
AHH...
AHH...
≡HUFF≡
≡HUFF≡

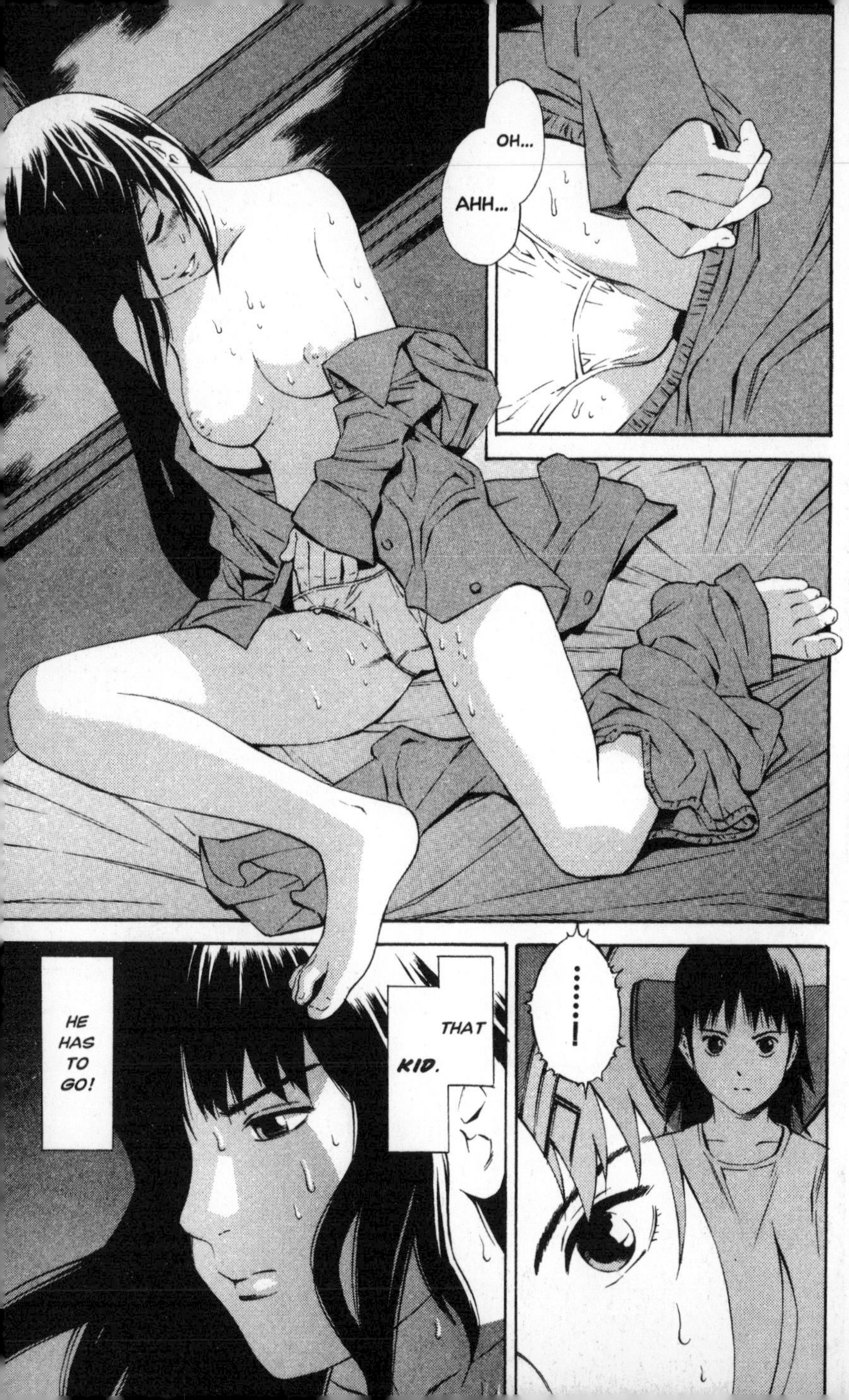
OH...
AHH...
......!
THAT KID.
HE HAS TO GO!

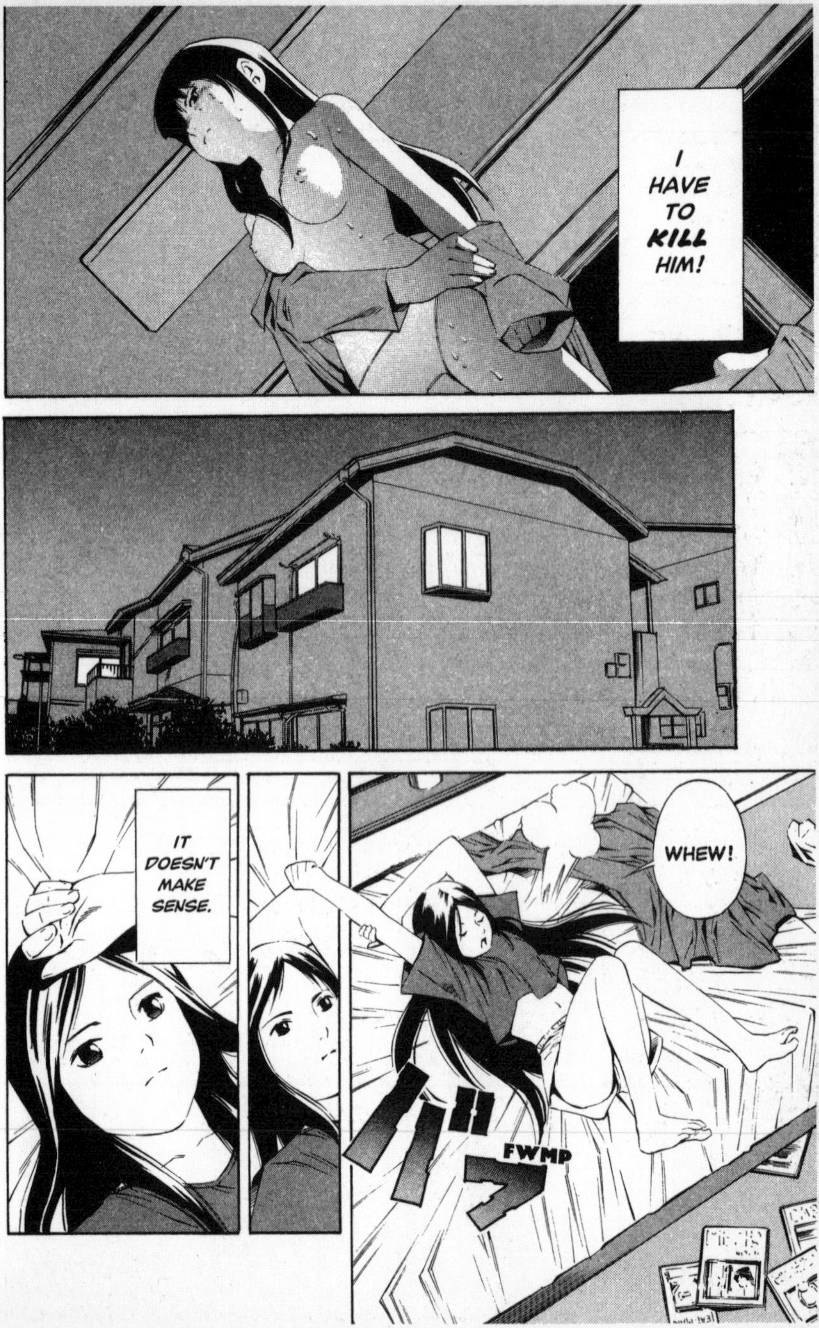
I HAVE TO KILL HIM!
WHEW!
FWMP
IT DOESN'T MAKE SENSE.

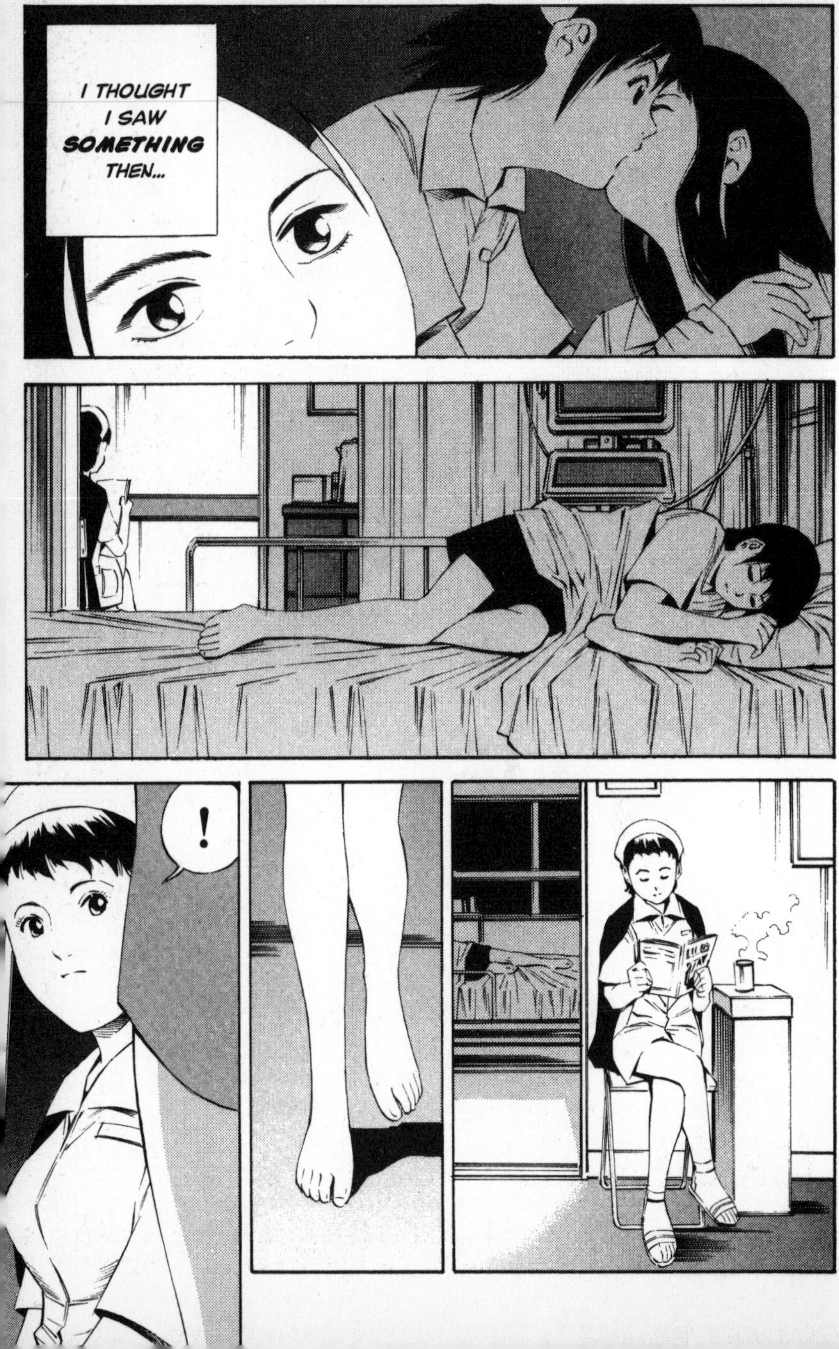
I THOUGHT I SAW SOMETHING THEN...
!

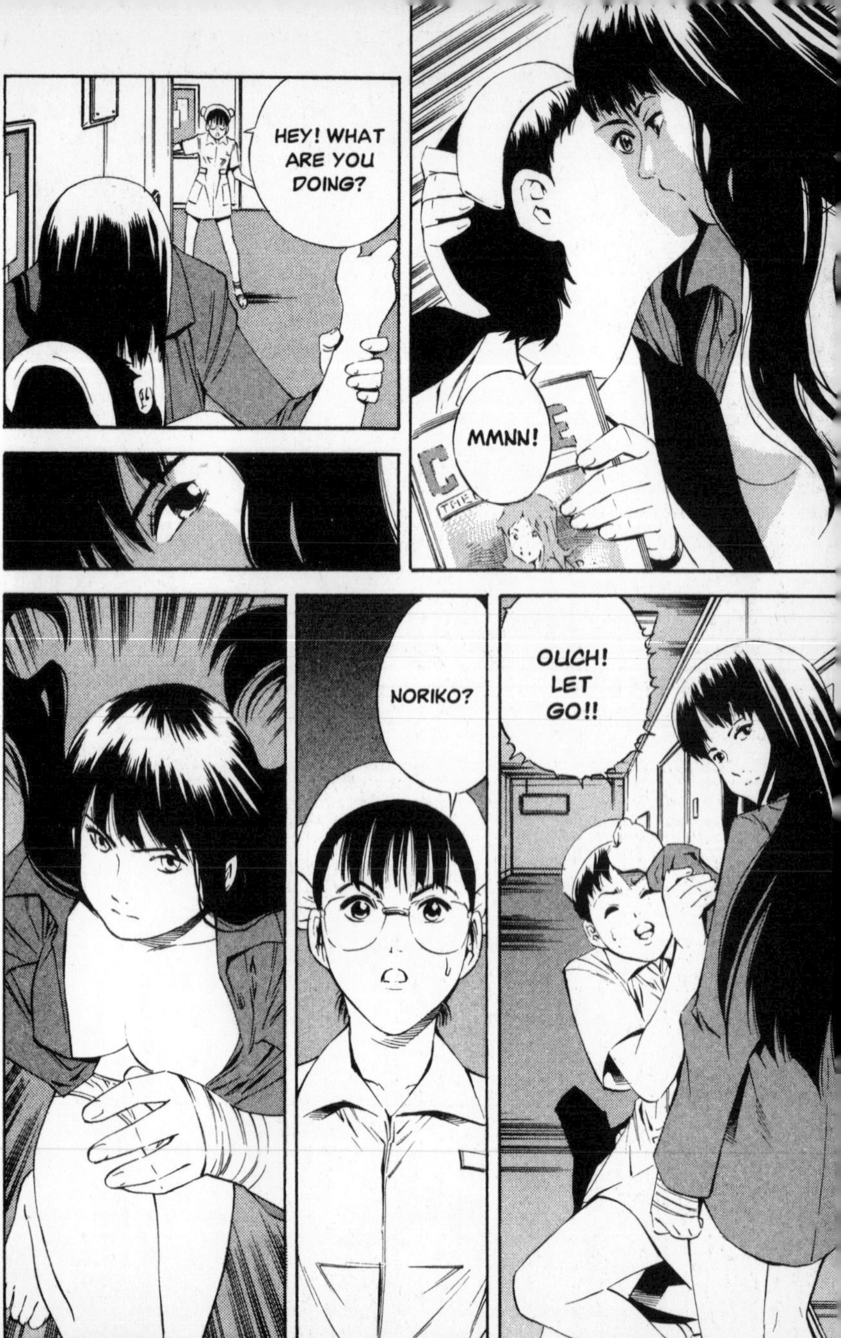
MMNN!
HEY! WHAT ARE YOU DOING?
OUCH! LET GO!!
NORIKO?

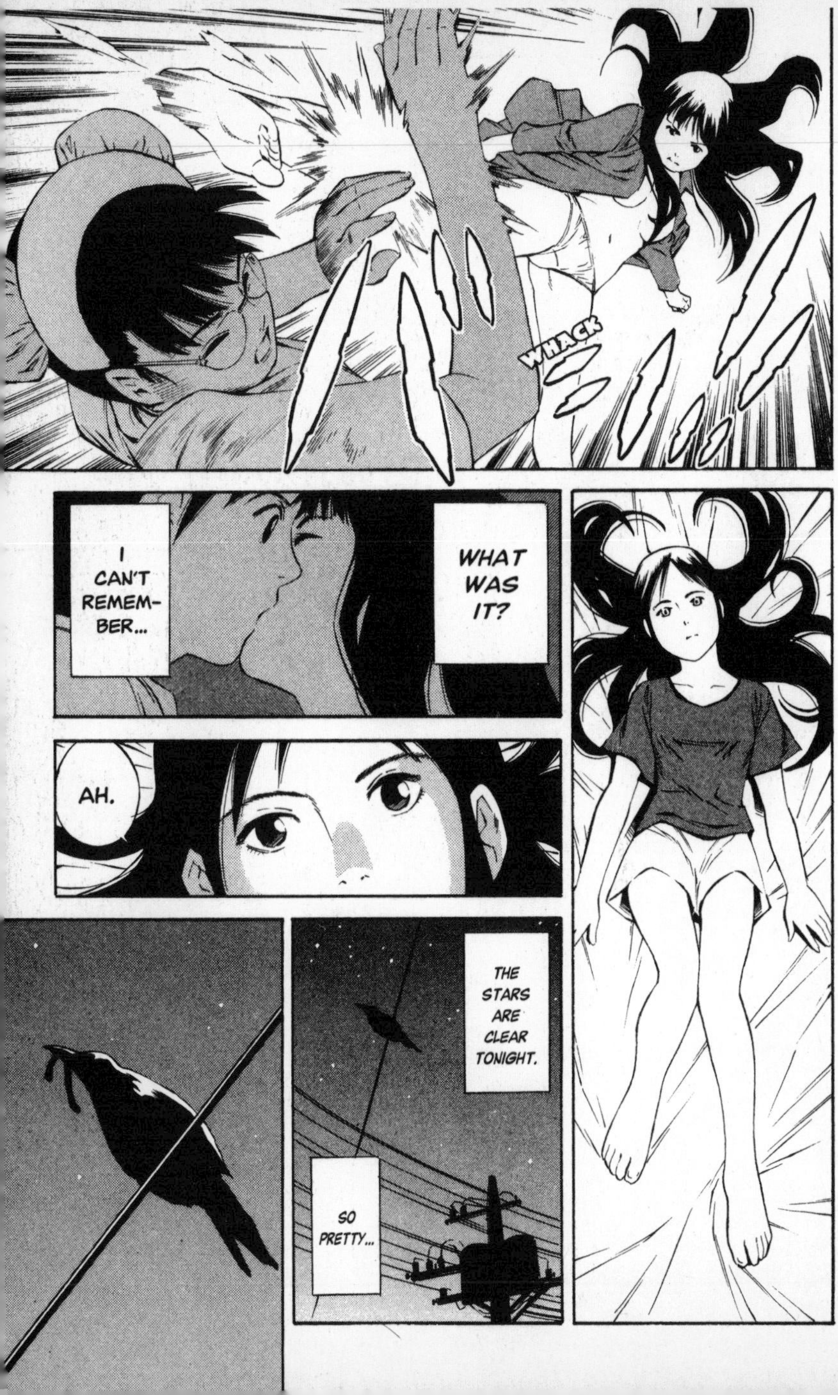
WHACK
WHAT WAS IT?
I CAN'T REMEMBER...
AH.
THE STARS ARE CLEAR TONIGHT.
SO PRETTY...

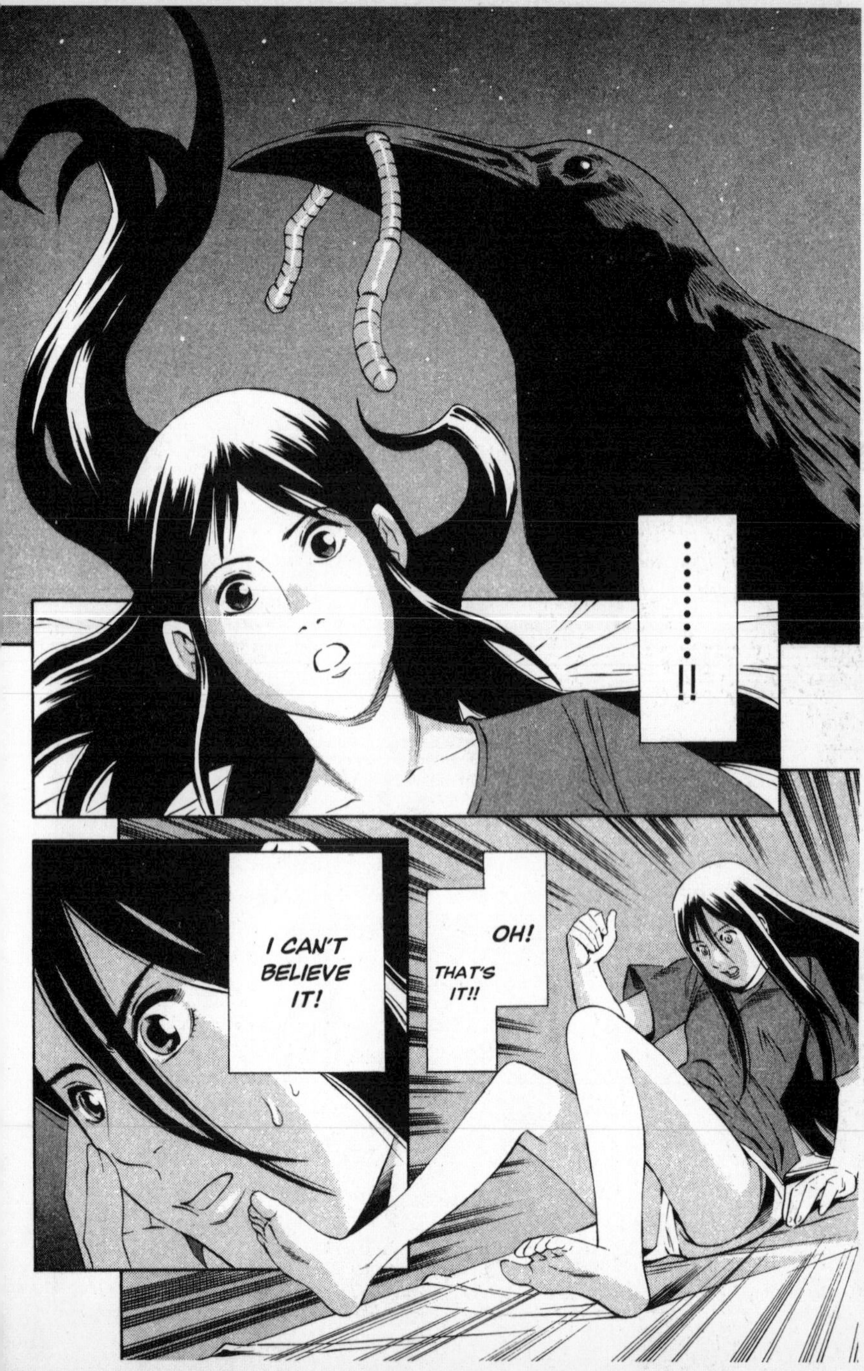

..........!!
OH! THAT'S IT!!
I CAN'T BELIEVE IT!

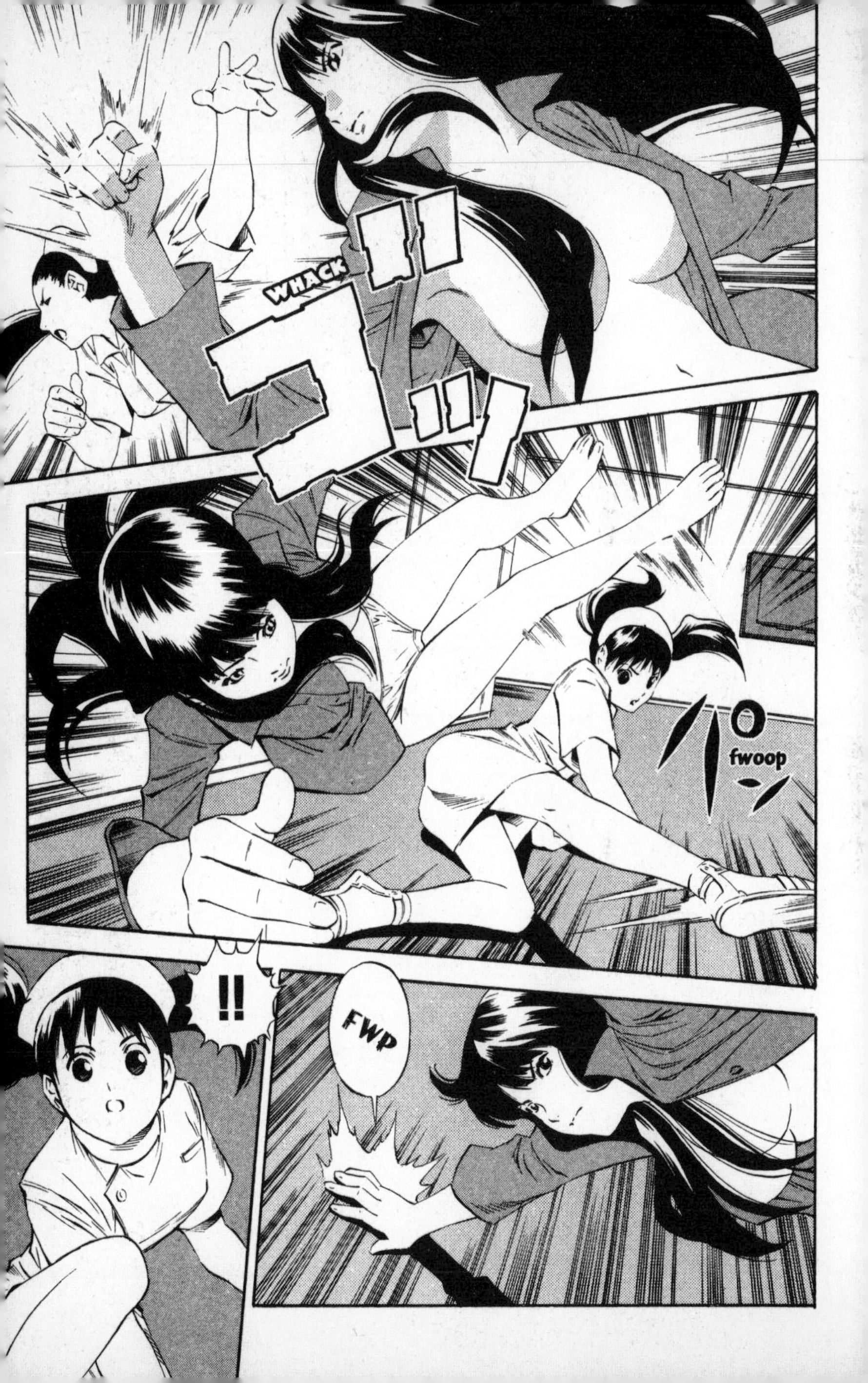
WHACK
fwoop
!!
FWP

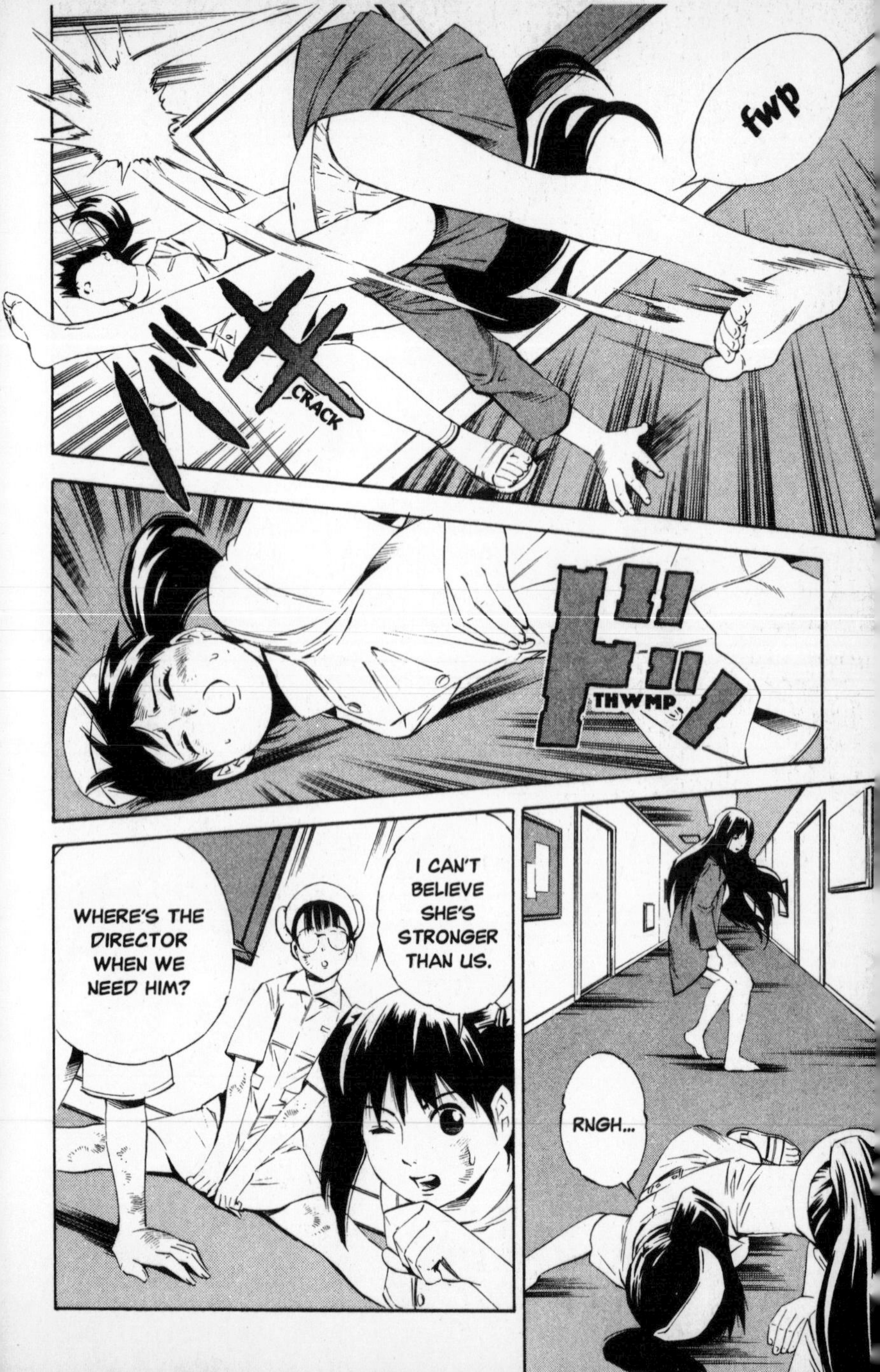
fwp
CRACK
THWMP
I CAN'T BELIEVE SHE'S STRONGER THAN US.
WHERE'S THE DIRECTOR WHEN WE NEED HIM?
RNGH...

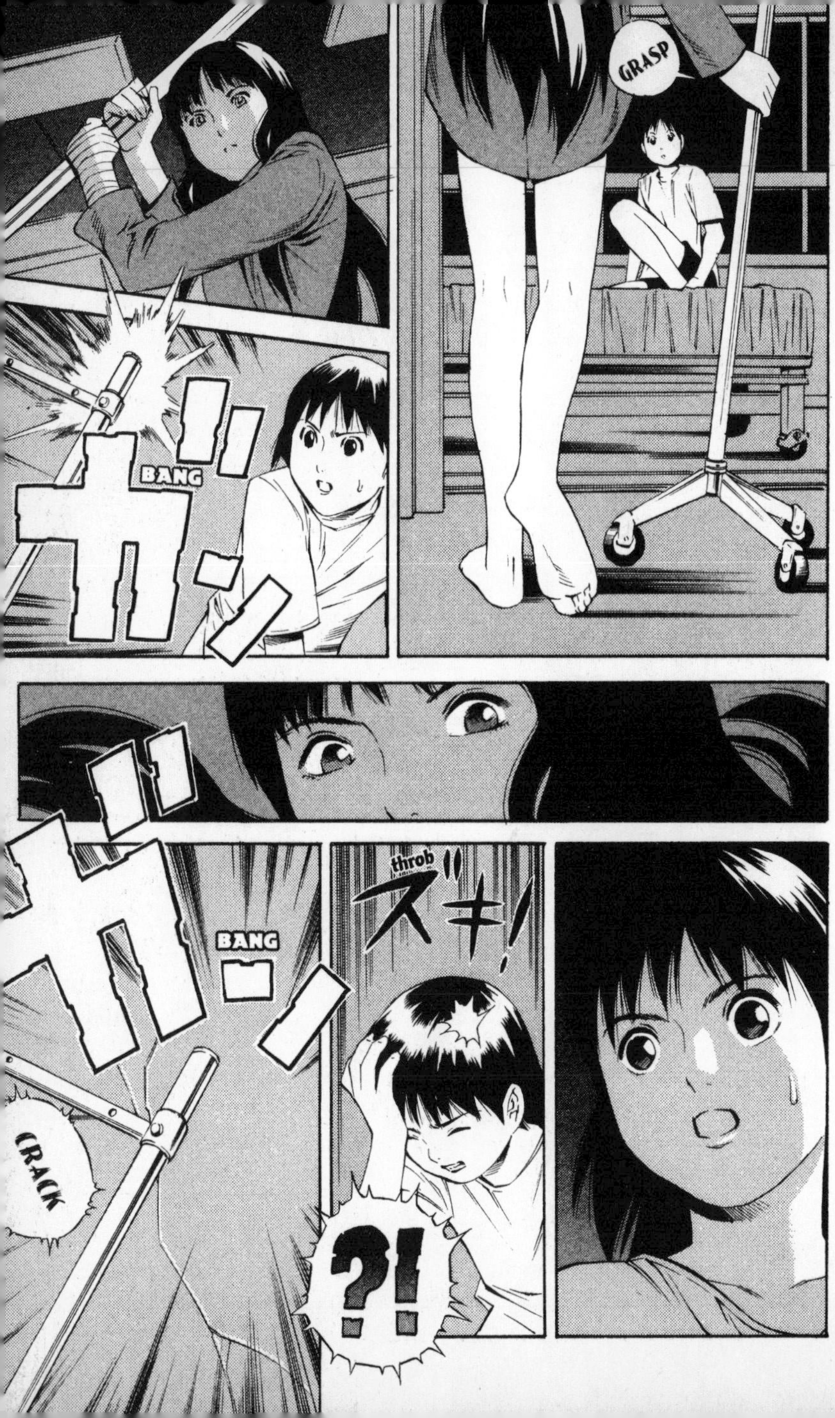
GRASP
BANG
ガン
BANG
ガン
throb
ズキ!
CRACK
?!

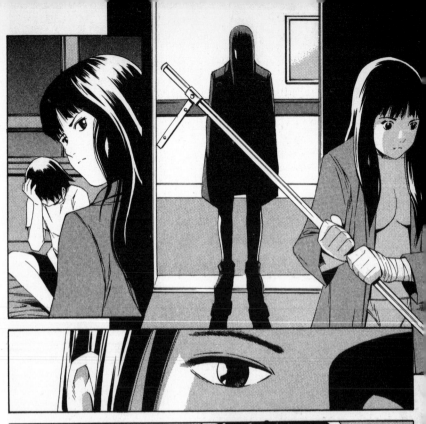

HEY...
YOU WANT TO GIVE ME A KISS?

······!

192

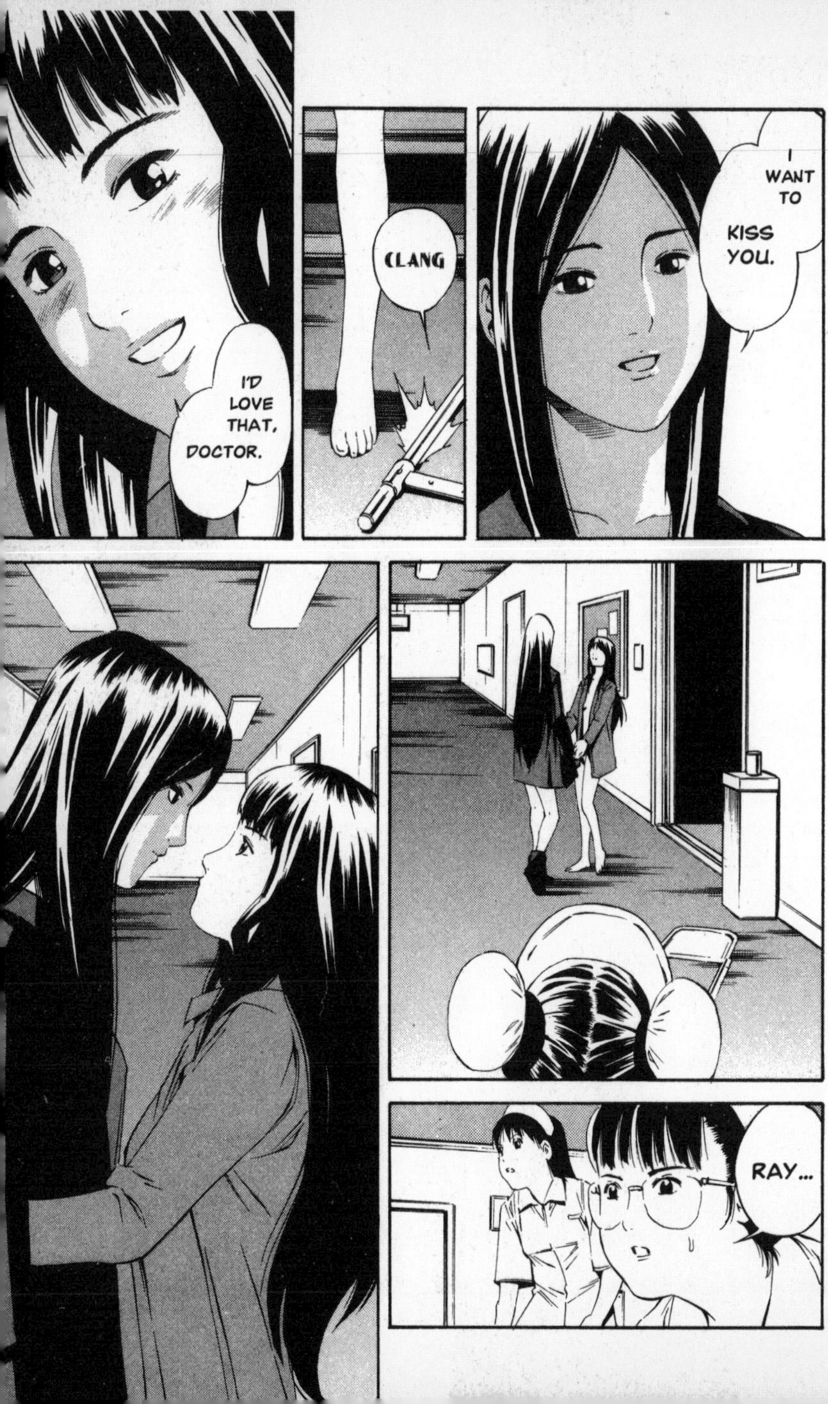
I WANT TO KISS YOU.
CLANG
I'D LOVE THAT, DOCTOR.
RAY...

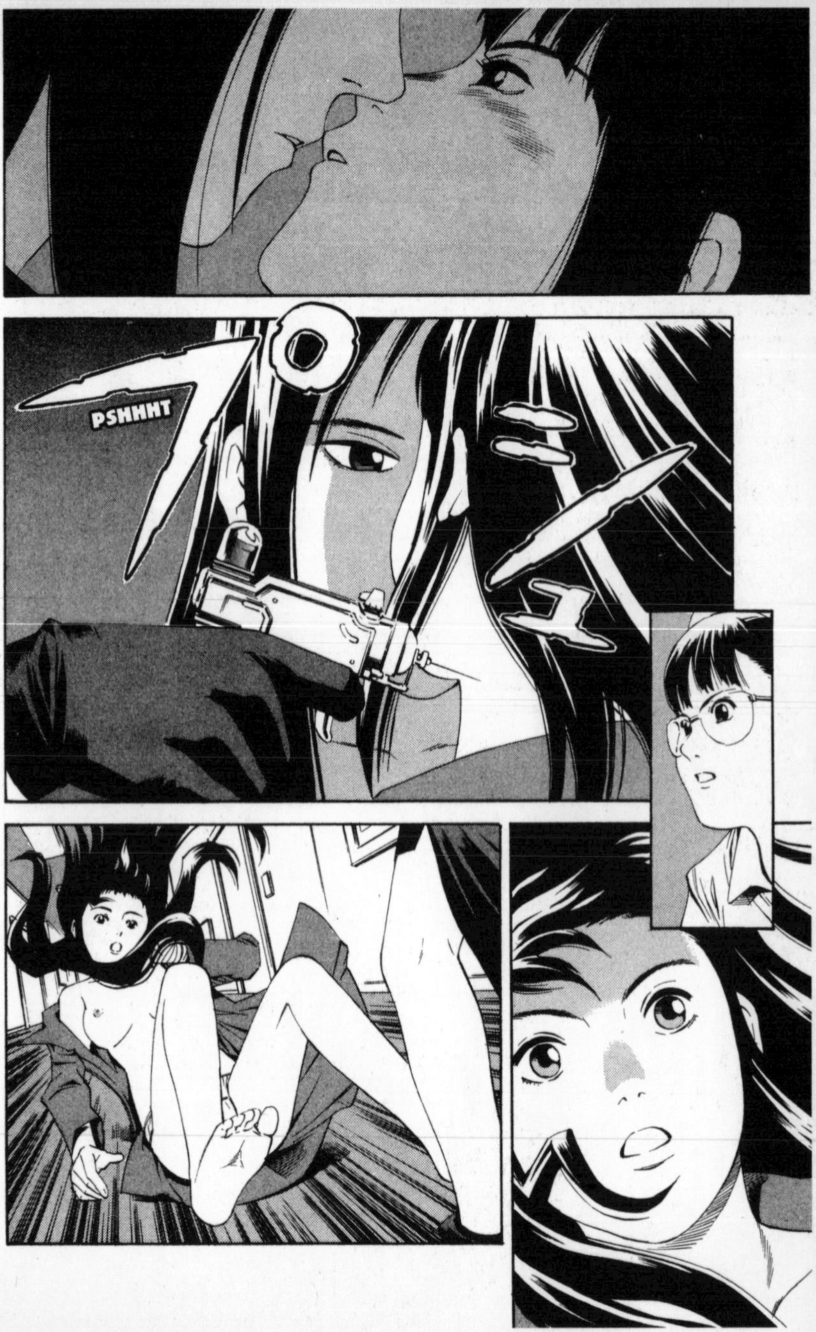
PSHHHT

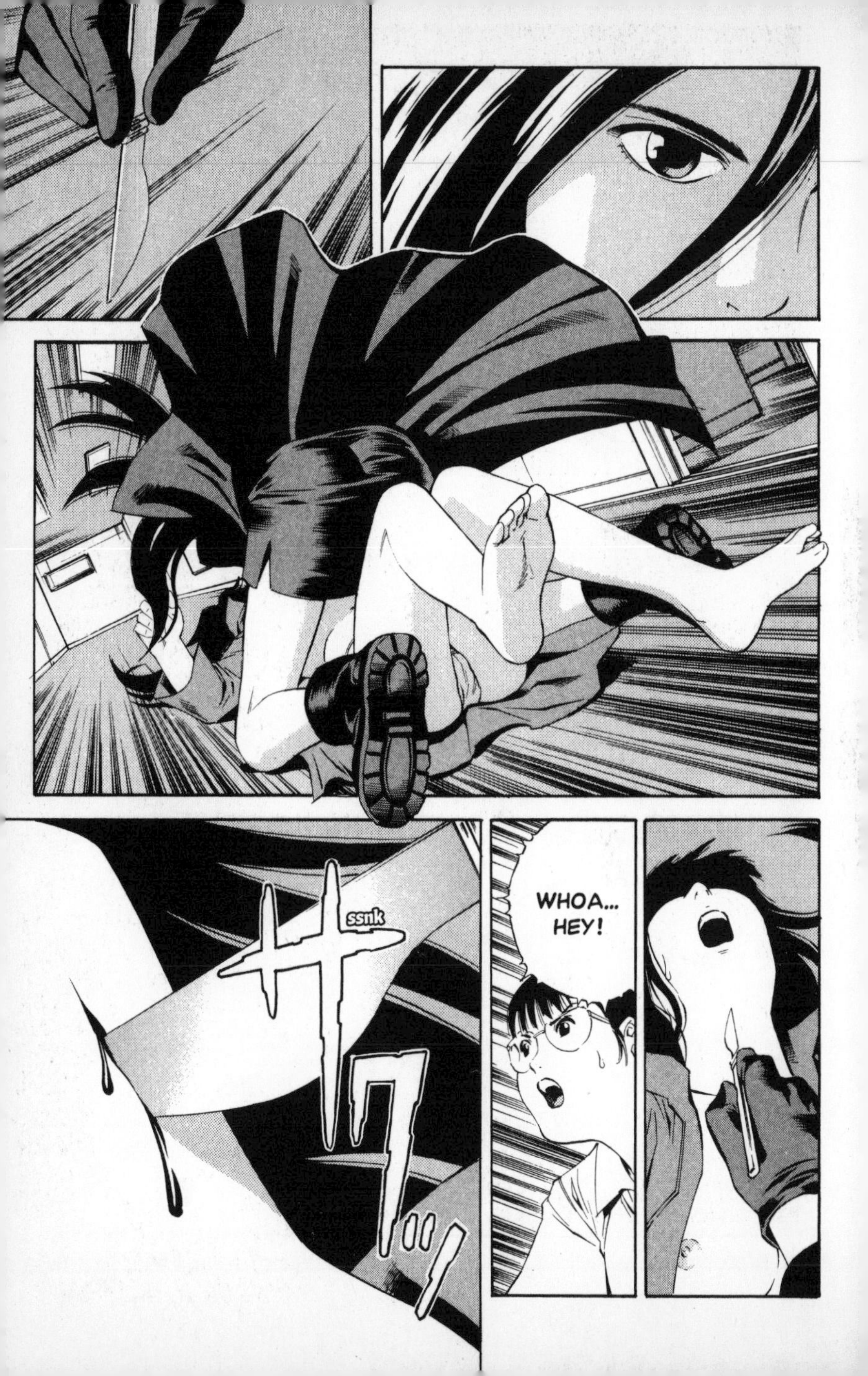
ssnk
WHOA... HEY!

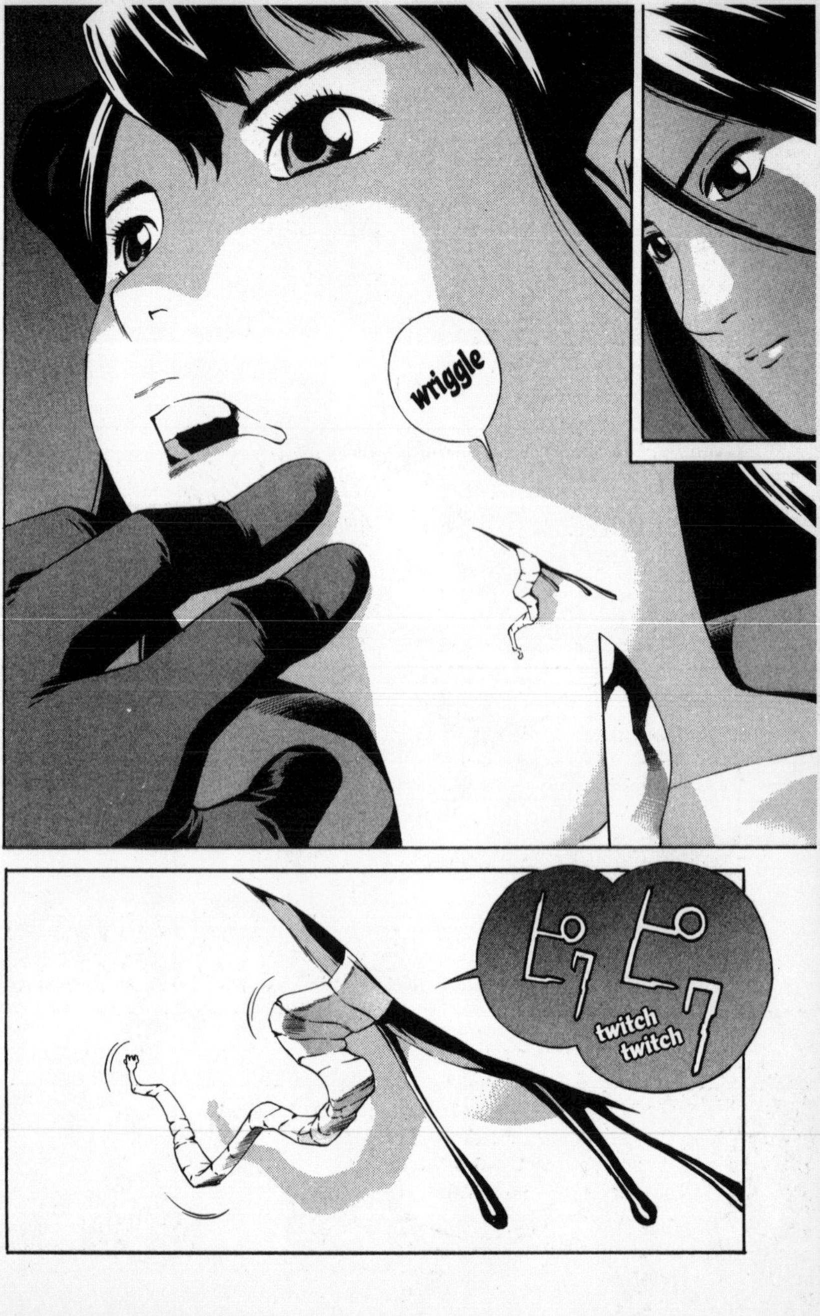
wriggle
ピクピク
twitch twitch

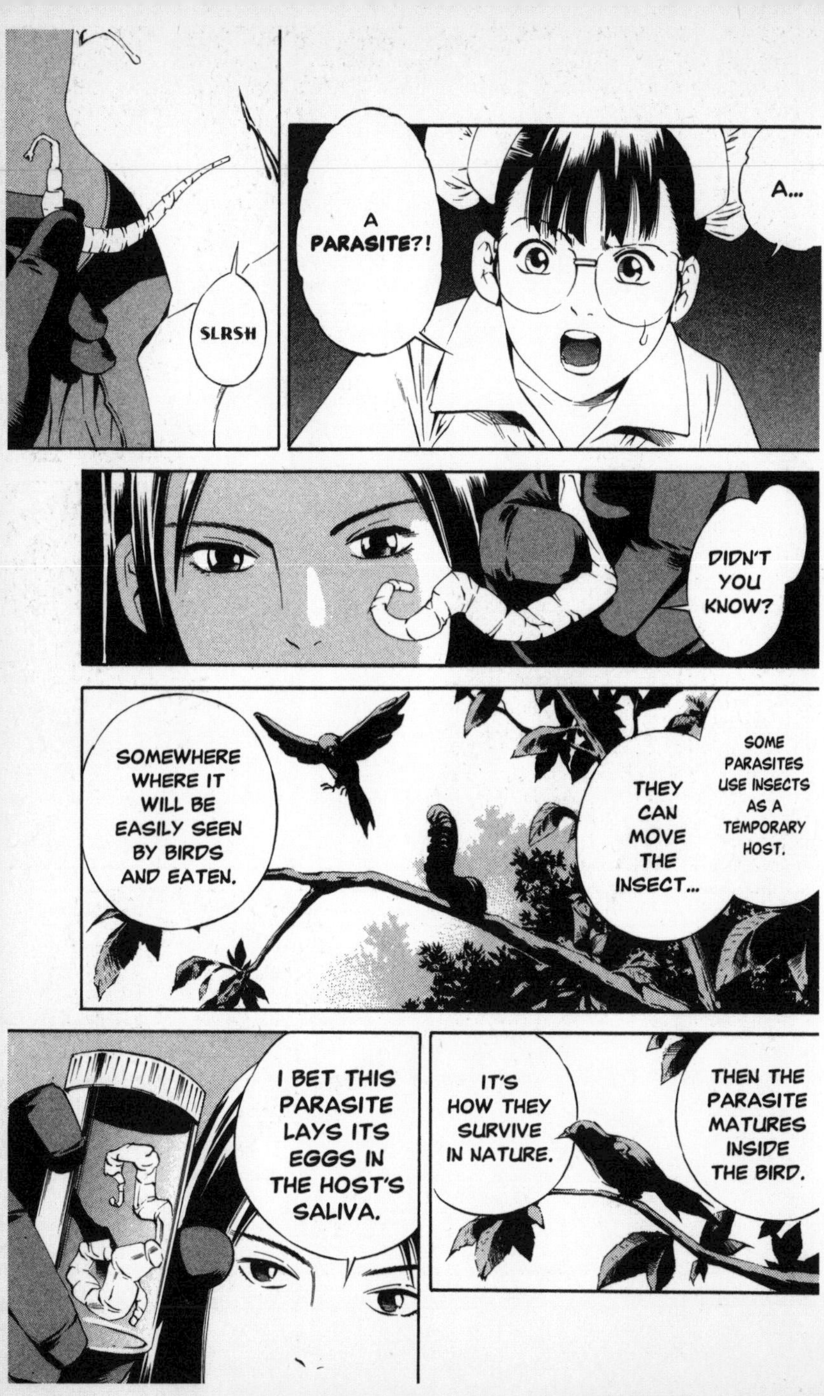
A...
A PARASITE?!
SLRSH
DIDN'T YOU KNOW?
SOME PARASITES USE INSECTS AS A TEMPORARY HOST.
THEY CAN MOVE THE INSECT...
SOMEWHERE WHERE IT WILL BE EASILY SEEN BY BIRDS AND EATEN.
THEN THE PARASITE MATURES INSIDE THE BIRD.
IT'S HOW THEY SURVIVE IN NATURE.
I BET THIS PARASITE LAYS ITS EGGS IN THE HOST'S SALIVA.

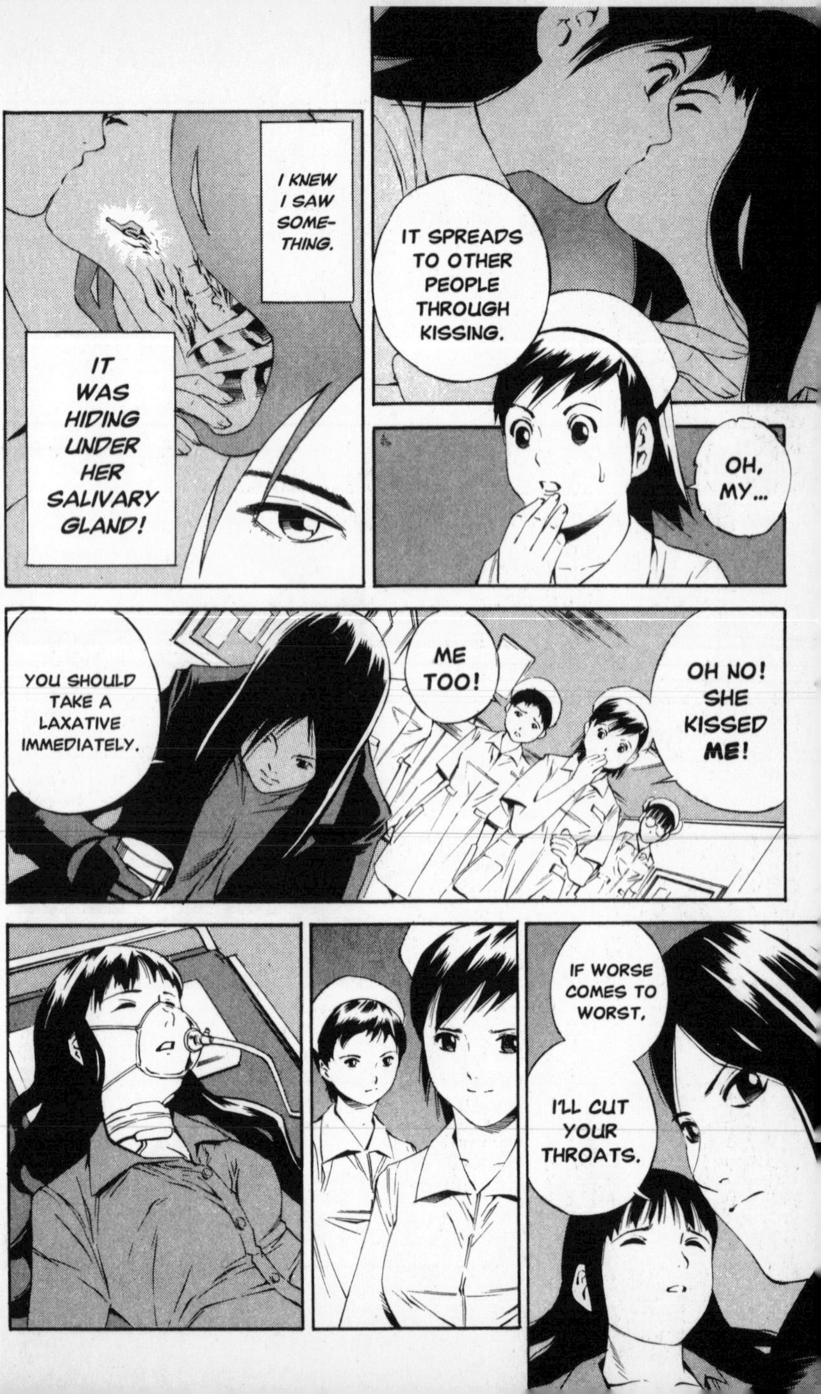
IT SPREADS TO OTHER PEOPLE THROUGH KISSING.
OH, MY...
I KNEW I SAW SOME-THING.
IT WAS HIDING UNDER HER SALIVARY GLAND!
OH NO! SHE KISSED ME!
ME TOO!
YOU SHOULD TAKE A LAXATIVE IMMEDIATELY.
IF WORSE COMES TO WORST,
I'LL CUT YOUR THROATS.

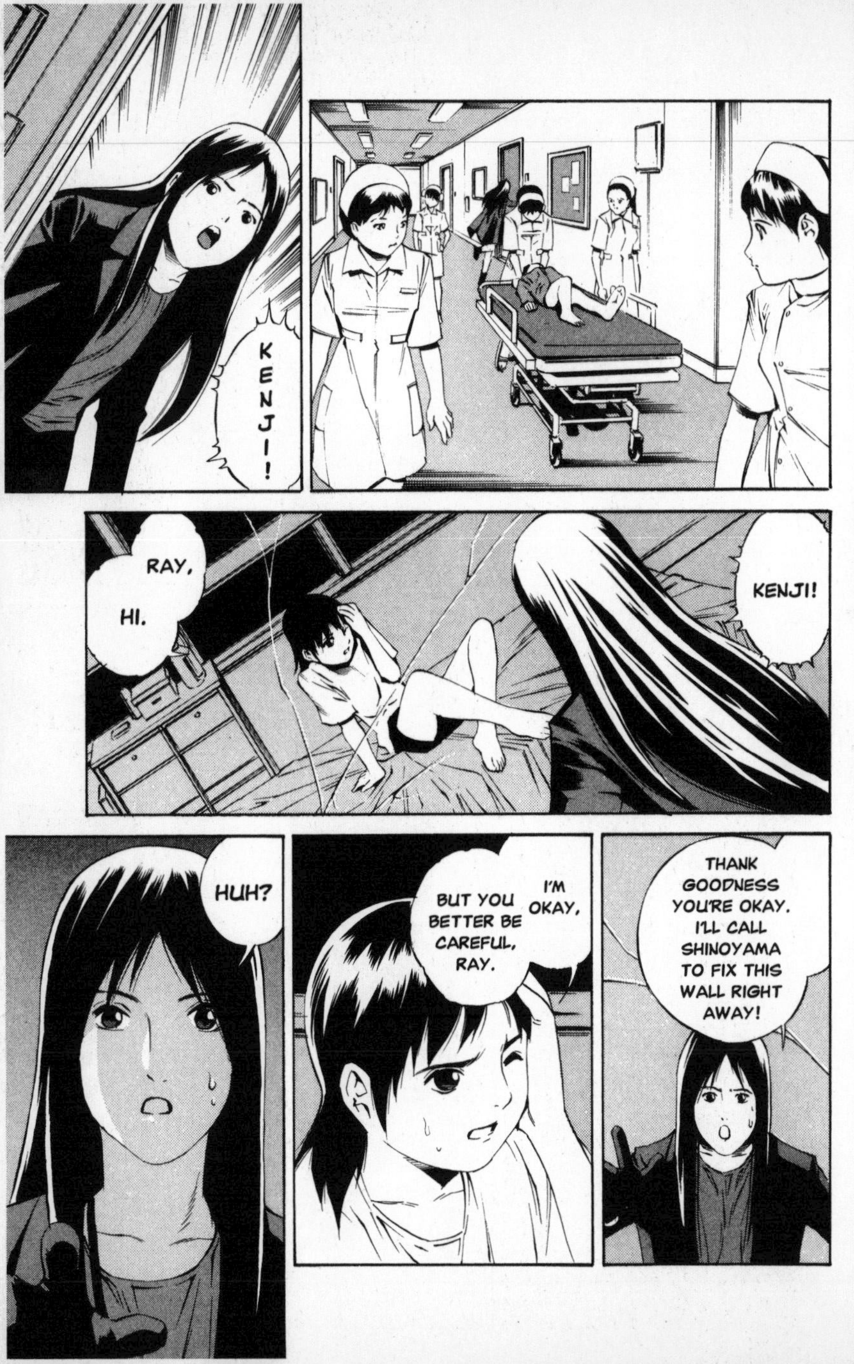
KENJI!
RAY,
HI.
KENJI!
THANK GOODNESS YOU'RE OKAY. I'LL CALL SHINOYAMA TO FIX THIS WALL RIGHT AWAY!
I'M OKAY,
BUT YOU BETTER BE CAREFUL, RAY.
HUH?

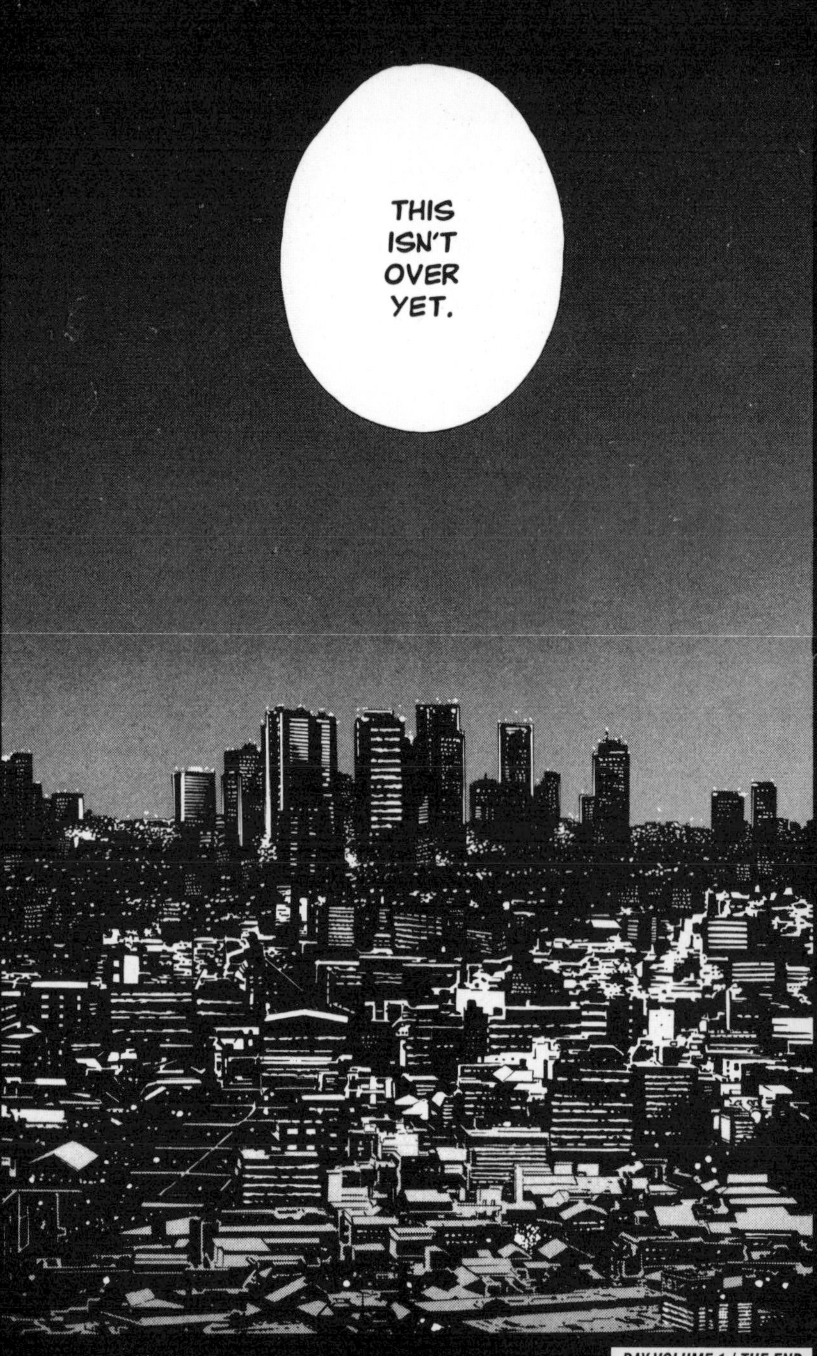
THIS ISN'T OVER YET.

RAY VOLUME 1 / THE END

零

RAY. 1

AKIHITO YOSHITOMI.

AFTERWORD

I'M REALLY EXCITED TO BE WRITING THIS MANGA. THE MORE I DRAW, THE MORE INTERESTING IT GETS! I HOPE YOU'RE LOOKING FORWARD TO THE NEXT VOLUME!

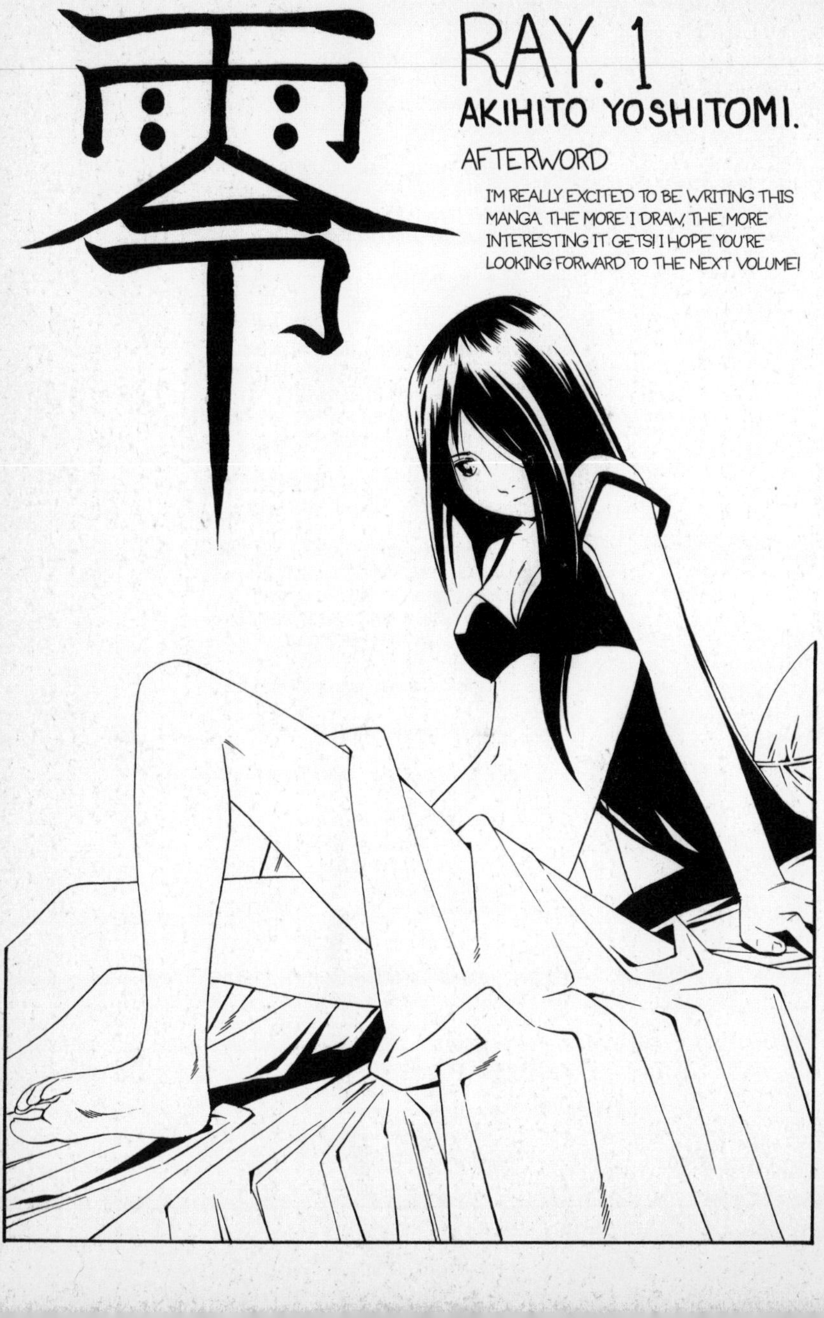

© Akihito Yoshitomi 2003
All rights reserved.
Originally published in Japan in 2003 by Akita Publishing Co., Ltd. Tokyo.
English translation rights arranged with Akita Publishing Co., Ltd.

Translator **HARUKA KANEKO-SMITH**
Lead Translator/Translation Supervisor **JAVIER LOPEZ**
ADV Manga Translation Staff **KAY BERTRAND, JOSH COLE, AMY FORSYTH, BRENDAN FRAYNE,
EIKO McGREGOR AND MADOKA MOROE**

Print Production/Art Studio Manager **LISA PUCKETT**
Pre-press Manager **KLYS REEDYK**
Art Production Manager **RYAN MASON**
Sr. Designer/Creative Manager **JORGE ALVARADO**
Graphic Designer/Group Leader **SHANNON RASBERRY**
Graphic Designer **HEATHER GARY**
Graphic Artists **SHANNA JENSCHKE, KERRI KALINEC, GEORGE REYNOLDS**
Graphic Intern **MARK MEZA**

International Coordinator **TORU IWAKAMI**
International Coordinator **ATSUSHI KANBAYASHI**

Publishing Editor **SUSAN ITIN**
Assistant Editor **MARGARET SCHAROLD**
Editorial Assistant **VARSHA BHUCHAR**
Proofreaders **SHERIDAN JACOBS AND STEVEN REED**
Editorial Intern **JENNIFER VACCA**

Research/Traffic Coordinator **MARSHA ARNOLD**

Executive VP, CFO, COO **KEVIN CORCORAN**

President, CEO & Publisher **JOHN LEDFORD**

Email: editor@adv-manga.com
www.adv-manga.com
www.advfilms.com

For sales and distribution inquiries please call 1.800.282.7202

ADV MANGA is a division of A.D. Vision, Inc.
10114 W. Sam Houston Parkway, Suite 200, Houston, Texas 77099

English text © 2004 published by A.D. Vision, Inc. under exclusive license.
ADV MANGA is a trademark of A.D. Vision, Inc.

ISBN: 1-4139-0204-9
First printing, November 2004
10 9 8 7 6 5 4 3 2 1
Printed in Canada

Ray Vol. 01

PG. 5 **B.J.**
This would appear to be a parody of Black Jack, the lead character in the comic of the same name (from manga great Osamu Tezuka). In the comic, Black Jack was (like Ray) an underground, unlicensed surgeon, and had a scar on his cheek similar to B.J.'s.

PG. 12 **Systemic Lupus Erythematosus**
An inflammatory condition that often brings with it a high risk of coronary artery disease. It is the result of bodily tissue coming under attack by the body's own immune system.

PG. 72 **(1) Shape-memory alloy**
Alloys that can be bent or twisted, but then (once heat is supplied) will return to their original shape.

(2) Peltier cooling
A system wherein electricity is run through two dissimilar conductors, with the effect that heat energy is transferred from one ("hot") side to the other ("cold") side, where the heat is absorbed.

PG. 201 **Japanese character (kanji)**
The *kanji* featured prominently on this page is pronounced *rei*, and is used in the original Japanese to refer to the main character (hence, "Ray"). While this *kanji* also means "spill (over)," it is undoubtedly being used here in its alternate meaning of "zero."

THE ADVENTURE CONTINUES IN
RAY Vol.2

True to her superhero form, Ray is coming to the rescue of those in need, but concerns with her two friends are occupying her time and talent. Fellow children of the organ farm, Ray needs both of them to bring down the inhuman organization that took her eyes. And while they both appear eager to help, one friend is holding back information. What dark and painful secrets must remain unspoken, even if they are the key to unlocking the organ donors from the farm's wicked clutches?

Ray must see through walls and hidden agendas to unleash her vengeance in *Ray* Volume 2.

COMING SOON FROM ADV MANGA!

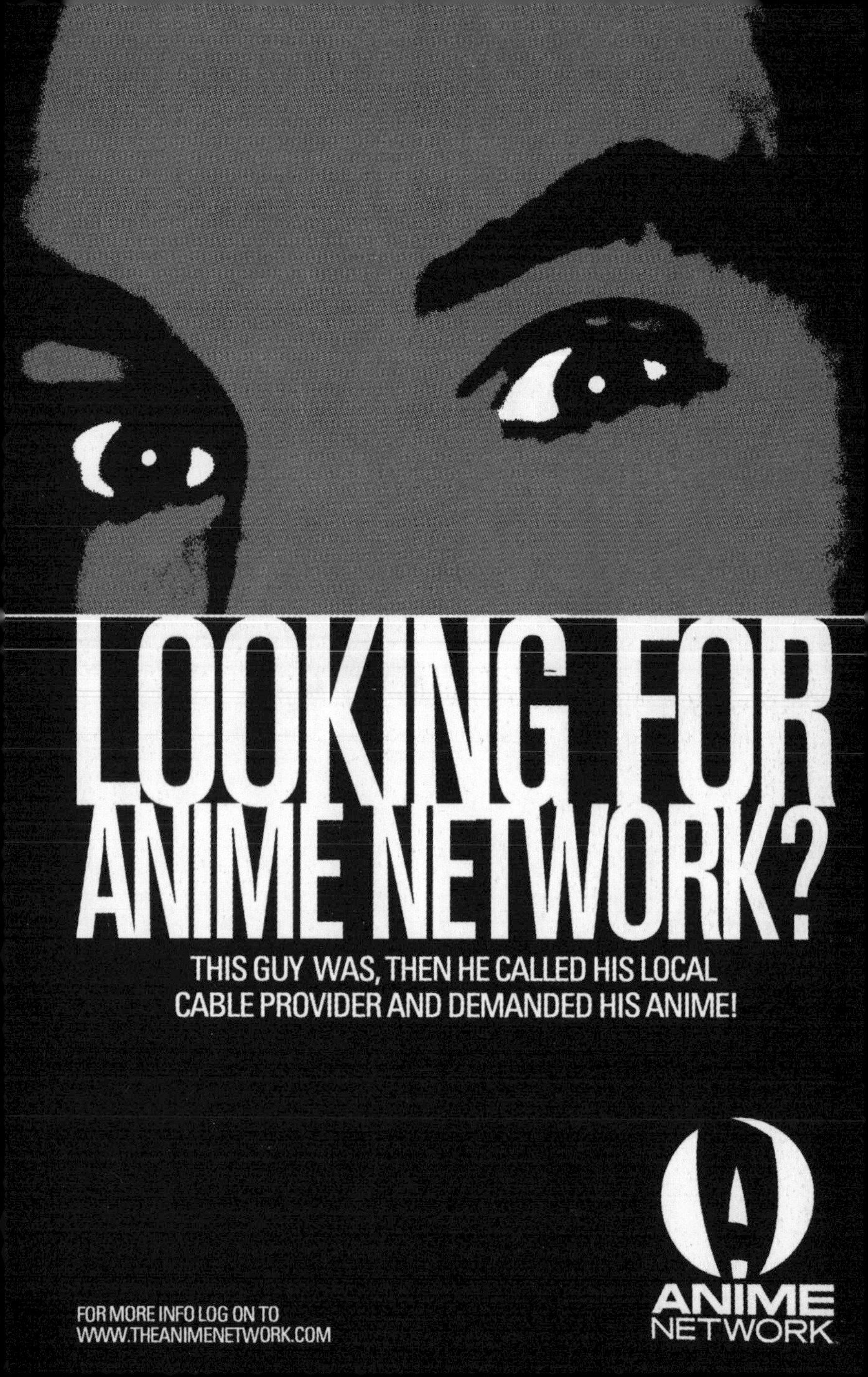
LOOKING FOR ANIME NETWORK?
THIS GUY WAS, THEN HE CALLED HIS LOCAL CABLE PROVIDER AND DEMANDED HIS ANIME!
FOR MORE INFO LOG ON TO WWW.THEANIMENETWORK.COM
ANIME NETWORK

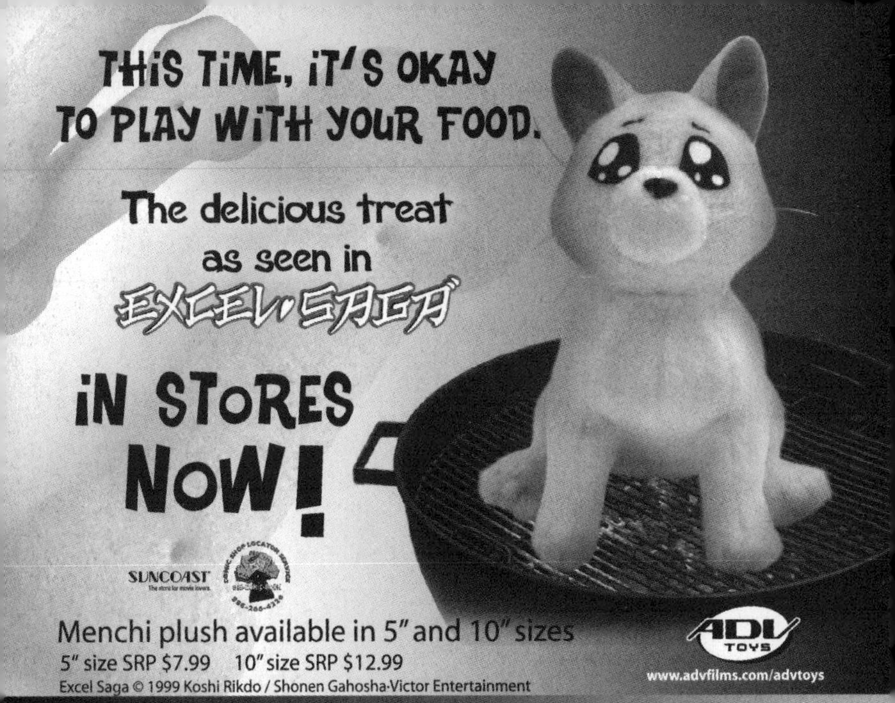
THIS TIME, IT'S OKAY
TO PLAY WITH YOUR FOOD.
The delicious treat
as seen in
EXCEL SAGA
IN STORES
NOW!
SUNCOAST
Menchi plush available in 5" and 10" sizes
5" size SRP $7.99 10" size SRP $12.99
Excel Saga © 1999 Koshi Rikdo / Shonen Gahosha·Victor Entertainment
ADV TOYS
www.advfilms.com/advtoys

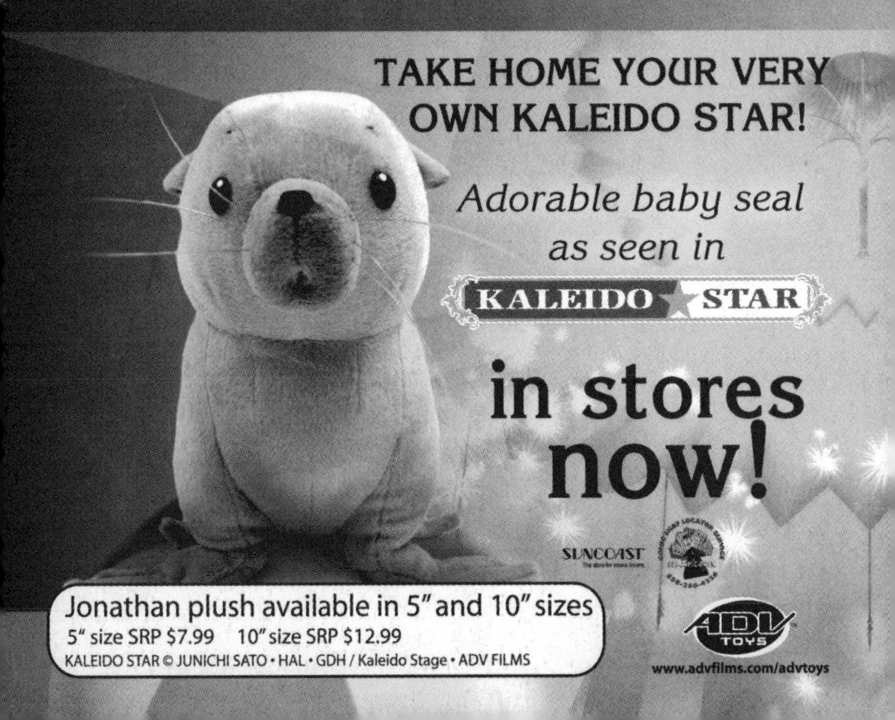
TAKE HOME YOUR VERY
OWN KALEIDO STAR!
Adorable baby seal
as seen in
KALEIDO STAR
in stores
now!
SUNCOAST
Jonathan plush available in 5" and 10" sizes
5" size SRP $7.99 10" size SRP $12.99
KALEIDO STAR © JUNICHI SATO • HAL • GDH / Kaleido Stage • ADV FILMS
ADV TOYS
www.advfilms.com/advtoys

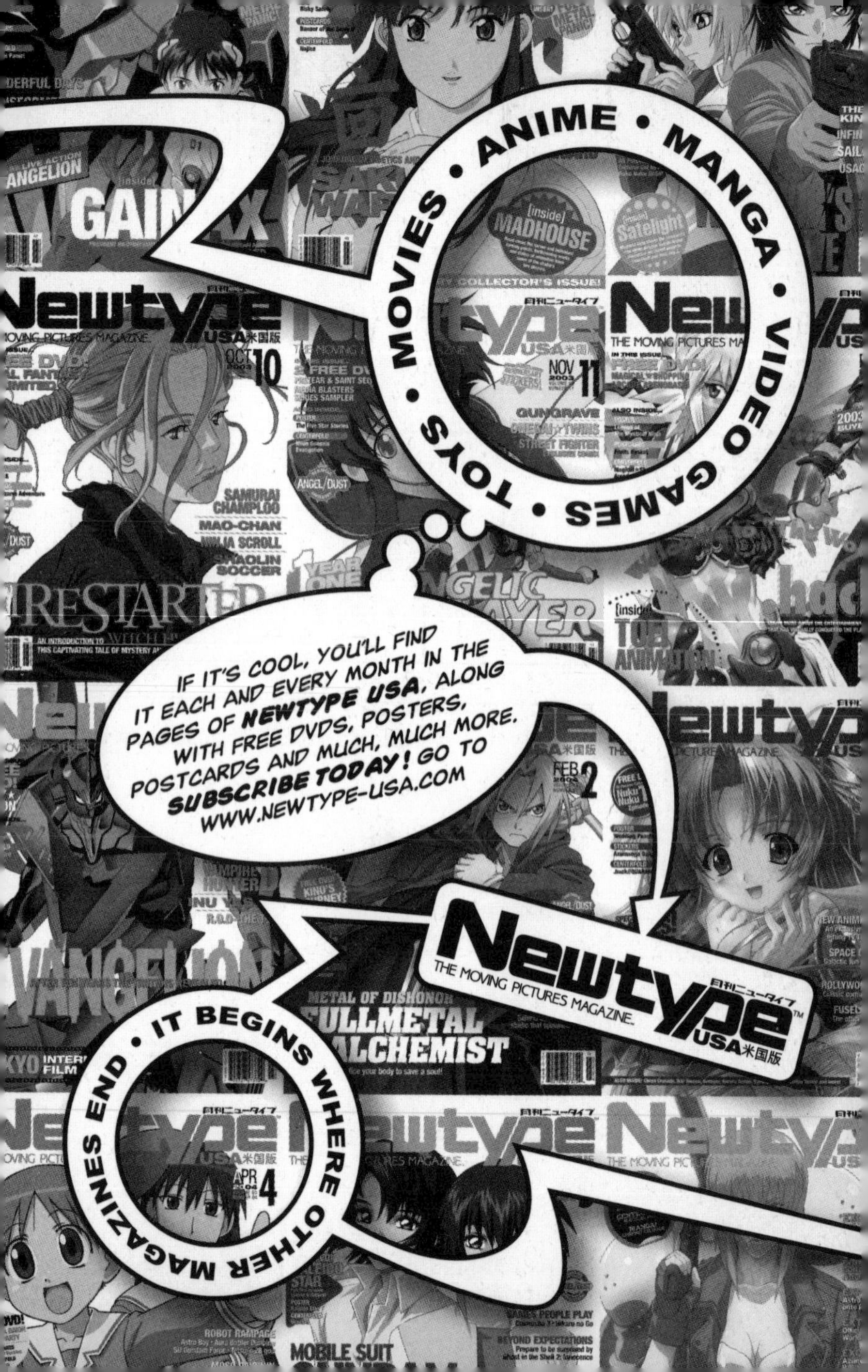
MOVIES • ANIME • MANGA • VIDEO GAMES • TOYS •
IF IT'S COOL, YOU'LL FIND IT EACH AND EVERY MONTH IN THE PAGES OF NEWTYPE USA, ALONG WITH FREE DVDS, POSTERS, POSTCARDS AND MUCH, MUCH MORE. SUBSCRIBE TODAY! GO TO WWW.NEWTYPE-USA.COM
Newtype
THE MOVING PICTURES MAGAZINE.
月刊ニュータイプ
USA 米国版
IT BEGINS WHERE OTHER MAGAZINES END •